DAWSON'S THE GOVERNMENT OF CANADA
SIXTH EDITION

Since its initial appearance some forty years ago, Dawson's work has been
regarded as an indispensable guide to Canadian constitutional and political
structures. This new edition has been revised by Norman Ward, as were the
fourth and fifth editions. He has brought the material up to date and reorganized
it to reflect contemporary students' approach to the subject.

Recognizing that today most students first encounter politics through
television, Ward begins with a TV scene. He has moved forward the sections
on political parties, the electoral system, Parliament, the executive, and the
Supreme Court. The sections on constitutional issues are now at the end, and
the book concludes with a commentary on the Charter of Rights and Freedoms.

The changes in the sixth edition make the book more current and more
accessible; the essential work continues to be the standard for its field.

NORMAN WARD, at the time of his death in February 1990, was Professor Emeritus
of Political Science, University of Saskatchewan.

NORMAN WARD

Dawson's
The Government
of Canada

SIXTH EDITION

UNIVERSITY OF TORONTO PRESS
Toronto Buffalo London

First edition 1947, 1948, 1949, 1952
Second edition 1954, 1956
Third edition 1957, 1958, 1959, 1960, 1962
Fourth edition 1963, 1964, 1966, 1967, 1968, 1969
Fifth edition 1970, 1972, 1973, 1975, 1977, 1979, 1981, 1983
Sixth edition 1987, 1990

© University of Toronto Press 1963, 1970, 1987
Toronto Buffalo London
Printed in Canada

ISBN 0-8020-5731-4 (cloth)
ISBN 0-8020-6644-5 (paper)

Canadian Cataloguing in Publication Data

Dawson, Robert MacGregor, 1895–1958.
  Dawson's The government of Canada

  6th ed.
  Includes index.
  ISBN 0-8020-5731-4 (bound). – ISBN 0-8020-6644-5 (pbk.)

  1. Canada – Politics and government. 2. Canada –
  Constitutional history. I. Ward, Norman, 1918–1990.
  II. Title. III. Title: The government of Canada.

  JL15.D39 1987   320.971   C87-093727-8

Contents

Preface

This revision of *The Government of Canada*, unlike its predecessors, is based on more than an addition of new subjects and an updating of old. It has been recast so that the topics of the earlier editions, while still discussed, are presented almost in the reverse of their original order. All earlier editions began with the constitution, worked their way through various major institutions, and concluded with the political parties. This book begins with the parties and ends with the constitution. Those preferring the earlier format for teaching purposes can, of course, still employ it; they will merely find the chapters are numbered differently.

The decision to alter the book's approach was not at first an easy one to make, and the revision was undertaken with some initial misgivings, shared alike by editors and the author. As the work progressed, however, the logic of the new sequence of chapters asserted itself. For me it did not embody a wholly new departure, since I had used a similar general approach twice, in shorter books aimed at different audiences. In both those books, and again in teaching a course designed for undergraduates not registered in a college of arts, I was motivated in part by the belief that there were obvious advantages in starting with a topic with which students had at least some acquaintance. The introduction of television cameras into the House of Commons strengthened that belief: students, I found, were coming to class with a greater awareness of politics than most of their predecessors had shown, and almost all of them had acquired it through television. This edition starts with a description of the television coverage of an event of both political and constitutional significance, and throughout tries not to lose sight of the impact that the electronic media have made on our perceptions of public affairs.

There are other reasons for changing the book's approach. When Dr Dawson produced the first edition, the available bibliography of secondary sources was meagre indeed, and he had to explain and expound many concepts on which there is now a substantial literature. For each chapter, and in some cases even parts of chapters, there are now more studies available than there were originally for the entire text. The growth of such a literature is gratifying; and it makes the creation of an encyclopaedic text that covers every major subject and the views expressed about each by scholarly commentators not only unnecessary but impossible. To keep this edition within reasonable limits, some developments relevant to the government of Canada have had to receive little more than serious introductions. I am sure that there will be readers who wish I had included more on such highly pertinent subjects as presssure groups, native rights, or guidelines on conflict of interest. To do justice to these and other topics would require in each case another full-length volume. But the retrieval systems of modern libraries will make it much easier to follow up any topic in the text than it was for users of previous editions. The number of notes considered essential for the support of the text has been sharply reduced, and for the first time there is no select bibliography.

Also missing from this revision are the texts of the former British North America Act of 1867, reborn as the Constitution Act of 1982, and the Statute of Westminster of 1931. With the additions to the constitution in 1982, the total text of the relevant enactments became too long, and the use of abridged versions was singularly unappealing. Parts of this book, therefore, had to be written under the constraints of knowing that I could not solve problems or evade difficulties by referring to appendices at the back of the book.

Writing a readable introduction to so vast a subject as the government of Canada is no longer – if it ever was – a task for one person. My family as usual rallied around, my wife cheerfully putting up with books and documents all over the house, and aiding in the countless ways in which she has always supported my work. Our daughter Nora typed the entire manuscript. University colleagues were always helpful when called on and one, Duff Spafford, went far beyond the call of duty to read and comment on every chapter. The offices of local members of Parliament were also responsive, and I must thank Bob Ogle of the NDP, and the Honourable Ray Hnatyshyn and Don Ravis of the Progressive Conservatives, for obtaining needed publications for me. Party insiders were equally helpful, and I am particularly indebted to Senator Keith Davey for Liberal materials not readily available to members of the public. The law clerk and parliamentary counsel of the Senate, Raymond du Plessis, QC, provided much valuable information on that chamber. Numerous other offices of government deserve mention, and I am one taxpayer who is content with publications provided by, among others, such varied enterprises as the Treasury Board, the Department of Finance, the commissioner of Official Languages, the auditor general, the chief electoral officer, the Public Service Commission, and Status of Women Canada.

The text has received the usual exceptional attentions of the University of Toronto Press; it was a pleasure to work again with R.I.K. Davidson, editor atop the social sciences, and for the first time with Diane Mew, who interpreted her role as copy-editor to include challenging every statement on my pages, even if the spelling, punctuation, and capitalization were beyond reproach.

This is the first edition of *The Government of Canada* not directly touched by Eugene Forsey, a remarkable circumstance that deserves special mention. Dr Forsey's influence is here, of course, for his clear (and freely expressed) opinions affected all its predecessors. This revision is the poorer for the want of his hand. But it does leave us free to dedicate the book to him, and it is fitting to record that the decision to do so was unanimous among editors and the author. We dedicate this book to Eugene Forsey as a mark of our deep respect and affection.

NORMAN WARD
Saskatoon
14 February 1987

THE GOVERNMENT OF CANADA

1
Political parties

No man in Canada has been more inconsistent than the man who has faithfully followed either party for a generation.
Sir John Willison, editor of the *Globe* (Liberal), 1890–1902, and the *News* (Conservative), 1903–17

Modern democratic government means government by party, and under all normal circumstances involves more than one party. A citizen's participation in his or her government may cover a wide range. It may be as a cabinet minister, so preoccupied with unavoidable duties as to leave almost no spare time. The citizen may, however, do little more than make a cross on a ballot paper every few years, casting a vote. He may not even bother to vote, liking none of the parties or their candidates, but reserving the right to criticize them all freely; and that, too, is an important function. Between the prime minister and the non-voting citizen are large numbers of others who serve publicly as candidates and legislators, or privately as party workers behind the scenes. Parties are pervasive, in short, and Parliament itself is organized to recognize their significance. The seating arrangements offer constant reminders of who forms the government and who the opposition, and parliamentary rules extend rights to parties that are not available to the occasional Independents who win seats. The party system has many critics, but nobody has yet produced a workable alternative.

How the public perceives the parties and their activities is naturally of fundamental concern, and it is now a fact that most observers gain their perceptions most immediately from television. As a medium for transmitting information about politics, television is unlike its colleagues, the newspapers and radio; by simply adding live visual coverage to political events it has altered many aspects of democracy, partly by influencing the selection of what events receive the coverage and how. In 1982, for example, after years of planning and negotiation, major changes were made to the Canadian constitution, and throughout the process relevant newsworthy parts of it received coverage in Ottawa, in the provinces, and in the United Kingdom, whose parliament also had to take action. As a news story, the constitutional changes of 1982, the greatest since Confederation, received much attention, parts of them (since the topic itself is not necessarily exciting) more than others. Total coverage was given the final ceremony, on 17 April 1982, which brought the queen to Ottawa to sign the official proclamation that gave legal force to a Charter of Rights and Freedoms and a clear formula for future amendments to the constitution entirely within Canada. The ceremony took place on Parliament Hill, in the presence of the prime minister and other dignitaries, and almost nothing of immediate significance to the signing was omitted from the coverage by all the media, print and electronic.

That coverage was typical of modern reporting on political affairs; and since television has become the most intrusive source of day-to-day news about politics (not just in Canada), it is important to emphasize what the cameras and their attached commentators can and cannot do. A simple ceremony such as that just cited not only showed what was officially of overwhelming importance, the actual signing; it also revealed such details as the style of Her Majesty's dress and the colour of the prime minister's tie, and gave them as much relevance as any observer cared to make of them. If the observer of such an event is a radio or TV commentator, minuscule details – especially if something untoward occurs, such as a dignitary stumbling and sprawling without dignity – can receive as much attention as the chief purpose of the event. Joe Clark, when Conservative party leader, travelling abroad on a mission that was important to him, once had his luggage lost for him at an airport: who now remembers anything else about that trip?

Television does not, and often cannot, reveal major matters: the fact that monarchy is one of the oldest known forms of government, for example, or that the Canadian prime minister is both the head of a cabinet and the leader of a vast and complex organization called a political party. Unless somebody in a position of influence considers it 'newsworthy,' nothing may be said about the parliaments that produced the document the queen signed, though they too have a tradition centuries old, as does the Charter of Rights, which contains ideas that can be traced to Magna Carta of 1215. It would be a gross exaggeration in such circumstances to say that television cameras – and the camera, according to legend, never lies – reveal only 'the tip of the iceberg'; what is ordinarily seen is a fragment of the tip, depending on which way the lenses are pointing. And in any case, tomorrow's tips may be from quite different icebergs.

The nature of television's view of the political scene must be recognized if the political parties themselves are to be understood, for it underlies much of what we see and affects the parties' own behaviour. Television seems to have had relatively little difficulty in coping with political parties, but the parties have had, and continue to have, great difficulties in coping with television. Some of their problems have arisen outside Parliament, for new methods of advertising, and thus of campaigning or otherwise attempting to attract public support, have had to be learned. It is possible, indeed, that television has created new differences between those parties which are able to exploit its potentials fully and those which are not.

The admission of television to Parliament has produced some obvious changes, such as turning the daily question period into what experienced MPs have called a 'circus.' An observer who sees opposition members gleefully (and legitimately) attempting to harass the government, and who does not also know that no opposition MP with any sense is likely to ask a question whose answer will make the governing side look good, can easily get an extremely distorted picture of the parties and of Parliament itself. Individual members on both sides of the House of Commons may be conscientious servants of their constituents, yet not look good on camera. There are other examples of the camera's effects on Parliament, and it is only fair to add that some of them have been beneficial. MPs have argued, for example, that it is a good discipline to know that one may be on camera, and they can point to a tightening of procedures that has saved precious parliamentary time.

But it remains true that the cameras, however skilfully manipulated, can show only a tiny fraction of what is actually going on in politics, and what little they show may be misleading. The mere attempt to reduce what may be an incredibly complicated issue to something that makes comprehensible viewing has many commendable aspects, but revealing important truths is not necessarily one of them. 'What is missing,' as a chief justice remarked of another medium's coverage of his court not long after his appointment, 'is in-depth assessment. Unless the press develops or engages reporters that can paint in the background of important cases or see them as part of an evolutionary process and explain this in their stories or a review column, the coverage is bound to be episodic and lack continuity.'[1]

If that is true of newspaper reporting of a stream of cases coming into a single court, how much more true is it when it comes to the televising of Parliament, with its involved agenda and timetable, its personnel drawn almost exclusively from political parties, each of which has an internal parliamentary caucus and an external organization stretching from coast to coast? Parliament, deep though its roots are, cannot now be understood without a consideration of political parties, and neither can most constitutional, legislative, and administrative activities. Even though the judiciary alone operates free of partisan bias, judges are appointed by governments and a high proportion of them are former political activists. Indeed, it can be said that parties lie beneath the discussion of almost all governmental affairs.

The workings of parties are such that there are few generalizations about them on which observers in Canada can still agree, for as the knowledge of parties continues to grow, so does discussion not only about what parties do but what they actually are. As will be seen, parties have always been indispensable as suppliers of candidates, issues, and manpower for high office; and as such they have had to be mobilizers of large armies of voluntary workers, paid and unpaid, raisers of vast sums, both from members and non-members, and spenders of those same funds. It is now clear that the very methods which parties use in performing their functions, and the nature of the support they thereby attract or repel, have profound implications for the parties' roles in Canadian society. Fund-raising, for example, can have significant centralizing tendencies, and fund-spending, particularly through the modern use of advertising agencies and the mass media, can play a part in breaking old allegiances and introducing new instabilities into party support. With the new instabilities comes a natural questioning of the parties' traditional roles as brokers between competing groups and as unifiers of dissident elements in a diverse population.

There are widely varying views on what has been happening to the political parties, as the following queries suggest. Are political parties in Canada divided on the basis of social class – for example, employers and property owners versus employees? If so, are the differences constant from province to province, or are the regional branches of the same party different from each other? That same question can be asked of other aspects of parties. Is religion a basis for variations in party support? Do the parties have differing appeals to ethnic groups? Is there a significant rural-urban split among parties? Do familiar terms used to characterize parties in other countries, such as right wing versus left wing, have a valid place in Canada? Seeking answers to such questions has led many observers to shed much light on the nature of our parties, but not to many conclusions on which they can all agree. New elements relevant to parties, such as the regular polling of voters on their preferences, raise new queries. Are the electors, for instance, in danger of being reduced to mere consumers, the parties viewing their supporters as 'their share of the market,' regardless of policies or principles?

Clearly, generalizations about political parties are at best difficult, at worst impossible. Yet one fact stands out: no matter what the observers' own points of departure, they all assume the existence of parties in the plural. The communist and fascist idea of a single party and the rigid suppression of all dissent have never made much headway in Canada, and all serious observers accept that the country has a multi-party system. They probably agree, too, that there are occasions when the actions of parties are reprehensible; but these must be accepted as necessary concomitants of free people governing themselves. Their problems are somehow worked out (at least they have been so far), and the nation presumably emerges sadder and wiser from the experience.

Some of the functions of political parties have already been cited, and the list can be extended. In all democracies they keep the public both informed and aroused by giving forceful expression to opinion and criticism on all subjects of general interest. They enable those who are concerned with these matters (whether they are actuated by selfish motives or otherwise) to organize for the more effectual propagation of their views and the more ready implementation of these views through practical political expedients. The parties are the outstanding agents for bringing about co-operation and compromise between conflicting groups and interests of all kinds in the nation; for as a rule it is only by a merging of forces that these can hope to become powerful enough to secure office. In Canada, indeed, the role of the national parties as a unifying agent in bringing together in amity some of the most powerful dissident forces in the country, despite contemporary argument to the contrary, can hardly be discounted. Further, the parties, pragmatically pursuing their own interests (chief among which is attaining power), sort out issues for special attention, and narrow down potentially long lists of candidates to modest proportions, thereby simplifying the task of the voter so that he is enabled to reach relatively simple decisions on a few major questions and a few leading people. The party (or parties) in opposition supplies an alternative government willing and eager to assume power the moment it begins to slip from the hands of the ruling party. Moreover, the new government comes into office with its leaders virtually chosen and its program largely prepared in advance, and the transition can thus be made with little uncertainty and with a minimum of friction. It is true that the party system also tends to bring with it many faults – a reliance on funds from sometimes questionable sources, an excessive selfishness, a distorted perspective on real problems, and favouritism, to name but four – and while it would be dangerous to idealize the party system, there can be no reasonable doubt that its merits decidedly outweigh its drawbacks. It is often overlooked that many of the faults of political parties are the faults of all large human associations, whether they are political, economic, or religious; like these other associations, a party can become corrupt only with the active co-operation of large numbers of people, some of whom on occasion profess a disdain for politics.

It has long been held that the party system, and particularly the party system under cabinet government, will find the best conditions for its operation where there are only two parties, or, at least, two parties capable of obtaining a clear majority in the legislature. Canadian experience at the national level provides at least three important reasons for being sceptical of the traditional theory. First, Canada has in fact had a multi-party system since at least the election of 1921; secondly, the administration of the Canadian state was unquestionably a good deal more corrupt and less efficient under the old two-party system than it has become since; and thirdly, Canada has had several minority governments since 1957 and they were very lively and interesting indeed, as well as productive.

It is true, none the less, that only two parties have ever attained power in Ottawa, and Canada has escaped some of the worst potential consequences of a multi-party system. If a legislature, for example, is under the shifting control of a number of parties, constantly seeking different alignments that will ensure a more permanent or more profitable majority, legislative programs tend to remain in a constant state of flux, executive leadership becomes hesitant, and short-term views unavoidably supplant more permanent policies. Under a two-party system the responsibility of the opposition can become more definite and inescapable, and the conflict of interests and the assertion of local views are less likely to be either so divisive or so intransigent.

But whatever the theoretical justification of the two-party system, every Canadian general election since 1921 has been contested by from three to a dozen or more parties, and each House of Commons in the same period has included representatives from at least three parties, and often more. Not all these groups qualify as major parties, of course, but it would be quite inaccurate to consider only the Liberals and Conservatives as major, and all the rest as minor. Some of the 'minor' groups, such as the Progressives of the 1920s, the Co-operative Commonwealth Federation after 1935, and the latter's successor, the NDP, in modern times, have had a great impact on the policies of the other parties; others, such as Social Credit after 1935, have had a less discernible impact, but have nevertheless been remarkably successful in retaining power in provincial legislatures, and in dominating provincial blocs of members elected to the House of Commons.

There is one genuine criterion which separates the Liberals and Conservatives from all the other parties, and that is age. Both these great parties have pre-Confederation antecedents; all the others are of much more recent origin. Since the media nowadays are so preoccupied with the immediate, the parties' origins deserve particular attention. In the discussion which follows, it must be remembered that the primary classification of the parties is, for convenience, based on 'older' and 'younger,' not 'major' and 'minor.'

THE ORIGINS OF THE OLDER POLITICAL PARTIES

The origin of the Conservative party can be fixed definitely at 1854, when a number of separate groups in the Province of Canada were brought together in a temporary coalition (which turned out to be permanent) under the contradictory but accurate title of Liberal-Conservative. It was composed of extreme Tories, who a few years before had fought against responsible government (which required the executive branch of government to be continuously supported by a majority of the elected members of the legislature), and moderate Liberals from Upper Canada, together with French-Canadian moderates (or *bleus* as they were called) under the leadership of George-Etienne Cartier and some English-speaking members from Lower Canada. The coalition soon fell under the influence of John A. Macdonald, who was able by his own personality and later by the strong urge of the Confederation movement, to weld the members, augmented by small groups from the other provinces, into a genuine political party. So successful was this endeavour that the party was able to retain office, with but one five-year interval, until 1896.

The outlook of Macdonald and his supporters meant a party of centralization: it identified itself with the propertied, commercial, and industrial interests, used these interests to advance nationalist as against local causes, and received in return the powerful support which they could give. The centralizing influences of Macdonald and the Liberal-Conservative party did not stop at Confederation. They found expression in the admission of new provinces on clearly understood terms, in the 'national policy' of a protective tariff, in the construction of the transcontinental railway, and in many other secondary policies which bore in the same general direction.

This was the work of a generation, and it was to a remarkable degree the work of one man. But Macdonald's bold schemes never allowed him to forget the details of politics, including the minutiae of local patronage; indeed, his wider schemes often appeared to be little more than the means of attaining his more immediate political ends. He possessed an exceptionally shrewd political sense of both timing and tactics, and was far from fastidious in the instruments and expedients he used to gain his victories. His greatest talent was a genius for conciliation, aided by a warm personality. He was able to gain the support of George Brown, his bitter enemy, for the Confederation project; he was able to induce Joseph Howe of Nova Scotia, another opponent, to join his cabinet; he was able to retain the backing of the English Tories, French moderates, Orangemen, and Roman Catholics. This trait was of inestimable value in the formative period of the Liberal-Conservative party; and later years were to show that leadership in any Canadian party, if it was to have any permanence, must continue to depend to an enormous degree on an ability to use conciliation and compromise.

The origin of the Liberal party is not so easily traced. Its ancestry undoubtedly goes back to the early reformers who fought for responsible government, but after Confederation the separate elements in the provinces were slow in coming together and forming a genuinely national body. Many of the Liberals had opposed Confederation, and this continuing lukewarmness, encouraged by the rival centralizing tendencies of the Conservatives, helped to make them the defenders of the rights of the provinces, a stand which in itself did not promote national party unity. Their belief in decentralized government drew support from a frontier agrarian democracy with distinct radical tendencies. The Clear Grits (as the Upper Canadian Liberals were called) were opposed to wealth and privilege in any form, and they favoured soft money, universal suffrage, frequent elections, and various other 'republican' measures well known south of the border. Another group which was included in or affiliated with the Liberals was the *rouge* party from Quebec. It was anticlerical and had aroused the opposition of the Roman Catholic church, and after Confederation it gradually declined in size and importance. To these two elements were joined some reformers, secessionists, and independents from New Brunswick and Nova Scotia.[2]

The first Liberal government came into power after the Pacific Scandal had broken over the head of Macdonald in 1873. This government was supported by the above groups, which acknowledged also a separate allegiance to their own leaders. But Alexander Mackenzie, the prime minister, was no Macdonald, and after almost five years the party left office still a party in name only. The unimaginative leadership of Mackenzie, the troubled genius of his chief lieutenant, Edward Blake, the administration's support of practical policies rather than those with popular appeal, its misfortune in holding office during an economic depression, its excess (at least at the federal level) of political rectitude and stern principles, and its disbelief in patronage and lavish public expenditures, all combined to accomplish its defeat and send the disunited Liberals into the wilderness for almost two decades.[3] Mackenzie none the less left three enduring monuments: under his leadership Parliament laid the foundations for Canada's national electoral system; it created the office of auditor general; and it brought to fruition a plan to establish the Supreme Court of Canada.

It was Wilfrid Laurier, who became Liberal leader in 1887, who made a genuine national party from the local and personal sections which gave him their support. He approached his task with deep misgivings, but with the conviction which was to be his guiding political principle all his life, that the overwhelming need was the co-operation of the French- and English-speaking in Canada, and his first public address after he became leader was an appeal for national unity. The immediate party problem was to carry the local party successes in the provinces over into the federal field. For although the Liberals lost the general election of 1891, they were at that time in control in every province with the possible exception of British Columbia. In 1893 the Liberals held the first national party convention in Canada with the obvious intention of consolidating the party's position, bringing the different elements together, and making the national leader better known to party workers all over the dominion. Laurier's first cabinet in 1896, which included three provincial premiers, was a clear demonstration of the same purpose.

'Laurier,' Professor Underhill wrote, 'had a more difficult and subtle role to play [than Macdonald], because he led a party in which the radical agrarian Grit tradition in Ontario and the radical anti-clerical *rouge* tradition in Quebec were still strong.' Laurier managed to discourage the extreme *rouge* tendencies, to establish better relations with the Roman Catholic church, and to capture a large part of the moderate element in Quebec, while he appealed to Ontario through the consideration which he showed for provincial rights and an imperial preferential tariff which his government introduced in 1897. Even in the 1893 platform the party had noticeably retreated from the extreme free trade position it had advocated earlier; and when it took office it tacitly accepted the necessity for maintaining the industries which had grown up under the protective system – a tendency toward maintaining the status quo that became even more marked in the early years of this century. The imperial preference was an ideal compromise as a party straddle. It was a move toward freer trade; it had a certain retaliatory aspect against the high American tariff; it retained many of the Canadian protective features intact; and it was a reassuring gesture to those imperialists who had suspicions regarding the empire loyalty of a French-Canadian prime minister.

If the Liberals had been unlucky in the time of their accession to power in 1873, they were amply compensated in 1896; for they caught the tide at the flood and rode into a period of prosperity unmatched up to that time in Canadian history. The enormous influx of immigrants, the railway expansion, the opening and settlement of western Canada, the creation of two new provinces, the expansion of internal and external trade, the continuing growth of Canadian autonomy – these were counted as Liberal achievements, and the winning of three more general elections was their reward. The fifteen years in office not only gave the party strength, they enabled it to acquire a character and tradition that were to prove very useful reserves in the years ahead. Although it is true that the tides were favourable and the winds fair, the success of the party voyage was nevertheless due in large measure to the capacity of the captain; for Laurier, like Macdonald, brought to his task a broad tolerance and a vision tempered with a skill in practical affairs that had had few equals in Canadian history. During Laurier's time the Conservatives rebuilt themselves as an organized opposition, and by 1911 both older parties were well-established institutions.

THE ORIGINS OF THE THIRD PARTIES

This is not the place to recount in detail the full history of the Liberal and Conservative parties, much of which remains unwritten, although some notable contributions to our knowledge of them have been made in recent years.[4] Paradoxically, the origins and histories of some of the parties that have been established since Confederation have received considerable attention, and a growing literature about them is now in print. All these parties, in one way or another, have reflected dissatisfaction with the older parties, and have been handicapped by the fact that when the dissatisfaction is soundly based and the new party threatens to become really successful, one or both of the older parties moves toward the appropriation of the new party's program, and sometimes its key personnel. The younger parties have thus been catalysts in the chemistry of politics, but have hardly ever been able to keep far enough ahead of their would-be swallowers to establish themselves as major threats in their own right; not one of them has convincingly succeeded in permanently absorbing any significant part of one of the older national parties.

As is shown in Table 1, only once, in 1921, has a third party briefly become a second. The Progressive party then enjoyed a unique success, for in 1921 it not only became the second-largest party in the House of Commons, but showed what was perhaps a prophetic grasp of its own future by declining to serve as the official opposition.[5] There had been several farmers' political movements in Canada since the days of the Clear Grits, and this one, like the others, arose from the same basic conviction that the interests of the farmers were being grossly neglected. That belief was (and is) all but chronic among those movements of political protest that have won seats in the House of Commons, and it gives to their parties several similar characteristics. They have distrusted the older parties and the policies they identified with them: for example, high tariffs, taxation favourable to large corporations, and corrupt political patronage. Historically the earliest third parties enjoyed a sporadic success, forming a Farmer-Labour government in Ontario in 1919, a United Farmers government in Alberta in 1921, and in the latter year scoring the federal victories noted above.

In due course they were either absorbed by the older parties (the Liberals proving particularly adept at borrowing their ideas), or were replaced by successors. The first provincial replacement came in Alberta, where Social Credit won an overwhelming victory in 1935 and remained in power until 1971. Where the United Farmers of Alberta had capitalized on the discontent following the First World War, the Social Crediters capitalized on the discontent which arose during the depression of the 1930s; where the former had promised to relieve the Alberta farmers through free trade and co-operation, the latter produced fancy monetary schemes toward the same end. 'The contest of the 1930's between the Social Credit government and the bankers was only one in the long series between east and west, city and country, banker and farmer, hard money and soft money, which had been going on ever since those early days when absences of hard cash forced

TABLE 1
Party standing in the House of Commons after general elections, 1921–84

Year	Liberal	Con-servative	Pro-gressive	Labour	UFA	Lib. Prog.	Social Credit	CCF/NDP	Reconst.	UFO/ Lab.	Unity	Bloc Pop.	Lab. Prog.	Crédi-tiste	Other	Total seats
1921	117 (41)	50 (30)	64 (23)	3											1	235
1925	101 (40)	116 (46)	24 (9)	2											2	245
1926	116 (46)	91 (45)	13 (5)	3	11	9									2	245
1930	88 (45)	137 (49)	2 (3)	3	10	3									2	245
1935	176 (45)	40 (30)				2	17 (4)	7 (9)	1 (9)	1					1	245
1940	181 (51)	40 (31)				3	10 (3)	8 (8)			2				1	245
1945	127 (41)	68 (27)					13 (4)	29 (16)				2	1		5	245
1949	193 (49)	41 (30)					10 (4)	13 (13)							5	262
1953	172 (49)	51 (31)					15 (5)	23 (11)							3	265
1957	107 (41)	112 (39)					19 (5)	25 (11)							2	265
1958	49 (34)	208 (54)					(2)	8 (9)								265
1962	100 (37)	116 (37)					30 (12)	19 (14)								265
1963	129 (42)	95 (33)					24 (12)	19 (13)								265
1965	131 (40)	97 (32)					5 (4)	21 (18)						9 (5)	2	265
1968	155 (45)	72 (31)						22 (17)						14 (6)	1	264
1972	109 (38)	107 (35)					15 (8)	31 (17)							2	264
1974	141 (43)	95 (35)					11 (5)	16 (15)							1	264
1979	114 (40)	136 (36)					6 (5)	26 (18)								282
1980	147 (44)	103 (33)					(2)	32 (20)								282
1984	40 (28)	211 (50)						30 (19)							1	282

NOTES: Until relatively recently election results were not officially tabulated in Canada, and for that reason tables such as this often vary in minor ways. Here, Independent Liberals, Conservatives, etc. are added to party totals, and the column showing Progressive popular vote includes figures for related groups. The table also ignores the changes of name the Conservatives have had. Figures in parentheses indicate percentage of popular vote.

resort to mooseskins, merchants' I.O.U.'s, or pieces of leather with holes in them.'[6] In its later years, Social Credit's monetary ideas were given a back seat, though the party apparently continued to believe in dark plots among the leaders of world finance and often combined the announcement of this discovery with anti-Semitic propaganda. Social Credit, despite a record tainted with authoritarianism, became an ardent upholder of free enterprise and individual liberty.

For many years the Social Credit party made little progress outside Alberta, though a Quebec version, the Union des Electeurs, appeared in the 1940s. In 1952 a Social Credit government took office in British Columbia (a triumph it repeated in 1975 and thereafter, after a brief spell in power for the NDP); and in 1962, having been eliminated from the House of Commons in the election of 1958, Social Credit returned thirty members of Parliament, twenty-six of them from Quebec. Thereafter the Quebec wing assumed the ascendancy, soon emerging as a new entity known as Le Ralliement des Créditistes, while the English-speaking wing once more disappeared from the House of Commons; in 1968 two of its former members won seats as, respectively, a Progressive Conservative (its one-time leader) and a Liberal, who shortly after appeared in Pierre Trudeau's cabinet. Whatever else can be said of Social Credit, the history of its supporters is unmatched in Canadian history.

Quebec has had a share of third parties unlike those of western origin. Federally, Quebec was predominantly Liberal from Sir Wilfrid Laurier's day until 1958, when the Conservatives won fifty of seventy-five seats. That breakthrough lasted only one Parliament, but in 1984 the Conservatives again successfully penetrated Quebec, this time electing fifty-eight MPs. The domination of its federal seats by the two older parties is misleading as an indicator of other aspects of political turbulence in the province. Quebec has been a natural breeding ground for parties that flourish for a while and then vanish, or reappear in another guise. All of them have been understandably pro-French-Canadian and (with the possible exception of Réal Caouette's Créditistes) rather confusingly considered themselves nationalist, by which they meant provincialist. An outstanding example was the Nationalist party in the early years of this century, which elected a group of members to the House of Commons in 1911, joined in a most unnatural alliance with the Conservatives, and was rewarded with three ministers in the cabinet; all three were soon gone, at least two of them to patronage appointments. The Union Nationale party in Quebec was often considered to be linked with the Conservatives, chiefly because it became the provincial Conservative party, though not in name. Actually it owed its origins to both Liberals and Conservatives, and federal representatives of both parties appear to have had little difficulty in co-operating with it on occasion, but it remained a provincial party with no acknowledged tie to its larger affiliate. It stayed out of the federal field, while the Progressive

Conservatives at the provincial elections conveniently did not contest seats. Under Maurice Duplessis's leadership it was aggressive, 'nationalist,' intolerant, and devoted to the task of defending French Catholic Canada against the machinations of her enemies in the religious, economic, and political fields. Duplessis's successors were more moderate, possibly as the result of having been relegated to the opposition for six years in 1960 after sixteen years in power, but more likely because of revelations of widespread scandals. The party's subsequent leaders tried a strong pro-Quebec though anti-separatist line, under considerable pressure from a genuinely separatist party under the leadership of René Lévesque. That group, the Parti Québécois, was formed after Lévesque had first tried to turn the provincial Liberal party (one of whose cabinet ministers he was) in a separatist direction; when he failed, he left the Liberals and was successful in forming a coalition from a variety of separatist factions. His coalition was phenomenally successful at the polls in 1976, winning an overwhelming majority of Quebec seats in 1976 and 1981, in the process eliminating the Union Nationale from the legislature and reducing the provincial Liberals to the fewest seats they had held in two decades. (Until the federal election of 1984 the Parti Québécois had no federal wing, but in that year, still emphasizing its separatist bent, it fielded some candidates.) The vigour of René Lévesque, and the radical nature of some of his party's separatist proposals, led to the raising of serious constitutional questions for all of Canada, topics that belong in a later chapter. In the 1980s the Parti Québécois suffered three major setbacks: it was defeated by the provincial electorate on a referendum over its separatist proposals; in 1985 the same voters elected a Liberal government with a huge majority led by Robert Bourassa; and in 1986 René Lévesque retired from his party's leadership. Separatist parties, it should be noted, have also appeared in the west with a variety of names and leaders, none of them remotely approaching the success of the Parti Québécois, possibly because none of them had a leader as colourful as René Lévesque.[7]

The Co-operative Commonwealth Federation (CCF) was formed in 1932 by members of earlier movements and a section of the old United Farmer (Progressive) organization, who believed that their political interests might be pooled to their mutual advantage.[8] Later the party was able to make a more general appeal to members of all occupations and to record substantial political progress in several parts of the country. It held office in Saskatchewan from 1944 to 1964, has been the official opposition in several other provinces, and always had an active aggressive group in the House of Commons. In 1961 the CCF was merged, with the help of organized labour, into the New Democratic Party (NDP), in an attempt to base the party more broadly on a farmer-labour foundation. The NDP's debut was undoubtedly successful, including the election of over thirty members twice to the House of Commons. It won provincially in Saskatchewan in 1971, 1975, and

1978, in British Columbia in 1972, and in Manitoba in 1969 and 1981, where as this is written it remains the only provincial government administered by the party. But concurrently it led the legislature in the Yukon, and made its first important gains in Alberta in the provincial election of 1986.

The NDP's policies constitute a modified and more conservative version of the CCF, which itself watered down its original program in a reappraisal in 1956. The CCF was born of the depression, and its first manifesto contemplated sweeping economic changes, socialistic in nature. Its purpose was stated in the Regina Manifesto of 1933, which is still worth quoting:

We aim to replace the present capitalist system, with its inherent injustice and inhumanity, by a social order from which the domination and exploitation of one class by another will be eliminated, in which economic planning will supersede unregulated private enterprise and competition, and in which genuine democratic self-government, based upon economic equality, will be possible . . . This social and economic transformation can be brought about by political action, through the election of a government inspired by the ideal of a Co-operative Commonwealth and supported by a majority of the people. We do not believe in change by violence. We consider that both the old parties in Canada are the instruments of capitalist interests and cannot serve as agents of social reconstruction, and that whatever the superficial differences between them, they are bound to carry on government in accordance with the dictates of the big business interests who finance them. The C.C.F. aims at political power in order to put an end to this capitalist domination of our political life. It is a democratic movement, a federation of farmer, labour, and socialist organizations, financed by its own members and seeking to achieve its ends solely by constitutional methods.

More explicitly the CCF proposed, as part of the planned economic order, the socialization of all financial agencies, transportation, communications, and public utilities generally; a national labour code; social insurance covering old age, illness, accident, and unemployment; freedom of association; socialized health services; crop insurance; removal of the burden of the tariff from the operations of agriculture; parity prices; encouragement of co-operative institutions; amendment of the British North America Act to give Parliament sufficient powers to carry out measures that were national in scope; and the abolition of the Senate. Some of these ideas have been adopted by the Liberals and Conservatives, and some of the proposals have thus been implemented, at least in part. The party's influence on the policies of the older parties has been considerable, but it is clear that the influence has not been so great as to lead the electorate to conclude that there is no further need for the NDP. The elections since the party's birth suggest the contrary, since the NDP has in successive elections outpolled the CCF's best showing. In doing so it has continued as a genuine paradox in Canadian politics: a party which has achieved some notable successes in having its policies adopted while remaining a solidly established third party that in Ottawa has not even formed the official opposition, let alone the government.

This brief sketch of third parties would not be complete without at least a mention of several more. The Communist party elected one member of Parliament in 1945, but his parliamentary career was abruptly terminated in 1946, when he was convicted of espionage. The party continues to field candidates in every election, but its success with the electorate is rarely impressive. The Bloc Populaire, a dissident nationalistic group from Quebec, returned two members in 1945. In 1935 the Reconstruction party, an offshoot of the Conservatives, set a record by polling 384,000 votes but electing only one member. (Social Credit in the same election, with less than half as many votes, secured seventeen.) At various times members calling themselves Labour, Liberal Progressive, United Farmers of Ontario-Labour, and Unity have appeared in the House of Commons, without starting any movement toward yet another party. The election of 1984 saw the usual multiplicity of smaller parties including the veteran Social Credit and Communist, the Rhinoceros, the Green Party, and CoR (Confederation of Regions). All of them attracted some votes.

PARTY DIFFERENCES

It may seem paradoxical to begin a section on party differences with reference to what most of them have in common, but it is important to make clear that all the major federal parties in Canada share many common principles. With variations (some of them wide and deep) within each party, all of them that are not separatist accept the federal system, and even the separatists appear to accept the parliamentary systems (except the monarchy), the party system, the necessity for broad health and welfare programs, and the recognition of fundamental human rights. All agree on the necessity of avoiding absorption by the United States, and recognize the need for policies that support the Canadian economy and maintain employment at the highest possible level, and they support national standards of education and governmental aid to the arts. The parties may differ on the timing of particular programs, and on the methods best suited to their implementation; by these criteria they can be classified from right to left, but by European standards only within a narrow spectrum. Parties vary in the nature of their internal organization, their financial support, the economic and social characteristics of their followers, and the motivations that stir their workers. A party long in power, such as the Liberals in the decades since 1921, may acquire special relationships with the upper echelons of the public service that are so close that the party and the state may be difficult to tell apart; a former opposition at last coming into power, as the Conservatives did in 1984, may have good reason to feel suspicious about some of its official advisers. A party long in opposition may have particular problems in finding a winning leadership, and will turn frequently to new leaders drawn from many different provinces. Until the 1980s the Liberals for a century had comfortably alternated their leaders between Ontario and Quebec, and kept each one for prolonged periods.

When all the facts that can affect the parties' fortunes are taken into account, it would plainly be unrealistic to expect that conflicts between well-established national parties should be pitched battles between opposing forces sharply divided on basic principles. The older parties have always disagreed; but they have not always fought their engagements on purely national issues, and the fate of governments has sometimes been decided on a series of local skirmishes that appeared almost unrelated. Nor, when wider and more fundamental questions have been at stake, have the two older parties been consistent; it is rarely possible to examine the course pursued by either party and from that deduce either one set of ideas which has been steadily pursued throughout the years, or two sets of ideas which clearly separate the parties. The reason is clear: each party, whatever its history, aims at the same target, the Canadian electorate and enough of its votes to win a majority of seats in the House of Commons. Thus each presents itself as the party of national unity, the party of economic prosperity, the party with the only truly national leader and platform, and so forth. The history of the more successful third parties in recent decades suggests that they are operating on branch lines of the same national system. While enjoying the luxury of pointing out how similar the two older parties are, so that only they offer any real alternative to those who desire a change, third parties can none the less broaden the basis of their appeal only by diluting the doctrinaire programs which attended their birth. Social Credit in its federal heyday became increasingly difficult to distinguish from any 'small c' conservative group. The NDP may have moved less from the early CCF beginnings, but it has paid a double price: it continues to have internal differences over its left and right wings; and it remains a small third party, its largest contingent of MPs to date comprising less than 12 per cent of the Commons. The impact of television on party differences is not yet entirely clear, but it is obvious that the Conservatives and Liberals have added to their similarities those that come from using the same packaging and merchandising methods of trying to attract the electorate. The third parties are free to speak critically of 'image politics' as compared with their own loftier emphasis on 'substance,' but there is so far no convincing evidence that the 'politics of substance' can be sold through modern campaign devices, or that the third parties are actually avoiding 'image politics.'

Historically, of course, it is not difficult to find genuine differences between the older parties. The Liberals were traditionally free traders and therefore in favour of a low tariff, though they maintained an unmistakably protectionist tariff after coming into office in 1896; the Conservatives were for high tariffs, suitably modified to placate those parts of Canada that favoured low tariffs. Similarly, both older parties vied in supporting the imperial connection while working toward greater national autonomy, and in taking turns at supporting and opposing stronger centralized powers for the federal government as against greater (or less) provincial autonomy. On public ownership, welfare legislation, conscription, and indeed almost any controversial subject, the older parties can be found to be divided at least sometimes, though over time neither will be found to have prized consistency as highly as campaign promises. How far the historical differences between the Liberals and Conservatives have survived is impossible to determine with precision; in the 1980s the parties' traditional stands on free trade and tariffs, for example, have been almost reversed, the Conservatives now for free trade, the Liberals expressing scepticism about it.

It does no great injustice to the newer parties to suggest that they too, with some reservations made necessary by both their youthful ebullience and their failure to gain power at Ottawa, fit into this same general pattern. Third parties when young tend to differ sharply from all others, but the differences get rounded off – partly because the other parties try in some ways to resemble *them*. Interestingly enough, the holding of power (and conversely the lack of it) can itself generate party distinctions. Parties successful in winning a long series of elections literally run out of MPs with experience of opposition, while members in opposition forget what it is like to hold power. The winners come increasingly to identify themselves with the national interest, the perennial losers naturally becoming more attractive to electors in regions that feel neglected by national policies.

One of the points on which all parties are identical is the insistence of each that it is different from all its rivals. Paradoxically, in that too they are correct. The Social Credit party is clearly to the right of the others in most issues, and the NDP is as clearly to the left; Liberals and Conservatives are demonstrably straddling the same centre, but always offering the electorate different leaders, and different formations of regional support. Regional support is, indeed, one of the major distinctions to be found among the parties, a fact which can be convincingly illustrated by reference to the varying fortunes of the Liberals and Conservatives in Quebec. In the days of Macdonald Quebec was almost invariably Conservative, although the party was shaken by the execution of Louis Riel in 1885; in 1891 the province transferred its allegiance and since that time has only twice failed to send a majority (1958 and 1984), and frequently an overwhelming majority, of Liberal members to the House of Commons. This may be attributed historically to the greater Liberal sympathy with provincial rights, in part to the leadership of Sir Wilfrid Laurier, Louis St Laurent, and Pierre Elliott Trudeau, and especially, in recent years, to the wider tolerance and sympathy the Liberals elsewhere in the country have shown to French-Canadian ideas and ambitions even when they did not agree with them. This willingness to allow differences of opinion and to make substantial concessions and alterations in policy in order to obtain a greater measure of agreement had far-reaching consequences in the conscription issue, which in both world wars set the Conservatives against Quebec with disastrous effects on national unity and on the Conservative party. Thus in the four general elections from 1917 to 1926 the Conservatives carried a total of only 11 seats in Quebec out of a potential 260; in the five general elections from 1935 to 1953 the Conservatives carried in Quebec only 12 out of a potential 343 – making a grand total of 23 out of 603, or less than 4 per cent. In the intervening election of 1930 they carried 24 seats and also, incidentally, attained office. In 1957, while winning office, the Conservatives carried only 9 of Quebec's 75 seats, but carried 50 in 1958; in 1962 the party's quota dropped back to 14, while the Liberals took 35 and Social Credit 26; from 1962 to 1984 the Conservatives' Quebec holdings remained small, but the party's victory in the latter year under its first bilingual leader from the province encouraged it to hope for a more lasting change in fortune. Prior to 1984 the Conservatives with some success made a virtue of necessity and often denounced as excessive the Liberal concessions to Quebec. It is, of course, obvious that a majority in the Commons without any Quebec members is still mathematically possible, but the mathematics of politics is not a matter of simple addition: a party that has little appeal in Quebec is unlikely to be able to attract enough support elsewhere to win a majority in the House of Commons.

Conservative problems in Quebec before 1984 were matched by Liberal problems in the four western provinces, where the party has all but disappeared from provincial legislatures and had no more luck in winning seats in the House of Commons than its rival in Quebec; but where in Quebec the Liberals were able almost to monopolize the seats, the Conservatives in the west had to share the constituencies with the NDP, so that the west's seventy-seven federal seats have not been available as an offsetting factor to Quebec. These regional divisions in party support have naturally contributed to the theory that the older parties are failing to form a national consensus, a theory that may be weakened by the Conservative victory in 1984.[9]

In a related way the regional basis of their support provides continuing distinctions between the other parties. Prior to 1962 the bulk of the Social Credit members came from Alberta, and those representing the CCF also came predominantly from the west, with particular emphasis on Saskatchewan. The elections of 1962 and after, however, produced groups of parties whose geographical sources seemed to defy all the accepted regional distinctions: 1962, for example, produced a Conservative party which swept the prairies and took a majority of Maritime seats; a Liberal party which drew four-fifths of its support from central Canada and held only two prairie seats; a Social Credit group of twenty-six Québécois, two Albertans, and two British Columbians; and a New Democratic party with no members from the only province where it held power, Saskatchewan, but nineteen urban representatives scattered across the country. The elections of 1979 and 1980 saw the Conservatives take every seat in Alberta, while the NDP were strong in the other two prairie provinces and in British Columbia. The pattern's only stable element appears to be a reliable instability.

PARTY COMPROMISES

The foregoing suggests what is probably the primary political generalization about Canadian parties: that no party can go very far unless it derives support from two or more regions, which are politically the Atlantic provinces (in 1986 with thirty-two seats in the Commons), Quebec (seventy-five), Ontario (ninety-five), the prairie provinces (forty-nine), and British Columbia (twenty-eight). To gain power any party must have as its primary purpose the reconciliation of what may be the widely scattered interests of two or more of these areas. For this reason party leaders must be ready to modify their principles and policies, favouring neutral shades over flamboyant colours, however attractive the bright ones may appear. The prime ministers with the longest terms in office – Macdonald, Laurier, King, and Trudeau – all possessed in one way or another the capacity to hold together people with differing concerns, and it is no coincidence that the last three especially devoted much attention to the aims of French-speaking Canadians. Sometimes they paid a high price, risking support elsewhere because of a necessary preoccupation with the central regions – for attention to Quebec always includes attention to Ontario. There is little evidence to suggest that their successors may be able to behave otherwise.

The differences within the parties can thus be more acute than between the parties themselves; and each party, if it is to command anything approaching general support from its members, must work out some kind of consensus within its own ranks. Extremes must be made to accept something short of what they consider the ideal; the prairies and the Atlantic provinces make concessions to central Canada, Ontario to Quebec, free traders to protectionists, corporations to unions, farmers to factory workers – all of these vice versa, and so on across the country. The inevitable result is that the most successful parties tend to be parties of the centre, swinging gently to right or left, differing about the means, but not the ends, of bilingualism, or of employment policy, with a slight urge towards centralization or back toward provincial rights, the pendulum never getting far beyond the point of stable equilibrium. Parties in the United States exhibit similar tendencies and for substantially the same reasons.

To these practical requirements electronic journalism has brought a new dimension; for now the parties, especially during election campaigns, must sometimes work out their compromises in public, under not only the eye of the camera but the relentless questioning of reporters. The temptation to escape into 'image politics,' where the meaning of what a party spokesman says may have less impact on the viewers than how convincingly he says it, is often obvious. But image politics has always been around, under other aliases. Although less sophisticated technology did not take every political leader into everybody's home every day, campaign literature of the past reveals a sturdy reliance on slogans and billboards not generally impressive for their comprehensiveness and clarity. The truth is that the platforms of the older parties in particular have always tended to be unsatisfactory documents; for they must always represent the highest common factor in a series of widely divergent terms, and that is apt to be a small number indeed. The comparative insignificance of this general accord, however, cannot be widely advertised, and inasmuch as there is always a large fringe of voters who might not agree with even the most modest statement, the party platform falls back on vague generalizations and ambiguous terms. Platitudes are wrapped up in an elaborate coating of words and symbols in the hope that few voters will attempt to pick them apart and so come to realize to what a small extent the party is committed to definite action. Everyone wants peace, control of pollution, wise measures of social reform, sound immigration policies, scientific conservation of natural resources, improved educational facilities, high employment, an adequate system of national defence, measures which will stimulate international trade and widen the markets for Canadian goods; and the parties have promised these and other so-called policies freely. In recent years the use of opinion polls by the parties has led not only to a narrowing of the range of appeals the parties make to the electorate, but also to a greater similarity in the devices and techniques used to present these appeals. Possibly for this reason party leaders in recent campaigns have sometimes shown caution about campaign promises and the costs of their implementation, as well as the time it might take. But the electors during campaigns expect promises, and still get them; and occasionally a party leader exploits his opponents' promises by pointing out virtuously how much less he is promising, thus sparing the taxpayers' purse.

One historical way of widening a party's appeal is none the less still widely used: each party seeks to include in its announced plans a number of statements, each of which refers to a special area of interest, in the hope that almost everyone will find something to his liking that will catch his eye and perhaps his vote. Thus platforms may contain paragraphs on labour relations and the St Lawrence

Waterway (for the benefit of Ontario and Quebec); on the fisheries, the use of Canadian ports, and offshore oil (for British Columbia and the Atlantic provinces); on the port at Churchill, Manitoba, freight rates on grain, wheat prices, and oil and gas development (for western Canada); on the future of the Northwest Territories; and on retraining for the unemployed, especially the young. The absence of sharply defined principles, the softening of those which do exist, and the general attempt to emphasize sectional appeals are apt to produce platforms which bear a close resemblance to one another or, at most, vary only in the matter of emphasis. If the platforms are drawn up for provincial elections, where the distinction between the parties is often nothing more than a choice between competing sets of persons or between the 'ins' and 'outs,' the differences frequently become so slight as to be farcical.

Professor Hugh Thorburn has written of New Brunswick politics in terms that apply to other provinces too:

For each provincial election both parties draw up platforms. These are remarkable more for their similarities than their differences. For example, in 1952 both parties presented fifteen-point platforms to the electorate. The following points were common to both platforms: industrial development, electric power development, aid to agriculture, greater forestry, mining and fishing development, good roads, promotion of the tourist industry, securing financial assistance from the federal government, a health plan, aid to education, improved labour legislation. The Liberals were exclusive in advocating co-operation with the municipalities, a housing programme, aid for the disabled, penal reform, and a provincial library. The Conservative points of uniqueness were: land settlement, good government, and a promise to try to do away with the 4 per cent sales tax. Obviously, no philosophic difference between the parties can be found by examining these election platforms, and they are typical – merely lists of 'bright ideas' that the party hopes will appeal to the public. It is not unusual to find an item (expressed in different words) appearing on four election platforms of the same party in a row. The fact that the party was in power throughout the entire period and might presumably have enacted the required legislation during this time does not seem to occur to those who draw up the platform.[10]

The newer parties naturally show considerably less inclination to compromise than do their more successful rivals, with the NDP showing the greatest rigidity thus far. But even the third parties have in recent years shown unmistakable signs of accommodating their campaign utterances to the exigencies of the national political scene; the broader the appeal, in short, the shallower the platform is bound to become.

Since no third party has yet attained power at the national level, none has had a full chance to reveal how far it might go to match the opportunism at which its older rivals have become so adept. That opportunism, firmly embedded in the Canadian party situation, tends to minimize the importance of the platform and emphasize the importance of the party leaders, who are the ones chiefly responsible for making the adjustments and compromises which are necessary for retaining support. 'Our platform is our leader, and our leader is our platform' is sometimes openly avowed, and it is a maxim that is almost always accepted in practice. It follows, therefore, that the leader is the master of the platform, and tends to accept it as a general indication of the way in which the party would like him to move when and if he finds it desirable to do so. And 'no man in Canada,' Sir John Willison, one of Canada's most astute journalists, once observed, 'has been more inconsistent than the man who has faithfully followed either party for a generation.' Both Liberal and Conservative parties have been experimenting with methods of enlarging the roles of both their parliamentary caucuses and their extra-parliamentary wings in the formation of policy; it will be interesting to discover how, if at all, Sir John Willison's observation may have to be modified.

In the meantime, to return to the theme on which this chapter began, campaign practices have been so altered since television began to be the major source of day-to-day coverage of politics that it is entirely possible that the party platform as it has existed since Confederation may become obsolete. The reliance on endless poll-taking and on merchandising methods of 'selling' parties and their leaders ('TV can make a stupid but handsome person seem intelligent,' a seasoned television critic wrote of Parliament in 1982[11]) is making party commitments in print seem increasingly unprofitable, not to say unsafe; and much will depend on decisions about television made by the parties themselves – advised, no doubt, by professional advertising agencies with nothing to lose by the successful use of whatever publicity devices become available. One of the most discerning historians of the Liberal party, Reginald Whitaker, has written of the advent of television in the late 1950s that 'the Liberals were quite lost in the new medium. While some solid empirical evidence would be needed to show that Diefenbaker rose to power [in 1957] on the strength of his television image – evidence that is simply not available – it *is* certain that television was an unmitigated disaster for the Liberals, a disaster so frightful that the party leadership itself was appalled and shaken.'[12] After that disaster the party won several elections and enjoyed many years in power – until the next disaster. Parties, whatever their policies, can obviously learn to compromise with misfortune, but permanent success is never guaranteed.

2
Party organization

Party came down to us as an inheritance of the theological and ecclesiastical age. Its organization resembled that of the adherents of a Church; its principles or programme constituted a creed invested, like the creed of a Church, with the sanction of orthodoxy and heterodoxy.

M. Ostrogorski, *Democracy and the Party System*

A political party, however lofty its principles, is as sounding brass or a tinkling cymbal unless it can persuade an appreciable number of electors to support it. Even to qualify as a registered party under modern electoral law, and thus become responsible for various actions and eligible for accompanying benefits, a party has to have enough support to field fifty candidates in a federal general election; and after an election, a party acquires further rights in the House of Commons itself if it elects twelve or more of its candidates.[1] Quite apart from the joys of office, clearly the nomination and election of candidates are of primary concern, equal and frequently superior in importance to principles. To succeed in an election on even a small scale demands organization; indeed, the entire effective life of a party is closely identified with organization. To keep the party ideas and principles attuned to public opinion; to persuade the voters to seek the realization of their aims through one party rather than another; to stimulate interest; to systematize and consolidate effort before, during, and after an election; to bring the views of the party members to the attention of the parliamentary representatives; to perpetuate and give continuity to endeavour; to enable the voters through the enunciation of common purposes and the selection of representative candidates to become effective participants in one cause; above all, perhaps, to raise funds to meet the insatiable demands of operating the party and conducting its campaigns – all these aims can be achieved or at least aided by party organization. And the form the organization takes will be determined in large measure by the zeal with which the members of the party desire them. Even so, organizations can vary so much that generalization about them is not easy; but enough is known to make several observations possible.

In the first place, the nature of party organization has changed markedly since Confederation, because the demands made on it have changed. In the early decades, the local organization in each electoral district (known also as 'constituency' or 'riding') played a key role in supporting its member, particularly if he was of the governing party. Not only were the individual electors continually courted one by one (in the early days the electorate in each constituency was by modern standards extremely small), but lists were kept of businesses 'qualified' to receive government patronage, and even of newspapers fit to receive official advertising. If the constituency had been so short-sighted as to elect an opposition member, the governing party's association still had plenty to do, often under the leadership of its defeated candidate from the last election. Opposition organization, bereft of a government MP and his status as the purveyor of petty patronage, had to rely more on hopeful aspirations for support. Until 1919 the MPs in caucus generally chose the party leader when the need arose, and he was always an immediate or a potential prime minister.[2] Both the local organizations and the elected members played roles which have since altered or disappeared.

Secondly, one of the major changes deserving of separate mention has been in the specialized area of raising funds. 'In bygone days,' the Liberal party's *Constituency Organization Manual* of 1984 said nostalgically of money, 'the limited needs of the constituency were met by the odd coffee party or annual dance, and the larger needs of the national level were met by donations from major corporations. The constituency effort was amateur, and the national effort shrouded in secrecy.' Nowadays, the manual explains to party workers, changes in electoral law have encouraged broadly based political contributions through a scheme of tax credits for donors, and 'instead of impoverished constituency associations depending on handouts from the national Party, the national Party suddenly found its financial health dependent on the fundraising efforts of constituency associations across Canada.' To make its point clear beyond cavil, the Liberal party (in a move typical of any party) augmented its organization handbook of 1984 with a second entitled *Constituency Fundraising Manual*, which described how to raise money by every device from direct canvassing to curling bonspiels and fashion shows.[3]

Thirdly, it is apparent that the organization of a party in power has different problems from those of a party in opposition. The acquisition of power brings with it rewards so obvious that no party would seek to avoid them because of the accompanying pressures on its organization. But power also brings with it inevitable centralizing tendencies that can make it the more difficult to satisfy local associations the longer a party is in office. A governing party is naturally preoccupied with governing, and that itself can create tensions within its extra-parliamentary wing of a sort less likely to disturb opposition parties. Ministers assume a particular importance, and in many instances their regional significance will far outweigh that of the party's other elected members. Additional pressures can arise during times of stress; for example, during wartime a government naturally must give priority to prosecution of the war, and in doing so may develop policies of rationing and restrictions that make the party locally unpopular.

Repeated success at the polls in even so-called normal times can make an organization complacent. The most successful Canadian federal party from 1921 to 1984 was the Liberal, and toward the end of that period its leader scolded a conference of supporters in these terms: 'You can't organize without fire in your bellies, without faith in something, and the reason we are not growing stronger in organization and drawing new sections of the population into our party may be a more worrisome sign of the fact that the Liberals don't have that sense of mission and a sense of desire to guide the destinies of this country in the next quarter of a century.'[4] Underlying those words is a plain implication: opposition parties never lack a mission to get out of opposition. The 'new sections of the population' referred to by Trudeau in 1976 became specific targets for the Conservative party which triumphed in 1984.

Fourthly, modern methods of campaigning have profoundly altered the nature of organization, and not all the changes can be attributed to the fundraising already cited. Materials prepared by the parties for use in national campaigns, and news coverage of each campaign, place heavy emphasis on party leaders and their images, to the point where a dispassionate observer could easily conclude that the choices being offered to the viewers were among a handful of individuals, not the several political parties they led. 'Our party,' one of its former national directors admitted in 1980, 'has dissolved into an election-oriented, leader-dominated, media-manipulated, marketing machine ... The role of party militants is to supply applause for party leaders, to serve as background for the 11 o'clock television news.'[5] Those gloomy words were, revealingly, spoken of a party in power; yet even the opposition parties, not reduced to keeping a winner winning, have to modify their campaigning to suit their own needs and the expectations of the television audience, and they too find the nature of their organizations affected. Local organizations of every party have had to adapt themselves to such elementary facts as these: a small northern television station may have a signal that reaches only three or four far-flung constituencies, while an urban station may cover thirty or more seats, only one of which each local party association may wish to spend money addressing. The kind of regional co-operation perceived to be desirable among local organizations will clearly be different in such circumstances.

Nevertheless, all parties remain united in a desire to offer the public an organization that at least appears to be democratic from the bottom up. There is general agreement among observers that in regions where one party has a strong hold on the constituencies, as in the Liberals' prolonged federal dominance in Quebec until 1984, its apparent local democracy may be the flimsiest of façades; and east of Quebec neither of the older parties has been noted for a sturdy egalitarianism as the main feature of its constituency organizations. But all the parties have constitutions which refer to local associations as a matter of course, and as if they were everywhere fundamentally the same. The Progressive Conservative party provides for the recognition of constituency associations by the national body, and empowers each to adopt its own constitution. The Liberal party's basic document refers almost at the beginning to 'Liberal associations on a riding, district, regional and/or other constituent basis.' The NDP constitution simply assumes that local organizations supporting the party exist, and delineates their powers. All three constitutions, in differing ways, try to ensure that democracy is not so defined as to exclude women and youth.[6]

Whatever the constitutions decree or permit, a party organization is essentially an empirical device for producing concrete results, and one of its most obvious characteristics, if it is to be successful, must therefore be easy adaptability to circumstances. Party constitutions are often suggestive rather than mandatory, and a great deal of local autonomy is permitted and even encouraged, probably more in the older parties than in the others. But in them all interference from provincial or national headquarters may be resented by local organizations, and higher party authorities usually intervene reluctantly and circumspectly even in the most damaging of internal constituency disputes. (A notable exception has been the Liberal party's Quebec wing, which has had an electoral commission charged with seeking and approving candidates for the House of Commons.) The Canada Elections Act now requires each party leader to endorse in writing the candidate nominated by each constituency organization, and that power can be used to assist in bringing out suitable candidates – or even, on rare occasions, to refuse to accept an unwanted individual, as the Progressive Conservative leader, Robert Stanfield, did in Moncton in 1974.[7] But the senior organizations do not generally impose candidates on constituencies, and in using 'influence' will avoid the appearance of interference.

All Canadian parties, it must be emphasized, pride themselves on their complete identification with democratic procedures, although there is little agreement on what party democracy really involves. Thus the Toronto *Globe* in

1893, in an editorial preceding the first national convention held in Canada, wrote as follows:

The fundamental idea of a freely chosen party convention is the application of the principle of popular government to party institutions. A country may possess all the forms of free government and law-making, and yet the benefit of these will be practically withheld from those who are bound by allegiance to a party despotically governed. A party convention such as that to be held at Ottawa recognizes the right of every member of the party to a voice in the making of its policy, and the means to be adopted to carry it out. As the convention cannot include every member of the party, it is important that it shall be as large as is convenient, and shall be freely chosen and thoroughly representative of the great body of Liberals. Those conditions, we believe, will be fulfilled. In order to be truly popular and democratic it is necessary that the discussion shall be free, and that every delegate shall have a real voice and a real share in the proceedings. We have no fear of this great convention being conducted in any other way. Finally the publicity of the proceedings enables those who cannot take part to be made fully acquainted not only with the decisions of the convention, but with the discussion leading up to them. There have been unmistakable signs of an awakened interest in public affairs, and we expect that the reports of the convention will be eagerly read and freely commented on.[8]

Yet this convention did nothing more than frame a platform and help its members 'go home with their political faith strengthened and their political zeal quickened.'[9] It passed, it is true, a resolution of confidence in the leadership of Wilfrid Laurier, but there was no suggestion that it should elect a leader or even confirm Laurier in his position. This function of the party convention has been of later growth: it became fairly common in the provincial field during the opening years of this century, but did not appear in national politics until 1919.

Until recent years, these and other signs of the influence of the party rank and file or the party representative bodies were always sporadic and uncertain in the two older parties, although lip-service was constantly paid to the inherent virtues of so-called democratic control. In actual practice, the extent to which the leaders and their chief assistants felt the need for refreshment or re-dedication at the source of all party power depended on the fortunes of the moment. Success at the polls and the control of a government, for example, were usually taken as a sufficient justification and authorization for continued leadership, even although the convention from which the power had been derived and which had laid down a program was many years removed. The continued success of Mackenzie King thus led the Liberals to ignore the national convention and its legendary prestige and authority for twenty-nine years after 1919; while the Conservatives, with little love for conventions but less luck in elections, had no fewer than three conventions during that period.

Under such circumstances, protestations of a belief in the active participation of all members in party affairs began to sound a trifle thin. It is but fair to add, however, that few Liberal supporters themselves felt the need to assert their rights in the midst of plenty. A winning team is a good team; and it would be considered sheer foolhardiness to risk a new captain or even new instructions which might quite conceivably break the happy succession of victories. In contrast to this, the organization and practices of the New Democratic party are devoted to the maintenance of a close identification of the party rank and file with its leaders. In recent years other parties have been holding national meetings fairly regularly; in 1960, for example, the Liberals held their first Study Conference on National Problems, and in 1961 their first national convention since 1893 that was not called to select a party leader. Meetings or conventions of the national associations of both Liberal and Progressive Conservative parties are now required every two years by their constitutions, and these are frequently supplemented by irregular 'thinkers' conferences,' at which the parties' long-range aims are discussed. It is now common for parties to hold 'accountability sessions' at which leaders are queried on their stewardship, and discussions of the leadership itself often precede, and sometimes dominate, party meetings. The modern Progressive Conservative party, indeed, set some sort of record by using party assemblies to replace consecutively three leaders – Diefenbaker, Stanfield, and Clark – the first and third of whom had been prime ministers. None of these changes, it should be noted, occurred while the party was in power.

Through all forms of Canadian party organization runs a current of influences from the United States, clear and persistent, yet not strong enough to be called imitation. But differences are also common. Delegates at Canadian leadership conventions, for example, vote as individuals, and not in provincial blocs. In the United States the frequency and regularity of elections, the enormous number of elective offices, and the common practice of fighting municipal contests on standard party lines tend to augment the importance of all party machinery to an extent unknown in Canada. Canadian party activity is not nearly as formal or as sustained: there are often long gaps between elections; and when the test comes, it is frequently unheralded, and hence must be met by quick improvisation without the benefit of a prolonged preparation which can gradually lead up to an electoral climax on a certain day specified in the constitution. The American direct primary, through which rank-and-file party members elect the candidates who later run for public office, has thus made no impression on Canadians. The convention system has never been sufficiently important or corrupt in Canada to create a need for the direct primary as a necessary substitute, nor does the government readily lend itself to the primary device. It could with difficulty be incorporated into a scheme based on uncertain election days; and the one elective office to be filled for each constituency would make a primary an extremely expensive instrument for the achievement of so modest an end as the nomination of one candidate from each party.

Any attempt to discuss party organization in detail must be undertaken with the knowledge that variation in local attitudes, customs, and even language is the norm rather than the exception. A party's apparatus, in short, is part of each community's political culture, and practices which may be considered usual in one area may be condemned in another. It is generally true that forms of organization within a particular party will bear a family resemblance from province to province.[10] It is clearly impossible within the scope of one chapter to hope to deal with all the forms of organization of parties operating within the federal area and in ten separate provinces as well. A further obstacle is the absence of sufficient information on the subject. Party organization in Canada is no longer the virgin field for study and research that it was until recently, and there is a growing number of excellent works; but any general description, to say nothing of analysis and comparison, is still restricted by the limited facts available.[11]

The following pages are thus not as specific as would be desirable: the intention is to give a reasonably accurate impression, not a microscopic analysis. It should be remembered that even within one province no party insists on adherence to a rigid uniformity in matters of organization. The main objectives are to maintain party harmony and produce the maximum support on election day; and if the party members in one constituency wish to depart somewhat from the normal practice, provincial headquarters will be inclined to regard such idiosyncrasies with a helpful tolerance. Then, too, it must be realized that all parties are trying, through their organization, to build substantially the same kind of pyramid: a broadly based system of poll organizations at the bottom, upon which are constructed constituency, district or regional groups, provincial and national associations, all culminating in a solitary figure at the apex, the national leader.

THE POLL ORGANIZATION

All parties regard the constituency as the basic element in organization, and the poll derives its importance from the requirement that every constituency is for electoral purposes divided into polling divisions – that is, an 'area fixed by the returning officer, for which a list of electors is prepared and for which one or more polling stations is or are established for the taking of the vote on polling day.' That definition from the Canada Elections Act is supplemented by instructions to each returning officer (the administrator in charge of the electoral machinery in each constituency) to ensure 'that each polling division, wherever practicable, contains approximately two hundred and fifty electors.'[12] Since the average constituency may contain upwards of 40,000 electors, each will have 160 or more polls. Most of them in urban areas will include only a few city blocks; those in rural areas may be geographically large.

The procedures that permit every elector to exercise the right to vote without undue inconvenience provide a political windfall. To prepare the lists of electors in every urban poll (rurally the procedure is different) the returning officer is required to appoint pairs of enumerators such that wherever possible 'they shall represent two different and opposed political interests.' Once the lists are prepared by these beneficiaries of local petty patronage, each party uses them to its own advantage. The lists can, by careful canvassing of electors, be divided into known supporters, known opponents, and 'undecided.' By comparing contemporary lists each party can tell which polls in each constituency show the most promise or need the most cultivating, and by the use of lists from the last election each can find where it is gaining or losing strength – an element of particular importance in districts where the turnover of residents is high. The names of known supporters on the lists can be marked so that each party can make sure their owners are encouraged to vote on election day.

All that (and more) is work that can best be done by party workers most familiar with the ground, and ideally each party hopes for an active group of organized supporters in each poll. A large percentage of such workers work without any remuneration beyond the satisfaction of competing in a contest while helping a cause one believes in, or the excitement of contributing to the election of a particular candidate or party leader. But there are a few cash rewards: enumerators are paid for compiling the voters' lists, and deputy returning officers for presiding over each ballot box on election day. Unofficially parties may pay for the driving of voters to the polls or the fulfilling of sundry other minor tasks, some of which may be frowned on by the law. Quite apart from the morale-building that usually accompanies political enterprise (especially if it is successful), local political work provides an excellent training ground for future party activists, and many organizers and MPs have started as poll workers.

The parties' poll organizations are thus clearly significant but, as in so many aspects of politics, the significance has changed. The day is over when local political enterprise provided the major form of social activity outside religion, with few alternative sources of entertainment. Modern methods of campaigning appear to be reducing some of the need for local activity, since both radio and television emphasize larger stages, concentrating on the candidates' constituency bases, or the party leaders' national image. But local work remains necessary, for the continued arousal of interest in the party, the recruitment of new members (who, unlike mere supporters, will be expected to pay a small membership fee), or the holding of any one of a variety of functions for both these purposes. As long as the electoral system retains its present form there will be work to do among individual voters; and the demands of urban organization will remain different from those of rural. The high concentration of city populations may require broader and more representative bodies than can be provided by individual polling divisions, but Canada will always have large polls with widely scattered populations outside the towns. Party organization at its most local knows no arbitrary forms or standards: the successful form is the one that suits each area and the wishes of its partisans.

THE CONSTITUENCY ORGANIZATION

It cannot be emphasized too strongly that the constituency is regarded by all parties as the fundamental unit, for polls exist only as parts of constituencies. Constituencies, in turn, exist only as parts of each province's or Territory's share of parliamentary seats (except for the Yukon, whose lone constituency necessarily comprises the whole Territory), and that is what makes them so significant: a constituency has one seat, and only one party at a time can win it. Although the winning of a seat by acclamation (i.e., without a contest) was not uncommon in the simpler two-party system that prevailed after Confederation, every constituency is now the scene of fierce competition among the parties whenever it needs a member.

The role of the constituency, like that of every part of the electoral and party systems, has changed markedly since 1867. At Confederation a constituency was relatively small, containing perhaps three thousand electors, all males, whose support was sought on an individual basis by the two political parties then extant. A modern constituency, by contrast, except in the smallest province and the territories has an electorate fifteen or more times the size of its earliest predecessors, though it still returns only one MP. To its traditional functions have been added its new role in raising funds. With careful management, expenses will all be legitimately covered by reimbursements under the Elections Act, so that the riding will be able to consider as its own income any money originally raised for the campaign. The result is that many local organizations have unprecedented private bank balances of their own, some of them substantial indeed. Two recent observers refer to these wealthy ridings as 'a chain of feudal fiefdoms that the parties find increasingly alarming – powerful riding associations that, from the parties' point of view, could turn into political Frankenstein's monsters.' These unforeseen results of modern legislation on election expenses have a secondary impact: not all constituencies, because of variations in size and the nature of particular expenses, have equally benefited.[13]

The growth in financial strength of some constituency organizations has paradoxically occurred during the same period that has seen a growing emphasis on the party leaders' positions during election campaigns, with a consequent diminution of the role of each constituency's individual candidates – a circumstance about which local politicians are wont to complain. Yet even in the field of campaigning, the constituencies' roles have grown, though perhaps no more in campaigns for seats in the House of Commons than in the parties' internal campaigns over the party leadership. Ever since the first national leadership convention, the largest single category of delegates at Liberal and Conservative meetings has come from the constituency organizations, each of which is entitled to provide at least six voters for the leadership; in fact, the constituency delegates have always comprised a clear majority of those eligible to select the new leader.[14] Ambitious would-be leaders naturally woo the support of these delegates and, with modern methods of organizing and campaigning, try to influence each constituency's selection of delegates in the first place. A modern leadership campaign can be as well organized, and as expensive, as general elections used to be, and in both types of campaign the constituency organizations have come to play key roles. Recruiting new members for constituency organizations when a party's leadership is at stake can take on some of the aspects of a business, with zealots actually being paid for new memberships in some instances, some of the acquisitions (in the absence of precise qualifications in party rules) drawn from 'derelicts, kids, and motorcycle gangs.' The competent observers who reported that also agreed that it was organization that won the leadership of the Conservative party for Brian Mulroney in 1983,[15] and organization was equally plainly behind John Turner's selection by the Liberals in 1984.

The internal party organizations which determine a party's choice of leader become more public when a party, however its leadership has been settled, enters a national election campaign, for the traditional roles of choosing candidates for the House of Commons and supporting the party still remain. Here too individual constituency organizations are sometimes the scene of spectacular activities, for desirable candidatures can be hotly contested, especially if the partisans involved scent victory in the next general election. What were formerly small, quiet meetings for the most part, attracting attention locally because they did in fact each produce a candidate, have shown in recent years that they can become 'media events,' erupting into mass meetings of two or three thousand people. One of the technical reasons for this has been the looseness of the definition of party member in both Conservative and Liberal constitutions, which has made it possible for would-be candidates and their adherents to recruit 'instant members' with voting rights almost to the day when the constituency nominating convention is held. The packing of constituency meetings under such circumstances has always been possible, and was by no means unknown in earlier times. Modern methods of communication, however, appear to have increased both the opportunities and the temptations to manipulate nominating conventions for a variety of cogent reasons, all of them legitimate: to by-pass a constituency executive which has fallen out of favour; to replace a sitting member of Parliament whose constituency supporters would like to see retire; to capture the nomination on a sitting member's voluntary retirement; or to demonstrate how strong is the local party's democracy. For these and other reasons, constituency conventions that attract as many of the faithful as a national meeting to select a new party leader (and are as noisy and contentious) have become a familiar happening in Canadian politics, most notably in large urban areas.

For all that, most riding organizations do go quietly about their affairs as indeed – in the intervals between rowdily choosing delegates to attend leadership conventions or nominees for the House of Commons – do the more conspicuous among them. The riding organizations are what politicians often mean when they refer to 'the grass roots,' a curious term to employ for bodies that could not fulfil their functions underground.

In every province the federal constituencies are outnumbered by the provincial, in the smaller provinces by several times; so nowhere are the two sets of ridings likely to have boundaries which coincide apart from each province's own boundaries, which no riding at either level can constitutionally cross. The result is that all parties must have some kind of organization which serves both federal and provincial electoral districts, and within each party decisions have to be made about which is to be the 'basic' unit of organization.

The practices of the several parties in this regard vary greatly across the country, although their written constitutions bravely set forth what at least ought to happen. The New Democratic party's constitution reads: 'Each province of Canada [province in that context includes the territories] shall have a fully autonomous provincial party, provided its constitution and principles are not in conflict with those of the federal party.' That implies that many details are left to provincial parties; but subsequent clauses empower the federal council of the party 'to rule on whether an organization shall continue to be a provincial party.' That could involve the individual constituencies, for the same document empowers the federal council 'to intervene with respect to a federal nomination if the interests of the federal party are involved and if the provincial party concerned had failed to take appropriate action.' Appeal procedures apply to any action taken under these powers, but they are rarely needed because the powers are rarely used.

Neither the Conservative nor Liberal constitution provides such centralizing authority over the local bodies to the national organizations. The Conservatives prescribe that each recognized constituency association 'shall have the right to nominate the official candidate' of the party, and ten party supporters can protest almost any action of a constituency association; but the national party cannot intervene on its own initiative. The Liberal constitution provides the national executive with no explicit powers over the activities of constituency organizations, although one might argue that some powers are implied in such phrases as 'The Liberal Party of Canada shall ... provide assistance and leadership to federal Liberal constituency organizations ...'[16] All party leaders, of course, as noted earlier, can now refuse to certify a particular nominee as the party's official candidate in an election.

In truth, riding organizations in all parties enjoy great freedom to conduct their own affairs, a not unreasonable practice if one can assume that local partisans are likely to know their local conditions best. With exceptions, for which there are always good party reasons, parties accept not only the candidates chosen by their constituency supporters, but also each local president, vice-president, secretary, treasurer, and so on. On these officers are laid many responsibilities, and since they enjoy so much autonomy in constituency affairs much depends on their energy and zeal for the cause. If these flag, or if there is a high turnover of personnel, as can easily happen, particularly in urban and suburban areas, a riding organization can become moribund. Paradoxically, a party long successful in winning national office, as was the Liberal from 1935 to 1957 and 1963 to 1984 (apart from a brief pause in 1979–80), may find its local associations relying on a 'sure thing,' and thus becoming less than aggressive in supporting the party.

But the ideal constituency organization is neither moribund nor lazy. It is the key link between those parts of the party outside the riding and the polls within it. If its last selected candidate is a sitting member, it transmits opinions and complaints to him or her, a task altered but not eliminated by the parties' growing use of private opinion surveys. It tries to attract favourable local attention and counteract the unfavourable. The Liberals' *Constituency Organization Manual* in use in 1984 listed as local continuing functions, in this order: policy development and advocacy; fundraising, election readiness; membership recruiting and main-tenance; internal communications, external communications. Other parties, both formally and informally, follow similar patterns.

Most constituency meetings, whether held to discuss organization, policy, or nominations, tend to be orderly and even sluggish. Closed meetings, which only party members of an approved seniority attend, may be lively; but open meetings to which anybody can go are not generally turbulent. A typical constituency nomination meeting, for example, includes much established ritual: local rules decide who can vote, and at the meeting anthems will be sung, greetings from party dignitaries read or delivered in person, names put into nomination, and speeches made while the votes are counted, the candidates invariably adding to the total output when the winner obtains a majority and the losers move to make the choice unanimous. When a constituency meeting lacks the excitement attendant upon the choice of a potential MP – and most are expected to hold at least annual business meetings separate from any nomination – the proceedings will concentrate on fundraising, recruiting, policy, and reports on past activities. Flamboyant they are not; but it is worth repeating that all parties still regard constituency associations as indispensable factors in attaining power. Despite new techniques for sampling opinion, few politicians could be found today who foresee the disappearance of the reliance on local sources of activity.

INTERMEDIATE ORGANIZATIONS

Party structures between the constituencies and the provincial and national organizations are designed to function on both regional and social levels. Regional bodies may serve the party in areas where many constituencies are bunched closely together, as in large cities. Social organizations are designed to enlist the special interests of women, or youth; as the population ages, it is possible that parties will develop institutions for the special concerns of senior citizens.

Regional and district associations
Whether or not a party develops this kind of intermediate organization depends entirely on how it perceives its needs. In small provinces returning a dozen or fewer MPs no need may be seen to supplement the riding associations. The larger provinces, whose constituencies range from compact metropolitan areas full of highrise apartments to vast northern expanses, will need special structures. One of the most clearly defined of these is the Toronto and District Liberal Association.

The T&D, as it calls itself, in 1984 served thirty-seven provincial and twenty-nine federal ridings. (The Toronto district, it is worth noting, contained more federal ridings than Saskatchewan and Manitoba combined, and only three fewer than all four Atlantic provinces.) The metropolitan organization covers one of four regions into which the Liberal party divides Ontario, and it has its own officers, chosen annually by delegates from the sixty-six ridings it serves. It regards itself primarily as a provider of services for its 'clients' and has an executive director with a small staff whose duties include liaison with the ridings and other regional associations. The T&D provides technical services, ranging from photocopying to address labels, and information and advice on almost any relevant topic, including detailed poll-by-poll results of past elections and 'organization and election readiness training material.' Historically T&D has also proved to be an excellent training ground for future Liberal activists, the springboard that propelled them into higher political echelons.[17]

Associations of special groups

For several decades after Confederation neither the Liberal nor Conservative party offered special recognition to any women's or youth groups in its organization, politics being traditionally regarded as the peculiar territory of mature males. The gradual extension of the franchise to women, and the lowering of the voting age accompanied by growing populations of young people assembled in places where they were readily accessible to each other, such as university campuses, made all parties increasingly sensitive to women and youth in politics.

The party that pays the least formal attention to women, in one sense, is the NDP, and the reason is that it has assumed from the start that men and women were politically equal, so that neither needed a special organization; 'individual membership,' the party's constitution says, 'shall be open to every resident of Canada, regardless of race, colour, religion, sex, or national origin ...' The NDP, none the less, requires that representation on its council must include 'at least one ... woman' who has 'the specific responsibility for sitting on the Participation of Women Committee,' a standing committee of the council 'to assist and encourage women's participation in all forms of political activity.' The Conservative constitution recognizes that in the provinces there are both Progressive Conservative Women's organizations and a National Progressive Conservative Women's Caucus, and ensures that there will be women involved in every key element of the party's national association. The Liberal constitution asserts that 'there shall be, within the structure of the Liberal Party of Canada, a commission established to represent and promote the interests of women within the party ...'; and again at all levels of the party the participation of women is guaranteed in the constitution.

Similar provisions for young people's associations are recognized by all three parties. In the NDP, for example, the organization of the youth group, the Young New Democrats, is left initially to each provincial party, but the party's federal council can also charter New Democratic youth clubs if a provincial party has not done so. The NDP's national constitution does not define 'young,' but the Liberal specifies '25 years of age or under,' and the Conservative refers to 'persons under the age of thirty' as eligible representatives of the party's youth at meetings of the national associations.

Other intermediate party organizations can always develop, and it is of historical interest that both women's and youth organizations first made their way into party structures through committees. The Young Liberal Federation, for example, was first integrated into the party's Ontario wing as a standing committee; the national party now provides for a Standing Committee on Native and Original People's Affairs, which may some day join the commissions the party now provides for women and youth. The constitution of the NDP allows for membership in the party of not only individuals but 'trade unions, farm groups, co-operatives, women's organizations and other groups and organizations which, by official act undertake and abide by the constitution and principles of the Party.' While these various associations are not part of the NDP's structure, their organizers often also work for the NDP, and are in that sense informal but often important sections of the party's organizational apparatus. Sometimes, it should be added, individual members of an affiliated group express grave reservations about their association's ties with a political party and the annual meetings of the Saskatchewan Federation of Labour, for example, are regularly the scene of lively debates on the subject.

The general effectiveness of the parties' intermediate organizations is not easy to assess, for each depends so much on the attitudes taken toward them by the parties' senior associations, and on the energy and determination of active individuals who may come and go. Youth organizations, inevitably, are always being sapped by the steady ageing of their members. Like the poll and riding associations, the intermediate structures do not have all the incentives that go with winning an entire provincial or national election (although of course they all contribute to the senior organizations' achievements) and for that reason parties sometimes encounter difficulties in keeping them alive. In earlier days, indeed, the older parties showed every indication of not wanting lesser organizations to be particularly active except as the proverbial hewers of wood and drawers of water: Reginald Whitaker has described the Liberal Women's Federation of thirty and more years ago as 'an organizational ghetto, a reservation where an important section of the electorate and of the party could be effectively contained and managed while any real participation in the party's leadership was prevented.'[18]

Such days are in general gone for intermediate associations; Christina McCall-Newman has portrayed in *Grits* the importance of the Liberals' Toronto organization in the party's history in the 1960s and 1970s, and the Conservatives' modern historians have cited the significance of PC Metro 'as a vehicle for disgruntled Tories to complain about their ongoing electoral failure in the area.' The same authors recount that before the Conservative convention of 1983 'the leadership of the Ontario youth wing was strongly behind the candidacy of Brian Mulroney.'[19] Not all these activities were necessarily to the liking of each party's national establishment, but what is revealing is that they took place at all. Formerly regarded as at best 'useful,' intermediate party associations in recent years have demonstrated that they can at times exert a strong influence from within.

THE PROVINCIAL ORGANIZATION

It is obvious that one cannot discuss polling divisions without discussing constituencies, or constituencies without reference to provincial and national organizations. This should not be surprising, for every party wants its organization to be an integrated whole. It is not unrealistic, indeed, to suggest that the provincial associations in most of the less populous provinces are also intermediate organizations, for a provincial party which, even if totally successful, can deliver at most only ten seats in New Brunswick, or fourteen in Manitoba, is unlikely to be listened to as attentively at the national level as an urban body based on substantially more ridings. Still, it is probably true that the provincial association, if it is effective at all, is the head of each party organization in Canada. Nevertheless, the national organization, which used to be no more than a loose federation of autonomous provincial bodies, has been growing in importance. It is of great significance, especially where the provincial party is weak, as a source of both direction and national leadership of the kind exploited in election campaigning. Poll, village or town or municipality or ward, riding, region or district, and province – these comprise the foundation of party-building proper, and the national organization forms a superstructure that looms above it. The top rank of the party is rarely independent financially: after the election of 1984, for example, both the NDP and the Liberals were in need of money, the first expecting to recoup funds 'mostly owed by its provincial sections,' the second hoping that 'some stubborn provincial wings of the party can be persuaded to join in a financial restructuring.'[20]

A fundamental reason for this kind of problem is simply that each federal organization commonly has contact with the voter primarily through the province and at other lower levels. It would, of course, be conceivable for the party to keep its federal activities apart from those of the party in the province, but this would necessitate the creation of one party organization at the provincial level and another in the federal constituencies, a duplication of effort and a confusion of activity that would be extravagant in terms of expense and effort and possibly bewildering to the voters. The constitutions of the Conservative and NDP parties assume that all provincial and territorial sections also work for the national organization, although the former is more casual about their place in the party's structure; the Liberals' names twelve 'member organizations' which comprise the party's federation (one each for the provinces and territories), and in its *Constituency Organization Manual* adds that three of these associations (in Alberta, Ontario, and Quebec) 'concern themselves with federal matters only.' Apart from those striking exceptions, it is normal for all three parties to work through the existing provincial organization if it is strong enough to carry the load; but this cannot be done without a frank recognition of the primacy of the provincial party in the field. Local patronage is so much less important than it formerly was that party workers now question its existence. In some provinces, however, acquiescence by the national interests in provincial leadership may still be given more readily in that the larger part of petty patronage is in the gift of the province, although the balance is to some degree maintained by federal control over the bulk of the really good jobs. Mutual interest and self-protection can usually be relied upon to keep the two interests working smoothly together, and dissension between federal and provincial sections of the same party can be disastrous. That does not stop it from happening: Prime Minister King had a legendary feud with Premier Hepburn of Ontario, another Liberal, in the early 1940s, and twenty years later Premier Thatcher of Saskatchewan had such poor relationships with the federal Liberals that his defeat in 1971 was welcomed both in Ottawa and among provincial Liberals who got along well with their national leader. Such incidents also reveal the degree to which relations between the provincial and the national organizations depend on particular circumstances.

While the parties' provincial organizations differ not only from each other but possibly from their own colleagues in other provinces, each for its own needs must follow a general pattern that involves representation from those with particular claims, as well as members of the public who wish to support it. Recognition within the association is commonly accorded to the party's candidates in the last federal and provincial elections (or sometimes the nominees for the next election); the party's senators, if any; delegates from ridings and women's and youth organizations; and in some cases delegates-at-large selected by the party's provincial executive, which is itself always part of the apparatus. In addition to the party establishment, any citizen who is not a supporter of another party can sign on as a member. All the loyalists are of course expected to honour the party's objectives, which range from upholding the party's principles to winning the next election by any means not actually illegal. The election itself is not necessarily directed by the expansive machinery outlined above, but by appointed officials (often professionals in some provinces) chosen by the party's leader, to whom they are responsible.

Provincial party organizations are required to hold at least one meeting annually, if for no other purpose than to elect officers. But such gatherings may also appoint committees on whatever topics are pressing, hear reports and speeches, and generally try to stimulate interest in the party's activities. What else the annual meeting does will depend on circumstances; the needs of a party in opposition will differ from those of the party in power, and an annual meeting of any party just after an election will display characteristics not commonly found if the next election is imminent. ('A party in power,' one distinguished Liberal once observed at a national convention, 'cannot pass resolutions with that fine free careless irresponsible rapture which is characteristic of the opposition.') Schisms are likely to surface at an annual meeting: outlying sections of the party complain of neglect from the more populous regions; supporters who want better relations with the federal wing vie with those who put the provincial organization first; the left and right wings battle to secure offices; the rank and file members urge that the executive pay more attention to their ideas; the party faithful indicate that it would be agreeable if the leader would listen more to the people who chose him. A provincial annual meeting can be a lively business, attracting useful coverage from the media. However, the Ontario Liberal party once did not hold an 'annual' meeting for eleven years, despite repeated demands from provincial supporters that one should be called.

A provincial convention for the purpose of choosing a leader, which usually means a new platform or revisions of the old, is the most colourful of party activities in the province. The leadership convention has now won acceptance in all provinces, and there is no doubt that it is now so firmly entrenched that any other method of choice would be almost unthinkable. It was not always so. The earlier method, which was used in all provinces as well as at the national level, was for the party members of the legislature to make their own choice, although as the convention idea gained ground, there was a tendency to adopt half-way measures. Thus in 1925 the Conservative leader in Nova Scotia was chosen at a joint meeting of the provincial party executive and the candidates nominated by the party for the coming election; and in 1929 the Liberal leader in British Columbia was chosen by the Liberal members-elect and approved by the executive of the provincial Liberal Association. In 1911 in Ontario the Liberal members notified the meeting of the Reform Association of the resignation of the leader, but the whip 'made it clear that the message he bore to the meeting on behalf of the legislative contingent was given as a matter of courtesy and was not by right.'[21] These early examples were exceptions to the understood rule that the party members in the legislature chose their leader, and thus the leader of the party.

That practice, undemocratic though it would now be considered, had some merits. The members, while they often represented only limited parts of the province or country, had an active sense of responsibility in the matter for they were themselves most closely affected by the leader's ability to perform his functions. If he proved competent, he probably became premier; if not, he could be quietly asked to resign and make way for a successor similarly chosen. His talents had already been put to the proof in the legislature and party councils where his colleagues could judge their quality; and while wire-pulling and manoeuvring for support by inside cliques were common, at least they were not reinforced by the demagogy and luck that often influence the choice by the present method.

There is no absolute guarantee that the use of a convention will enable the party to institute a new system of democratic control by breaking away from the official or semi-professional element, and that is true at both the provincial and national levels. In most instances it is the steady party workers who form the mainstay of such meetings. Responsibility for party policies and decisions can thus be lifted from the shoulders of those who should bear it, the party leaders, to those of the convention, which in no way can be considered to have responsibility in any real sense at all. Over half a century ago the late John W. Dafoe in his biography of Sir Clifford Sifton stated substantially the same argument:

Sir Clifford knew enough about conventions to know that unless public opinion was vigorously stirred up the convention would fall under the control of the official element in the party . . . In theory, the holding of a party convention returns the control of the party as to policy and leadership into the hands of the rank and file; in practice, it often means an opportunity to get an apparent endorsation from the rank and file for leaders and policies that are ripe for retirement. This perversion is possible owing to the manner in which delegates from the polls are usually chosen − not by a public gathering of electors, but by slimly attended meetings of the local party associations, which are usually made up of workers and members who are keenly interested in the party. A party convention, unless care is taken in the election of delegates, is apt to reflect not the opinions of the great mass of voters, but the wishes and purposes of the ultra-partisans − the 'hard-boiled' practitioners of the political game.[22]

Those words were written before modern methods of communication and persuasion made the manipulation of a convention easier. The personnel of conventions may have changed, but recent studies suggest that those who become delegates, while no longer 'under the control of the official element in the party,' are nevertheless drawn from remarkably small fractions of the populace at large, as are members elected to legislatures. Leadership conventions (and this appears to be equally true of provincial and federal bodies) 'are useful,' John Courtney has found, 'in reducing some of the demographic imbalances that obtain in the parliamentary groups of both parties and in making the bodies responsible for selecting the Conservative and Liberal leaders noticeably less biased toward the areas of the parties' electoral strengths.' But, Professor Courtney adds, 'glaring deficiencies nonetheless remain when compared to the total population.' Another trio of scholars has reported that the delegates at conventions they examined 'were representative of the more privileged groups in Canadian society.'[23]

That is but to say that conventions are full of people selected in ways which, depending on the party and the region, may represent some segments of the populace to the virtual exclusion of others. And conventions can be criticized on other grounds. Although a convention is expected to make decisions on exceptionally difficult matters, each calling for careful consideration, the weighing of various alternatives, and the exercise of dispassionate judgment, neither the qualifications of the delegates nor the conditions under which they must work are at all adapted to the tasks in hand. The time and facilities for gaining information at the disposal of the delegates are limited; some of the candidates are frequently unknown to many of those present; the feverish surroundings are almost certain to react unfavourably on the delegates' capacity to make wise decisions; and there is always a danger that the convention may be rushed off its feet by the emotionalism of the moment. Thus arguments concerning party representative democracy carry but little weight when applied to an overwrought crowd of two thousand or more people trying to transact business of this nature and importance in the space of a few hours of frantic activity, which commonly also includes a good deal of strenuous partying in the non-political sense. The convention may also throw a heavy burden of expense on people seeking the party leadership, thus excluding some possible candidates, for extensive organization and travelling in the months preceding a convention are increasingly expected of candidates.

The provincial convention (as distinguished from the meeting of the provincial association) was formerly not called at stated intervals, but only when there was a leader to be chosen, and the custom has been steadily growing that a convention should be held to confirm or reject any leader who has been chosen by any other method, and at regular intervals in any event. (The Liberal party of Ontario has had constitutional provisions for three separate kinds of conventions: the leadership convention, whose purpose is obvious; the annual meeting, which conducts business and may discuss but not resolve policy; and policy rallies, to be called 'once every two years to develop and determine policy.' At these rallies, the leader was held accountable for his actions on the decisions of the previous rally or annual meeting.)[24]

If for any reason the members of a legislature have to choose an interim leader, it is now common for the leadership to be confirmed or otherwise settled at a convention. A famous case arose in Ontario over forty years ago when Mitchell Hepburn retired from the premiership and advised the lieutenant-governor to send for G.D. Conant, although the latter had not been chosen by even the Liberal members of the House. So great was the general dissatisfaction among the Liberals throughout the province that they demanded a convention to make the choice, expressing their discontent through riding and regional associations; and when the meeting was held, the mantle did not fall on Conant. In Ontario and in most of the other provinces, the fact that a party leader has not been chosen or confirmed by a convention is now a reproach which can be adequately answered in only one way – approval by a convention called for the purpose.

The responsibility a leader who has been originally elected by one convention owes to another convention is not fully established, and there are too few precedents from which to generalize. He (or she) may feel that if he resigns the leadership, only a convention can accept the resignation. It is not uncommon for a leader to submit his resignation to the party executive, but only the most acute dissatisfaction could cause a convention to be called to force him out. For example, open hostility to Premier Anderson in Saskatchewan led to the submission of his resignation to the Conservative convention in 1933 as a way of clearing the party air, and he was thereupon re-elected by the convention with enthusiasm. An effort to avoid this awkward situation appears in the Conservative constitution, for it provides for the calling of a convention not only 'upon the death or retirement' of the leader, but any time the party fails to win an election.

While a convention may be called for purely provincial purposes, the party representatives whose interests lie largely in federal politics are not expected to remain aloof. It is usual for provincial conventions to recognize the 'federal presence' at their proceedings by seating MPs and officials of federal constituency associations, who may or may not be voting delegates on all matters. National party leaders are also sought as convention speakers, and if the party is in power, cabinet ministers are frequently in attendance. The federal wing may indeed have particular reasons for wanting to secure the choice of a friendly provincial party leader.

The choice of a leader follows a recognized pattern, and the standard practice is to lay down rigid rules to prevent any one candidate from gaining an unfair advantage. Names are formally submitted in writing, nominating speeches are usually made, the candidates themselves are allowed to speak for a specified time, and the convention makes its choice by a series of secret ballots, usually with the provision that the lowest candidate drops out after each ballot until one candidate has received a majority of the votes cast.

This bald account gives no hint of the tense excitement that runs through all these proceedings, which are reminiscent of both a revival meeting and a football game.

THE NATIONAL ORGANIZATION

'National organization' is a term which may suggest some special kind of leadership in party affairs, the national association enjoying a dominant position over those at the provincial, regional, or riding level. That is in fact not so: the allegedly lesser groups all enjoy a great deal of autonomy, and while they are all expected to be loyal supporters of their respective parties' federal wings, that does not in itself give 'the feds' a continuing hegemony. As previous pages have emphasized, the fortunes of a party's national association are inextricably tied in with those of other sections. The federal president of a party has been known to refer to the national organization as the party's orphan, and successful political leaders (as distinct from party officials) have sometimes been scornful of their party's own bureaucracy, as if they could somehow, having attained high public office themselves, get along without it. That is not true either.

Part of the frequent overshadowing of the national organizations stems from the nature of parties in Canada. Canada is a federal state, and all the major party organizations are federal too. The parties' member organizations, whatever each party's constitution calls them, are all closer to the ridings, and thus the electorate, than national offices located in Ottawa. The national offices now generally depend heavily on the lower levels for financial support. In earlier days, when the national offices of both the Liberals and Conservatives raised their own funds, it was too often from donors who contributed in ways that the parties' political leaders did not even want to know about.[25] The political leaders, and not the party officials, whether the former sit on the government or opposition benches, are the winners of elections, the people who receive national coverage from the media. Occasionally a party president for particular reasons may have what is fashionably called a 'high profile,' but it is never so high as to obscure the party's political leader.

An entirely separate set of reasons for the national organization's lack of power derives from the nature of the parliamentary system. A prime minister or a leader of the opposition, or a provincial premier and his or her opposite number, all have public responsibilities which come from the constitution of the country, and would exist whether or not party organizations did. The leader of even the weakest opposition in a legislative chamber often has to react quickly to public events, whatever his party's platform may say. A prime minister or premier has a double responsibility to the crown, the source of his commission, and to the legislature whose majority keeps him in office. Mackenzie King, who was prime minister of Canada for more years than any other individual, told a large audience on his retirement: 'A Prime Minister is not responsible to a party organization or to a political party; he is responsible to Parliament, and through Parliament to the people of the country as a whole. Unless we are to abandon the basis on which constitutional government rests, and substitute the decisions of a single political party for the authority of Parliament, and for the respect owing to the Crown, we cannot guard too closely against any course which, even to appearances, might tend in so disastrous a direction.' The body King warned off that disastrous direction was his own Liberal party, which he had led from 1919 to the convention he addressed in 1948 – its first such meeting, incidentally, in all King's time as leader. Joe Clark, who was prime minister for a much shorter period in 1979–80, was by that time accustomed to regular meetings of his party, the Progressive Conservative; but chroniclers of its modern history found that 'throughout Clark's tenure as national leader, he and his party had never really paid much attention to the National Executive Committee.'[26] No leader of the New Democratic party could be as cavalier toward the organization, as its constitution requires a convention 'at least once every other calendar year,' at which the party's officers, including the leader, are elected.

The two older parties, as suggested above, have also been trying to bridge the gap between the political leaders and their organizations, not only through more regular meetings which allow for leadership reviews and accountability sessions, but also more informally by electing active politicians as party presidents. The Liberal president of the mid-1980s, for example, was a former MP and cabinet minister who unsuccessfully sought re-election in 1984. The Conservative party president in the same period was a sitting member of Parliament. Nevertheless, at least one prime minister invented new ways to find advisers outside the conventional party machinery: Pierre Trudeau, building on precedents that were established by his predecessors, made of the Prime Minister's Office so formidable a branch of government that it aroused public criticism by his opponents and more quiet concerns among his supporters.

All parties none the less are paying increasing attention to their national organizations, a statement which is perhaps misleading where the NDP is concerned, for that party always has emphasized its internal democracy. The Liberals will not again be able to go twenty-nine years without a national convention. The Conservatives, quicker to hold meetings because of the perceived necessity of changing leaders (at least until the choice of Brian Mulroney in 1983), have had considerable experience in the working of their own machinery, and their national constitution will serve as a representative example for others. Party constitutions, it must be reiterated, vary greatly in details, and even within a single party the working structure does not always follow slavishly the dictates of the constitution.

All three parties' constitutions begin with preambles that summarize the party's philosophy. The NDP cites 'democratic socialist principles' in its opening paragraphs. The Liberal begins with the assertion that the party 'is committed to the view that the dignity of each individual man and woman is the cardinal principle of democratic society.' The Conservative opens with a declaration of practical purpose aimed at facilitating the participation of all supporters in promulgating the party's aims which, as defined in 1956 and reiterated in the latest edition, put first: 'We believe in freedom of worship, speech and assembly; loyalty to the Queen of Canada; and the rule of law.'

At first sight these preambles may seem to place the three parties far apart (the Conservatives' being especially noteworthy as the only one that mentions the monarchy) but once past their statements of principle the constitutions get right down to the listing of who can belong to the party, what they can do, and how they can do it. The two older parties especially show similar characteristics, and while their constitutions vary in names and details, the Conservative can fairly represent them both. The longest article in the Conservative constitution is entitled 'Voting Membership,' and describes an association whose members range from all the party's privy councillors, all senators and MPs and defeated candidates from the last election, to delegates from any approved group supporting the party. (The total voting membership of the national association amounts to many hundreds of people.) The Conservative constitution lays few specific duties on what the association is to do when in convention, but does describe in detail who may be on the national executive and its executive and steering committees. The president of the national association, if not being already remunerated as a member of either parliamentary chamber, is entitled to an MP's pay 'in direct proportion to the amount of time the president gives to the responsibilities of office.' The constitution also requires the creation of a headquarters at Ottawa under a national director 'appointed by the Steering Committee on the recommendation of the national Leader,' the national office 'to serve as the organizational, administrative and co-ordinating centre for all branches of the Party.' The headquarters staff performs all the usual functions of distributing information and assisting other party organizations when asked. The Liberal party has essentially the same kind of national organization performing similar functions, although structures and the names given them vary.

The relatively sophisticated extra-parliamentary associations which are now common to Canadian parties have behind them a difficult process of birth and maturation. When the annual party meeting, whatever form it took, was in its infancy, it had some difficulty securing nourishment, possibly because the upper echelons of both parties included people who were not anxious that their child should thrive. In 1947, for example, the resolutions of the Liberal Federation were buried for three weeks before being made public, an interval that was presumably devoted to their revision and possible emasculation by the parliamentary members. When they finally appeared, even so sturdy a Liberal paper as the *Winnipeg Free Press* gave only half of them in any detail, and the report was tucked away near the back of the paper – a treatment which showed either alarm or contempt for the formal opinion of the highest council of the Liberal party. The Progressive Conservative Association in 1947 passed resolutions which did not seem to be particularly startling in any way; but they apparently caused consternation at Ottawa. For although the party had all the scope in these matters which comes from being in opposition, the resolutions were advanced with the astonishing proviso that there was no intention of committing the whole party membership to the association's proposals. The meeting, it was added, was not a policy-making convention, because its sessions were too short to permit of adequate research, consultation, and consideration. Why the national party organization should waste its time in passing resolutions which have no official character and which any party follower or leader could disown at any time was not explained; but the statement almost certainly indicated some uneasiness on the part of the parliamentary group at the prospect of having its hands forced by a rival party body.

The national convention (as distinct from a meeting on policy) is a special and formerly irregular manifestation of party activity called together either to construct a platform, or to plan for party organization, or to elect a party leader, or to do all three. Its future, like that of its more humble relation in the provinces, is apparently assured, and both older parties are showing a tendency to call more, not fewer, conventions, and at settled intervals. Before 1956 the Liberals had held only three conventions, and only two of those to choose a leader; the Conservatives had held four, all leadership conventions. Since then both parties have held so many meetings – to elect leaders, construct platforms, or just to think – that it is not always clear what should be classified as a convention and what should not.

The national convention, copied from American practice, was first brought to Canada by the Liberals, who held the first general policy discussion in 1893, and the first leadership convention in 1919,[27] when in a resolute effort to rehabilitate the shattered fortunes of the party and to choose a successor to Sir Wilfrid Laurier they called upon all members to unite in support of the cause of Liberalism. The results of the next election in 1921 were as encouraging as they had been a quarter of a century before, and the value and prestige of national conventions were greatly enhanced by the convincing manner in which this one had apparently passed the test at the polls. *Post hoc ergo propter hoc* may not carry conviction in an argument; but any political party will gladly accept the sequence of events and forgo the logic.

The Conservatives for many years had little liking for or confidence in national conventions, although in 1910, at what appeared to be a very low point in their fortunes, Robert Borden succeeded in securing party consent to a meeting as a source of inspiration and a means of bringing the party leaders into closer touch with their followers. The early Liberal convention furnished the encouraging precedent. 'The Liberal party was never so strong,' ran an editorial in the *Toronto News*, 'as during the three years immediately following the famous convention of 1893. It had ideals worth fighting for. The leader and his aides stood upon firm ground and laid about them in an ecstasy of bludgeoning. They knew the temper of the reserves.'[28] The proposed Conservative convention, however, was for a variety of reasons postponed; and the electoral success of 1911 removed the most urgent inducement for a meeting.

Borden had been chosen leader of the Conservative party in 1901 by the usual method of a caucus of Conservative senators and members of Parliament. On his retirement in 1920 his successor was selected by a curious system which was invented for the occasion by Sir George Foster.[29] Each party member of the Senate and House of Commons submitted, as his suggestion, a list of names in order of preference with the reasons for his choice attached; and Sir Robert Borden, having considered these carefully and consulted with his cabinet, was then to make the selection.[30] After much difficulty, frequent discussions with Conservatives outside as well as inside Parliament, a serious divergence of views between ministers and members of Parliament, and the refusal of the position by one candidate, Sir Robert finally selected Arthur Meighen, the popular choice of the caucus, who a few days later became prime minister.

On Meighen's retirement in 1926, his resignation was accepted by a 'Conservative Conference' of senators, members-elect of the House of Commons, and defeated candidates; and a temporary successor, Hugh Guthrie, was chosen to lead the party in the House. The disastrous reverse the Conservatives had just suffered in an election, and the contrasting success of the Liberals, convinced the majority of the conference that some greater effort should be made to identify the Conservative party as a whole with the selection of a new national leader. The obvious way to achieve this end was to hold a national congress of the party. The call was accordingly issued, and the first Conservative national convention assembled at Winnipeg in 1927. R.B. Bennett was chosen leader, and the next election returned the Conservatives to power. Once again, a convention had been followed by victory.

But the system could not guarantee immediate results. On Bennett's resignation, another Conservative national convention met in 1938 and selected Dr R.J. Manion as his successor, only to see the party meet virtual annihilation two years later. After another singularly unsuccessful experiment with a modified version of the old system of choice by elected politicians, the party in 1942 turned once more, though with some reluctance and little confidence, to the national convention. But neither the 1942 convention, which chose John Bracken, nor that of 1948, which chose George Drew, was able to produce a winner, and it was not until the choice of John Diefenbaker in 1956 that the convention system of choosing a party leader led the Conservatives to victory at the polls. Since then conventions have produced winners and losers for both parties, and the practice of selecting the leader in a large representative convention is established beyond doubt. An incidental by-product worthy of note is the reduction of the role of the parties' supporters in Parliament in the choice of their own leader, whom they are none the less expected to serve loyally.

It is probably still true that there are a few Liberals and Conservatives who have not yet been fully convinced of the virtues of the system of choosing a national leader by a convention. Most people believe that it is efficacious as a publicity device, vote-getter, and rouser of enthusiasm, and that a candidate who can carry a convention successfully is also likely to be the kind of person wno can carry an election. But these beliefs were long tinged with a lack of confidence in the reliability of the convention's judgment on men and measures, particularly with the new dimensions added by television. Nor is it possible with the present loose party organization to 'manage' the meeting and bring it under any kind of effective control. This was not always so; Meighen was apparently the chief instrument in securing the choice of Bracken at the Conservative convention in 1942 and King the one whose influence resulted in the election of St Laurent in 1948. St Laurent, in his turn, was scrupulously careful to choose no favourite as his own successor in 1958, as was Lester Pearson in 1968 and Pierre Trudeau in 1984. Diefenbaker, making an unprecedented bid to succeed himself in 1967, after the Conservative party's extra-parliamentary wing had succeeded in calling a leadership convention against his clearly expressed wishes, did not choose his successor either, nor did Joe Clark, fighting for his own job in 1983.

For all parties, the composition of a national convention is bound to be varied and complex, for it is highly desirable to have all elements in the party represented. However, there has always been a decided tendency to provide generously for the official section of the party, the members of federal and provincial cabinets and legislatures. The practice not only gives these members a large number of seats, but because of their experience, broad acquaintance, prestige, and familiarity with the issues and candidates, it places them in a position where they may exercise considerable influence over the convention. But this group, based as it is on a dozen legislatures in the provinces and territories, is far from homogeneous, and dissension, if it should arise, is not as likely to appear between official and non-official sections as among the political leaders themselves. The presence and influence of this element can, however, scarcely be regretted. They represent much of the practical wisdom of the party and constitute its more experienced members; their future lives and conduct will in large measure be determined by the decisions of the convention – a fact which is, admittedly, as likely to lead them to be short-sighted as long. Neither party has apparently considered the possibility of apportioning delegates on a basis of votes cast for the party in the last election.

The resolutions passed by the convention, which become the party platform, are drafted and considered with care, although not necessarily at the convention itself. Any party association may send in suggestions, and a resolutions committee is appointed and at work some days before the convention assembles, sorting out the proposals and preparing the material for consideration by the convention committee on resolutions and the convention itself. The committee eventually reports to the convention, and the platform it proposes is debated and passed, item by item. In many instances, this approval is cursory and largely formal; but in others, the discussion may be keen and amendments may be moved and in rare instances carried. The real platform-maker may thus become the resolutions committee, and a genuine effort is therefore made to have it both large and representative of all interests and geographical areas.

The election of a leader by the national convention follows with substantial exactness the procedure already outlined for provincial conventions engaged on the same task. In the 1919 leadership convention the Liberals did not allow the candidates to speak in their own behalf, but the restriction was made almost meaningless by the candidates being given an opportunity to display their wares in the discussion on proposed resolutions. The Conservatives, however, preferred to follow the more common and straightforward practice of allowing candidates to address the convention under a strict time limit, and it is now the practice in both parties for candidates to be allowed equal time, the order in which they speak determined by lot – the whole, of course, planned with an eye to television coverage. The election is made by secret ballot – a vast improvement on the American open declarations by states – and the balloting proceeds until a candidate receives a majority. A substantial number of delegates are usually pledged in advance, but there is nothing to show that this is a serious restricting influence in enabling a convention to come to a decision. All kinds of external aids to emotion and general enthusiasm are present, as they are in provincial conventions: pretty girls (both French and English) register the delegates; musicians play inspiring airs; rousing speeches go on and on interminably. More variations have appeared with the advent of television, which provides such vivid portrayals of what is going on that delegates now can often be seen, at the site, watching on television the convention they are attending.

The atmosphere of the convention is best given by an eye-witness; the following newspaper account of the concluding stages of the election of Mackenzie King at the first of them is still representative of them all:

The decisive vote was cast and the electric period of waiting begun. There remained a tag end of resolutions to be passed and orators bellowed and perspired in the faces of an audience that was thinking of something else. The great majority was jammed in the corridors, coatless, panting, eating messy ice cream cones, sucking at pop bottles through straws and talking, talking interminably. Here and there a woman delegate, uncurled and damp, talked prohibition or wandered through the crowd. The heart of the assembly was in the Ontario committee room where the scrutineers were translating the will of the assemblage into figures. Outside, a brass band performed amid the dust unregarded.

There were half a dozen false alarms. Bursts of tired cheering from the main hall caused a stampede through the narrow side entrances. But bit by bit the big hall filled as the time drew near. Brown of Alberta was making a rousing speech when the time came, but he might as well have been making it in Cree in his native province, for all the attention he was getting. There was only one thing the audience cared about, and that thing was being rushed in by the door in front of the Quebec delegation. Brown swallowed his peroration and hustled into the background, and a hush fell over the great crowd as Premier Stewart of Alberta stood up with the fateful paper in his hand. There was silence till Mr. King's selection was announced, then pandemonium broke loose. Mr. King had no reason to complain of his reception as leader. There may have been a lack of abandon in the Ontario cheers, but Quebec and the West made up for it. It had to be done all over again when the figures were given.

Then came one of the really nicest incidents of the convention, the motion by Mr. Fielding that the election be made unanimous. While it is the customary thing to do that, it takes real grit, and an innate sporting spirit to do it, as Mr. Fielding did it. Unquestionably, he would have liked to crown his long career with the greatest honour his party had to bestow, but there was not a hint of bitterness, not a shadow of anything but whole-souled sincerity in his short, manly but graceful speech. Mr. Graham followed, back in his old form, mentally debonair as ever, equally eager to offer his services in the ranks ...

Mr. King's speech was adequate and careful, nicely appreciative, duly modest. He omitted nothing; he said nothing he should not have said. He perorated effectively. He did not get across quite as completely as in his speech of the previous night when he was fighting for the prize he had won, but the speech he delivered was quite satisfactory to his audience, or at least to that part of it which was given to satisfaction at all.

The convention came to an end, appropriately enough with 'God Save the King.' Taking the political interpretation of the National Anthem the crowd sang 'send him victorious' with especial fervour. There was a last cheer, a stampede to the platform where the successful candidate underwent the penalty of greatness by shaking a multitude of hands, and the Liberal Convention of 1919 passed into history.[31]

Add buttons, hats, sandwich-boards, walkie-talkies, and microphones and cameras, and one has the 1980s' version of the same thing.

The choice of the convention is frequently narrowed by the necessity of choosing not only an able leader, but one whose qualities and background are such that he is likely to appeal to the voters and secure the return of his party to office. Personal integrity is indispensable, but the so-called popular qualities have certainly not been conspicuous in all the leaders chosen in recent years. Political experience in the House of Commons rather than in the provincial legislature is one of the most common qualities, but it need not be long. Provincial premiers often run strongly, and sometimes win, as Robert Stanfield did in the Conservative convention of 1967. But a provincial premier, by his close identification with one province, may not be well known or acceptable to delegates from elsewhere. Mother tongue (as between French and British) is often of paramount significance, but the role attached to it is apt to turn primarily on the political situation at the time of choice rather than on any permanent principle. The folly of attaching too much importance to many of these personal factors is best illustrated by the unfortunate fate that overtook Robert Manion in 1938. He was a thoroughly likeable man, with a long parliamentary experience which included five years in the cabinet; he was a war veteran and an eloquent speaker; he was a Roman Catholic from Ontario married to a French wife, a combination which might well have appealed to both Ontario and Quebec. Yet although he was the choice of the convention, he led his party to overwhelming defeat.

Manion's experience remains a striking demonstration of the pitfalls that await any leader, however chosen. Especially when in opposition, parties are likely to be scrambling for a winner, and the Conservatives until 1983 had tried leaders from every part of the country except Quebec (if one overlooks the brief and rather eccentric prime ministership of Sir John Abbott in 1891–2). The Liberals, comfortably accustomed to being thought of as 'the government party,' found all their winners after Confederation alternately from Ontario and Quebec. The selection of John Turner in 1984 may have breached that informal rule, for he was a resident of Ontario for many years but had family connections with British Columbia. In that province he sought a seat in 1984, to further Liberal fortunes west of Ontario; he won his own seat, but the party made no other gains in the west. The Conservatives in the same election were led by their first leader from Quebec chosen in convention: Brian Mulroney's family was of Irish origin, not French, and he led his party to an overwhelming victory.

A concluding reflection on the national convention suggests yet another similarity to the conventions which choose the provincial leaders. Although there can be no doubt that the environment is unsuitable, the time for consideration deplorably limited, the delegates' knowledge of the contestants frequently inadequate, the danger of a candidate sweeping a convention off its feet always a grave possibility – despite these and other circumstances working against success, the selective function of the national convention, judged on its record, has been astonishingly well performed. The parties have shown that they can in convention generally choose people of outstanding ability and character. One would find it difficult to assert with confidence that any other method would have given better results.

THE NEW DEMOCRATIC PARTY

The New Democratic party has been frequently mentioned in the preceding pages, but it is entitled to at least some undivided attention because both historically and in its relations with various segments of Canadian society the party can with truth claim to be different from the Liberals and Conservatives. The Co-operative

Commonwealth Federation, from which the NDP was in part formed, prided itself on being 'not just another party but ... a new venture in the technique of applied democracy.' But the party always showed a sturdy and even conservative interest in the realities of political life, which the NDP has inherited. Certainly the general organization of both CCF and NDP groups has shown a number of old party characteristics. There are undoubtedly great differences between the organization of the NDP and that of the other parties, but the resemblances in all three are many. After all, the general aim of each is to elect candidates to office by inducing the voters to give them vigorous support, and these efforts must be made over a given area under certain conditions. It is therefore not surprising to find that the general machinery each party constructs for this task is similar. It is true that the CCF and NDP have insisted on their unique character, as indeed have all parties at all times; and they have frequently scorned (again in the best party tradition) the loose organization, and the techniques and spirit of their rivals. In some measure the CCF was able to demonstrate the truth of these contentions, although many of the differences would not appear to be as profound or as significant as the statements of the party would indicate. The NDP, while its organization is clearly the heir of the CCF, is somewhat more like the older parties than its honourable ancestor.

The most distinctive feature of CCF organization was the assorted grouping of its members at the lowest level, a product of its history rather than its philosophy. In the early 1930s a number of separate protest groups and minor parties came together in a coalition designed to secure more effective political action; but they insisted on maintaining their individuality and making it essentially a co-operative endeavour. After some years these separate parties disappeared; but the CCF remained in local clubs or units (the terms were interchangeable), and other organizations, such as trade unions and farmers' societies, might affiliate for political purposes. The NDP recognizes the importance of supporting groups in a more formal way. The federal constitution of the New Democratic party, first adopted in 1961, provides for two classes of membership: individuals who agree to accept the constitution and principles of the party, and whose application for membership is approved by the appropriate provincial party; and organizations that undertake to accept and abide by the constitution and principles of the party. Individuals pay a small membership due determined by each provincial party, of which part is transferred to the federal party; special arrangements are made for family memberships, and for those on social assistance. Affiliated groups pay fees also, which go to both the federal and the appropriate provincial party. The NDP's system of raising funds from trade unions particularly has caused considerable controversy in areas where, for example, trade unions are associated with governments whose legislatures are dominated by other parties; but it should be noted in fairness that the NDP's methods of raising funds are at least open to public view, and that the bulk of the criticism comes from newspapers and other sources associated with the party's opponents. Until the report of the Committee on Election Expenses in 1966, little was known of the sources of funds, or the methods of raising them, used by the other parties.

As with the older parties, the key element in the party's organization is the provincial party, and the basic unit within that is the provincial constituency organization. Thus in Saskatchewan every individual member of the party automatically belongs to a constituency organization, and affiliated groups participate in the activities of the constituency organization on a basis mutually agreed upon. (Any person belonging to an affiliated organization who does not wish to support the NDP may be able to opt out.) Each provincial constituency organization has an executive elected from among the party's qualified members, both individuals and affiliated groups. Each federal constituency organization has a similar executive, one of whose chief duties is to co-ordinate the provincial organizations within the federal constituency into an effective unit. In Saskatchewan, where the party has its oldest roots, there are fourteen federal seats and over four times as many provincial, and co-ordination of activities can be complex; but if the provincial constituency organizations are in good shape, the work is greatly facilitated. Each provincial constituency organization is charged with 'the general administration of the affairs ... at all times between conventions, and at the time of the convention or at subsequent meetings [will] divide the constituency into zones,' where members are empowered to elect a zone chairman and appoint organizers.

The governing body of the Saskatchewan NDP (which continued to use 'CCF' in its title until 1967) is the annual provincial convention, which has the power to amend the party's constitution and program, and elects the party's chief officers, including the leader, each year. (As with the CCF, the actual practice is to re-elect the existing leader; but formal machinery for deposing a leader has always existed.) The personnel of the convention, as with all parties, is broadly representative of the party, and includes all members of the provincial council; the party's MPs and MLAs; at least ten delegates from each constituency chosen in convention; and delegates from affiliated and young people's organizations. The provincial executive, which meets bi-monthly, consists of the officers of the provincial association (that is, the leader, the president, and vice-presidents); five members from the provincial council; one from the young people's section; and an appointed secretary-treasurer. The provincial council, which meets at least twice yearly to review the activities of the executive and give directions concerning them, consists primarily of the officers of the provincial association; the presidents of the constituency organizations (or substitutes for them); the province's two members on the party's national council; three from the youth section; one

Saskatchewan MP and three MLAS, each elected by their fellows; and three from the provincial women's committee.

The preceding mass of detail is necessary to emphasize some peculiarities of NDP organization. The party goes to elaborate lengths to maximize internal party democracy, and to keep the party's politicians as far as possible under some kind of control. The leader is annually elected; no party member while serving as MP or MLA can be elected to other party office; the provincial executive is dominated by ordinary party members, the only political officer being the leader himself. In addition, the party's constitution has a strong article on discipline, which forbids anybody to publish or circulate what purport to be the party's views without the council's approval. Any five members of the party can request disciplinary action against a sixth which may, after a hearing by the appropriate constituency organization, result in admonition, suspension, or expulsion of the erring member by the provincial executive; a final appeal lies to the council. The restrictions on publishing party views, and the process of expulsion, it is to be noted, both rest in the hands of the party's lay leaders, not the political. Finally, and most interestingly because of its implications for the principles of responsible parliamentary government, there is the legislative advisory committee, whose description deserves quotation:

Article 14

   Section 1: An Advisory Committee composed of four members appointed by and from the Provincial Council and one member appointed by and from the Provincial Executive who shall be advisers to and observers of the Members of the Legislature concerning the implementation of the program of the Association ...

   Section 3: The chairman shall report to the Executive and to the Council (a) concerning the implementation of the program of the Association and – (b) on the attendance at caucus meetings of the Members of the Legislature and of the members of the committee ...

   Section 6: Whenever appointments to a Cabinet are being made, the Political Leader shall submit the names of his proposed Cabinet Ministers to this Committee, which shall act in an advisory capacity, realizing that final responsibility for Ministerial appointments must rest with the Premier.[32]

The final quoted clause reveals as clearly as any single statement could one of the fundamental problems of all party organization in Canada: the reconciliation of some measure – perhaps no more than a façade – of party democracy with recognition of the essentials of responsible government. Responsibility, in the public interest, can only mean responsibility to all the members of a duly elected legislature, not just to the members of a single party. Yet the political leadership of a party with what it considers a unique and even indispensable program may find itself caught between the wishes of the party, on the one hand, and the requirements of parliamentary principles, on the other. The older parties, despite recent innovations in their constitutions, still solve the potential problem simply by giving, in effect, vast powers to the party's political leadership, powers that are enhanced even more when the leader is a premier or prime minister. The NDP, and before it the CCF, have tried to enlarge the powers of the party per se, but in practice appear to have had to accept in one important area a modified but substantially similar version of the older parties' solution. This general problem is referred to again in the next chapter.

3
Party activities and problems

We won't need any human sacrifices for some time. We've just had an election.
Ben Wicks cartoon, 13 November 1984

The two preceding chapters have outlined the historical and organizational backgrounds of parties, on the assumption that one must have some knowledge of where parties have come from, and what they consider important in their own structures, to comprehend some of their main activities. Chronicling the development of the parties' more formal manifestations can be misleading if one stops there; but each individual working within a party inherits and becomes a piece of its history, and participates within its organization. This participation is by no means unimportant, and it shows every sign of becoming more so as organization develops and as popular expression through party channels becomes increasingly common. But, as has already been suggested, the success of the party in its major task of winning votes and thereby attaining office does not by any means depend solely on these formal committees and showy gatherings. Without discounting the personality of the leader as a factor in his party's success, a great deal depends on the prosaic labours of the canvassers and field workers and their ability to make an impression on the individual voter. A party is above all a fighting organization; and while it must be firmly founded on the opinions and goodwill of its members and must provide occasional open demonstrations that it can attract public interest and support, it must also adopt the army practice of keeping its own counsel on many matters and directing a substantial number of its operations in private. Thus by far the greater part of a party's labours in organizing the constituencies – in providing canvassers, in checking voters' lists, in adopting means to get its supporters to go to the polls, in raising money, in procuring support by promises of special jobs or general employment (and perhaps, in older times, in buying votes, a far rarer method than is generally supposed) – is accomplished as unostentatiously as possible and is entrusted to those workers who through inclination or self-interest will give the party unquestioning support. This part of the organization and those who direct and operate it constitute the party machine, a name that optimistically suggests the mechanical efficiency with which the party is presumed to deliver the vote on election day.

THE PARTY MACHINE

The word 'machine,' like 'patronage' and 'politics,' in popular usage often connotes sinister enterprise of some sort, and the parties do not help to clarify the terms when they use them to accuse each other of indulging in undertakings they all find necessary. But a machine is only an organization, and patronage, while it can be abused, is an indispensable factor in what the organization does, especially when a party is in power. The activities of all the parties are indispensable factors in politics, and politics is essential in any government with even modest claims to be 'free.' (Machines and patronage, of course, can exist in any government, free or not.) One of the striking developments in the rise of the modern democratic state has been the adaptability of parties to such varied changes as the extension of the franchise, the waging of war with extremely sophisticated technical devices, and the invention of policies to guarantee minimum standards of health and welfare to entire populations. The modern state has so multiplied its activities in the past century that it is now common for groups of all kinds to turn first to a government when they need assistance or protection. At the governmental level the major vehicles of change have been the parties.

What citizens expect from government in the last years of the twentieth century is a long list of protections, services, and benefits, and the electorate's expectations of government are thus expectations of the parties who seek responsibility for conducting government. One of the modern ways in which parties have learned to compete with each other, indeed, is to offer the electors new benefits or extensions of old ones, and a common way for one party to criticize another is to accuse it of planning real or fancied reductions in popular governmental services. Inevitably, reactions against assistance from the state for everybody crop up from time to time, and one of the natural reactions to them is the creation of a demand for yet more services, to compensate for the losses caused by any reductions that may have resulted from changes in government policy. The parties are inextricably a part of all such movements, for it is the parties who take, and are expected to take, the major initiatives in offering and implementing change. Any Canadian prime minister down to at least the 1920s, for example, would have been surprised and puzzled by the suggestion that it was his duty to accept responsibility for the condition of the national economy, for the creation of work for unemployed citizens, and the caring for those who cannot find work. His modern successors do not question that 'job creation' is a responsibility of the state: they merely argue over how best to go about it. If a modern government fails to come up to expectations, possibly because a problem may actually be insoluble, it is likely to find itself, however hard it may have tried, being treated as a scapegoat. So far little attention has been paid to the increasingly obvious possibility that one of the unsuspected functions of an electoral system is to choose not only a government for the immediate future, but to single out a group for future banishment.

Parties, even when most successful, are always aware that the next election is never more than a few years away, and the preoccupation with their own internal organization, already noted, is one of the indications of their concern over being prepared at all times. The steady development of party organization in recent decades, as suggested, has itself produced problems, of which tension between the political and the extra-parliamentary wings is probably the most important. The argument over who really determines party policy is in turn the most significant element in that, and it is relatively easy for a party in power under a parliamentary system to decide that the last word must rest with the political leaders. But a party in power has to decide whether the extra-parliamentary section should have any say at all in policy – a question that was more readily answered in the negative before internal democracy overtook the parties. And a party in opposition, lacking the prestige that accompanies having cabinet ministers among its prominent members, may want to seek from its rank and file any help it can get. Yet a party in power can have difficulty deciding whether, for example, the real heads of a party in any particular province should be the federal ministers elected as MPs from the area, or the executive of the organization that helped them accomplish victory. Patronage offers a special aspect of that problem: the ministers, as the responsible leaders under a constitution presumed to provide for 'responsible government,' will naturally feel that they alone should be in charge of whatever perks there are, while the organization will equally naturally feel that it should at least be consulted, if not deferred to, about the same largesse.

No party ever settles such problems permanently, for changing circumstances and the frequent addition of fresh personalities keep relations between its political and extra-parliamentary wings in constant flux. In the early days of extra-parliamentary organization, when a minister would normally regard any party structure that existed as his anyway, some establishments of almost classical symmetry could be found. All the most famous (or notorious) of these political private armies were of provincial origin, and some of them, such as Maurice Duplessis's Union Nationale in Quebec, or the Conservatives' Big Blue machine in Ontario, were legends in their time. One of the best-known organizations, unusual in that its head was able to use it to serve him both provincially and federally, was that of Saskatchewan's James Gardiner; and as an example of a well-co-ordinated fighting unit, in this case Liberal, it is worth describing. Gardiner was fortunate in that he came from a province whose population was small enough to support only one dominant minister at a time, whether he was the premier or in the federal cabinet. (Larger provinces often have more than one 'boss,' each with his own fiefdom.) Gardiner also drew strength from the presence of his party's national leader, Mackenzie King, as a Saskatchewan MP for several years: King lent prestige to the party, but sensibly left the province's local affairs in provincial hands. In provincial Liberal affairs Gardiner's voice had no serious competitors, while at the federal level Gardiner's recommendations on patronage in Saskatchewan usually carried a convincing authority. Gardiner's record as a politician (he spent over twenty years each as an MLA and MP) gives many insights into the historical role of the political leader in relation to his party, and his use of patronage as an instrument in his own and his party's fortunes.

The Liberal machine in Saskatchewan before Gardiner went to Ottawa in 1935 had always depended on skilful use of those departments of government which afforded widespread and frequent contact with the electorate. In the province's earliest years after entering Confederation in 1905, when a new school system was being created to cope with the children of immigrants, the Department of Education was also useful in facilitating the development of the governing party's organization. By Gardiner's time the key bureaucracy was in the Department of Highways, where many public servants were often indistinguishable from party workers. The highways inspectors, for example, were among the most active of the partisans; and though they did not often discuss politics with the voters, they were most sensitive to any party problems in their districts and were a constant source of information for the party authorities. Road supervisors, sanitary inspectors, liquor store managers, and many others were loyal supporters of the party and usually energetic party workers as well. Appointments to the service were made, of course, largely from staunch Liberals; public works, especially roads, were undertaken with a clear eye to party advantage, and the contracts were granted in exchange for party support. The power of the Liberal machine was eventually broken; and although the party later returned to power, its organization was never as highly developed or as successful as in the earlier period.[1]

An interesting by-product of the Liberal organization appeared when the CCF government assumed office in Saskatchewan in 1944. One of its pledges was the elimination of patronage and the institution of a merit system, but the proposal to carry this into execution precipitated a struggle within the party, some of whose supporters demanded that patronage be retained. The reason advanced was the natural but far from original one that the old gang had all the jobs and that the new government would find itself thwarted in its work by an unco-operative public service. A reform act was eventually placed on the statute books, to such good effect that in 1962 the CCF-NDP provincial convention passed a resolution critical of the numbers of civil servants who were not sympathetic enough toward the party.

There is little reason to suppose that party machines have disappeared; they have merely become less conspicuous and more discreet. It was part of the electoral process to reward partisans for their contributions to the maintenance of the party in power. It assumed that the extra-parliamentary wing of the party, whether provincial or federal, was not expected to be influential in the formation of party policy, except in so far as extra-parliamentary influence was interpreted by the political leaders. Gardiner, for example, was convinced that his management of patronage followed the correct method: how could a minister be truly responsible if he could not control his own workers? And what kind of responsible minister would rely on appointees chosen from among his opponents, or even from the politically neutral? On that he was at one with Canada's first prime minister, who wrote shortly after Confederation: 'I think that in the distribution of governmental patronage we carry out the true constitutional principle. Whenever an office is vacant it belongs to the party supporting the Government, if within that party there is to be found a person competent to perform the duties. Responsible Government cannot be carried on on any other principle.'[2]

The 'principle,' it must be emphasized, was ancient and honourable, pre-dating by centuries the invention of responsible government. The struggle for responsible government in Canada, extolled in the history books as a triumph of colonial democracy over executives sent out from imperial Britain, was itself in part a struggle over patronage, the elected legislators wanting control over what governors had. It was in another sense one more step in the transfer of patronage powers from monarchs to elected members of parliaments, a step leading in due course to twentieth-century attempts to work out devices and institutions that would transfer to acceptable modern policies the same problems that used to be solved through the use of patronage. Patronage today is a survivor of a tradition in which rulers not only appointed their trusted supporters to positions of power, but also encouraged artists to pursue their creative impulses. If, indeed, the world were to be deprived of all the literature, painting, sculpture, and music produced under political patronage in the past, it would be an impoverished place. Modern governments are still striving to find the ideal way to provide for patronage of the arts now that monarchs and wealthy aristocrats have lost their authority.

Political patronage, then, is not necessarily bad; nor is it corrupt, although, like many another institution, it can become so. When a party in power exploits its position to benefit its own supporters it is using public funds, not its own. It is also adhering to the constitution, for it is that body of documents which gives a prime minister the real word in the appointment of judges and senators, among others; and gives his administration the authority to govern, which includes overseeing the expenditure of public funds in myriad ways. Patronage means that when a party enjoys years of power, its opponents are effectively cut off from any significant share of favours. This may result in a judicial bench stocked with former supporters of one party, and a Senate the majority of whose members may be of an opposite persuasion to the majority in the House of Commons. The upper echelons of the public service, in both departments and crown corporations, are staffed by appointment, and an incoming party will find itself with many confidential advisers chosen by its predecessor, now in opposition. These are no mere theoretical possibilities: they were encountered by Diefenbaker in 1957, and by Mulroney in 1984. In both cases (and there are older precedents) Conservatives then received their turn at appointing people sympathetic to Conservatives, a swing of the pendulum obviously agreeable to the two older parties since Confederation. If, as the editors of one pertinent book aver, patronage is 'the process by which governments award employment or contracts on the basis of partisan support rather than on the basis of merit,'[3] both older parties could justifiably retort (with the silent acquiescence of the ghost of Macdonald *et al.*) that partisan support is itself a form of merit, and not one to be lightly discarded.

Dissent to the system might be expected from third parties who do not attain power federally; but they, when they win provincial elections, also invariably find support among their partisans. After all, public offices have to be filled somehow. If heredity and conquest are virtually obsolete as methods, and election and 'merit' are found inappropriate, how else does one choose judges, senators, administrators, board members and others than through appointment by somebody? And what more appropriate somebody could be found than those trusted to govern the whole country?

In any event, patronage remains an important adjunct of government throughout Canada, a fact not boasted about by parties in power. It has certainly not lost its appeal for provincial governments. No province has a complete merit system in the public service, though several have passed statutes apparently designed to put up at least a pretence that such a system is in force. The federal service, as will be seen, is in considerable measure under a merit system; but there are those in authority who, while reconciled to a life of virtue, still recall with nostalgia the old uninhibited days which, while undoubtedly troublesome and even at times embarrassing, nevertheless had compensating advantages in the constituencies. Thomas Van Dusen, in a revealing paragraph, has described what happened when the newly elected Diefenbaker government attempted to eschew patronage in 1957–8: a number of Conservative members found themselves handicapped in their constituencies while the patronage, gravitating naturally to the civil service level, showed a tendency to benefit Liberals because of traditions established under a long Liberal reign.[4] The prime minister who took office in 1984 clearly inherited his predecessor's staffing problems.

Closely allied to the party patronage system is what is known as the 'pork barrel,' a kind of large-scale patronage and bribery offered to a community in the hope of winning support, an appeal to what President Cleveland years ago called 'the cohesive power of public plunder.' These promises are not pledges on matters of general policy which the party, if elected, will redeem; they are special concessions dangled before a particular interest or area in exchange for the election of the 'right' candidate. In any such bidding, the party in power enjoys a substantial advantage; for it is not only in a position to implement its promises, but it can, if it desires, spend the money first and trust to the collective gratitude of the community to repay the debt on election day. 'The "pork barrel,"' one writer once said in words that still have applications, 'dispensed with equal rapacity by all parties and governments since Confederation, has been the worst penalty of our Canadian democracy. It has been the chief source of whatever of corruption has degraded our public life during the past fifty years. It has sinned more than all other agencies combined against efficiency and honesty in politics. And it stands to-day as one of the chief reasons for the extravagance and waste that father taxation and debt.'[5]

That statement is probably too strong for much of contemporary Canada, although there is no evidence that the millennium has been reached. In older days, tariff protection used to be the most widely used of these inducements, for a protected industry could mean much to a constituency's prosperity. In both world wars, MPs competed with each other in seeking for their ridings whatever munitions factories, airfields, or military camps were being established. At all times public works (a post office, a dam, a bridge, a dry dock – anything to which a sitting member or a party could point with pride) have had an irresistible appeal. In more recent decades health and welfare policies have been at least suspected of including a pork barrel component, for while the resulting programs are not commonly considered as 'pork' in the usual sense of the word, they undoubtedly benefit all citizens and are, equally undoubtedly, very popular; it is often impossible to tell whether individual policies are pork, or are legitimate responses to genuine needs. Many expenditures aimed at the voters in particular ridings might be expected to be denounced by opposition parties, but parliamentary rules in Canada historically made it easy for a party with a majority to slip items into its spending proposals, commonly at the end of session when members were anxious to go home.[6]

In fact, an opposition party can do little but criticize or make promises, awaiting the day when it will be its turn to draft estimates and vote them through an acquiescent House. Deserved improvements in anti-government constituencies can be neglected, while patronage is lavished in areas where a government is supported. The following exchange, unusually explicit in its detail, is over half a century old, but its essence could be repeated today. The main speaker is a Conservative, whose party had been returned to power, after a decade in opposition, a year earlier:

MR. McGIBBON: The riding which I have the honour to represent, and which is an important one from the revenue standpoint, has been literally starved for about ten years. We think it is time that members on this side of the House should have some of the requirements of their constituencies considered. We are not pressing for appropriations this year, but we cannot understand the minds of some hon. gentlemen opposite. After having fed so freely from the public estimates for the last ten years they are still hungry .... When the time comes, when we can loosen the strings of the treasury, his [the minister's] first consideration should be those constituencies which have received nothing for some years past.

MR. HANBURY: Conservative constituencies?

MR. McGIBBON: Yes, Conservative constituencies. I am one of those who believe in being frank about these things. I took my medicine when I was sitting on the other side of the House and could not get anything; we all had to take that medicine ... We take the ground that we are not going to have hon. gentlemen opposite collect the fees while we write the prescriptions. I want to press very strongly upon the Minister that this action be taken, and I do not think any member of this House will object to it. We are all human; we all know what we are here for and most of us are pretty good party people. We follow our party sometimes when we differ from it, because of the greater good to the country, but when the time comes, as we hope it will come, when this depression lifts and the treasury contains a little money, we want the needs of the people in those parts of this country which have been neglected looked after before there are any railway stations built in Temiscouata, or new wharves or anything of that kind.[7]

A modern version of the same complaint may include whole regions, as in the years before 1984 when Liberal governments with almost no representation on the prairies were frequently accused of neglecting the west; or whole sections of the population, as in the case of native peoples who, with only an occasional seat in Parliament, consider that progress toward satisfying their needs is unconscionably slow. In 1986, on a more specific level, Mulroney's government managed within the space of a few weeks to arouse antagonism even among his own supporters by awarding a public contract in Quebec rather than Manitoba (where the bid was lower), and moving the site of a large new prison building from one part of Quebec to another, the latter being in his own constituency.

FINANCING POLITICAL ACTIVITIES

The preceding passage deals with public money. Parties, as outlined earlier, also spend their own money; and elections, as more than one politician has observed, 'are not won by prayers.' Until relatively recently the money parties spent was not as blameless as that collected in churches either. No informed person would ever deny that parties have always needed money: for campaign literature, radio and television time, the taking of opinion polls, newspaper advertising, lecture halls, billboards, travelling expenses, paid organizers, and assistance to needy candidates and to those running in doubtful constituencies. These and other legitimate outlets dotted across the continent make heavy demands; and any party that is fighting nearly three hundred engagements simultaneously will use up ammunition in enormous quantities. An additional reason for high campaign costs is that it has been customary for all those patriots who had something the parties need at election time to charge generously for their services. Thus many newspapers, for example, charged top rates for political advertising and, according to a former national party organizer, some newspapers would not cover a candidate's meetings unless he purchased advertising.[8]

Partly because of the large sums of money parties need, and partly because they have no products or services of their own to sell to raise funds, parties until the 1970s had to turn to those who could afford to contribute to their coffers. But what did these contributors get in return? Before new legislation on election expenses was passed in 1974, Canadian political history was dotted with scandals about campaign funds, and in the 1960s a fresh outbreak, not all concerned with elections, raised an alarming spectre of sinister elements gaining access to the highest offices in the land.[9] The 1960s scandals were sensational in themselves, and they happened to coincide with sharply rising costs in media advertising, something the parties could not of course do without. In 1964 the government of Prime Minister Pearson established an Advisory Committee on Election Expenses, whose creation was considered of sufficient importance to be announced in that year's speech from the throne. The committee was expected to report on 'the best practicable way to set enforceable limits to expenditures in election campaigns,' and to carry out its broad mandate was given a generous budget to study relevant electoral practices generally, not just in Canada.

Since the committee's recommendations were superseded by legislation, its two-volume report is now a historical document, but one that remains a valuable compendium of those aspects of party activities it was directed to address. It found itself faced with an archaic electoral law which assumed that only individual candidates, not political parties, fought elections, and based its report on considerations which would now be thought commonplace, but which in the 1960s envisaged fundamental changes in existing practices:

I Political parties should be legally recognized and, through the doctrine of agency, made legally responsible for their actions in raising and spending funds.

II A degree of financial equality should be established among candidates and among political parties, by the extension of certain services and subsidies to all who qualify.

III An effort should be made to increase public participation in politics, by broadening the base of political contributions through tax concessions to donors.

IV Costs of election campaigns should be reduced, by shortening the campaign period, by placing limitations on expenditures on mass media by candidates and parties, and by prohibiting the payment of poll workers on election day.

V Public confidence in political financing should be strengthened, by requiring candidates and parties to disclose their incomes and expenditures.

VI A Registry under the supervision of a Registrar should be established to audit and publish the financial reports required, and to enforce the provisions of the proposed 'Election and Political Finances Act.'

VII Miscellaneous amendments to broadcasting legislation should be enacted to improve the political communications field.[10]

The committee's report, published in 1966, buttressed by a thousand pages of studies, was welcomed generally by all those concerned (although it naturally also aroused criticism) and its subsequent treatment provides a salutary object lesson in how a democracy undertakes a major unopposed change. In June 1971 a committee of the House of Commons recommended legislative amendments which followed the intent of the Committee on Election Expenses but went further; and in 1972 an actual bill reached the floor of Parliament. Its timetable was brought to a halt by the general election of 1972, and in the following year another bill was introduced which, after a good deal of able and remarkably non-partisan discussion in yet another House committee and in the House itself, became law in 1974, ten years after the original announcement in the speech from the throne of 18 February 1964. The statute of 1974 was amended in 1977 and 1983, but no amendments were aimed at altering the basic structure by then in place; the amendments followed discussions in an ad hoc committee of representatives of all parties in the House of Commons and the staff of the chief electoral officer.[11]

The legislation on election expenses will no doubt be subject to continuing amendment as both conditions and costs change, for the subject is dear to the hearts of MPs and a complex measure for election officials to administer. In essence the relevant statutes in 1984 provided as follows (for convenience the order below follows that of the considerations of the Advisory Committee on Election Expenses presented above):

I Political parties are now recognized as legal bodies which have agents, in much the same manner as individual candidates have had agents for over a century; parties and candidates also have auditors. Parties, candidates, and their agents are legally responsible for their actions in raising and spending money. (Canada Election Act, 1984, ss. 13, 13.1, 61.1–63 inclusive.)

II Parties and candidates who otherwise comply with the law receive reimbursement for certain legal election expenses. A registered party which qualifies receives back $22\frac{1}{2}$ per cent of its election expenses (s. 99.25). A candidate who polls at least 15 per cent of the valid votes in the election he contested receives back 15 per cent of the maximum expenses allowed him by law (s. 63.1).

III Any person can contribute money to a party and receive in return a tax credit, on a sliding scale. A contribution of up to one hundred dollars earns a tax credit of 75 per cent of the donation, and a contribution of five hundred dollars earns a credit of 55 per cent. It costs an ordinary citizen, that is, only twenty-five dollars to give a party one hundred. The same citizen could contribute any amount, but the maximum tax credit stops at five hundred dollars. (These provisions are not part of the Elections Act, as they concern individual tax returns.)

VI and VII Limits on broadcasting costs are set by provisions which maximize the amount of time stations must make available to registered parties by purchase in a fixed period between the twenty-ninth and second days before a general election; and also by requiring stations to provide free time as a condition of their licence to broadcast (ss. 99.13-14, 99.21). The actual allocation of time is shared between the parties under complex arrangements which never satisfy everybody. (Consider, for example, whether parties should receive time on the basis of seats won in the last election, or votes polled. In either case what of new parties that as yet have no electoral record?) Reducing campaign costs by shortening the election period runs up against a hard fact: the system takes a minimum number of days to prepare and revise the lists of electors. Each returning officer is ordered to start the process 'on Friday, the thirty-eighth day before polling day' (s. 18.1), and the election itself will have been called several days before that. The suggestion that Canada adopt permanent lists of electors, to be maintained in readiness at any time, is attractive to many, but it has disadvantages for a large, thinly settled country with a mobile population.

The main limits the legislation sets on spending by parties and candidates consist of fixed ceilings. Each registered party may spend a total of thirty cents for each elector on all the preliminary lists of voters in the constituencies where the party has approved candidates (s. 13.2); in round numbers (in 1984), that gave each party with a full complement of candidates a limit of over $6,400,000 for each general election. Each candidate may spend one dollar for each of the first 15,000 electors on the preliminary lists for his constituency, fifty cents for the next 10,000, and twenty-five cents for the remainder. Extra arrangements are made for those running in far-flung constituencies which average fewer than ten electors per square kilometre (s. 61.1). The totals permitted candidates vary with the population of electors in each riding; the preliminary lists for the election of 1984, as reported by the chief electoral officer in his *Statutory Report* for that year, ranged from 21,000 in Prince Edward Island, to nearly 54,000 in Ontario and 56,000 in Quebec. Only about one-quarter of all candidates, in the legislation's application so far, spend as much as 90 per cent of their permitted limits; the two older parties have spent 85 per cent or more of theirs, with the NDP well behind at around 70 per cent.

v and vi Both parties (ss. 13.1 ff) and candidates (ss. 63 ff) are obliged to file detailed audited financial statements after an election, and they are available to the public through the electoral administration.[12]

That brief summary of how parties have tried to cope with the problems of raising and spending campaign funds is not intended to draw attention away from the parties' clear accomplishments in the field. It was a party in power that created the original advisory committee in 1964, and the co-operation the committee received from all sides of the House was matched by the parties' subsequent roles in devising, enacting, and amending the legislation in force. It remains to be added that, as is often the case, the well-intentioned attempts to control election costs to make participation for candidates and parties easier in a variety of ways, and to encourage public involvement in the electoral process, has produced some unforeseen results. They do not arise from unworkable legal regulations, or from non-compliance with them: the chief electoral officer reported that of 1,449 candidates in the general election of 1984, for example, 1,438 submitted their expense statements on time, leaving only 11 subject to possible penalties. In a sense, some of the most conspicuous problems created for the parties by legislation on election expenses arose because it worked too well.

One of these has already been mentioned in the preceding chapter: individual constituency organizations can use the law to become individually powerful financially within their party; while this is no doubt a democratic development in important ways, it also means that constituencies can be vastly unequal within even their own party. How this may affect the parties (in manoeuvrings, for example, among candidates for a party's national leadership) is not yet known, but it appears that any national party organization, however led, may find it harder to follow policies which assume all constituencies are equal. A related problem stems from the strikingly uneven success of the parties in attracting public financial support – a situation which is not yet a concern for the electorate in general but for the parties themselves.

All the major parties have naturally tried to attract financial support from the public, and all have devised similar procedures for soliciting contributions by mail: the standard forms sent out strongly resemble those long used by recognized charitable organizations. The differences are in the responses. The NDP has always relied on large numbers of small donations, and the legislation on election expenses has not materially changed its practices beyond making them public. The party has, however, in recent years received much larger amounts of money from approximately the same number of donors. In 1984 the NDP received $4,156,000 from 80,027 individuals, and an additional $2,393,680 from other contributors, $2,159,055 of that from 947 trade unions. In the same year the Liberals received $5,181,097 from 29,056 individuals, and an additional $5,372,219 from other contributors, only 8 of them trade unions and 6,494 of them business organizations; the last-named donated $5,339,729. The Progressive Conservatives received $10,142,398 from 93,199 individuals and $11,003,522 from 21,286 business organizations, but nothing from trade unions.[13]

In 1984 the three parties combined had a total number of 231,377 contributors of all kinds, hardly an impressive figure when one adds that for the general election of 1984 there were 16,775,001 names on the official voting lists; this makes a contributing percentage of only 1.38. Many of the contributors, however, are organizations such as companies (for the two older parties) and unions (for the NDP), who collectively represent an unknown number of individuals. What is more striking about the statistics is their sensitivity to the parties' fortunes leading up to the general election of 1984; the contributors, as the statistics show over a period of years, seem able to sense the upcoming winner and loser between the two older parties and measure out their money accordingly. If that sensitivity in the financial health of the parties prevails over time, analysts may have a tool for predicting what expensive polls will predict.

One other sidelight on the parties' financial picture deserves mention. Parliament in 1983 acted to prevent any person other than a legitimate candidate or a registered party from incurring election expenses (s. 70.1), a provision originally recommended by the advisory committee of 1964 to forestall the establishment of 'fronts' for candidates and parties who could bypass the legal restrictions imposed on them. In 1984 an interested group that was not a party, the National Citizens'

Coalition, sought to have the clause declared in contravention of the Canadian Charter of Rights and Freedoms. After an unusually informative trial in which counsel for the Coalition, on the one side, and the Attorney General of Canada, on the other, canvassed many important issues related to the holding of free elections, a justice for the Alberta Court of Queen's Bench agreed with the Coalition: in its present form, the restriction on election spending by 'third parties' which are not parties as envisaged throughout the Elections Act was held to be unconstitutional.[14] The crown decided not to appeal the decision, and the relevant legislation as it now stands may have become a dead letter. For the future, both the clause in the legislation and its fate raise questions that may be of major significance, of which the most important is a simple one: is the electoral system to be controlled by the courts, or by Parliament? Is it to become the norm, when the parties in Parliament have tried through legislation to regulate spending and police those who use the electoral system, for groups outside the parties to be uncontrolled? In 1983, before the legislation of that year and the court case of 1984, the chief electoral officer referred to people who 'spent unlimited sums of money to promote or oppose a particular candidate or registered party, sums which they do not have to account for in terms of sources or amount.'

The effectiveness of the legislation on election expenses, and the use of it by candidates and parties, has so far been tested for only a decade, but it is carefully monitored by election officials and party representatives, and its first ten years showed great promise. Certainly it seems to minimize the possibility of sensational scandals over monetary gifts to political partisans in return for favours; it has also reduced controversy over political giving, and indeed has made it respectable. It is now not only possible, but usual, for the parties to be able to raise publicly considerably larger sums than the law allows them to spend in a general election: the ceiling for a party contesting every constituency in 1980 was $4,546,192, a sum considerably smaller than is now donated to each party every year. Parties are free to set their own rules for leadership conventions, and contesting the leadership in at least the two older parties often leaves veteran members heavily in debt. That is another source of controversy; but controversy is part of the lifeblood of politics.

PARTIES, OTTAWA, AND THE PROVINCES

Anybody who wants evidence of dissention within a party needs only to look at yet another aspect of political activity. It concerns parties and governments – not just relations between each party's parliamentary and extra-parliamentary wings, but the areas where a party leading the national government must deal with a party in power in a province. Although there are three main levels of government in Canada, federal, provincial and municipal, party activities and therefore party problems have rarely taken hold of the municipal level. In some parts of Canada parties keep out of municipal politics only by not using their names, and many municipal politicians are well-known supporters of provincial or federal parties, some having served as candidates or elected members. Many observers believe that municipal politics could be improved if aldermen and councillors ran openly under the auspices of parties which could be held responsible for their actions; but that proposition remains almost untested. What is tested almost every day is the parties' roles in federal-provincial relations.

Since relations between Ottawa and the ten provinces often appear to involve dealings with separate governments as such, it must be remembered that each head of government is a prime minister or a premier, with one or more political parties supporting him in power. (Canada has not yet had a female head of government in this sense, although there is nothing in the law or the constitution to prevent it.) Each 'First Minister' (a modern euphemism which lumps all the political heads together) thus has a large constituency of supporters he must serve as a political leader, as well as head of government; and as a head of government he must also guard his own legal jurisdiction jealously. The political side of federal-provincial relations includes several anomalies. The eleven heads of government meet as equals, but only the Prime Minister of Canada can claim to speak for the whole country. The other equals are in fact very unequal. The smallest provinces have populations that are only a small fraction of the largest, and while the provinces control their own natural resources, the disparity there is at least as great as in the populations. Yet each premier at a conference has one vote. In the House of Commons in 1984 one province had 4 members and one had 105. Who speaks for a province – its premier and his ministers, or the prime minister supported by MPs from the same province?

The dimensions of political problems at the federal-provincial level are obviously enormous, and so continually changing that they are not always clear. It can be assumed that normally the maximum co-operation and friendliness can be expected when federal and provincial governments are controlled by the same party, although this is by no means certain: one of the leading critics of both the Pearson and Trudeau governments in the 1960s was the Liberal premier of Saskatchewan, Ross Thatcher.[15] Any co-operation will include also the granting of any special favours by Ottawa to the province, and Canadian history is full of examples. Thus H.A. Robson, Liberal leader in Manitoba, speaking in 1927 on the subject of an agreement regarding the transfer of the natural resources of Manitoba stated: 'We claim to be in a position to have this matter settled satisfactorily with despatch and without any risks of litigation. We hold the advantage of position in this by reason of our affiliations with the federal Liberal Party. From this very important standpoint, the existence in Manitoba of a

Government in sympathetic contact with the federal Government will undoubtedly give the province an advantage in all matters of negotiation.'[16] Three years later Mackenzie King, speaking in the House of Commons, accepted the same principle:

So far as giving money from this federal treasury to provincial governments is concerned, in relation to this question of unemployment as it exists to-day, I might be prepared to go a certain length possibly in meeting one or two of the western provinces that have Progressive premiers at the head of their governments, but I would not give a single cent to any Tory government ... May I repeat what I have said? With respect to giving moneys out of the federal treasury to any Tory governments situated as they are to-day, with policies diametrically opposed to those of this government, I would not give them a five-cent piece.[17]

When the Progressive Conservatives party won the general election of 1984 it found that most of the provincial governments were of the same political persuasion, and much optimism was expressed over the anticipated settlement of thorny issues ranging from offshore mineral rights for provinces with extended seacoasts to better agricultural policies for prairie provinces with none. By 1986, however, Conservatives in several provinces had expressed their unhappiness with federal Conservative actions. A curious aspect of federal-provincial party relationships is that it is by no means certain that a party is better off when it is in power in both places. Under such circumstances the dominant party cannot shift the blame for inaction, mistakes, or unpopular policies, for it is clearly bound to accept responsibility through its control of both federal and provincial governments; whereas any unfortunate consequences that may occur under a separation of party control can usually be ascribed to the neglect or the errors committed by the other side. It has even been said that Sir John A. Macdonald believed it was no disadvantage in having his opponents in power in the provinces, although the care he took to keep his provincial fences intact does not seem to justify such a statement. Certainly Sir Wilfrid Laurier paid exceptional attention to Liberal fortunes in the provinces and he never doubted that solid provincial support was a great bulwark for the party in the country at large.

The reverse, however, may not be true. While it may be advantageous for a national government to have its own party in power in the provinces, it may well be that a provincial government is more secure if it is politically opposed to the party in power in Ottawa. Here and there, no doubt, a provincial government in such a situation may lose through a lack of federal cordiality and assistance. But even in these circumstances, fate, working through the federal government, has placed a magnificent electoral weapon in the hands of the provincial cabinet which it can scarcely fail to use to its advantage. The election issues that have always been most successful in the Canadian provinces have been those directed at the encroachments of Ottawa, and these can be urged without restraint if the provincial cabinet is not handicapped in advance by belonging to the same party as its federal adversary. Unity of party control may arouse the suspicion in the province that its ministers are unduly acquiescent in national policies and that they are afraid of antagonizing their friends in Ottawa by fighting fearlessly for the rights of the province. This was the opinion, for example, voiced by a western paper in a classic statement:

These western provinces have had sharp conflicts with Ottawa in an endeavour to secure full equality with the other provinces in Confederation, and are still suffering in a very considerable degree from discrimination in federal legislation. Too close relationship between federal and provincial parties in the past has been a potent factor in preventing the removal of this discrimination, and undoubtedly the maintenance of such relationship will prove a handicap in the future. It may be difficult at times to maintain a clear-cut distinction, but the needs of this country will be better served if provincial parties as far as possible adhere to provincial matters and avoid those relationships with federal parties which have proved to be detrimental to the welfare of these western provinces.

That complaint happens to be over sixty years old, but its descendants are still with us. Of historical interest is a similar complaint made a few years earlier in the maritimes: 'We are ignored by the Dominion Government; the West gets whatever it asks for.'[18]

When one adds the long history of Quebec's feelings as a French-speaking enclave surrounded by an English-speaking North America, the political tensions that have arisen between parties in power federally and those in power provincially are not difficult to comprehend. That a provincial electorate may be little moved by a desire to choose a government of the same party as the federal cabinet receives a substantial degree of confirmation in the records, and elections have shown cyclic party movements which seem to follow a pattern. In the first instance, the great majority of the federal and provincial governments will belong to the same political party; then the provincial governments will begin to fall away to the opposition party or parties until these are in a majority; finally, there is an overturn in the federal Parliament which brings it once more into sympathy with the provinces, whereupon the cycle begins anew. No sure conclusions can be drawn from these sequences, and the pattern is not a consistent one, but one generalization seems possible. The records suggest that provincial electorates have shown a decided tendency to fall away from the party which gains control of Parliament.[19]

While provincial elections are normally fought on provincial issues, questions involving federal-provincial relations (and particularly financial relations) have been very common, although these too may be considered to be provincial issues. There are also numerous instances where national issues have virtually forced the provincial questions out of the field, especially when either party has felt it would gain by such a manoeuvre and turn attention from less popular topics. Thus a Saskatchewan Liberal government, wishing to capitalize on the popularity in the province of a reciprocal trade agreement with the United States as shown in the 1911 federal election, fought the provincial election in the following year on the same question. 'The issue in the election,' said the Liberal leader, 'will be the trade question'; and in his manifesto of sixteen paragraphs, the one dealing with reciprocity was given as much space as the other fifteen combined. A second manifesto, proclaimed just before the election, declared that reciprocity was 'the whole issue.' Yet such a trade policy was not even under provincial jurisdiction.[20]

While there are sound reasons for divorcing local from federal politics, the fact remains that it does not always happen, and many Canadians politicians have declared forthrightly that total separation is impossible. Nor is it unknown for a provincial issue to loom large in a federal election. For example, the medical care insurance plan introduced by the government of Saskatchewan in 1961–2 was an influential factor in the province in the federal election of 1962, and NDP supporters outside Saskatchewan also used the issue during the campaign.[21] The low sales of wheat and the federal government's white paper on taxation, both national matters, were lively issues in all three prairie provinces in 1969–70. The mixing of federal and provincial issues in elections on both levels is probably more common than otherwise; fresh mixtures have followed the federal election of 1984, which produced a government of the same party (in names at least) that was in power in most of the provinces.

Part of the mix results from the participation of the same personnel in electioneering. Party candidates, federal and provincial, often support one another on the hustings, on the principle that it is mutually advantageous to make the party supporter a consistent voter in both fields; 'Political chameleons' clearly do not make for party solidarity and reliability. The same reciprocal exchange of talent does not extend so commonly to federal and provincial cabinet ministers, although it is by no means unknown. The support of members of a provincial cabinet in the past was given freely and eloquently in a national election; and it was appreciated and frequently recognized by appointment to the federal cabinet.[22] Federal ministers, however, do not participate in provincial elections with anything like the same frequency, for such intervention is apt to be misconstrued and resented as an interference in provincial affairs.[23] It has become increasingly common, too, for provincial leaders to hold themselves aloof from federal campaigns for prolonged periods, usually because of a desire not to damage their province's position in the complex of federal-provincial relations. Since the national convention has become the standard method of choosing each party's national leader, provincial leaders have often been coy about publicizing their own choice, on the ground that, whoever the new national leader is, every provincial leader of the party will have to work with him.

THE PARTY PLATFORM

The nature of the platform and its influence on party measures are in some respects still a matter for disagreement. Certainly the older parties do not regard their platforms with the same apparent respect as does the NDP, which follows in this regard its predecessor. Some significance may attach to the prominence each party gives to its own formal pronouncements. The Liberals did not hesitate from the start to publish the proceedings of their conventions and with them the full statement of their programs. The Conservatives, before their first convention, derived great enjoyment and possibly some political advantage from sniping at the Liberals with their 1919 principles, and avoided presenting their enemies with the same kind of ammunition when their program was drafted in 1927, for in a published report running to 436 pages they were unable to find room for a verbatim statement of the platform. Other Conservative national conventions were not even honoured with a souvenir book of pictures. Indeed, in the 1957 election, the mass of resolutions passed at the party's 1956 convention was not only not used as a coherent platform, it was reportedly ordered burned by the party's new leader, John Diefenbaker. In 1966 Prime Minister Pearson announced that he considered resolutions passed at party conferences as guidelines only. The CCF party had the courage – or foolhardiness – to publish the proceedings of their conventions, provincial and national, the most conspicuous section of which was the impressive list of resolutions proposed and considered.

The NDP, like the CCF, is willing to be explicit in its general aims and in many of the measures it puts forward. This may be due in part to its realization that the opportunity to carry them out is still remote; but it arises chiefly from the system the party uses and the remarkable fertility of its conventions at all levels in producing proposals of infinite number and variety. The older parties are inclined to be more cautious, and until recently their constitutions said literally nothing about the formulation of the party platform, or the leader's responsibility in regard to it; both national associations now have standing committees on policy, and provisions for regular policy meetings have been added to their constitutions. It has already been pointed out that the Canadian situation frequently leads both these parties to follow contradictory policies in the drafting of platforms: some sections are kept very general in order to avoid antagonizing different groups of voters, while others deal with a wide variety of particular topics on the assumption that each of these will appeal to a special element or area. Even so, both the older parties admit the desirability of phrasing all paragraphs, with few exceptions, in vague terms, so that when the party eventually goes into action it will have the advantage of flexibility in interpretation and not find itself hampered by bonds which it itself has tied. 'The convention,' a newspaper commented cynically of the Conservative enterprise of 1927, 'has got the right idea, i.e., that the best platform for a hurried, haste-driven and heterogeneous gathering to adopt is either a blank piece of paper or one to which even the most cantankerous Grit could not take exception.'[24]

Even when the platform is fairly specific, the official party leaders, when they attain power, will use their discretion as to how much of it shall be executed and whether the time or the occasion for action has yet arrived. This might fairly be dubbed the 'chart and compass' theory, for the metaphor was used by Mackenzie King at the time of his election as leader, and he reverted to it on several later occasions. King insisted that the 1919 platform of the Liberal party was given to him and the leaders for guidance only, and that if elected to office he would not attempt to follow it literally but would exercise a wide discretion.[25] The great majority of Liberals and Conservatives would adopt such a position with little hesitation. They acknowledge an obligation to observe in general fashion Liberal and Conservative principles (although these may at times become a trifle elusive), and they accept broadly the party platform,[26] though it is not to be construed as mandatory as to time or extent. Leaders of both parties have generally been in the position of having been selected *after* the platform has been settled, which candidates for the leadership rarely try to influence; Diefenbaker's stout opposition to the 'two nations' concept at the Conservative convention of 1967, at which he was seeking re-election, was a notable exception.

On the other hand, members of these older parties will support with reasonable certainty any election manifesto the leader issues to the country immediately before an election. The leader's manifesto is not as common as it was but in its heyday it tended on occasion to override the party's platform. Modern electronics allow each leader to keep making suitable pronouncements on policies as a campaign develops, and as the opinion polls reveal which policies are attracting, or not attracting, support. Whatever the party's platform says, in effect a leader can now issue manifestos on an almost daily basis if it seems desirable. The leader's interpretation of the party's course thus remains, as it has been since Confederation, of paramount importance. Historically, the Conservative party has been both the chief sufferer and the chief beneficiary from the dominant position the leader has acquired over the party policies and many of the accepted party principles. Time and again Conservative leaders have cut loose from traditional Conservative policies – not without some justification, but frequently at the cost of creating a disunited and dissatisfied element in the party following. Sir Robert Borden's experience as prime minister during the First World War led him into nationalistic tendencies at variance with Conservative ties with the British Empire, as did a speech made by his successor, Arthur Meighen, in which the latter advocated holding a general election before Canadian troops should be sent abroad to fight another war. R.B. Bennett, who had the misfortune to lead the government during the depression years of 1930–5, endorsed a program of social legislation which consternated many good Conservatives. John Diefenbaker, who led the party for a decade which included six years in power, had to survive many suspicions that he was a dangerous prairie radical, and in 1967 became the first leader to be publicly rejected by his own party. Brian Mulroney's accession in 1984 was followed by an encouragement of American investment in Canada that seemed a far departure from his party's traditional affection for protectionist policies for Canadian industry; and his subsequent interest in free trade, fully articulated by the late 1980s, took him even further from his party's history.

Yet if party solidarity and support are to be maintained, a close liaison between leader and party must be established and continually maintained, and today both the Liberal and the Progressive Conservative parties are making an effort to bridge the gap by means of more frequent meetings of their national representative bodies. 'The Prime Minister,' Dalton Camp wrote in 1966, in a critical mood which has become increasingly representative of the older parties, 'recently told his party supporters ... that he would stay on, so long as his strength and health were maintained, as if continuing his leadership were a matter between himself and his Maker, and not between himself and his supporters.'[27] Camp was then national president of the Progressive Conservative Association, and one of the leaders of a movement that may revolutionize two fundamental relationships in the Liberal and Conservative parties – that between the leader and the party, and that between the leader and the platform.

Constitutional limitations on the absolute majesty of party leaders in the two older parties are now accepted as normal, but there was a time when they were regarded as revolutionary, and even today a winning leader remains in a strategically powerful position no matter what the party's constitution says. In the NDP, as in the old CCF, limitations on the leader's authority have always been routine; for many years the national convention, which must be held at least once every two years 'at a time and place determined by the Council,' not the leader, has been defined as 'the supreme governing body.'[28] No national leader has been deposed when seeking re-election, but on at least two occasions (in Ontario and Manitoba in 1968) provincial conventions became genuine leadership battles.

Such contests can produce bitter divisions within parties, and it is common for the victor in any party leadership race to seek to placate or otherwise accommodate his unsuccessful rivals; nevertheless, it is not easy for a leader to take a charitable view of a colleague who has openly tried to overthrow him. The same is true in the older parties when many candidates seek the leadership: if the winner becomes prime minister, he has to consider how many of the rivals for his leadership belong in his cabinet.

The NDP conventions give a frequent opportunity to the party rank and file to review the work of the leaders and to stimulate them, if need be, by criticism and suggestion. The idea that underlies the acceptance of the convention as 'the supreme governing body' is fundamentally healthy, and if the process of review is used with common sense, should benefit leaders and ordinary workers alike. The NDP is heir to a lively tradition. In 1945 in Ontario, for example, the CCF leader accused the provincial government of operating a secret police force, and the government was vindicated at the polls. One of the resolutions submitted to the next CCF convention questioned the wisdom both of precipitating an election and of making the charges, and it constituted a virtual vote of want of confidence in the leader, E.B. Jolliffe. The convention went into closed session, the leader spoke an hour and a half in his own defence, and the whole matter was debated at length, resulting in Jolliffe's vindication by the convention. The NDP's national convention of 1969 was a controversial affair, pitting a strong left-wing group against the established leadership.

Given the basic principles of parliamentary government, a convention's power must be used with restraint, and it was never entirely clear whether the CCF party as a whole had appreciated what this involved. There was, for example, the emphasis placed on the convention's power to pass resolutions supposedly binding on all members of the party and particularly on those who sit in the legislature. While it is true that these resolutions were first discussed to some extent by groups and meetings at a lower level and then discussed by the convention itself, this latter consideration was almost always of a most cursory nature and in many instances could not fail to be based on insufficient information. Thus one Ontario CCF convention was expected to pronounce upon the merits of no fewer than 199 proposals dealing with almost every subject under the sun, including the National War Labour Board, cattle, tourist trade, the atomic bomb, old age pensions, immigration, the CCF constitution, publications, nursery schools, religious freedom, university scholarships, federal-provincial relations, sewage disposal, sale of war assets, arts and crafts, and Palestine. To accept the opinion of local units on many of these questions as authoritative is on the face of it preposterous, and to accept the collective opinion of the convention as being of any greater value is even more so, for the time which the convention was able to devote to these resolutions was quite literally on an average not more than three or four minutes each.[29] The resolutions passed by the conventions of the other parties are obviously open to attack on the ground that they frequently receive the most casual consideration by the delegates; but they are few in number, are usually general in character, and are rarely expected to be binding immediately and in detail on the party leaders.

The outpouring of collective wisdom by any convention cannot prove very embarrassing as long as the party remains in opposition; but accession to power and acceptance of office may increase rather than stem the flood, to the potential discomfiture of the premier and his cabinet. The only province to have a CCF government was Saskatchewan, and the experience there was instructive, for it revealed clearly the paradox that a party leadership can find itself in when it is responsible both to a legislature, in accordance with the country's constitution, and also to a non-legislative body, under the party's constitution.[30] The party convention was apparently willing to issue a multiplicity of orders to its ministerial representatives and demand that they be implemented without delay. On a few issues, indeed, the Saskatchewan cabinet and members of the legislature balked at implementing immediately the dictates of the convention, and their prior responsibility to the legislature as a whole had to be insisted upon. That the NDP has once more inherited from the CCF was indicated in 1962 when the Saskatchewan provincial convention of the party passed, among many others, two resolutions requiring the dropping of the legal drinking age to correspond to the voting (that is, from twenty-one to eighteen), and a loosening of the religious restrictions surrounding the adopting of children. Whatever else might be said for the merits of these proposals, they were at the time politically explosive and, when added to convention criticisms of the political attitudes of the civil service, aroused considerable unfavourable comment at a time when the government was already deeply engaged in the medicare dispute.

The CCF government in Saskatchewan lasted twenty years, from which it appears that the demands of parliamentary government and party democracy are not irreconcilable, though the questioning of the former by zealots who believe in the latter seems to be an inevitable by-product of any serious conflict. From the point of view of parliamentary government, it must be conceded that the assertion of what may easily be an immature and ill-informed judgment over the more careful and considered opinion of the leading representatives of the party, in the name of democracy, contains dangers. Procedure of this kind does not necessarily permit reasoned discussion; it fails to utilize the expert knowledge and judgment of an experienced civil service and ignores administrative and other difficulties which are frequently of decisive importance. It is not designed to produce deliberate and tentative progress toward a desired end; it disregards authority and decision by those who are best informed and who are willing to be judged by their record and performance, and substitutes ill-informed verdicts and instructions by those who have no responsibility and have little to lose by failure. The CCF always asserted, and the NDP would undoubtedly agree, that the vital considerations in all these matters were the principles and the policies and that the persons who carry them out are entirely secondary. But human institutions can work successfully only if they are being operated by people who are able to devote their utmost efforts and best talents and judgment to their task.

Words such as those are no doubt unacceptable to the ultra-democrat; and it is also true that the CCF-NDP procedures are still unquestionably more democratic than those of the other parties. That democratic practices can be accommodated to the realities of responsible leadership is suggested by the fact that the CCF-NDP combination in Saskatchewan lasted twenty years its first time in office, and eleven years the next, not only without serious breaks between the political leadership and the party as a whole, but with repeated votes of confidence in the leader at annual conventions. To think otherwise, indeed, is to raise profound questions about whether democratic government in Canada, with or without parties like the NDP, is possible at all.

On the surface, at least, the common factor underlying all the attempts at control of party leaders and platforms appears to be distrust of organized authority. This has a positive side: another common factor is a firm belief in the validity of the opinions of the ordinary citizen. It is undoubtedly true, as Professor Laski argued years ago, that 'the business of the modern citizen is not to ask, what shall I do? But rather, whom shall I trust?'[31] But those words were written before the rise of the modern state, with its complex technical and welfare programs and the inevitable aggrandizement of executive authority. The modern citizen must add to Laski's admonition at least two other pragmatic questions: 'How shall I trust those I trust? And how can I ensure that my trust is not abused?' The CCF and NDP, following in the footsteps of earlier radical movements in Canada, have one answer to these questions. But the other parties, too, have been gradually meeting a new political environment by increasingly complex national organizations which meet oftener, and more systematically, than their predecessors. A decade ago, the leader of the opposition told his party's Study Conference on National Problems that 'politics in Canada is becoming a contest for a single category of citizen, the "liberally-minded" man.' One may argue about what a liberally minded man is, but the validity of the underlying assumption that parties must be ready to adapt themselves to changing conditions has never been more obvious.

Parties are continually, and optimistically, seeking control of changing conditions, and they have never found the task more difficult than it is now. Whether or not to use expensive polling techniques, and how to interpret the results, confront a modern party with one set of problems that did not exist until relatively recently. A related but different set of problems, also costly to settle, arises from the current reliance on advertising agencies which has created, among other things, a whole new field of patronage. The parties each have their own favoured firms, who can expect to benefit further if their client wins, and even individual departments and their political heads, the ministers, are coming to regard public relations as an indispensable part of running a government. Public relations policies make available enormous amounts of valuable information, but they are sometimes also intended to allay what may be well-founded criticism, or divert attention away from it. When adopted by political parties and the governments they operate, they raise profound questions about how citizens can keep themselves fully informed about their own affairs. The parties, paradoxically, are among the citizens' most useful helpers there: a governing party will always be ready to explain, defend, or justify what it is doing and the opposition parties will be equally ready to express doubts and issue challenges. The political history of Canada suggests that out of this adversarial approach, peculiar though it may appear to a dispassionate observer, much good can come.

4

The House of Commons:
representation

Let's not worry about whether the man in the street will vote for a woman, will *you* vote
for *me*?
Judy LaMarsh, *Memoirs of a Bird in a Gilded Cage*

The political parties are at work all the time, but the public is most aware of their
performances on two stages: the election campaign and the House of Commons.
The first, through a familiar action in which some twelve million Canadians, at
irregular intervals, mark a cross on a small piece of paper, is probably the most
direct contact the majority of the electorate has with a party. (Another four million,
incidentally, do not bother to vote.) The second, whose performers are chosen
through the first, has a cast which has survived the reduction of fourteen hundred
or more candidates, almost all of them chosen in the first place by parties, down to
the current membership of the Commons. Once in the House, the elected continue
to wear party labels, one party (and so far only one party) forming the government,
the rest the opposition. Neither the electoral system nor the House of Commons as
we know them could operate without the parties; and while the partisanship that
dominates both is often deplored, nobody has yet come close to inventing a
democratic system based on anything else.

The parties are themselves shaped in part by the systems they operate. A party
seeking power in a society where only males over the age of twenty-one could vote
(as was the case in Canada until the First World War) would not have the same
organization, or offer the same policies, as a party seeking the support of
everybody over eighteen, male and female alike. A party seeking power in a
system where every constituency elects only one member, whether the winning
candidate does it with 25 per cent or 75 per cent of the popular vote, would not
work the same as a party in a system of proportional representation using
multi-member constituencies in which each party earned seats approximately in

proportion to its popular vote. The same considerations affect the nature of the House of Commons. Today, for example, there are both male and female MPs and cabinet ministers, as was not the case before women were legally granted the right to vote. The party in power, the Progressive Conservative, has the largest majority in Canadian history – 211 seats of 282 – and it won that 75 per cent of the House of Commons with barely 50 per cent of the votes cast in the general election of 1984.

Both the electoral and parliamentary systems, as will be discussed below, are also affected by their provincial bases: seats are shared among the provinces, not the population at large regardless of provincial boundaries, and no MP represents a constituency that crosses any provincial boundary. The parties, the electoral system, and the House of Commons, although they may have vastly different histories, are also in the broadest sense all indispensable sections of the same thing: a complex apparatus of representation that permits each elector's voice to be heard in the selection of the individuals, and therefore the parties, who will supply the members of Parliament. Everything those members enact into legislation also has to pass the Senate and receive royal assent, but neither the senators nor the queen (or her Canadian representative, the governor general) is chosen through the representative apparatus being discussed here.

The ultimate goal of any national party is of course to win the support of enough MPs to form a government. Most Canadian governments have found their majorities among members of one party, but since the rise of third parties that were neither Conservative nor Liberal it has not been uncommon for governments to be sustained in power with the support of what would otherwise be considered opposition members. The crucial test is the support of a majority, no matter where it comes from, and governments that control fewer than half the seats in the Commons through one party are popularly – and inaccurately – labelled 'minority governments.' However a government is supported, it obtains its power through the representative apparatus, and party organization and election campaigns can justly be regarded as means to the end enshrined in the House.

The House of Commons, with all its human strengths and weaknesses, has been called 'the grand inquest of the nation,' the one place where all citizens are represented. It is the body to which the political members of the executive branch of the government, the prime minister and his cabinet, must continually turn for justification and approval, its chamber the place where they must appear in person to explain and defend what they are doing. Opposition members devote a great deal of energy trying to demonstrate that the ministers, whatever they are doing, are not doing it well. The whole process, and especially those fragments clipped for the media, is easy to criticize, but impossible to replace.

The fundamental importance of the House of Commons is its essential representative character, the fact that it can speak, as no other body in the democracy can pretend to speak, for the people. It presents in condensed form the different interests, language groups, religions, classes, and occupations, whose ideas and wishes it embodies (sometimes with approximate exactness, sometimes not). One of its greatest merits is derived from the fact that it is not a selection of the ablest or most brilliant men in the country, but rather a sampling of the best of an average run that can survive the electoral system, an assembly of diverse types and varied experiences, the members of which are genuinely and actively concerned with the promotion of the national welfare as they see it. A cabinet that grows out of touch with the Commons is courting disaster, and while a government will frequently be embarrassed by the need for satisfying the many demands which the House will put forward, it will also derive considerable benefit from these encounters. Mackenzie King was by no means a convincing champion of Parliament, but he declared in the gloomy days of 1940:

I can say frankly to hon. members that it is a source of comfort rather than the opposite to have Parliament in session at a time such as this. I say that quite sincerely. There is comfort in the sense of knowing that where the situation is as serious as it is, the body of the people's representatives are here and can express freely their views, as can the Government its views and what it is doing, in a manner which it is not possible to do through the press ... I would not wish a long period to elapse, with the country and the world in the state in which it now is, without having an opportunity of consulting with members of Parliament and having them fully informed with respect to what the Government is doing.[1]

The companion function of the Commons, and one which can scarcely be separated from the first, is that of educating and leading public opinion. This is a task which has been changed, and possibly made more difficult, by the selectivity of television coverage, which emphasizes some aspects of the House and virtually ignores others. The House cannot become a mere mouthpiece to repeat and advertise the views of the constituencies, although it will, of course, do that to a large extent. But it will also discuss many questions on which the voters have as yet no certain convictions or on which they may need further information and guidance. The House will talk, argue, investigate, oppose, decide, and frequently postpone action on many matters, and in doing these things it arouses interest and helps to create a more enlightened opinion throughout the country. With society growing more complicated at an accelerating rate, Canadian governments are increasingly concerned about both receiving and disseminating accurate information, and new institutions to supplement the Commons' traditional role are continually in the making.[2]

The House of Commons, under the unremitting leadership of the cabinet and with the co-operation of the Senate, also sets its formal seal of approval upon legislation and matters of state policy. (Here the Senate takes a decidedly subordinate part.) Decisions of the legislative chambers pour out in various forms: (1) statutes; (2) taxation regulations and the authorization of expenditures (which are only a special kind of statute); (3) resolutions, which may range from initiatives aimed at amending the constitution to specific requests that the executive remove a judge or public official; and (4) formal declarations of state policy, which the executive will certainly carry into effect, such as those dealing with treaties or the declaration of war.

When a government has a majority among its own party members, the House invariably consents to all the measures submitted by the cabinet. But the timetable followed may be that of the House, and especially of the opposition, rather than that of the cabinet, since even when giving consent the House insists on exercising its important function of criticizing. Here the participation of the ordinary members depends on their party affiliations; and although their share is largely indirect and often inconspicuous, the influence they exert on government measures is far from small. If they belong to the majority party, they make themselves felt in the privacy of the government caucus where, separately or in association with other members, they may carry enough weight to bring about substantial modifications in the cabinet's proposals. If they belong to an opposition party they can vent their criticism on the government's measures when these come before the House, and they may sometimes be able at this time to secure concessions. But the opposition has a more far-reaching and significant impact than this, for normally the cabinet will have done its utmost to forestall opposition criticism by drafting proposals in the most acceptable terms possible. Of course, the criticism of the opposition may not pay dividends until the next general election, although in the meantime it will serve as invaluable material to use against the government, not only on the floor of the House but in the media and in the country generally. In short, the cabinet is always aware of the danger of allowing its opponents any base from which they can launch their attacks.

A vital aspect of the critical function of the House of Commons is its power of general supervision which, as will be seen later, takes many forms. The House asks the minister endless questions, conducts investigations into the administration of the departments, scrutinizes the financial statements and proposed taxes and expenditures, checks to a limited degree departmental orders and orders-in-council, listens to ministerial statements on government policy, and receives petitions for redress of grievances. Many of these matters are related to cabinet functions, and the responsibility of the cabinet to the House of Commons is always both present and active. As a last resort the House of Commons can withdraw its confidence from the cabinet, and thus obtain a new government or force a dissolution. This is no mere theoretical possibility, or even a rarity. It has happened five times since Confederation – in 1973 (an unusual case since Sir John A. Macdonald then resigned in anticipation of defeat), in 1926 (King), in 1926 (Meighen), in 1963 (Diefenbaker) and in 1979 (Clark).

Finally, the House of Commons has considerable powers of selection. It does not actually pick the cabinet, although the fact that the cabinet, chosen by the prime minister, must always be able to retain the support of a majority of the House may be considered as giving the chamber a negative power of choice. It is somewhat more correct to say that the House selects the prime minister, although here the party convention (and, in unusual circumstances, the governor general) has more initial authority in the matter. Once again, however, the Commons must give its seal of approval after the choice has been made. But the House selects ministers indirectly in yet another way. It provides the rigorous environment in which ministerial talent must prove its worth and establish its right to office. The prospective ministers usually serve an apprenticeship in the House; and while many cease to be serious contenders long before their party comes to power or vacancies occur in the cabinet, the few able survivors have had ample opportunity to develop their capacity before they are called upon to assume office. The result is that even a cabinet drawn from a party newly in office will include a fair percentage of able people, what they lack in ministerial experience offset by other training which has repeatedly been shown to be an effective substitute.

ALLOCATION OF SEATS

The federal basis of representation in the House of Commons has been part of the constitution since Confederation, and it includes not just representation *per se* but also decisions about how large the House is to be. The membership of the House is based on representation by population. Clearly, any system of representation which sets a ceiling on the total membership of the House, and at the same time shares seats among the provinces according to their populations, will inevitably put pressures on the parliamentary share allotted to the smaller provinces. If Ontario, to take an example that has many times arisen, continues to grow while the smaller provinces (even though they too may be growing) become relatively smaller fractions of the total, Ontario will get more and more seats in the Commons as the smaller provinces get fewer and fewer. Special protection for the smaller provinces is of course always available, but only if the principle of 'rep by pop' is sacrificed. If, however, the constitution provides for a Commons that grows in size as the country grows, quite other kinds of problems arise. For example, the room available for members to sit in the chamber itself is a fixed quantity, and if the number of MPs exceeds the available space, as well as the available offices outside the chamber, what does one do with the extra members? A steadily growing

Commons also means more constituencies, and hence more organizational problems for the parties. For the taxpayer, each MP means an annual cost of over $300,000 in salaries and office expenses.

Canada, without finding a permanent solution, has in the main accepted the idea of steadily increasing the number of MPs, although it has also experimented with a fixed ceiling on the House; in 1986 the matter had to be grasped again, the chamber now, to put it simply, being full.[3] In 1867, starting with a new building as well as a new country, the Fathers of Confederation deliberately chose a Commons whose membership could grow, largely because they had great expectations that the Canada of 1867 was as small as it was ever going to be; new provinces and enlargements of old ones were anticipated, so they devised a system of representation that was adapted to their expectations. Each time the national census was taken (in the first year of each decade) the membership of the House had to be suitably adjusted; and if good reasons, such as the addition or creation of new provinces, developed between censuses, MPs for them could be constitutionally added too.

The adjustment of representation after the census was made mandatory, and the original system set up to accomplish it endured, with some tinkering, until 1946, when the redistribution of seats based on the census of 1941, postponed for the duration of the Second World War, took place. The original scheme was simple in its main outlines, and the tinkering perceived to be necessary by succeeding generations of politicians affords another instructive instance of the difficulty of finding a lasting solution to changing and unforeseen problems. In 1867 Quebec was given 65 members (the same number she had had in the pre-1867 assembly), and this number remained fixed for decades. Representation from other provinces was to vary as their populations varied with that of Quebec. In other words, a quota of representation was obtained after each census by dividing the population of Quebec by 65, and this quota was then divided into the population of each province to determine the number of its representatives. The total number of members in the House as well as those from each province (except Quebec) might thus vary from decade to decade.[4] Once a new province was admitted, on whatever terms, it came under the same rules as the others. The only areas which were not provinces, the Northwest Territories, originally received seats in 1887, and when Alberta and Saskatchewan were established out of the Territories in 1905, the Territories retained one seat, which was raised to two in 1952, and to three in 1974.

The representation system thus created, however simple, produced a few anomalies. Despite the fact that the House could grow, for example, the addition of the four western provinces and the extensions of the boundaries of Ontario and Quebec made the smallest provinces relatively still smaller, and in 1915 Parliament acted to guarantee that no province could have fewer MPs than it had senators: at the time this was intended, in effect, to peg Prince Edward Island's share of the Commons at 4, and the other two maritime provinces at 10 each. A complex provision originally intended to protect those smallest provinces actually turned out to aid the province that needed it least, Ontario, which after the census of 1941 would under strict 'rep by pop' have had 74 seats, except that successive applications of the protection afforded to all provinces had kept Ontario's share at 82. By the census of 1941, in fact, five of the nine provinces (Newfoundland had not yet entered Confederation) were in one way or another being assured extra seats.

A general rule that applies to fewer than half of the entities it covers is never easy to justify or defend, and in 1946 Parliament took advantage of the wartime postponement of the readjustment of seats in the Commons to try a new system (also simple). The House membership was fixed at 263, and Quebec ceased to be the fulcrum on which the representation of the other provinces rested: it was to be treated the same as the others (that is, on 'rep by pop'); the smaller provinces were still guaranteed at least as many MPs as they had senators. In legislative terms the ink was barely dry on those enactments when fresh anomalies appeared. The new system, according to the census of 1951, meant among other things that one province, Saskatchewan, would suffer a drastic drop from 20 to 15 MPs; and Saskatchewan had a powerful and vocal spokesman in the federal cabinet, James Gardiner.

Saskatchewan was not alone in being threatened with a loss of seats in the House of Commons, but it had the most dramatic case and, given the frequency with which strict representation by population had been avoided in Canada's history, Parliament had little difficulty in 1952 in inventing new departures. The first was that after a decennial census no province's representation should be reduced more than 15 per cent below the representation to which it was entitled at the last redistribution. The second change was that there should be no reduction in the representation of a province as a result of which that province would have a smaller number of members than that of any other province which according to the most recent census did not have a larger population.[5] The second change was clearly intended to remedy any embarrassment that might arise from the operation of the first. But it also had another effect: it raised the minimum of each of the four western provinces, as long as their populations exceeded New Brunswick's, to 10 (the New Brunswick minimum under the 1915 amendment). That is, as long as any province could retain a population larger than that of New Brunswick (or Nova Scotia, for that matter) its minimum number of representatives was 10 by virtue of the combined operation of the 1915 and 1952 amendments. An interesting by-product of these changes was that since any extra seats allotted to provinces by the new protections were to be added to the Commons' fixed ceiling of 263, no House of Commons in fact ever had exactly 263 members.

The new system worked until the census of 1971, when it was abandoned to meet new pressures on the smaller provinces, and with it went the concept of a Commons with a more or less fixed ceiling on its membership. Also abandoned was the concept of simplicity; for while earlier adjustments of provincial representation in the Commons had paid at least lip service to the principle of treating the provinces equally, with admittedly special exceptions for special reasons, the Representation Act of 1974, enacted after a good deal of parliamentary inquiry and consultation, frankly treated the provinces differently. From 1971 to 1986 representation in the House of Commons, using a device known as the Amalgam Method, was based on a complicated division of the provinces into several categories, depending on their populations. (The Territories were as usual awarded seats independently of the rest of the country.) Quebec was again chosen as the pivotal province, this time allotted 75 seats to start with, with 4 to be added after each census. Large provinces, with over 2.5 million people, were given seats in proportion to Quebec's. Intermediate provinces (between 1.5 and 2.5 million) whose populations were still growing received 1 new seat for each 2 they would have earned if they had been, in effect, small provinces. Small provinces (below 1.5 million) were treated partly as a statistical pool for purposes of representation, and were allocated seats by a formula all but incomprehensible to those without legal training. One point was clear, no province could lose seats as a result of these rules, so that the smaller at least knew what their minimum quota of seats was.

That system's true fault turned out to be not its complexity, grievous though that was to citizens who wished to understand the bases of their House of Commons, but an unforeseen and startling growth in the size of the institution, from 282 to 310 members. After the 1971 census, under the formula, the House grew from 264 to 282. After the 1971 census only three provinces (Prince Edward Island, New Brunswick, and Saskatchewan) would have remained the same. Three small provinces (Nova Scotia, Newfoundland, and Manitoba) would have gained 1 seat each. Quebec received its statutory 4, and British Columbia went up 5 to 33, Alberta went up 6 to 27, and Ontario went up 10 to 105. By 2001, on the basis of contemporary projections, Canada would have 396 MPs. The Liberal government in power to 1984 seemed to have misgivings about these real and potential results, and during the thirty-second Parliament the House of Commons Standing Commitee on Privileges and Elections canvassed several aspects of representation, including the size of the House. The Liberals nevertheless permitted the actual drawings of constitutency boundaries to proceed, and the task was all but completed when the general election of 1984 intervened. The incoming Conservative government had its own ideas, and after further careful study by the Commons committee, whose subject-matter now included an amendment to the constitution embodying another system, new legislation came into effect in March 1986.

The rules currently in force still allow the House of Commons to grow, but only to 295 until the census of 1991. The new rules are mercifully simple:

1 The base figure in the calculation is 282, the number of MPs resulting from the previous redistribution.
2 Three seats are set aside for the Northwest Territories (2) and the Yukon (1).
3 The remaining total of 279 is divided into the total population of the ten provinces.
4 The quotient obtained from the foregoing division is then divided separately into each province's population, to determine each province's initial share of seats.
5 The initial share for any province may be altered because no province can have fewer seats than it had when the new legislation came into force. This rule assured extra seats to Quebec and Nova Scotia (1 each), New Brunswick and Manitoba (2 each), and Prince Edward Island and Saskatchewan (3 each). Only four of the ten provinces, in short, currently receive representation on a close approximation to 'rep by pop,' and across the country the average populations of ridings still vary considerably. The seats after the redistribution of 1986–7 have these averages: Ontario, 87,122; Quebec, 85,764; Nova Scotia, 77,040; New Brunswick, 69,640: Manitoba, 73,302; British Columbia, 85,764: Prince Edward Island, 30,626; Saskatchewan, 69,165; Alberta, 86,066; Newfoundland, 81,097; Northwest Territories, 22,870; Yukon, 23,153. Table 2 shows the statistical history of representation in the House of Commons.

CONSTITUENCIES

Sharing seats among the provinces is only half the solution to the problems discussed here. Once each province has its quota, the province must then be divided into the constituencies allotted to it. Changes in constituency boundaries will always be necessary whenever a province's representation changes; but even when it does not, alterations may be needed to accommodate population movements within a province, such as those obvious in recent decades with rapid urbanization. Drawing constituency boundaries always follows a decennial census, and the word 'redistribution' is the Canadian term used to describe the double task of allotting seats to provinces and then drawing the constituency boundaries. The sharing of seats among the provinces is provided for in the constitution, but the drawing of constituency boundaries is under the control of Parliament. How Parliament performs the task is therefore of paramount importance.

TABLE 2
Changes in representation in the House of Commons as a result of recent censuses

	1921	1931	1941	1951	1961	1971	1986
Prince Edward Island	4	4	4	4	4	4	4
Nova Scotia	14	12	13	12	11	11	11
New Brunswick	11	10	10	10	10	10	10
Newfoundland			7	7	7	7	7
Quebec	65	65	73	75	74	75	75
Ontario	82	82	83	85	88	95	99
Manitoba	17	17	16	14	13	14	14
Saskatchewan	21	21	20	17	13	14	14
Alberta	16	17	17	17	19	21	26
British Columbia	14	16	18	22	23	28	32
Yukon Territory	1	1	1	1	1	1	1
Northwest Territories				1	1	2	2
Totals	245	245	262	265	264	282	295

SOURCE: *Canada Year Books*; Chief Electoral Officer, *Representation in the Federal Parliament* (Ottawa 1986)

The early method of dealing with the problem was for the government to introduce into the House a bill outlining in detail the altered boundaries of the constituencies, which was then put through Parliament like any other government measure. Invariably, the party in power engaged in some gerrymandering. For example, the Conservative cabinet in 1872, 1882, and 1892 used the opportunity to draw the constituency lines so that they greatly favoured their own members.[6]

The system was altered by Sir Wilfrid Laurier at the redistribution in 1903, when the detailed determination of constituency boundaries was referred by the House to a select committee on which both political parties were represented. The size and procedure of the committee varied considerably over the years, but essentially the same plan was followed on all subsequent occasions until the 1960s. It was somewhat fairer to the opposition, for while a majority of the committee members always came from the government side, every party had an opportunity to voice its views and influence the final decision. The result was that a gerrymander on a comprehensive scale disappeared, although it did occur in a small way and sometimes gave rise to wrangling and accusations of sharp practice. It is improbable that coincidence alone in 1947 was responsible for the fact that 'the three seats most adversely affected in the entire country had ... been held by three leading members of the Progressive Conservative party.'[7]

Since before Confederation proposals have been advanced to overcome this kind of difficulty by giving the power of redistribution to some impartial body, and in the 1930s serious suggestions to move the operation away from the immediate direction of MPs and into the hands of judges began to appear.[8] Annually from 1958 to 1962 Douglas Fisher of the NDP introduced a bill to provide for an independent commission; and finally in 1962 the prime minister produced a government bill for an 'electoral boundaries commission' which survived first reading but was not proceeded with because of the dissolution of Parliament.[9]

The short-lived Parliament elected in 1962 was too preoccupied to carry the plan further, but that elected in 1963 shortly gave its attention to redistribution, and after a protracted debate that broke out sporadically for most of a year, settled on a wholly new method for drawing constituency boundaries, under a new set of rules.[10] In essence, the new legislation created a new public office, the representation commissioner (whose duties were later assigned to the office of the chief electoral officer), and ten ad hoc boundary commissions, one for each province (later one was added for the Territories), which were empowered to draw up maps for their area. Each commission now has three members: a chairman, chosen by the chief justice of each province from among the members of the high court, and two members chosen by the Speaker of the House of Commons. Each commission publishes its map, holds hearings to receive representations about it from the public, considers any proposed changes, and then sends the map, as amended, to the chief electoral officer, who refer it to the Speaker. Any ten MPs can object to, and precipitate a debate about, any maps, after which the map, with a copy of the objections and the record of the debate, is returned to the relevant commission. The commission in each instance has the final word on the boundaries, and after the proclamation of a 'representation order,' the new maps become effective at the next general election, provided that the representation order is at least a year old when a dissolution of Parliament occurs. The year is needed to allow both the election administrators and the parties to organize the altered constituencies.

The commissions do not have a free hand in drawing the maps, but are obliged to follow rules that eliminate the enormous discrepancies formerly common in Canada. (The census of 1961, for example, showed that Ontario ridings had populations that ranged from 29,000 to 267,000, each returning one MP.) The commissions are instructed to make each constituency in the province as near the average as possible in population, which can still mean that constituencies within one province can vary greatly as geographic entities: all the provinces west of New Brunswick have huge northern seats whose populations are smaller than those that can be encompassed in a few city blocks. The commissions have some leeway to cope with such distinctions; they can give recognition to density or sparsity of population, or local community or diversity of interest among the inhabitants. But in no case can a constituency have a population more than 25 per cent above or below the average for the province.

The political parties themselves contend over both the size and use of that permitted variation, since their members can often perceive how they might benefit locally from a larger or smaller departure from the average. It is now common for the electoral boundary commissions, which were originally set up to reduce discrepancies in constituency sizes and to minimize partisan considerations in drawing boundaries, to be criticized because they have been successful. The success of the modern system of drawing boundaries is none the less clear. Major discrepancies in constituency populations now rest on differences among the provinces themselves and the special safeguards provided for the representation of the smaller provinces.

REPRESENTATIVE CHARACTER OF THE HOUSE

All the constituencies discussed in the preceding section now each elect one MP, although until after the census of 1961 there were two that returned two members, and in the first decades after Confederation there were ten such ridings.[11] It is this single-member system, coupled with the multiplicity of parties offering candidates, and not variations in the size of constituencies, that still provides major anomalies in election results. Mention has already been made of the gap between the large majority of seats won by the Progressive Conservatives in 1984 and their share of the popular vote. Almost any general election can produce that kind of gap, and there are some striking examples worth noting. In 1930 the Conservatives polled 49 per cent of the vote to earn a comfortable majority of 56 per cent of the House, and five years later the Liberals won an even larger majority (73 per cent) with a smaller vote (47 per cent); the Liberals' overwhelming victory in 1935 was based on almost the same popular vote that saw them ignominiously defeated in 1930. In 1957 the Conservatives, after twenty-two years in opposition, returned to power by winning 42 per cent of the House with 39 per cent of the vote; in 1958 they won what was up to that time the largest majority in Canadian history (78.5 per cent) on 53 per cent of the vote. An increase in fourteen percentage points in their vote, that is, all but doubled their share of the House of Commons. In the 1960s the Liberals twice earned status as a 'minority government' by winning 49 per cent of the House on 42 per cent and 40 per cent of the vote, but by increasing their vote to 45 per cent in 1968 they won 59 per cent of the House. Among all these anomalies probably the oddest is that the party winning the most votes may not win the most seats: this happened in 1957.[12]

Nothing has yet been done to solve the problem of representation that is raised by this condition. There is a natural reluctance to adopt any system of proportional representation which might give further encouragement to the multiplication of political parties, and even the alternative vote in single-member constituencies (i.e., the elector votes his preferences 1, 2, 3, etc. instead of marking one choice with an x) has been suspect. There is an understandable reluctance on the part of any party in power to conclude that the system which put it there can be wholly bad. Nevertheless, voting reform has been a perennial subject of debate for at least sixty years in Canada, and before the election of 1984 it received added stimulus from the fact that the Conservatives, although always attracting votes in Quebec, could hardly win a seat there, while the Liberals were having the same difficulty west of Ontario. This phenomenon was profoundly altered by the Conservatives' winning in both Quebec and the west (and everywhere else) in 1984, and it appears likely that electoral reform as a subject of controversy will for a while receive a low priority at the federal level. Among the provinces, where electoral reform has often begun, the government of Quebec has been the modern leader. It was the first to take up the control of election expenses in the 1960s, and since then has seriously studied other electoral changes, producing one major paper in 1979 and another, entitled *Territorial Proportionality, A Fair Approach to Voting,* in 1984.[13]

The membership of the House of Commons shows in some ways a remarkable stability, regardless of elections, although a massive turnover (as in 1984 when eighty-two members of the previous Parliament were defeated and another forty-six did not seek re-election) can disturb what appear to be established trends. Most members enter federal politics in their thirties and forties, although there are now always at least a few in their twenties. There is not even a rough correspondence between the age composition of the House and that of the total adult population, nor is there yet an approximation of the sexual composition: the number of women elected in 1984 nearly doubled over the previous election, but the total was still only twenty-six MPs. The turnover of members at every election is always substantial, rarely dropping below 40 per cent, which means in turn that many have a short tenure as MPs, so that every House contains inexperienced individuals who may feel inclined to follow their leaders out of ignorance as well as conviction. The job of the member has become so complex that the newly elected are no longer left to their own devices to learn on the job but are given an orientation course, during which they hear from experienced politicians and parliamentary officials, are shown films, and given a file of pertinent documents.[14] The course is particularly helpful because fewer members than formerly now enter federal politics after having served in a provincial legislature.

Apart from age, sex, and previous political experience, the House of Commons membership reveals the same kinds of social bias already seen in national party conventions. As a group members have a high level of formal education, far beyond the general public; the House elected in 1984, for example, had 109 MPs with undergraduate degrees and 121 with some form of postgraduate education.

That education is reflected in the occupations and professions of those elected. In 1979 a commission (the first of its kind) was appointed to review members' salaries and allowances, and collected data on their non-parliamentary activities. Among 293 listed occupations (some members reported more than one) 67 MPs were lawyers or notaries, 32 were businessmen, 31 teachers, and 23 farmers or otherwise engaged in agriculture. But the same list revealed only one each in the categories of electrician, foreman, industrial worker and labour representative, and no waiters or waitresses, barbers or hairdressers, ditchdiggers, or truck drivers. More summary figures from the 1984 election showed the same pattern: 80 MPs with business backgrounds, 55 law, 48 education, and 19 farming: all the rest of the House, 26 per cent of the membership, was in other occupations.[15]

It would not of course be desirable for members to look upon themselves as representatives of, or delegates from, any special economic or social group, and few of them do. Women MPs may feel an understandable desire to take a particular interest in the status of women, as farmer MPs do in agricultural matters. But all MPs perform for their constituents a variety of services that have little or nothing to do with the members' personal or partisan backgrounds. No member, for example, feels confined to representing only those who voted for him or her on election day. None the less, as election after election produces the same kind of Commons, it is difficult to believe that a distribution of members which corresponded more with the occupational census of the nation would not furnish a more useful Parliament for at least some purposes. But the electoral system, however open it is theoretically to all citizens, and however aided those citizens can be by recent changes in the laws of election expenses, remains highly selective. Anybody *can* stand for election, but with some exceptions only political parties and their supporters can avail themselves of the opportunities afforded by the system. The parties are the institutions which select virtually all candidates who reach the House of Commons.

Once there, a successful candidate is assumed to represent the whole nation. There are always those who argue that a member, having been chosen by one constituency, should be the mouthpiece for it – its delegate, in effect – but Parliament has never accepted that notion. In the 1920s and 1930s attempts were made by third parties to bind their candidates through such devices as undated resignations which could be used whenever an individual, in his party's view, stepped out of line, but Parliament moved to prevent any such interference with its members. The Canada Elections Act in 1984 still proclaims (s. 104): 'It is an illegal practice and an offence against this Act for any candidate ... to sign any written document ... if the document requires the candidate to follow any course of action that will prevent him from exercising freedom of action in Parliament.' A cynic might observe that every member is prevented from exercising freedom of action by membership in a party. But members often do criticize their own parties, although not always in public; and they do defect with – if one takes a long historical look – surprising frequency. Even when they slavishly support their parties, members as individuals are still doing so by choice.

THE FRANCHISE

The section of the Constitution Act of 1982 entitled Democratic Rights begins with an unequivocal assertion: 'Every citizen of Canada has the right to vote in an election of members of the House of Commons or of a legislative assembly and to be qualified for membership therein.' The Canada Elections Act in 1984, continuing ancient practices, still listed as disqualified to vote several classes of citizens, including the chief electoral officer, the returning officer in each constituency except when two candidates tie for first place, all federally appointed judges, and inmates of prisons (sections 14(4) and 15(1)(2)). These same classes of people generally could not be candidates, along with additional folk such as sheriffs, members of provincial or territorial legislatures, and in general all those on the federal payroll (section 21). Public servants may not run for office while working, but they can get leave of absence without pay to do so. The list of the disqualified, in the light of the declaration that all citizens can vote and be candidates, is substantial, and in his statutory report for 1984 the chief electoral officer urged that the Elections Act should 'be seriously examined with a view to determining whether, in light of the Canadian Charter of Rights and Freedoms, some or all of its provisions are justified.' The government responded with a White Paper on Election Law Reform in June 1986. At that, the number of citizens currently disqualified from voting can hardly be compared with this at Confederation. Then only males could vote, and not even all of them. The franchise, in short, is another of those portions of the electoral system that has had a long development, and the right to vote has gone from a narrow to a broad base, en route often being manipulated by rival parties to make life inconvenient for their opponents.[16] Because of its singular importance, the history of the franchise is worth tracing in some detail, and it falls into convenient periods:

(a) *1867–85, when provincial franchises were used in federal elections.* The Constitution Act, as the British North America Act of 1867 is now called, provided that all electoral matters in the first national election were to be governed by existing provincial laws and would remain so for the future until they were changed by the Canadian Parliament. The reason for this provision was stated by Macdonald in the Confederation debates in 1865:

Insuperable difficulties would have presented themselves if we had attempted to settle now the qualification for the elective franchise. We have different laws in each of the colonies fixing the qualification of electors for their own local legislatures; and we therefore adopted a similar clause to that which is contained in the Canada Union Act of 1841, viz., that all the laws which affected the qualification of members and of voters, which affected the appointment and conduct of returning officers and the proceedings at elections, as well as the trial of controverted elections in the separate provinces, should obtain in the first election to the Confederate Parliament, so that every man who has now a vote in his own province should continue to have a vote in choosing a representative to the first Federal Parliament.[17]

Five federal elections were held under the provincial franchises. For although Macdonald believed that the federal Parliament should determine the qualifications of all those who voted in its elections, he was unable to persuade all his followers, and the Liberals stood firmly for provincial control which they considered to be more in accord with the idea of federalism. Several circumstances eventually brought a change. Some provincial governments had begun to disfranchise employees of the federal government. As these were appointed by patronage, and as Conservative governments had been in power at Ottawa for most of the time since Confederation, the great majority of those affected by these provincial laws were Conservatives. It not unnaturally irked a Conservative cabinet to see the most reliable of party supporters (including many on the payroll of the government-owned Intercolonial Railway) deprived of an opportunity to show their gratitude to the party that had given them their positions. Furthermore, a number of the provinces were abandoning the early property qualifications for the suffrage, and were thereby transplanting these electoral practices into federal politics. By modern standards the property qualification required of voters was never large, ranging at Confederation (in terms of real estate, for example) from $100 in New Brunswick and $150 in Nova Scotia to $300 in Ontario and Quebec. But $300 was in fact half a year's pay for an MP at the time, and the number of people then qualified to vote was only 16 per cent of the total population. Macdonald and the Conservative party generally had little sympathy with advanced ideas of democracy and wished to retain a property or income qualification. But a national franchise would necessitate national election lists, and these in turn would involve widespread patronage in their preparation and frequent revision, an advantage not to be overlooked by the cabinet. Taken together, the arguments for a single federal franchise were considered to be conclusive.

(b) *1885–98, the first federal franchise*. The Electoral Franchise Act was enacted in 1885 after some of the stormiest scenes in Canada's parliamentary history. It set up uniform qualifications for voting in a national election, which were based on a low property test. Its original draft extended the franchise to widows and spinsters who could meet the property qualification, but that clause was defeated in committee and dropped. The Liberals opposed the bill vehemently on theoretical grounds and also because of the cost, the party jobbery, and the manipulation which it encouraged. In practice it did, indeed, prove very expensive. The Liberal opposition continued unabated for years afterwards, and at their national convention in 1893 they promised repeal if returned to power. In 1898 the new Liberal government repealed the Franchise Act.

(c) *1898–1917, a return to provincial franchise in federal elections*. The 1898 act eliminated the single national franchise and returned to those of the different provinces. It provided, however, that no person could be disqualified from voting at a federal election because he was an employee of either the federal or a provincial government. When the Conservative government came to power in 1911, it made no move to change the existing law, which remained intact until the passage of two special measures brought about by the First World War.

(d) *1917–20, a mixed federal-provincial franchise*. For a few years the franchise was both fish and fowl: it used the old provincial franchises with additions and subtractions made by the Military Voters Act and the War Time Elections Act of 1917. The general purposes of these acts were plain and unmistakable: they were to give the vote to those who would support the government, to take it away from those who would oppose it, and to create a floating military vote, a large part of which would almost certainly be given to government candidates. The Military Voters Act thus enfranchised all Canadian men and women on active service, and made it possible for a substantial part of the military vote to be moved around, and cast in such constituencies as might be suggested to the voters at the time the poll was held. The War Time Elections Act denied the vote to conscientious objectors, enfranchised the wives, widows, and other female relatives of men overseas, and disfranchised both those of enemy alien birth and those of European birth speaking an enemy alien language who had been naturalized after 1902. A year later, the election being over, the vote was extended to all women who were otherwise qualified.[18]

(e) *1920 to present, a final return to a single national franchise*. In 1920 Parliament passed a new act, which straightened out the confusion created during the previous years and once more set up a national franchise for all national elections. Since then all parties have accepted the general principle, and there is no reason to suppose that there will be any attempt to revert to the provincial basis. The provinces still, of course, control the franchise for provincial elections.

Canada today has full adult suffrage. Generally speaking, the Canada Elections Act (section 14) provides that every man and woman may vote if he or she is qualified as to age and is a Canadian citizen. Certain persons are, as noted, disqualified for special reasons, and doubt remains as to the validity of at least some of the disqualifications under recent constitutional additions. Canadian Indians, who had been excluded from the franchise since shortly after Confederation, were made eligible as voters in 1960. In May 1970 the government introduced legislation to lower the voting age to eighteen, and the only remaining untapped pool of voters lies in people younger than that.

THE ADMINISTRATION OF ELECTIONS[19]

Much has been said so far about specific details of the representative system and the role of the chief electoral officer, but no attempt has been made to describe the office as such, and no account of representation would be complete without it. Elections after Confederation, particularly in the days when the House of Commons was relying on provincial franchises, were at first held in a casual, almost happy-go-lucky manner, and both the Liberal and Conservative parties exploited the system with considerable spirit. They happily collected evidence on each other's malpractices so that after each general election the results of several dozen constituency contests would be disputed on legal grounds; it seems incredible today, but in the Parliament elected in 1874 petitions protesting the right to sit were filed against sixty-five MPs, and forty-five of them were unseated for corrupt or illegal practices. The parties quickly adapted to such events by making deals: they said to each other in so many words, 'We'll withdraw our suit against your man in A if you'll do the same for our man in B.' These saw-offs, once a fascinating element in Canadian democracy, have disappeared, and controverted election cases, now rare, go to the courts like any legal dispute.[20] In their day they provided one of several good reasons for having a federal administrator put in charge of the whole electoral apparatus, and the position of chief electoral officer was finally created in 1920.

It is no exaggeration to say that the office is today one of the most important in government, and it and the system it operates are one of Parliament's great achievements. The chief electoral officer is provided for in the Canada Elections Act (section 3(8)): he is appointed by a resolution of the House of Commons, and can be removed before the usual retirement age of sixty-five only 'on address of the Senate and House of Commons.' The internal organization of the office is not strictly relevant here, although it should be noted that as new duties have been added the administration has grown and changed. For technical purposes, such as the provision of a pension, the chief electoral officer has the rank of a deputy minister and the same legal status as other public servants (section 3 (2)(5)); but he has otherwise a tenure much like that of a judge, and he is paid at the same rate as a judge of the Federal Court of Canada (section 3(4)). As long as he performs 'all the powers and duties specified in this Act as exercisable and performable by him' (section 3(1)), he enjoys a remarkable independence: like the auditor general, no minister can tell him what to do. He is assigned clear duties and expected to perform them, and he reports (section 59 (1)) only to the Speaker of the House of Commons. He is in charge of all federal general elections and by-elections and he is charged not only with reporting in detail on them, literally poll by poll, but on anything else 'that he considers should be brought to the attention of the House of Commons' (section 59 (1)(a)). Chief electoral officers take their reports seriously, and the result is an extraordinarily valuable series of annual statutory reports; working with his own staff and at times with committees of MPs, he produces not only facts but a running commentary on the Canadian electoral system.

Some of the details of the system, considering the sheer magnitude of any device that permits twelve million or more Canadians to elect the membership of the House of Commons all on the same day (except for the few using advance polls), are minute; but somebody working under the chief electoral officer somewhere has to see to them all. Every candidate, for example, whether or not he is backed by a party, must secure on a prescribed form the signatures of twenty-five electors qualified to vote in the constituency, and the signatures must be witnessed. The candidate must swear (also before a witness) that he consents to be nominated, and file a deposit of two hundred dollars with his nomination (section 23). The deposit is returned if the candidate earns at least 15 per cent of the vote cast in his constituency, the intent being to discourage frivolous candidatures (section 63.1(1)). In due course each qualified candidate's name appears in alphabetical order on a prescribed ballot paper, together with the proper political affiliation, if any. The paper on which each ballot is printed is supplied by the chief electoral officer, and must be 'paper that is of a mass of not less than one hundred and five grams per square metre' (section 31 (4)), the intent being to preserve the secrecy of each elector's choice by ensuring that it will not show through to the back. All the foregoing details (and they are but a selection) concerns only getting names and marks on pieces of paper which are supplied, one each, to every qualified elector who chooses to vote. When one adds such other necessities as the drawing of constituency boundaries, the making of voters' lists, the counting of the votes, and the reporting and auditing of election expenses, it is not difficult to grasp that the representative system is, to put it mildly, complex. It also works very well.

It is pertinent to conclude with a reminder that all this work only makes a huge machine available for use. The constitution limits the life of a Parliament to five years, but within that period it is a government that decides when a general election will be held or, short of that, any by-elections. Once a decision is made, nobody officially directs anybody to start using the electoral system: parties and individuals use it, but in the unimaginable circumstances that no party or individual volunteered to use it, no election could be held.

It is further pertinent to raise as a relevant consideration the potentialities of voting by electronic devices, and the use of public opinion polls as supplements to the contemporary electoral process. Electronic voting is no doubt technically possible, but although the subject is often mentioned so far no party has tried to insist it be used in the relatively simple community of the House of Commons' membership, let alone in a coast-to-coast election in a country where in remote areas ballot boxes and the necessary papers have had to be dropped by parachute. Public opinion polls, however, are clearly taken seriously by political parties, and to some extent they are replacing by-elections as methods of sampling the electorate's political thinking. Before opinion polls, by-elections were the surest indicator a government could have of its strength or weakness, and parties considered them gravely. Some by-elections were often routine; but they can be crucial to a party's assessment of its own position, for a government win in what was considered a safe opposition seat, or a series of losses by the governing party itself, may well affect not only the parties' responses, but the general electorate's responses in subsequent opinion polls. Although nobody can ever be certain what the results of any by-election really mean, parties will undoubtedly continue to regard them as essential parts of the representative system. It is often argued that a governing party ought not to be free to leave a constituency unrepresented for months at the government's convenience, as now happens; but that argument, however valid, is rarely heard from governing parties. It provides one more reminder that, while the representative system as a whole is non-partisan, the use of it is not.

A similar point can be made of other important elements in the government of Canada. An impartial decision by the learned judges of a court, for example, or an objective analysis by the auditor general of the government's management of public funds, can arouse distinctly partial and subjective reactions in the electorate. That does not alter the significance of the original non-partisan institution.

5
The House of Commons: personnel matters

One moment it's a cathedral, at another time there are no words to describe it when it ceases, for short periods, to have any regards of the proprieties that constitute not only Parliament but its tradition. I've seen it in all its greatness. I have inwardly wept over it when it's degraded.

John Diefenbaker, *The Wit and Wisdom of John Diefenbaker*

QUALIFICATIONS AND DISQUALIFICATIONS

Many aspects of representation, as previous chapters have shown, are covered both in the constitution and in laws passed by Parliament. The constitution declares unequivocally that every citizen is qualified for membership in the Commons, but the law expressly disqualifies certain classes. Since the Charter of Rights and Freedoms added to the constitution in 1982 also says that its terms are 'subject only to such reasonable limits prescribed by law as can be demonstrably justified in a free and democratic society,' those disqualified by the Elections Act will almost certainly have recourse to the courts. When the ballot is secret, can preventing *anybody* from voting, or from membership in a legislature, be considered a 'reasonable limit'?

Historically, until 1982, Parliament had no difficulty answering such questions, partly because the constitution after 1867 did not determine who could be an MP. The qualifications of members in the early Commons were fixed by the same provincial laws that set forth those of provincial legislators (which meant, incidentally, that for a few years the qualifications for MPs were not exactly the same in all the provinces); but in due course Parliament exercised its right to decide who would be elected to the Commons. The modern requirements could hardly be simpler: with the kind of exceptions already mentioned, anybody who can vote can run for Parliament. This meant that in the days when whole classes of citizens were disfranchised they were usually also disqualified as candidates, and thus as members. (In the days before candidates had also to qualify legally as electors, they were technically not even required to be residents of Canada.) For prolonged periods exclusions as electors applied to females, Indians, people of Oriental origin, and, for a single bizarre election in 1917, 'all naturalized British subjects born in an enemy country and naturalized after March 31, 1902 [and] all who even spoke an enemy language habitually and were naturalized after that date.' Nowadays the young are the only Canadians disqualified as an otherwise unspecified group; the others are disqualified because they hold particular jobs, for example, or are already members of a provincial assembly or a territorial council, or are confined for criminal reasons or because of mental health.

Parliament cannot change any of these rules without passing amendments to the law, but it has always had the right to rid itself of even properly elected persons: the House of Commons did so with Louis Riel twice in 1874–5, with Thomas McGreevy in 1891, and Fred Rose in 1947. In two of these cases the House did not pass a formal motion of expulsion: in Riel's second expulsion the House merely observed that he appeared to have 'been adjudged an outlaw for felony' and was therefore disqualified, while Rose was found 'incapable of sitting or voting in this House' when he was sent to jail. (In 1986 the right of the legislature of Nova Scotia to expel a duly elected member who had pleaded guilty to an indictable offence was challenged under the Charter of Rights and Freedoms.)

Offices of profit or emolument under the crown
It has long been a general rule that no person can hold an office of profit or emolument under the crown and remain an MP: in plain terms, one cannot simultaneously hold a government job (or contract) and a seat in Parliament. The original reasons for this arose in England at a time when it became necessary to protect members from being subject to sinister executive control. That kind of abuse, common when monarchs had real political power, dates most specifically to the efforts of Tudor and Stuart sovereigns to acquire parliamentary support through a not too scrupulous use of the power of appointment (a practice finally stopped in 1700). If applied without exception today, the rule would clearly exclude from the House not only judges, civil servants, and other officials (which is desired) but also any cabinet minister who received a salary – an absurd and impossible restriction under the British system of cabinet government. (It worked at least once, none the less: in Prince Edward Island a law zealously applied kept the whole cabinet as unpaid ministers without portfolio for four years after 1859.) Following the English precedent, a Canadian statute for many years declared that if a member of the House accepted a portfolio (that is, a position in the cabinet and the headship of a department) he could regain his seat only if, as minister, he

submitted to re-election to the House. In short, the constituency had to give its approval to the member *while holding the office of a salaried minister*. Thus if the members of a cabinet who were already in office were returned at a general election, they would not have to be re-elected; if, however, as a result of a general election the government changed, or if at any other time one or more new ministers took office, the extra elections would become necessary. Special provisions were made to permit a mere exchange of portfolios taking place within the cabinet without the necessity of an additional election.

This curious arrangement provided another example of a law based on an undeniably sound principle which produced unforeseen side-effects. It had one great merit: it caused from time to time a number of by-elections at which the record of the government was brought into special prominence, inasmuch as the immediate issue was the election or rejection of a cabinet minister. But certain other features were not so easily defended.[1] It was, for example, meaningless to have a general election and overthrow a government, to swear in a new cabinet immediately, and then to have the new ministers, fresh from an election, return to their constituencies and submit to further elections. These by-elections were so superfluous that usually the ministers were returned by acclamation.

Another awkward situation could arise when a cabinet was changed in the middle of the parliamentary session. On the new cabinet assuming office several seats would become immediately vacant. Since there would be no cabinet to meet the House, usually the most feasible alternative was to adjourn the House for some weeks until the by-elections could be held and the ministers had had an opportunity to regain their seats. If the new government's majority was uncertain (and, under the circumstances, it was almost bound to be so) it might easily have vanished after the fifteen or twenty vacant seats had been filled. It was to avoid these delays and embarrassments that Arthur Meighen, when he accepted office in 1926,[2] formed his ministry. This was composed of Meighen, who had by the operation of the law automatically vacated his seat on becoming prime minister, and several others, who were made ministers without portfolio and acting ministers of the several departments; as such they received no salary and could therefore retain their seats. This kind of cabinet was legal, but (although known in Australia and New Zealand) new to the government of Canada. Its position was questioned by King, and enough Progressive support was detached to bring about its defeat in the House three days after it had taken office.

The law was changed in 1931, so that today any member of the House of Commons may become a minister or a parliamentary assistant to a minister without such action affecting his seat.

The general rule which makes a person who holds an office of profit or emolument under the crown ineligible to sit in the House of Commons remains unimpaired, even though (as is shown in more detail below) the number of MPs receiving payments above their basic indemnity is increasing.

Residence

There are no constitutional or statutory residence qualifications for members of the House of Commons, although there is a marked tendency for parties and constituencies to prefer their candidate to live in the riding. But cases are not uncommon (particularly in Quebec, and in large cities) where members do not live in their constituencies and they occasionally represent constituencies in other provinces. The latter is most apt to occur when a seat must be found for a party leader or a cabinet minister who has been defeated or who is entering the House for the first time. The absence of any residence requirement gives a useful element of elasticity, for defeat does not necessarily mean exclusion from Parliament, nor is an able member kept out simply because he happens to live in a district which is politically opposed to him. Until the end of the First World War, eccentric though it now seems, the absence of a residence requirement permitted a few leaders to hold two seats in the Commons simultaneously, the Canadian record in this regard belonging to Sir John A. Macdonald, who in the general election of 1878 contested three seats losing one in Ontario and winning two, in Manitoba and British Columbia. Laurier had two seats from 1911 to 1917.

The overwhelming majority of members reside in their constituencies, a fact that has begun to raise interesting questions about how, given modern costs of living, one can fairly compensate MPs who must also maintain a second domicile in the capital for a good part of each year. Any system that treated all members with rigid equality might yield unfair benefits to members representing seats in or near Ottawa. The commission on members' salaries, which reported in 1980, recommended that seven MPs in that position be ineligible for any residence allowance, while the others would be reimbursed 75 per cent of the cost of maintaining a residence in Ottawa, 'to a maximum of $500 per month.' As this is written, no action has resulted.[3]

LIFE OF PARLIAMENT

The maximum duration for a Parliament is five years, which runs from the day on which writs are returned; but there is no minimum. During the First World War Parliament was extended to six years by constitutional amendment: the Charter of Rights and Freedoms, affirming another amendment of 1949, now states (section 4(2)) that 'in time of real or apprehended war, invasion or insurrection,' the life of a Parliament may be extended provided the 'continuation is not opposed by the votes of more than one-third of the members of the House of Commons.' (A similar power is given to provincial legislatures.) The shortest Parliament, in 1957–8, was technically less than six months, while those of 1925–6 and 1979–80 were a little longer.

Although there may be periods when for particular reasons elections occur frequently (as in 1962, 1963, 1965, 1972, 1974, 1979, and 1980), the usual Parliament lasts about four years. It is, indeed, a tradition of Canadian political life that no prime minister will allow a Parliament to run for the full five years if it can be avoided. This is based on experience as well as on other practical considerations. Three times Parliament has run its full five years:[4] on two occasions (1896 and 1935) the government was then beaten, and on the third (1945) it had a narrow escape. Moreover, a cabinet that puts off the election to the last possible moment is sure to be faced with the embarrassing accusation that it has postponed the day of reckoning because it was afraid to face the people. It also runs the risk of failure in getting its measures through Parliament; for on such occasions time is a powerful ally of the opposition, who may be able to filibuster government proposals until the life of the House runs out. Thus the Liberals in 1896 prevented the remedial bill on Manitoba schools being passed by resorting to systematic obstruction. In the last months of a Parliament's life the government may find itself running out of options.

From the cabinet's point of view, the weightiest objection to allowing a Parliament to run a full five years is that it loses control of the political situation. As long as there is an alternative time for an election, the prime minister is free to pick his own issues and seize the most favourable moment for the contest. This is a tremendous advantage which no astute leader will ever relinquish unless, as occasionally happens, the present and immediate future appear so discouraging that nothing can be lost by postponing the election as long as possible. In all three instances of the five-year periods mentioned above, the risks incurred were apparently preferable to the difficulties which an earlier election might have precipitated; Mackenzie King, in 1945, was particularly desirous of avoiding a wartime election.

The prime minister's power to decide within broad limits the length of each Parliament has one conspicuous merit, namely, that while it cannot guarantee that there will be a genuine issue to be decided at an election, it increases greatly the likelihood of such a fortunate synchronism. The combination may come about through skilful manoeuvring by the prime minister, or because the political situation forces an election, or because both factors work together to produce the same result. Canadian history supplies several excellent illustrations. In 1873–4 the Conservatives were caught accepting campaign money from the Canadian Pacific Railway (with whose construction the government of Canada was assisting), and the Liberals used the scandal to win the election of 1874. In 1911 the Liberals proposed a trade agreement with the United States which the Conservatives successfully exploited to make it appear that Canada was being sold out to its large non-British neighbour. In 1926 the governor general, Lord Byng, refused a dissolution of Parliament to the prime minister, Mackenzie King, partly because there had been an election just eleven months before; King made it appear that an appointee of the United Kingdom was interfering in Canada's internal affairs. In 1963 a conflict over defence policy developed within John Diefenbaker's cabinet, and it helped the prime minister to decide to seek the electorate's opinion. In all four instances the election was called to settle a controversy; there was a real issue to be decided, and the government made an appeal to the electorate for support, in three instances after a real or anticipated defeat in the Commons. With the rise of the national convention as the method of choosing party leaders, a new prime minister may want to test his strength as soon as possible, regardless of the current Parliament's age, as happened in 1968 and 1984. It is possible, too, that dissolutions may be called because of the incumbent party's standing in current public opinion polls.

There is clearly an appreciable risk in lodging the power of dissolution with the prime minister, and the Byng-King dispute of 1926 turned in part on the propriety of the prime minister making his demand for a dissolution. But even when the circumstances surrounding the demand are more normal than they were in 1926, there is always the temptation for a prime minister to use his power to promote party ends, for few in such a position are able to distinguish clearly the exact place where the party prospects end and the public good begins. There is, however, fairly general agreement on two points: first, the governor general should in the vast majority of cases allow the prime minister to exercise the power of dissolution without interference; and second, the power is an important weapon to a prime minister in enabling him to keep his party and Parliament under control. The weakness of cabinets in prewar France has been ascribed in no small measure to the lack of such a power.

Finally, while the uncertain life of each Parliament and a sudden election call may at times have a disturbing effect on the economic and political life of the nation, it is questionable whether this is more injurious than the elaborate preparations which precede an election which is known and planned for long in advance. The elements of speculation, hesitation, and suspense, the dramatic appeal of the government for vindication at the hands of the electorate, the frequent emergence of a genuinely controversial issue, are all calculated to attract attention, to induce discussion, to make people realize their importance as active and indispensable participants in the democratic process. Routine elections appear, by comparison, somewhat stodgy and uninspiring affairs; they are also, because of the long campaigns that the parties are likely to run preceding fixed election dates, very expensive for candidates and parties. Parliamentary elections may also appear costly, of course, but as a fraction of the total costs of modern government the expense is almost minuscule; and in any event, there is no workable substitute for them.

Parliament must hold a session (that is, a formal meeting) 'at least once every twelve months,' a constitutional provision that says nothing about how long it must be; the first session of 1940 lasted only a few hours. More than one session may be held in a year, and this has occurred in emergencies and sometimes following a change of government or a general election.

RESIGNATION

A member of the House of Commons, unlike his fellow member in Great Britain, is allowed to resign. (British MPs can none the less leave Parliament: they apply for the Chiltern Hundreds, a handy office of emolument with virtually non-existent duties, and then resign from that.) Even so, the act of resignation may be attended with certain complications. If the member's election is under dispute or if the time during which it may be questioned has not yet expired, his resignation is forbidden. There may be in the minds of some an implied restriction that resignations are not to be made except for serious reasons. 'A member,' said Mackenzie King (though mistaken about a Canadian practice established from the start), 'is elected to serve during the life of a Parliament. Unless there are grave reasons compelling him to return to private life, or he receives some appointment under the Crown, he is, I believe, in duty bound to keep the mandate he has received from his constituents.'[5]

When the member has actually decided to resign, he has more than one method open to him. He may give notice from his place in the House of his intention to resign; or he may send a written declaration of his intention, attested by two witnesses, to the Speaker of the House. If the member is himself the Speaker or if there is no Speaker at the time, he may make the same written declaration and send it to any two members of the House, provided enough time has elapsed since his election to comply with the law concerning controverted elections.

Resigning members usually give reasons for their action, but they are not obliged to, nor do they have to respond to a suggestion from somebody else that they ought to quit. (In 1890 a Canadian MP moved to England without relinquishing his seat.) Members who accept an office emolument such as a judgeship do not have to resign: acceptance of the office automatically vacates the seat.

Members of the House of Commons and Senate are not yet formally paid a salary: their pay is now legally itemized as a sessional allowance, and historically it was called an indemnity – that is, compensation for leaving their own affairs temporarily to devote time to the public weal. At the start that was true; the first session of the first Parliament, with the legislators getting a new country organized, lasted 199 days, but for the next four years the average was 70 days. Nowadays an MP has a full-time job, and must be reimbursed accordingly.

The members of the first Assembly in Canada in 1758 were paid nothing, and those of the first Parliament received $600. The amount was thereafter raised at irregular intervals (often because of pressures that developed when desirable candidates were reluctant to accept nomination just in case they won, and then found their income sharply reduced), and in more recent years increases have become systematic, not only linked to rises in the cost of living, but accompanied by additional allowances. Even so, the first commission to assess the emoluments of members of Parliament reported in 1980 that 'the country can no longer tolerate a system that seems likely to attract mainly the independently wealthy to seek public office. Rather the system must encourage all capable and interested individuals to embark on a political career irrespective of their financial circumstances.'

In 1986 (most of the following figures now change annually) an ordinary member received a basic indemnity of $56,100 and tax-free expense allowance $18,700. In addition, MPs in 1986 received travel allowances for travelling to and from their constituencies or on other public business. All were members of a pension scheme to which they contributed 11 per cent of the basic indemnity, but from which they could draw no benefits unless they had served in the House a minimum of six years: in other words, under all ordinary circumstances they would have had to be elected at least twice.

Apart from these direct monetary benefits, the contemporary MP receives a variety of support services which the complexity of modern government has made necessary. In the 1960s a member had an office in Ottawa and a secretary and, apart from the usual mailing and telephone privileges available to an elected official who was expected to keep in touch with others, little else. In 1986 each ordinary MP had an office allowance of $100,400 for personal staff in Ottawa and in his constituency, and also had at his or her disposal the large regular staff of the House of Commons, which in 1986 approached two thousand persons, including security guards, librarians, restaurant aides, law clerks, and various kinds of administrators. A glance at the parliamentary telephone book suggests that Parliament Hill is a sizable village with, among other amenities, several restaurants, several health offices, computer and other electronic services, a carillonneur, cleaning and repair services, and two barber shops and a beauty salon. Parliament has its own post office, and the necessary staff and equipment to record, translate, print, and distribute the regular debates, journals, and committee proceedings which the House produces.[6]

The considerable budget of the House ($167,507,000 for 1986–7) is not the responsibility of a single minister, for the excellent reason that Parliament is not a branch of the executive. Since Confederation the financial management of the House has rested with the Commission of Internal Economy, a committee of four ministers who are also MPs, and the Speaker, who presides at meetings. The commission has never included opposition members, but since 1975 the House has had a committee on management and members' services which is empowered to advise both the Speaker and the commission on administration and the provision of services for members.[7] As an administrative unit the House is departmentalized into staffs under a variety of servants, the most conspicuous among them the Clerk of the House and the Sergeant-at-Arms, who both sit at tables in the centre aisle of the Commons.

All these services and emoluments are available to all members, but in 1986, 77 of the 282 MPs also received extra remuneration. The prime minister received $64,000 and all other ministers, the Speaker, and the leader of the opposition, $42,800. (It may seem unusual to pay not only ministers to execute the business of the country but also an opposition leader who often does his best to stop them, but Canada has recognized the principle since 1905.) The leader of any third party with at least twelve members was paid an extra $25,800, and various other parliamentary functionaries received extra compensation: on the government side, ministers' parliamentary assistants received $9,400 and on both government and opposition sides it was worth $11,700 to be a chief whip, and lesser amounts to be lesser whips. ('Whip' is borrowed from hunting: in the field a whip manages a pack of hounds, and in Parliament a whip keeps his MPs informed on Commons business and sees that they are on hand when needed. Joe Clark's defeat in 1980 was attributed by some to the failure of the whips to have enough Conservative votes in the House.) The Speaker, the prime minister, and the leader of the opposition have official residences.

Apart from payments to ordinary MPs and others for their individual services, it is relevant to add that the recognized parties as such also are supported. Each party in Parliament has its caucus, in which its members meet behind closed doors to assess their policies and strategies, and since 1969 the caucuses have received money for staff, including research workers. The amount for each party is related to the number of members it has in the House, which means that the governing party, which already has at its disposal the entire public service, somewhat ironically has the richest caucus. In 1986 the total amount available for research and operating expenses was \$1,516,160, the government's research grant being set at \$618,000, and the other two parties receiving research allocations based on their standing in the House. All three parties share an operating budget divided on a simple formula. Each qualified opposition leader's office also received a grant related to a similar formula.

The foregoing financial details (and the list is not complete) accurately reflect how complex the duties of a modern member of Parliament have become. As in many professions, a member is remarkably free to work as much or as little as he pleases, and it remains difficult to assess objectively how much members should be paid, or even whether they should all be treated equally. Members have always been subjected to penalties for absenteeism from the House – attending in the chamber is one of the few things MPs do that can be seen and counted – but the penalties are not impressive for their severity. In any case, the more involved the job becomes, the more legitimate reasons a member can have for being elsewhere. Whether serving constituents, explaining and defending policies, studying public issues, or keeping up with fields in which the member or his electoral district has particular interests, a conscientious MP will always have plenty to do; and to that in most cases must be added family responsibilities. There is nothing in the history of Canada's Parliament to suggest that good representatives have ever been overpaid.

PARLIAMENTARY PRIVILEGE

The ancestor of the Canadian Parliament in the United Kingdom has for many centuries enjoyed certain special privileges, immunities, and powers which apply both to individual members and to Parliament as a whole. Parliaments in the former colonies that are now independent countries have all inherited privilege. 'Parliamentary privilege,' in a classic British statement which is quoted or paraphrased in the documents of parliaments throughout the Commonwealth, 'is the sum of the peculiar rights enjoyed by each House collectively as a constituent part of the High Court of Parliament, and by members of each House individually, without which they could not discharge their functions, and which exceed those possessed by other bodies or individuals. This privilege, though part of the law of the land, is to a certain extent an exemption from the ordinary law.'[8] It is privilege, for example, that permits members to express themselves freely on the floor of the House without running the risk of being sued for slander. It does not, however, protect them outside Parliament.

A power such as that is clearly capable of abuse, and occasionally it is misused; but it is an essential attribute of a free parliament. It and other privileges developed originally as part of parliamentary defences against meddling monarchs in the days when sovereigns had political power; they derived their initial force not from Parliament's role as a lawmaker and talking-shop but as a court. Parliament gradually asserted control over matters affecting its own members and its own business, and the ordinary courts grudgingly admitted its right to do so. When legislatures were set up in the colonies, questions naturally arose over whether parliamentary privilege could be claimed by them, or whether as colonial bodies they were subject to British courts. Time again settled such controversies, and there is now no uncertainty about the reality of parliamentary privilege in Canada.[9]

The privileges inherited by the Canadian Parliament when it was created were of the same modest proportions as those allowed to other British colonies. The original British North America Act of 1867, however, in a section whose history is informative about privilege, made explicit provision for the immediate addition of statutory powers and privileges on a substantial scale. Section 18 read as follows: 'The privileges, immunities, and powers to be held, enjoyed, and exercised by the Senate and by the House of Commons and by the members thereof respectively shall be such as are from time to time defined by Act of the Parliament of Canada, but so that the same shall never exceed those at the passing of this Act held, enjoyed and exercised by the Commons House of Parliament of the United Kingdom of Great Britain and Ireland and by the members thereof.'

In 1868 the Canadian Parliament enacted a law which gave to each of the houses, in almost the identical words used above, the powers, immunities, and privileges enjoyed by the British House of Commons at the time of passing the British North America Act, 'so far as the same are consistent with and not repugnant to the said Act.'[10] A further section stated that these were part of the general and public law of Canada and 'it shall not be necessary to plead the same, but the same shall in all Courts in Canada and by and before all judges be taken notice of judicially.' The act also protected the publication of any proceedings against civil or criminal suit if these were published under the order or authority of the Senate or House of Commons.

This was followed in the same year by an act professing to give to the Senate or to any select committee on private bills of the Senate or of the House the power to examine witnesses on oath. In 1873 the power to examine witnesses on oath was extended to any committee of either house. This latter act was disallowed by the British government on the ground that it was ultra vires, in that it tried to give powers to the Canadian houses which were not possessed in 1867 by the British House of Commons. The earlier act had been, in fact, ultra vires also, although it had been allowed to stand. The sequel came in 1875 with an amendment to the British North America Act, which repealed the original section 18 and substituted another to the effect that the privileges, immunities, and powers of the Canadian Parliament and its members were never to exceed those enjoyed from time to time by the British House of Commons. Another section confirmed the earlier Canadian act of 1868 noted above. Inasmuch as the British House of Commons in 1871 had given to its committees the power to examine witnesses on oath, the Canadian Parliament was able in 1876 legally to endow its committees with the same power.[11] The provision tying Canadian privileges to those of the United Kingdom was never again to be as significant as it was in the 1870s, and the passage of the Constitution Act in 1982 almost certainly abolished it, although that is not explicitly stated. Before 1982, Canada could probably have added to its parliamentary privileges at any time through the use of a conpstitutional amendment of 1949, to be discussed in a later chapter.

The privileges, immunities, and powers of the Canadian Parliament fall into two chief categories: those of individual members of either house; and those of the Senate or of the House of Commons as a body.[12] They are virtually but not quite the same for each house (the Commons' early privilege of settling controverted election cases, for example, has no parallel in the Senate), and the discussion which follows will, for the sake of convenience, deal only with the privileges (including 'immunities and powers') of the Commons.

Privileges of the individual member
Some of these are designed to enable the member to attend to parliamentary duties without interference. An MP cannot be arrested or imprisoned under civil process while Parliament is in session or within a reasonable time going to and returning from the session. This gives him no protection against arrest in any criminal action or for an indictable offence,[13] although, if he should be arrested, that fact must be at once reported to the Speaker. A member does not have to serve on a jury during the session; nor at such times can he be compelled to attend court as a witness although, if necessary, the House will give its permission for him to absent himself for such a purpose.

Other privileges are meant to encourage the member to speak and act freely without fear of undesirable consequences. The most vital of these has already been mentioned: the right of freedom of speech – that is, an immunity from any legal prosecution for anything said as a member in the House or on its committees. The assumption is that occasional abuses of this privilege will be more than compensated for by the gain in complete frankness in discussion. A few restrictions do, in fact, exist, but these promote more orderly debate and the proper and seemly conduct of government. Members cannot be assaulted, or insulted, or threatened in the House or going to or from the House.[14] To offer a bribe to a member – or for a member to accept a bribe – is a breach of privilege and regarded as a 'high crime and misdemeanour.' These privileges may also be extended to any who attend the House under its orders (such as, for example, a witness before the House or a committee of the House) and the House's own officers on occasion.[15]

Collective privileges of the House
These privileges concern the House as a corporate body, and their breach is usually designated by the word 'contempt,' a term used in much the same sense as the more familiar 'contempt of court' applied to judicial proceedings. Contempt is an invasion of the rights of the legislature as a whole, disobedience to its orders, or disorderly conduct before or within it.

The fundamental collective privilege of this nature is the maintenance of order and discipline in the House; for clearly the legislature could not function if it had no authority to compel obedience from its members. The mildest exercise of this power is when the Speaker calls a member to order, and this will occur a number of times before the Speaker moves on to sterner measures. If necessary, the Speaker will then threaten to 'name' the offender, that is, to call him by name instead of using the name of his constituency. If the member is named, he or she is thereupon led from the chamber by the Sergeant-at-Arms and the House decides what disciplinary measures shall be taken, the initiative being with the senior minister present. The House may suspend the offender for the sitting, or for a much longer time, or may even expel him or her. Members are rarely so disciplined, but it does happen occasionally, the last suspension being that of Ed Broadbent in 1983.

The House of Commons has always had the power to regulate its own internal concerns. The power of expulsion is closely associated with the refusal to admit, and in either situation the rejected person may run again as a candidate and be again elected – and conceivably be again refused admittance. The House had formerly the privilege to try all controverted election cases, but this right has been passed over to the judiciary in order to secure a more impartial and expeditious trial.

Another kind of contempt proceeds from outside the House, and may consist of scandalous or libellous reflections on the proceedings, or on the members in their capacity as members. Inasmuch as attacks of this kind on a member may be construed as attacks on the privileges of the House as a body, the line between personal and collective privilege is here not very clear. Members are, indeed, inclined to overwork this privilege by raising a wide variety of petty questions as alleged infractions,[16] although, on balance, these protests do little harm and may enliven the proceedings so that the House starts on its day's work in a more cheerful frame of mind.

Breaches of privilege committed by persons outside the House may be followed up by summoning them to appear before the Bar to explain or to justify their actions.[17] If guilty they may be punished by a public reprimand, delivered by the Speaker, or even imprisoned, although they cannot be kept in custody after the House has prorogued. There is nothing to prevent the House at its next session from re-committing the offender to jail for further punishment. Here again, future interpretation of the Charter of Rights and Freedoms may have implications for parliamentary privilege which cannot be clearly foreseen. When the House of Commons calls a person to the Bar of the House, for example, it has on occasion acted as both prosecutor and judge. It is not obvious that this is consistent with clauses in the Charter; but Parliament alone can amend the constitution on matters 'in relation to the executive government of Canada or the Senate and House of Commons.'

6

The House of Commons: organization and procedure

Here is Edward Bear, coming downstairs now, bump, bump, bump, on the back of his head, behind Christopher Robin. It is, as far as he knows, the only way of coming downstairs, but sometimes he feels that there really is another way, if only he could stop bumping for a moment and think about it.

A.A. Milne, *Winnie-the-Pooh*

The House of Commons has functions that are in addition to its role as a representative body, although they are partly related to representation. All societies seem at times to require elaborate ceremonials, which can range in type from massive military demonstrations in Moscow's Red Square to the singular stage rituals that accompany pop singers. The House cannot approach either of these in intensity, but it does have annual celebrations that open each session of Parliament, and every new Parliament adds to that the election of a Speaker. The shape of the chamber itself produces behaviour different from what might develop if the members all faced the same way instead of so plainly facing each other, the government on the Speaker's right, the opposition to his left, and the prime minister and the leader of the opposition sitting directly across from each other. With the advent of television, House happenings have joined the world of entertainment, and that makes it unlikely that the House would ever schedule its question period to compete with prime time dramas and athletic events.

At the other end of the political spectrum lie the House's serious functions, one of the least of which, most observers now agree, is the actual making of laws through discussion and negotiation. John B. Stewart, now a senator, was for six years an MP closely attached to parliamentary leaders charged with organization and procedure. In an illuminating study, he lists four opportunities available to the House of Commons for the discharge of 'its democratic function':

First, the House can prevent the clandestine exercise of power by the government ...
Second, the House can serve as a proving ground for the administrative policies and legislative proposals of the government ...
Third, the House can constrain the government between elections ...
Fourth, the House can serve to inform and educate the electorate.[1]

All of these, it is important to note, John Stewart qualifies with the word 'can.' How well a particular House of Commons discharges all or any of the above depends in part on elements beyond the reach of mere organization: the relative size of the government majority, the size and vigour of the opposition parties, the skills and experience of the party leaders.

But much depends also on organization and procedure, and some of the informal but relevant parts are so informal as to be all but invisible. The private discussions MPs have in their offices or over lunch, for example, make important contributions to the workings of Parliament, but they are hardly ever recorded, and systematic study of them is impossible. Equally essential, and only slightly more visible, are the pressure groups, those 'organizations whose members act together to influence public policy in order to promote their common interest.'[2] The nature of the Canadian parliamentary system is such that most pressure groups find it more profitable to devote their energies to trying to persuade ministers and high-ranking public servants of the eternal rightness of their aims. But ministers in turn depend on the support of MPs, and administrators can be called as witnesses before parliamentary committees; with members increasingly well informed, and more adequately equipped with offices and staffs, ordinary MPs cannot be ignored by any group trying to influence public policy. Members of Parliament themselves, incidentally, are forbidden by law to accept any kind of direct or indirect compensation for, in effect, trying to further the cause of a pressure group.[3] That of course does not prevent a member from Nova Scotia from championing the Atlantic fisheries, nor are Saskatchewan MPs silent about wheat, or Albertans about oil.

The most important parts of the Commons' informal organization when the House is in session are the party caucuses, which meet secretly, and regularly. The partisan nature of Parliament's work requires each party to be organized, and it is the responsibility of the whips to keep members of their own caucuses informed and on hand to vote. How well each caucus is organized depends on the same factors cited above about the House of Commons. A large government caucus under a successful and strong-minded prime minister can quickly become demoralized if the leader merely tells the caucus what he is going to do – and keeps on winning elections. A small opposition caucus can be enthusiastic and lively, happily free of responsibility for its criticisms of the government's activities. The caucus of the official opposition party, with enduring hopes of winning an election some day, is commonly so well organized that it grooms its members to become future ministers. The Progressive Conservative party before the election in 1984, expanding on established opposition practices, in addition to such indispensable positions as leader, deputy leader, and the whips, assigned two MPs to study each portfolio in the cabinet, the leading member of each pair belonging to what is popularly called the 'shadow cabinet'; and a number of these individuals moved into the portfolios they had been watching when the party became the government. The party also had nine caucus committees on major governmental topics (for example, External Affairs, Fisheries, Agriculture) and was also divided into regional caucuses, each having as its chairman an MP from the region.[4]

All these activities, many of which give members of Parliament plenty to do without even stepping on the floor of the House, are as important to the government of Canada as the more observable activities about to be described.

Enough has already been said to establish that the rules of the House, governing what is generally referred to as parliamentary procedure, are part of the apparatus which, like privilege, permits the members individually and collectively to carry out their duties. The House is unique in that it must be efficient, but in ways that recognize minority opinions, which in turn means that it must also permit the delaying of making decisions while members speak their views. The rules are almost always under pressure: the government wants its policies, expressed in bills, implemented expeditiously; the opposition wants more time to expose and criticize. Fundamental change in the rules is invariably resisted fiercely, and if one side of the House is satisfied with proposed changes, that in itself virtually guarantees that somebody on the other side will not be.

The first major alterations in procedure generally did not happen for a century after Confederation, but with the enormous growth in governmental business in recent decades the rules are now under continuing discussion. They still reflect their British origins, and until the 1980s the standing orders even specified that in all cases not otherwise provided for, 'the usages and customs of the House of Commons of Great Britain and Northern Ireland as in force at the time shall be allowed so far as they may be applicable to this House.' Members came increasingly to regard the rule as obsolete: in 1986, as part of a major revision, it was amended to instruct the Speaker to base decisions on 'the usages, forms, customs and precedents of the House of Commons of Canada and on parliamentary tradition in Canada and other jurisdictions, so far as they may be applicable to the House.' The discarded rule had the advantage of being precise, and the latter part of the new one is so general that it is hard to imagine circumstances in which it could be useful.

Not all the relevant provisions are in the House's own rules, which are solely under its jurisdiction. It is constitutional practice, for example, that allows the prime minister to advise the governor general when to summon Parliament and when to send the MPs home. From 1867 it was the constitution that decreed that 'The House of Commons on its first assembling after a General Election shall proceed with all practicable Speed to elect One of its Members to be Speaker' – a provision now enshrined also in the House rules. Since the election of a Speaker is associated with some of Parliament's most familiar and venerable ceremonies, it is a convenient subject with which to open a more detailed description of the House's formal procedures.

OPENING OF PARLIAMENT

Until, and including, the first session of the thiry-third Parliament, which occurred after the election of 1984, Parliament opened as it had since 1867. The members of the newly elected House of Commons come together when summoned, and they sign the roll and take the oath administered by the Clerk. Soon three knocks are heard on the door of the Commons chamber, and it is opened to admit an official of the Senate, the Gentleman Usher of the Black Rod. He announces in English and French that the deputy of the governor general (the chief justice or the senior puisne judge of the Supreme Court) desires the presence of the Commons in the Senate chamber. The members of the Commons then proceed to the other house, where the Speaker of the Senate announces:

I have it in command to let you know that His Excellency the Governor-General does not see fit to declare the causes of his summoning the present Parliament of Canada until a Speaker of the House of Commons shall have been chosen, according to law; but this afternoon, at the hour of three o'clock, His Excellency will declare the causes of his calling Parliament.

The members of the House thereupon retire to their own chamber to elect a Speaker. This occurs only for each newly elected Parliament or, of course, at other times if there is a vacancy. The House, which is as yet unorganized, is presided over by the Clerk, who until 1986 merely pointed to the proposer and seconder (commonly the prime minister and the leader of the opposition) of the candidate for the speakership.

Prior to the Parliament elected in 1984 there was never a contest for the speakership, although occasionally a nominee received some negative votes. For a century the process invariably produced a Speaker chosen from the MPs supporting the government. In 1968 the House began to experiment with a continuing Speaker – in other words, a new Parliament re-elected the Speaker from the last if he was available. That practice was not rigidly adhered to, partly because under it the alternation of the speakership between incumbents from English- and French-speaking backgrounds became difficult.

In 1986 the House abandoned most of its existing method in favour of choosing a Speaker by secret ballot from among the members. This system was used for the first time in September of that year, after Mr Speaker Bosley resigned. The new rules required any MP who did not want the job to say so in a formal notification, and when the balloting for the election of a Speaker began on 30 September thirty-nine candidates were still in the running. The counting of votes proceeded on the basis of dropping each time those coming last, and voting again until one of the survivors received a majority. That sounds simple but the process in 1986 took eleven separate ballots, and occupied the House from 3 p.m. to 1.48 a.m. the next day. Some members expressed dissatisfaction with the method, but the alternative of requiring candidates to be nominated for the speakership raises the question 'nominated by whom?' and that opens the door to the same controversies that occurred when the Speaker was plainly the government's choice.

The length of time taken by the election of the Speaker in 1986 also raised questions about what modifications may be needed in the opening rituals. Until 1986 the choice of Speaker and the formal opening of Parliament with the speech from the throne all took place on one day. But in 1986 the process took two days, the first for the election, the second for the speech. Unless the rules are amended, future parliaments may have to assemble the day before the session is actually opened. Under the established practices until 1984, the House with its new Speaker would receive another message, again delivered by the Gentleman Usher of the Black Rod, who this time bows three times as he approaches the Speaker; he repeats the bows after telling the House that their presence is desired in the Senate. This time the MPs proceed down the hall in a more orderly fashion, preceded by the Sergeant-at-Arms (bearing the mace), the Speaker, and a small retinue. On arrival at the Senate, the Speaker informs the governor general of his election, and immediately claims on behalf of the MPs 'all their undoubted rights and privileges, especially that they may have freedom of speech in their debates, access to Your Excellency's person at all reasonable times.' These the governor general confirms (through the Speaker of the Senate), after which the speech from the throne is read. The speech, drafted by the prime minister and approved by the cabinet, usually reviews the state of the economy and recites in fairly general terms the government's programs for the coming session. It is invariably destined to be criticized later by the opposition parties for its vagueness and omissions.

The Commons then repairs to its own chamber, where the Speaker tells the members what they have just witnessed in the Senate. The prime minister then moves for leave to introduce Bill no. 1, a phantom proposal about oaths of office whose purpose is to demonstrate the immemorial right of the House of Commons to attend to its own business before taking up that of the executive as contained in the speech from the throne. The bill is read the first time, after which the Speaker announces that a copy of the speech ('to prevent mistakes') is with the chair, and it is presented to the House, which then determines when it will take up the contents. Then follow some routine proceedings, the most important of which is usually the establishment of a bipartisan committee to determine which MPs will sit on all the standing committees provided for in the rules. The real work of the House begins with the next sitting, when the House takes up the speech from the throne, and in an eight-day debate (not necessarily on consecutive days) the House will entertain an address in reply moved and seconded by two MPs supporting the government, while from the opposition side will come critical attempts at amendment of the address. All the voting almost always follows on party lines.

The Speaker's task, it should be added, is not easy. The Speaker occupies what looks like a position of authority, an elaborate chair on a dais, and from there looks down on a House organized on party lines. When the government supporters are very numerous, they fill not only the entire space to the Speaker's right, but overflow to the far left as well. The members, unlike their British counterparts, have individual desks, and their equipment includes the microphones used in the remarkably efficient simultaneous translation system, by which speeches made in one official language can be heard almost concurrently in the other. Galleries occupy all four sides of the chamber, and the translation system is available in them too.

All these physical aids do not remove from the Speaker the onus of trying to keep order in an assemblage that has a variety of opportunities – and reasons – for getting out of hand, or appearing to. The Speaker's duties are always spoken of impressively whenever a new one is chosen, and the leader of the opposition, after the first election by secret ballot in 1986, put it succinctly: 'We know what we demand of you, Mr. Speaker. Perfection! We want fairness, independence, decisiveness, patience, common sense, good humour, upholding the traditions of the House, knowledge of the rules and an intuition for the changing mood and tone of the House as we move through our days.'[5]

If the repetitious opening ceremonies for Parliament seem like the waste of a parliamentary day (except for the election of a Speaker, they open every session), it should be remembered that they are colourful and impressive, orderly and peaceful. They happen also to include, offstage, great events in Ottawa's social calendar, but that is not their purpose. What they do is annually reaffirm ancient rights won by our ancestors in days that were not peaceful for them.

COMMITTEES OF THE HOUSE

The House of Commons appoints a variety of committees which, like all committees, are expected to report back to their principal, whose creatures they are. The last two decades have seen a remarkable increase in committee activity, as the House tries to grapple with the steady growth of government activity by delegating work to committees. Some MPs, because of the needs of their constituencies, or their own particular interests, are at least as active in committees as they are on the floor of the House, and it would be unfair to assess any member's performance, or even that of the House as a whole, solely by what transpires in the chamber.

The *standing committees,* each with seven to fifteen members, are called that for the same reason that the rules are called the standing orders; the committees also stand ready to consider whatever the House refers to them. There are at present (1987) twenty-five of them named in the standing orders, and their titles cover all the general areas of government policy, such as Aboriginal Affairs and Northern Development, Agriculture, Communications and Culture, Research, Science and Technology, and Veterans Affairs. They all have general assignments to oversee the work of the departments assigned to them, but several have specific mandates. For example, the committee on elections privileges, and procedure is to review and report on House rules and procedures, including the committees themselves; that on multiculturalism is not merely to examine policies but encourage the departments to be sensitive to multicultural concerns; that on public accounts is to receive automatically the public accounts and the auditor general's reports on them, without annual reference by the House.

There are also three *standing joint committees,* with senators added to MPs, on matters of common interest: official languages, Parliament, and regulations and other statutory instruments. Membership on the committees reflects the party strengths in the House, and with two exceptions (public accounts, and management and members' services) the chairman is generally a government supporter. Members may serve on more than one committee, and all other members are free to attend but not to vote. When several committees are active, smaller parties have difficulty attending to all their committee assignments because of inadequate numbers.

The committees generally are smaller than in the years following Confederation, when some had over one hundred members. Even until the present system was adopted in 1968, committees of up to sixty were not uncommon; one reason for the reduction in size was to make the committees more effective. But apart from that, the work and scope of the committees have been enlarged and systematized in an unprecedented manner, and while complaints about individual committees, and the whole system, continue to be heard, the present committees are unquestionably superior to their predecessors. Progress in parliamentary procedure is slow, as a single major sequence will show. In the 1950s the House occasionally referred some estimates (the government's spending proposals for the next fiscal year) to a special ad hoc committee; then the special committee became a standing committee; now all estimates are referred to the relevant standing committees. It is unusual today for an important standing committee to let years go by without meeting, as was formerly the case; now any four members of a committee can secure a meeting on request. The appearance of witnesses before committees has begun to produce its own small literature, as members and those summoned to appear before them reflect on their experiences.[6]

When the standing committees were less active they naturally enjoyed less of the House's confidence, and the House often turned to committees which were not standing but set up to meet a special need. Sometimes special committees became standing committees (as in the special committees on estimates mentioned above) and even, on occasion, provided the impetus for further studies by royal commissions, which are instruments of the executive, not Parliament. The standing committees have grown so much in importance in recent years that the special committees, as an institution, will possibly take their turn at being eclipsed. But it was a special committee that produced the report which led to major procedural changes for the Commons in 1986. Special committees are small, consisting 'of not more than fifteen members.'

Joint committees of the House and Senate may also be special, as distinct from standing, and some of them have produced interesting and influential reports. In the 1940s there were joint committees on a Canadian flag, on Indian affairs, and on human rights; in 1950 there was a joint committee on old age security; and in 1966 one on the public service. More recent joint committees have been that on the constitution, which in 1972 produced a report after hearing approximately one thousand witnesses; and that of 1984 on reform of the Senate, which added to the voluminous chronicles on that subject.

The special committee on the reform of the Commons in the early 1980s led to innovations that included another kind of committee, the legislative. The work of a *legislative committee* is neither general, as with most standing committees, nor aimed at a general study of one topic, as with most special committees; it is narrowly confined to specific pieces of proposed legislation referred to it by the House after second reading. A legislative committee may have up to thirty members, and its chairman is not elected by the committee members, as with the other types, but chosen from a panel of MPs appointed by the Speaker. Like other committees, the legislative have budgets and are empowered by the standing orders 'to retain the services of expert, professional, technical and clerical staff as may be deemed necessary.'

A more unusual committee, one of vast significance in parliamentary history, is the *Committee of the Whole House*, which consists of the entire membership of the House sitting more informally than when the Speaker is in the chair. The chairman is the Deputy Speaker, and the procedure allows MPs to speak repeatedly, and even chattily, on a measure, although no speech apart from the main party leader's may exceed twenty minutes. In former days the Committee of the Whole was the main device used by the House to discuss both the raising and spending of public money, but, with the reference of the estimates to the standing committees, the Committee of the Whole has become more a receiver of reports. The House can of course refer any matter to itself as a committee, and the Committee of the Whole still plays a major role in financial legislation, one of particular use to the opposition parties.

RULES OF THE HOUSE

Enough has been said already to suggest that the rules by which the House conducts itself must facilitate the passage into law of the government's programs, for whatever else happens, the government of Canada must go on. When the government has a majority in the House consisting of its own party members, that strength is reflected in the composition of all the House committees; the committee system is naturally modified during the life of a minority government, and for that reason many opposition members speak well of such periods in parliamentary history. Whenever revision of the rules is under discussion much is said about ways of enhancing the roles and opportunities of the private member, as is seen in the tendency since the 1960s to give the committees, and hence the MPs, more work.

The rules of the House set aside fixed periods for the special use of the government and private members respectively. For many years eight full days were set aside early in each session for private members' business, but in the 1960–1 session the House moved toward setting aside a single hour on four days a week. The current rules give private members from 5 to 6 p.m. on Monday, Tuesday and Thursday of the parliamentary week, and from 4 to 5 on Friday. The same rules also give other business precedence over the private members' under certain circumstances.[7] With time so short, alloting the available hours takes place by lot: at the start of each session, a 'random draw' is held to establish the precedence of 'twenty separate items of which at least twenty separate members have given notice.' There is no guarantee that even the twenty items will all receive consideration.

The business of Parliament – and of the government – is also greatly expedited by the rules of debate. Only certain specific motions are debatable; speeches cannot be read (though the practice is much abused); members cannot speak twice on the same question. These and other rules of a similar kind eliminate much needless discussion. In 1927 the House introduced a drastic curtailment, whereby no one was allowed to speak for more than forty minutes except 'the Prime Minister and the Leader of the Opposition, or a Minister moving a Government Order and the member speaking in reply immediately after such Minister, or a member making a motion of "No Confidence" in the Government and a Minister replying thereto.' (Those exceptions still exist.) When the Speaker is in the chair, the basic time allowed MPs is now twenty minutes, and an additional ten minutes is allotted to allow other MPs to speak to what was said in the first twenty minutes. The rules ring several changes on these basic provisions: on second reading of a government bill, for example, no limits are put on speeches by the prime minister and his opposite; the first three 'ordinary' members receive forty minutes, and the rest of the field twenty if they speak 'within the next eight hours of consideration,' and ten after that. The members are also allocated fifteen minutes early in each parliamentary day for statements of 'not more than one minute.' (SO 19 and 21). The Speaker's equipment in the chair now includes a stop-watch.

The pressure on the House's timetable has not unnaturally created a need for methods of cutting off debate altogether: in other words, closure. To get a closure rule into a set of standing orders that has none is not easy, but in 1913 Sir Robert Borden's government, exasperated by a non-stop two-week debate that saw the House silent only on Sundays, by a tricky manoeuvre, used its majority to bring in a way of cutting off the talking. The rule, in essence, allows a minister after due notice to move 'that the debate shall not be further adjourned' (no. 57), and if the motion passes, a vote must be taken by one o'clock in the morning. The House has experimented with other types of closure, notably in amendments brought in in 1968–9, but the original rule, with slight modifications, still stands. No member can speak more than once or for more than twenty minutes after a closure motion has been accepted by the House.

The closure rule gives the initiative to the government, which in itself irritates the opposition. In March 1982, however, the opposition discovered an ingenious form of closure of its own. By a long-standing custom not specifically covered in the rules, the bells summoning MPs into the chamber to vote continue to ring until the government and opposition whips signal to the Speaker that their members are, in effect, ready for the vote. In 1982 the chief opposition whip simply stayed away, and the bells rang for fifteen days, paralysing the House and putting the Speaker in an impossible position. Any action by the Speaker to either stop the bells and have the vote, or let them ring indefinitely, would appear to be taking sides for or against one of the two main parties in the House. The bells on the first occasion were finally stilled by agreement, but the basic problem remained. Clearly an unlimited bell could bring the work of Parliament to a standstill, while restraints would not only add a new rigidity to House procedures but, since control of the bells could be entrusted only to the Speaker, could easily put that officer into an impossible situation. An unlimited bell, it should be noted, does not merely permit an opposition to go on strike against the government; it also gives a government in difficulty an opportunity to avoid a possibly adverse vote. The committee on reform of the House produced a solution: the rules now specify that, depending on the business before the House, the bells cannot ring for more than fifteen or thirty minutes before the business is proceeded with. It will take unusually ingenious MPs to find a way around the current rules.[8]

The older forms of closure, while not used lightly by any government, have always caused controversy, even on those occasions when the opposition appeared to be taunting the government into using closure so that its autocratic tendencies could be clearly seen. In the elections of 1957 and 1958, which followed a Liberal use of closure in 1956 that was widely decried, the Progressive Conservative party campaigned on a platform calling for its abolition; but although in 1958 and again in 1984 the Conservatives won the two largest Commons majorities in Canadian history, closure is still with us.[9]

The hostility that usually accompanies the use of closure and the combativeness that shows in the daily question period are not typical of much that goes on in and around the House. Individual and party rivalries never disappear, and sometimes a particular member, whether in the cabinet or not, can become heartily disliked or distrusted for the same reasons that would create those reactions anywhere. But members also admire hard work and tenacity, and ambition and deep conviction, and in general treat each other courteously —as the rules, indeed, formally oblige them to. Co-operative devices such as 'pairing,' whereby two members from opposing parties agree not to vote on partisan divisions, thus leaving either or both free to be absent, are typical of the common arrangements through which the peaceful transaction of parliamentary business goes on. And while all informal arrangements can break down when feelings run high, the House throughout most of its history has been a congenial place, 'the best club in the country,' as more than one MP has said. Experienced members usually come to regard the House as a special place, and many distinguished Canadians as varied as Chubby Power (a Quebec Liberal), John Diefenbaker (a Saskatchewan Conservative), and Stanley Knowles (a Manitoba CCF-NDPer) have found in the House profoundly rewarding careers.

THE PASSAGE OF BILLS

The basic procedure in the passage of public bills (which deal with matters of a public or general nature and can be introduced by any member) is that they should receive three readings in the House, three in the Senate, and then go to the governor general for royal assent. If the bill originates in the Senate, the order of passage in the two houses is, of course, reversed. If one house amends a bill passed by the other, it is returned to have these amendments considered and approved; and if these are not accepted, the house which originated the bill will state the reasons for rejection. Communication between the houses is by message; but if no agreement occurs through this medium, a conference may be held between representatives of both houses to discuss and, if possible, to reconcile differences. If agreement is not reached, the measure is, of course, lost.

The House of Commons by its very nature cannot often be taken by surprise on procedural matters (although it may be startled by related happenings, as in former bell-ringings) and the introduction of a bill must be preceded by forty-eight hours' notice. The notice appears in the *Votes and Proceedings,* a daily diary of what takes place in the House without the words spoken in debate. The bill cannot be either 'blank or in an imperfect shape,' and its sponsor, when asking for leave to introduce it, may give 'a succinct explanation' of its purpose. Leave is almost invariably granted, although refusal is not unknown. First reading is not contentious, as all it does is get the bill started on its way.

The second reading of a bill is normally its most important stage, and it presents the opportunity for full and lengthy discussion. The debate on the second reading, however, is confined to the principle of the proposal and any attempt to discuss details or to deal with the clauses seriatim will be ruled out of order. The bill cannot be amended on second reading, but it may be defeated, although that is extremely unlikely if the bill is sponsored by a minister whose party has a majority in the Commons.

If the House gives a bill a second reading, it has expressed its approval of the general aim of the bill. The next logical question to be answered is whether the measure as proposed will best carry out this purpose. The following stage must therefore be devoted to a discussion of the detailed provisions. To accomplish this, the bill now goes to one of the legislative committees, unless it is a financial bill, which automatically goes to a Committee of the Whole. The committee goes through the bill clause by clause, possibly calling witnesses or otherwise collecting relevant information, and then reports it back to the House, with or without amendments. A lapse of forty-eight hours then occurs (unless the House takes action to shorten it) after which the House considers the bill as reported from the committee, accepting or rejecting the bill as it came from the committee and amending it at the report stage if it wishes. The bill is then finally given third reading. Third reading is by no means a formality, although the rules assume that all amendments the House desires will have been made in committee or at the report stage – that is, after the bill has returned from a committee. The only debatable point is whether the bill should or should not be read a third time.

Occasionally, the opposition at this stage will make a last desperate effort to encompass the defeat of a government measure or at least to establish its own position beyond any possible doubt. But a bill which has progressed thus far is not likely to be defeated as it comes into the home stretch.

The apparent simplicity of the procedure described above – for financial legislation it is more complex – should not lead one to assume that every bill has an easy passage through the House. (Private bills, those dealing with such matters as the incorporation of a company or a charitable organization, follow a somewhat different and ordinarily quieter procedure, though one similar in principle: fees ranging from $100 to $800 are charged for different stages of private bills.) Highly controversial debates can occur both in the Commons chamber and in the committee room on public bills; they do get withdrawn by cabinets in the face of opposition criticism; the parliamentary timetable is often such that bills die on the order paper; and once through the House of Commons a bill has to survive passage through the Senate. If the Senate makes any amendments, as noted, the bill has to come back to the Commons for consideration. The actual passage of any bill can be traced in detail with the aid of the two houses' respective official diaries; a comparison of any bill's voyage through the House of Commons before recent amendments to the rules will show that current standing orders have enormously simplified procedure. But it remains more complicated than the simplified general outline described here.[10]

FINANCE

No single proceeding more dramatically illustrates the difficulties of adapting democratic devices to rapidly changing and increasingly expensive governmental policies than parliamentary attempts to supervise the raising and spending of the taxpayers' money. The first fiscal year after Confederation saw the Commons providing for annual expenditures of roughly $15 *million*. Now every fiscal year sees expenditures well in excess of one hundred *billion* dollars. Nevertheless, the principles on which the Commons bases its management of the public finances have remained remarkably constant:

1 There is an annual budget (occasionally, for special reasons, two) which is systematically presented to the House for public as well as parliamentary scrutiny.
2 The cabinet accepts responsibility for preparing both estimates for future expenditure and ways of raising money for them.
3 Parliament, and especially the House, accepts the responsibility of receiving the government's financial proposals, studying them, and approving them.

4 Cabinet and Parliament fully understand that parliamentary approval in no way relieves the cabinet of the responsibility for its own proposals, or for any changes made after debate.

5 The cabinet is not free to alter the proposals after their parliamentary approval, although there is some flexibility allowed within major items of expenditure, and the cabinet may, on its own responsibility, abstain from making an approved expenditure.

6 Once the plans are approved, there is adequate machinery provided for carrying them out. Most of the machinery is under the jurisdiction of the cabinet (although there are important exceptions), which takes responsibility for the necessary accounting, reporting, and auditing facilities, and for producing clear documents that a body of laymen such as the House of Commons can understand. The House has its own auditor and an audit committee, that on public accounts.[11]

One department of government, the Treasury Board (in essence a committee of cabinet members presided over by a minister who is now one of the most powerful figures in the government), is primarily responsible for seeing that each branch of the administration prepares its spending plans for the future and submits them to the board. (More detail on financial matters will be found in Chapter 11.) Each department will know, through its minister, whether the cabinet's mood is one that favours reductions or increases in its various categories of spending, although it is a safe generalization that most estimates at the early planning stage are optimistically prepared with increases in mind. The estimates work their way upward from the department's various branches to the deputy minister, who after discussions with his more junior administrators (and no doubt changes in the proposals) presents the final draft to the minister. That individual, who is the person who may have to defend or explain the proposals in public, may have suggestions to offer or even insist on. The estimates then go to the staff of the Treasury Board (whose officials may have already greatly influenced the plans while they were in preparation) and finally to the board itself. The financial management of government is in principle simple, in practice complex, but the departments generally tend to see the Treasury Board's chief function as one that can be expressed in a single word: no. Composed of the ministers primarily involved in financial matters, and particularly with the raising of money, the board is implacably opposed to extravagance, and its members must argue with other ministers and MPs who are not necessarily of like mind. One conservative-minded Liberal minister of finance, J.L. Ilsley, told the House on 18 December 1945, in timeless words:

We talk about putting a watch on expenditures, but how much assistance do we get in this House in watching expenditures? Nine-tenths of the speeches in this House are asking for bigger and better expenditures. That was the case all through the last Parliament. While this session did not start out in that way, it finally got that way. If the Government is making large expenditures, it is not because the Ministers are trying to make those expenditures, it is because of public and parliamentary demands for those expenditures. That is why the expenditures are being made. At times I feel as though I am against the whole world when I try to keep a lot of these expenditures down. We just do the best we can, that is all, and keep them down.

After their troubled passage through the Treasury Board, the estimates are approved by the cabinet (where a disappointed minister may make a last stand for a larger appropriation), and are recommended to the governor general for his approval, which is given as a matter of course. They are then transmitted to the House of Commons early in the parliamentary sessions, and are at once referred to the relevant standing committees.

The estimates are not presented simply as enormous blocks of funds assigned to each department, for this would make it impossible for Parliament either to understand the expenditures or to exercise oversight of any consequence. Even a moderately effective control must be based on an intelligent appreciation of the exact purposes for which the money is to be spent, and this involves breaking down the proposals into a large number of comparatively small items. But Parliament must not make its statutory provisions too rigid, for it would thereby greatly embarrass the administration in its task of applying the funds effectively to the need which is to be met. Ideally, the whole process combines flexibility for the executive with an adequate measure of control for Parliament, with all the necessary documentation appearing in comprehensible publications that are readily available. The estimates now come out in a variety of volumes that present proposals for expenditures under the names of departments or other agencies; the actual legislation that emerges is, by comparison, short and simple, authorizing the government, in effect, to spend money as the books of estimates say it can.

The *main estimates* for each incoming fiscal year must now by House rule be referred to standing committees by 1 March, and the committees, after examining them item by item, must report back by 31 May, thus having three months for the completion of their study. This practice, begun in 1968 after a good deal of serious criticism of traditional financial procedures by successive committees, does not prevent the House as a whole from considering supply – that is, the money to be supplied by law for approved purposes. The rules provide for the setting aside in each session of twenty-five days (five on or before 10 December, seven more by 26 March, and thirteen more by 30 June on which only members in opposition can present motions, on 'any matter within the jurisdiction of the Parliament of Canada,' thus preserving the ancient privilege of 'grievances before supply.' A maximum of six of these opposition motions, two in each period for which allotted days are provided, may be 'no-confidence motions against the government.' To facilitate the work of all members, but especially those in opposition, the estimates are presented in a form that shows comparative data for the previous year, thus permitting members to assess increases and decreases in the expenditure proposals. The final legislation becomes an Appropriation Act.[12]

The main estimates do not comprise the whole of the cabinet's requests for money. The rules provide for *supplementary estimates,* to be treated in much the same way as the main ones, because it is not possible to know by 1 March what unforeseen expenditure needs may arise in, say, September. There are also *final estimates,* introduced just before the close of the fiscal year, to tidy up items perhaps not foreseen in the supplementary estimates. There are obviously dangers in presenting the House with three sets of estimates instead of one, since they make it difficult for the members to obtain an overall picture of the cabinet's expenditure program. Since the supplementaries usually come late in the session when the House is under pressure to finish all of the session's work, they can also be abused. More than one auditor general has complained about a cabinet's practice of slipping into hastily passed supplementaries items that might not have been readily acceptable in the main estimates.

Emergency and unforeseeable expenditure that has not been provided for by Parliament may be made by a governor general's warrant, a special authority issued under an order-in-council. It cannot be issued if Parliament is in session, and its use is severely restricted by other statutory provisions. Prior to 1958 it was customary for expenditure made under governor general's warrants to be included in the next supplementary estimates, so that Parliament was still able to review the expenditure ex post facto; since 1958 the practice has been required by statute.[13] Warrants have been used on occasion to finance virtually the whole of ordinary governmental expenditures for short periods.

The estimates deal with the spending of money. The other side is raising the money, and this is considered in the presentation of the budget – the balance of the contemplated expenditures with a corresponding income (derived from current revenue or loans), so that spending and raising public money are, at least theoretically, kept in balance. When the whole House is considering the estimates, it is said to be in *Supply,* and when it is studying revenue the process is *Ways and Means.* Annually the minister of finance gives notice that he will move for Ways and Means, and when he presents the motion (which must be on another day than the notice) he proposes, 'that this House approves in general the budgetary policy of the government.' The Commons then celebrates one of its annual festivals, the budget debate, to which six days are allocated. The main topics in the minister's opening speech have become fairly well standardized and embrace the following:

1 A review of the economic and financial conditions during the past year and the effects of government policies on these conditions.
2 A review of the financial operations of the government during the past fiscal year (or, it may be, the year which is almost concluded). This lays the necessary foundation for what is to come.
3 A tentative weighing of the existing and, to some degree, known elements of the situation: the probable revenue to be derived from taxation at present levels, and the almost certain expenditures as indicated in the estimates already presented and by the financial demands arising from existing statutory grants. Statutory grants are expenditures authorized in legislation that requires money (as in family allowances or old age pensions) to be paid out regularly, and are thus outside the annual sets of estimates. The minister must provide the revenues for total expenditures, regardless of the form in which Parliament approved them.
4 The adjustment in revenue-raising which the above tentative computation has made desirable, in the government's opinion. If a surplus is indicated, the minister will probably either change the taxes in certain respects or reduce or abandon some of them. If a deficit is indicated (as is now the norm), the minister may close the gap by tax adjustments, tax increases, new taxes, or capital borrowings, depending partly on how the government may be attempting to influence the business cycle. The government may, of course, choose the budget to announce any drastic changes, such as a departure in tariff policy, which are likely to have important financial consequences.

The Ways and Means motion is debatable and subject to amendments, and it usually receives both. This is one of the most important debates of the year and it will naturally stress in particular the economic difficulties and outlook for the future. The motion is eventually carried, or the government will either have to resign or seek a dissolution. Legislation based on the budget proposals can of course also be debated under the usual rules for processing bills, so that the members have a minimum of two opportunities for discussing the government's proposals.

The elaborate and complicated system of authorizing, auditing, and checking that forms an essential part of the financial administration as it affects the receipt and, particularly, the disbursement of the public funds cannot be discussed here in detail. The primary responsibility for the system is of course vested in the cabinet. The methods used vary, but expenditures are pre-audited before being made, to ensure that Parliament has actually voted the money for the proposed expenditure and that the money has not already been spent; but the individual departments and agencies are of course the bodies initially responsible for spending properly the money granted to them. There has been for years a continuing discussion of how to reconcile centralized control with departmental autonomy so that neither gets out of hand, or moves beyond the reach of Parliament. Two major investigations in recent decades are the Royal Commission on Government Organization (the Glassco Commission) which reported in 1962, and that on Financial Management and Accountability (the Lambert Commission), 1979; after serious research, these two studies revealingly reached differing conclusions on some major matters.

The expenditures are also post-audited by the auditor general, whose office was established in 1878. He is an official of Parliament, not of the cabinet, and he holds office during good behaviour, subject to removal only by the cabinet after the passage of a joint address by both Houses of Parliament. His original function was to check on all receipts and payments of the Consolidated Revenue Fund, to ensure that money has been or is to be paid for the purposes intended, and generally to investigate every aspect of the public service as it affects finance. His decisions can also be overruled by the Treasury Board, but these cases must be submitted to the consideration of Parliament in his annual report. In this report he is further bound to call attention to any irregularity, any exceptional procedure, any special payments by warrant, any refund of a tax or similar payment under statutory authority, or any matter which he feels he should bring to the attention of Parliament; and Parliament may, of course, take what it considers to be appropriate action. In 1977 Parliament enacted a significant addition to the auditor general's power, which empowered him to move well beyond the traditional duties of his office: in the words of a former auditor general, he is now 'required to report to Parliament on cases that he has observed where there has not been due regard to economy and efficiency in the expenditure of public funds and where adequate procedures to measure and report on the effectiveness of publicly funded programs have not been applied where it was reasonable that they should be.'[14] As part of these new duties, the auditor general in March 1985 took the government to court to sue for the production of information that he felt was being improperly withheld from him.

Parliamentary consideration of the auditor general's report, primarily through the Standing Committee on Public Accounts, has had an exceedingly erratic history, though in recent years it has become increasingly systematic. In 1958, following British practice, a member of the opposition was elected chairman of the Public Accounts Committee, and shortly thereafter the committee undertook to follow up its own comments and criticisms to see what executive action had been taken on them. The committee's work and authority was shaken by the long period of minority government from 1962 to 1968, and it is clear that the House of Commons, as has already been remarked, is still searching for further reforms of itself which will improve (among other activities) its scrutiny of financial affairs.

Reform of the House of Commons has indeed become a regular item on every session agenda. The new rules adopted in February 1986 were to expire if not extended by the end of the year, but they were in the event extended to April 1987 when again a decision (not yet made as this is written) had to be made to extend, or amend, or replace them. Opening up the House rules for reconsideration is time-consuming, and not the kind of topic to which members are likely to give a high priority with the next general election almost in sight. The trial run of the 1986 rules, that is, may become a marathon.

7

The House of Commons
and the executive

In the absence of a firm hand one expects uproar in such an assembly as the Commons, but one does not expect to find things scrawled all over the walls in chalk. Hopscotch and marbles again are harmless enough, but for M.P.'s to bully and maltreat those of their number who are weak in the head (especially if of Cabinet rank) is outrageous.
D.B. Wyndham Lewis, *Daily Mail*

Earlier passages of this book have referred to some aspects of relations between the House of Commons and the cabinet its majority supports, and the purpose of this chapter is to present a systematic description of some specific instruments necessary to those relations. It has already been suggested that the connection between the legislature and an executive backed by a secure majority can become virtually identical. An MP who is a government supporter may be unhappy with his party's policies or its leadership, and behind the scenes and in caucus be a vocal critic, but in the public arena he has always to consider that there may be one course worse than voting with the cabinet: voting with the opposition, of which he must generally disapprove even more or he would not be in the governing party.

The prime minister and cabinet thus wield extensive authority in the House. Parliament is summoned and dissolved on the advice of the prime minister, who will often (though not always) exercise his powers after consulting members of his cabinet. The cabinet has a ruling influence on all legislation and exclusive authority over the initiation of all financial legislation. The cabinet controls the time, regulates the business, and apportions the energies of the House almost from hour to hour during every day of its meeting. There is virtually nothing the House does in which the cabinet does not have some interest, and in most of these matters it exercises a paramount control. The functions of Parliament to some seem to have degenerated until all that it does is to pass on the measures the cabinet chooses to offer within the time the cabinet chooses to allow; to raise and spend the money the cabinet desires without the opportunity of increasing either revenue or expenditure; to fall in constantly behind the majority, which in turn automatically falls in behind the cabinet. Responsible government would appear to have suffered a strange and alarming inversion: the cabinet is no longer responsible to the Commons; the Commons seems instead to have become responsible to the cabinet.

That there is a substantial measure of truth in this, no one can deny. The cabinet does dominate Parliament, and it is largely because of this masterful leadership that Parliament is able to make its expenditure of time and energy produce results that are moderately satisfactory. A House of two or three hundred members which wanders where it pleases will undoubtedly be able to cover a lot of territory, but it will not accomplish much. If it is to perform its functions as a useful part of the government, it must be willing to place some limits on its freedom and submit to direction. It does not thereby become of necessity subservient to the cabinet, nor is the cabinet on that account unable to derive from the House much counsel and guidance. To regard the rare defeats of the cabinet by the House as a reliable indication of the efficacy of parliamentary control is to judge the efficacy of parental control by the number of times the child is punished. The House of Commons does control the cabinet – rarely by defeating it, often by criticizing it, still more often by the cabinet anticipating criticism before subjecting itself and its acts to the House, and always by the latent capacity of the House to revolt against its leaders.

Many elements of the relations between the House and the cabinet are not visible to observers in the visitors' galleries, nor are they available to the television cameras. The work of parliamentary committees can usually be seen by outside observers, but it is not yet generally covered by electronic media. The party caucuses meet behind closed doors. More obvious is the parliamentary work of the opposition, whose responsibilities include open criticism and attack. It wages perpetual war on the government, finding out its faults, critically dissecting its policies and proposals, offering substitutes and amendments, and lying in wait for any sign of weakness or dissension. The rules of the House tend to favour the cabinet and to give it a general right of way for its business, but there are also many rules which are designed to aid the other side.

It remains now to glance at those opportunities which allow the opposition – and, indeed, any private member – to vent its criticism, woo its public, and test its strength in the votes cast on the floor of the House. These opportunities, it must be remembered, are only the visible parts of a process: as with an iceberg, the tip can be misleading about what remains unseen.

The first opportunity available to the House of Commons each session follows the speech from the throne. The speech itself is invariably a general statement, but its very vagueness gives MPs tremendous latitude in debate. With the formality of a classical dance, the leaders of the opposition parties direct the attack on the government's policies, past, present, and future, through the device of moving amendments to the main motion. Such amendments were not moved before 1893 but are now the normal practice, and the rules specify the timing for the disposition of sub-amendments and amendments. (The recognition of sub-amendments is also a roundabout recognition of the existence of more than two parties in the modern Commons.) The prime minister then defends the government's policies at length. After the big guns have spoken, those of smaller bore are free to be heard.

Some idea of the diversity of subject-matter allowed may be gathered from a speech of the leader of the opposition (R.B. Hanson) on the address in November 1940. Setting what may still be a record, he spoke on: the summoning of Parliament at that time; responsible government in Canada; the Canadian attitude to the war; the possible invasion of Britain; the manufacture of aeroplanes; the Canadian war effort in general; a speech made by General Crerar; the training of troops; Canada's external relations; finance; soldiers' hutments; wasted potato bags; the Montreal railway terminals; imports from the United States; the Rowell-Sirois report. He then added:

I did intend to say something about the St. Lawrence Waterway, but I do not think I should trespass much longer on the time of the House. The Prime Minister today tabled the correspondence, and I have not had opportunity to look at it. I shall therefore reserve what I have to say on that matter. I had also intended to say something about leadership in Canada, but also reserve my remarks on that subject until a later date. I cannot, however, refrain from saying something about the position of truck transportation in the province of Prince Edward Island.[1]

The debate on the address used to ramble on almost indefinitely, the government often accused of permitting dawdling because it had no legislation ready. In 1955 a limit of ten days was set, and it is now eight. The basic problem with even eight days is not the consumption of time, but the pointlessness of many of the speeches. The full measure of their worth is to be found in the fact that frequently nowadays they are not even prepared by the members who speak, but by hired hacks. They do, however, give backbenchers an opportunity to get on the record in a speech that can then be printed up and distributed to constituents.

QUESTIONS ADDRESSED TO MINISTERS

The standing orders that cover questions have remained much the same for years, but the impact of television on the House has profoundly altered the use of question period. On paper the rules permit each member to have up to three questions daily marked for an oral reply, and unmarked questions are answered on papers handed to the Clerk of the House and then printed in the debates. (In practice, 'oral' replies are commonly typewritten too.) If the information required is lengthy or is apt to be delayed, it is passed as an order for return and is tabled in due course.

For many years the rules provided only for written questions, although in practice the Speaker permitted oral questions, theoretically those confined to matters of some urgency. The rules now permit an oral question period of up to forty minutes daily (again for matters of urgency), and any member not satisfied with a response to any question can on three days a week give notice 'that he or she intends to raise the subject-matter of his question on the adjournment of the House.' Standing order 64 says that 'in putting any such question or in replying to the same no argument or opinion is to be offered, nor any facts stated, except so far as may be necessary to explain the same; and in answering any such question the matter to which the same refers shall not be debated.' Observers of question periods may find those words hard to reconcile with what they see, but in fact MPs elicit from the cabinet through questions vast amounts of information related to their constituencies, their own particular interests, or almost any topic they can bring up in a manner that appears relevant to any public matter. The minutiae that appear in such abundance in MPs' questions (and both questions and answers become part of the public record) are a useful reminder that much of Parliament's work lies outside the robust give-and-take one can see almost daily between the front benches in the House.

The purposes behind the interrogation are varied. It may be a simple inquiry for information; it may represent a covert attack on a minister; it may be a search for material to use in a later debate; it may be an attempt to win favour in a constituency; it may be an endeavour to call public attention to a grievance; or it may be a scheme to induce the government to commit itself to a policy, or force it to take a stand. Question period is undoubtedly valuable, especially since dissatisfied questioners have been able to transfer their inquiries to the debates on adjournment motions. The whole process draws the acts of government out into full publicity and threatens at all times to submit the most obscure happenings to a sudden and unexpected scrutiny. It is one of the most formidable devices the opposition has at its disposal.

The question, invaluable though it is, is clearly open to abuse unless it is surrounded with substantial safeguards. The minister is thus permitted to decline to answer any question and cannot be compelled to furnish a reason for doing so, although a blunt refusal would place him in a vulnerable political position. A common reason for silence is that an answer would not be in the public interest, and this is deemed adequate if the question demands confidential or secret information, which might occur in the course of a war, or with privileged correspondence, for example. Inquiries involving future government policy are also considered to be improper, as are trivial or hypothetical questions, those seeking information readily obtainable by members through other channels, and many others. A frequent abuse of the question privilege in the Commons is the demand for information that is of doubtful value, and the securing of which involves a tremendous amount of labour.

As with so many aspects of parliamentary affairs, the use of question period varies with the personalities involved. In his first year of office, Brian Mulroney was sometimes criticized for answering questions that opposition MPs thought were the responsibility of other ministers. In 1968 Trudeau tried to save the time of busy ministers by platooning them so that not all needed to be present for all question periods. The experiment proved at best only partially successful: opposition members found it difficult to adjust themselves to the planned absences of ministers they wanted to get at and, as one experienced parliamentarian asserted roundly while the 'roster system' was young, 'Anybody who has been in government will recognize that for a minister to be in the house every day is the best thing in the world for him.'[2] Besides, nowadays an absent minister might miss being seen on television.

A MOTION OF ADJOURNMENT TO DISCUSS 'A SPECIFIC AND IMPORTANT MATTER REQUIRING URGENT CONSIDERATION'

This device enables the private member to break into the routine proceedings of the House and precipitate a discussion on an urgent current matter that he believes should be brought to the attention of the government and Parliament. The member (who must give the Speaker notice of the urgent matter at least one hour before raising it) asks leave to move the adjournment of the House and presents without argument the statement he has already given the Speaker. The Speaker decides whether or not the matter is a proper one, and is enjoined by the rules to consider 'the extent to which it concerns the administrative responsibilities of the government or could come within the scope of ministerial action and [he] also shall have regard to the probability of the matter being brought before the House within reasonable time by other means.' If the Speaker decides that the question is urgent, he asks whether the member has the leave of the House. If the member obtains leave, or at least twenty support his motion, the member may proceed; if less than twenty but more than five support it, the question of leave is at once referred to the House for a decision. The House does not, of course, actually adjourn, and it is customary at the end of the discussion for the member to withdraw his motion. The motion is simply the means to enable the matter to be brought before the House. A member will probably succeed in doing more than force a discussion, for the cabinet can scarcely abstain from offering some comment on the issue that has been raised.

There are a number of restrictions on the use of this motion for adjournment. The most controversial is that concerning the question of urgency. This is taken to mean that the matter is so pressing that the public interest will suffer if attention is not at once directed to it. The Speaker is the sole judge of the question of urgency, and there is no appeal from his decision. The matter to be discussed cannot be one that has already been before the House that session. With all these restrictions on it, the device is one not often successfully exploited by members; the important point is that it is there.

OTHER ADJOURNMENT MOTIONS

Three days a week (Monday, Tuesday, and Thursday) any member who has given the Speaker proper notice can bring up at the 6 p.m. adjournment virtually anything he has on his mind. He has seven minutes in which to make his point, and a minister or a parliamentary secretary may reply for three minutes. The total time allotted to these adjournment debates is thirty minutes, so that at least three members, on three occasions each week, have an opportunity to speak.

The adjournment device, first experimented with provisionally in the 1960s and now part of the Commons' standing orders, is regularly used by members to take up questions to which they have earlier received what they consider unsatisfactory answers, and to raise matters that need public attention. The members make excellent use of the time available, and the adjournment debates not only provide them with free time not formerly at their disposal, but also take a good deal of pressure off other proceedings of the House. The subjects aired at this time are so varied that it would be impossible to select representative examples.

ALLOTTED DAYS

Mention has already been made of the practices by which twenty-five days, spread over three defined periods in the parliamentary year, are set aside as periods in which motions by opposition members take priority over government motions; two such opposition motions in each of the three periods may be motions of want of confidence in the government. Prior to the adoption of amendments to the rules in

1968, the chief similar opportunities available to members were motions (now abolished) to go into Committee of Supply, or Committee of Ways and Means. Both these motions, but particularly the former, provided ample scope for the discussion of almost any conceivable subject for, as M.J. Coldwell, an experienced MP who led the CCF party for many years, once said: 'There is one place and one place only in this Parliament where private members are supreme, namely, in Supply when discussing the estimates. This is His Majesty's purse, and the age-old right of members of Parliament is to decide to what extent His Majesty's purse shall be filled. This is what we are doing now, and I certainly wish to protest against any precedent being established that would curtail the right of this Parliament to discuss any matters in connection with the administration of the minister's department.'[3]

The abolition of the Committee of Supply has altered but not abrogated Parliament's ancient rights. The sending of all estimates to standing committees, instead of through a Committee of Supply, was expected to enhance the members' opportunities for scrutinizing expenditures; and of course all committees must report back to the House, where their reports can be discussed. All financial legislation, as distinct from the estimates, must still pass the whole House. How effectively the 1968 reforms have worked has been controversial. Some veteran members continued to yearn nostalgically for the larger stage of the Committee of the Whole: some complained that when estimates go to small committees only a few MPs get a chance to comment on them. An experienced observer of Parliament wrote in 1982 that the Commons' financial system was 'an unleavened disaster. MPs have neither the time nor the interest to do the homework to probe details of complicated expenditure programs. The Government protects itself by controlling the choice of committee chairmen and exerting tight discipline over its supporters on each committee ... In the old days, the Opposition could withhold approval of the estimates until the Government ran out of money.'[4]

That indictment was of a system intended to enlarge, not restrict, the opportunities for opposition members to criticize the government. The opportunities now not only include the twenty-five days when 'opposition motions shall have precedence over all government supply motions,' but one additional occasion when the leader of the opposition is permitted to select 'the main estimates of one named department or agency' for more extensive consideration within the parliamentary timetable by the committee to which they were referred.

BILLS AND RESOLUTIONS INTRODUCED BY PRIVATE MEMBERS

This is one of the simplest and most obvious ways for an ordinary member of the House to influence and to attack the government. The private member will have great difficulty in securing the necessary time on the parliamentary calendar for the consideration of his proposals, but hours are always found for some of them, and a debate develops. The subject is likely to be a special hobby or interest of the member (such as Senate reform, public ownership, federal aid in matters under provincial jurisdiction, nuclear power) and its introduction gives the House an opportunity to express its views and perhaps vote on the question. It provides an opening for an attack on the government if the member wishes to use it for that purpose, for if the suggested change is desirable and if nothing is being done about it, some degree of blame can be attributed to the cabinet for its inaction. The normal government attitude is one of official indifference with no restrictions being placed on how its supporters speak or vote. If the government should wish to suppress such a measure, arrangements can be made to have it talked out (that is, debated to the full amount of time available, thus leaving no time for a vote), or voted down. The limited hours for private members' motions are always a reliable ally fighting on the side of the government. Occasionally a private member's bill, if it has attracted considerable support after being brought up session after session, will be adopted by the government; or the government may accept the principle of the proposal in legislation of its own. The roots of federal aid to post-secondary education first grew in such a climate.

THE BUDGET

The budget furnishes the private member's second main sporting event of the session. Economic issues are so pervasive and the remedies for all economic ills so well known and so clearly comprehended that everyone will have a contribution to make to the budget debate. As in the debate on the speech from the throne, virtually all contributions can be considered relevant. Almost all will involve some part of the government record as well as its budget proposals. The necessary practice of keeping all budget provisions a secret until the minister of finance presents his statement to the House makes preliminary consultation in caucus impossible, and occasionally the cabinet may be moved to make some modification in the original recommendations. In 1963 an interesting budget debate developed when opposition members discovered that the minister of finance, Walter Gordon, had consulted three non-departmental experts in the preparation of his proposals; and in the ensuing debate the opposition was able to score some solid points about the violation of secrecy. Since the budget also included plans that turned out to be highly unpalatable to influential elements in the business community, and were subsequently withdrawn, the 1963 budget was probably the most unusual in Canada's history.[5] With the development of third parties interested particularly in employing the state's resources for the support of welfare policies, and in monetary reform, and with enormous growth in governmental deficits in the 1980s, the budget debate has tended to become increasingly important. But it is still limited by the rules to six days.

A MOTION OF WANT OF CONFIDENCE IN THE GOVERNMENT

This is the most direct method of launching an attack on the cabinet, and the allotted days guarantee that there will be at least six opportunities available in every session. Other no-confidence motions can arise outside of the financial procedures (by an amendment to a government motion, for example, or an attack on a policy which the government defends), and a cabinet may itself take the initiative and demand a vote of confidence from the House. Thus in January 1926, when no party had a majority, the Liberal government, before the speech from the throne was considered, asked for a vote of the House to confirm its right to office. A defeat on a clear confidence vote is of course a defeat for the government.

Despite their importance, votes of want of confidence receive scant attention in the standing orders. Apart from stating that 'the election of a Speaker shall not be considered to be a question of confidence in the government,' the rules are not specific about what a vote of no-confidence is, or what consequences follow if one is passed. The rules do provide for numerous motions that may or may not involve confidence in the government, and every government has by custom a good deal of discretion in deciding whether it considers any particular motion crucial. That is not true of motions clearly labelled by the opposition as a no-confidence motion, and a minority government has more to fear from such procedures than one with a comfortable majority. But even a minority government can under the right circumstances evade the consequences of a defeat. Ordinarily any loss on a financial proposal would be seen as a withdrawal of confidence by the House, but on 19 February 1968, Lester Pearson's government, in the prime minister's absence, lost on third reading of a budgetary bill by 84 votes to 82, but stayed in office. When the prime minister returned, the government introduced a motion asserting that the House did not regard its rejection of the financial bill 'as a vote of non-confidence in the government,' and it passed. With a precedent like that, it is not easy to generalize about what a vote of want of confidence really is, beyond what a government may say it is.

RECENT ADDITIONS TO MEMBERS' POWERS

The last chapter outlined how Commons' committees have been strengthened by being assigned budgets and the authority to employ staffs, and by other noteworthy changes. The standing orders were enlarged to include two new chapters, one of which, entitled 'Review of Delegated Legislation by the House,' enlarged the powers of the existing Joint Committee on Regulations and Other Statutory Instruments. (Delegated legislation, briefly, consists of regulations and orders issued by branches of the executive authorized to do so by statute; its review by Parliament is obviously necessary.) The chapter empowers the committee, no more than once during each sitting of the House, to select 'one specific regulation or other statutory instrument, which the Ministry has the authority to rescind,' and recommend that it be rescinded. A second new chapter, 'Review of Order in Council Appointments,' for the first time permits the standing committees to examine governmental appointees (other than judges) on their 'qualifications and competence ... to perform the duties of the post.' The rules permit review only, and the committees have no power to reject an appointee; but the mere establishment of a recognized authority to review patronage appointments is a substantial addition to committee powers.

It is too early to tell how effective these innovations will be. Cynical observers note that the governing party has the same kind of majority on each committee that it has in the Commons, and that majority can be used to dissuade committees from an overly enthusiastic use of their powers. Others point out that huge majorities, such as those elected in 1958 and 1984, always need make-work projects to keep the government's backbenchers out of mischief, so that parliamentary reform is not necessarily taken for altruistic reasons. However, ordinary MPs do have enlarged scope for examination of executive actions, and some individual members and some committees have shown considerable initiative in raising matters to which the cabinet, for its own reasons, does not give a high priority. Recent reforms of the Commons point consistently in one direction: both MPs and committees have powers they did not have previously, and the use made of them depends on the members.

These are some of the formal conditions under which the political war is fought, and there is general agreement that the essentials cannot be changed suddenly. Commons procedure as such is a permanent assignment of one standing committee. The importance of all committee work is now generally accepted, and the committees continue to work on principles long recognized. A Committee on the Revision of the Standing Orders of the House of Commons declared in 1944: 'Two fundamental principles govern the procedure of the House. They are, that the Government shall, so long as it can maintain a majority, be able to secure such legal powers as it considers necessary for administration, and that minorities, however small, shall be able to criticize that administration ... These rights cannot be alienated even if the House, in maintaining them, may protract sessions and lay itself open to severe criticism.'

Occasional appearances to the contrary, the basic condition under which the

House operates thus has to remain a genuine spirit of tolerance and fair play, and an unwillingness to take undue advantage of the power which political fortune has temporarily placed in the hands of the majority. Indeed, time and again a party leader will be found to forgo the momentary advantage and maintain a principle that strengthens the position of his adversary. A cabinet minister may intervene, for example, on behalf of an opponent if he believes the ruling of the Speaker to be wrong or to have given insufficient weight to interparty arrangements that may have been agreed upon.[6] The leader of the opposition will prove an even more zealous defender of the minority privileges, for his position – and interests – make him their special guardian. In the words of a man who was both prime minister and leader of the opposition:

I occupy a position in which I am placed by statute, and one of my duties is to do exactly what I am doing, to try to safeguard the liberties of Parliament from encroachment by the Government of the day. That is my duty. That is one of the difficulties of the position which I occupy, and I will discharge that duty whether it be on behalf of a member of the Opposition or of any other party when there is tyrannical exercise of power on the part of the Government by reason of a great majority, enabling the administration to destroy the liberties of this Parliament, which have been secured in the manner we all know. When that happens it is my unfortunate duty to protest against such an encroachment upon the liberties of members of the House, and I propose to do it so long as I am here.[7]

Intervention on the part of a cabinet minister may not be all undiluted sportsmanship blended with a love of minority rights. No government can be unmindful of the fact that in protecting the minority today it is protecting itself tomorrow; and this sober reflection affects its relations with other parties. Moreover, no government wishes to affront the basic political tolerance in the electorate, which would resent, and probably actively resent, anything it considered flagrant interference with freedom of speech and criticism. This was dramatically illustrated in 1956–7 during one of the most celebrated debates in Canadian history, on the use of closure in the debate on the Trans-Canada Pipe Line. Finally, the members of the minority always have their own defences, and a wise cabinet will know that it can often persuade far more successfully than it can drive. 'Is it the Government's fault,' asked a wartime minister at a time when he seemed to expect the House to be co-operative, 'that so much discussion goes on, that it takes so many days to get through a particular item? I tried just before the Easter recess to crowd the House a little. I will not do it again. If the Government starts to crowd the House, the House crowds the Government. That always happens. The moment we indicate to the House that we want to get ahead, we simply precipitate speeches about the right of the House of Commons to discuss matters and to discuss them thoroughly.'[8] Inexperienced ministers, needless to say, are more likely to run afoul of the House in this regard than are the seasoned veterans.

While the rules and customs of the House will protect the rights of the rival forces, they can win no engagements for them. All contestants must therefore be conditioned and disciplined and equipped for service. Here the parliamentary organization of the parties plays a very useful part. Some mention has already been made of the control which the government is able to exercise over its members; and the government has the tremendous advantage also of having leaders who are in actual authority and not merely at the head of party councils. To a useful prestige they can add the practical virtue of being in a position where they can dispense favours and consolidate power. Ministerial leaders have also great ability at their disposal. They can draw freely on the talents of public servants, who will supply them with ideas, prepare and execute their programs, and furnish the debating material necessary for their vindication. For it is virtually impossible to draw any distinction between ministers as ministers and ministers as party leaders, between the government's proposals and the party's proposals. While the non-parliamentary sections of all political parties are becoming increasingly vocal, a cogent argument in the past for allowing the policy-forming functions of the non-parliamentary section of the party to fall into desuetude during the party's tenure of office was always the comparative inefficiency of that section when contrasted with the well-informed and well-schooled ministerial group.

An opposition party is rarely so generously provided with leaders and never so well equipped with assistance as the government. All members can, of course, employ the reference services of the Library of Parliament and the parties are now granted money for research. Any opposition group can always enhance its effectiveness by a carefully planned scheme of organization, and the Conservatives, from their prolonged presence on the Speaker's left for so much of the twentieth century, have been especially productive in the field of caucus organization. An impressive commentary on the Conservative caucus of the 1980s, written by a caucus committee before the party attained power, is full of trenchant observations such as this: 'The discussions have produced the conviction that no Leader, under the present structure, can secure the contentment of all the Caucus and the extra-Parliamentary Party, because the Leader is made the focal point of all disputes and target of virtually all resentment.'[9]

Those words were written in 1983. Consider them in the light of these:

The House meets, and in march the Opposition, and sit there ready to attack Ministers and their measures; never, if possible, to make a concession, by word or vote, to official shrewdness or skill. For the time being they are Her Majesty's loyal sappers and miners, not to be very particular if only they can hack and hew their way to the treasury benches. They are waiters upon Providence – all animated with the most exalted, never-say-die patriotism. If they only had a bandage on their brow inscribed 'organized fault-finders,' and a symbolical grid-iron, to be transferable, like the seals of office, the equipment would be complete. Broiling is a part of their special functions; and woe to the Minister when a chief with the spirit of an untamed Indian is at the head of his foes. For party aims, he is understood to be clothed with forked-lightning invectives; and in debate, wonder not, if he substitutes epithets for arguments and deals more with the motives than the logic of Ministers. In brief, he and his lieutenants must be quick to detect the joints in the armour of those in power; and, above everything, they are bound to cultivate the most wakeful and morbid suspiciousness.[10]

Those words were written in 1871; and while hypersensitivity to accusations of error and 'wakeful and morbid suspiciousness' can have its absurd side, they nevertheless lie at the base of responsibility and good government. For the cabinet remains efficient primarily because the searchlight of publicity never ceases to play upon it, and the opposition directs the beams of the searchlight. The final objective of the opposition is a majority of seats in the House of Commons; and while this can rarely be obtained by the direct alienation of government supporters in the House, it can most certainly occur as a result of the next general election. A shifting of a small number of popular votes from one side to the other may under Canadian conditions bring about a change in government, and the eyes of the opposition are ever searching for material to win over this detachable vote. The criticism, the amendments to motions, the divisions in the House, the long debates, the theatrical denunciations, the examination of the estimates, and scores of other manoeuvres have this as their ultimate goal; and no expedient or weapon is so insignificant that it can be neglected in the unceasing engagement for prestige, for reputation, and eventually for power. Here again the televising of Commons' activities has added new dimensions whose uses the parties are still exploring. For the first time the parties are having to cope with the dilemma of frequent exposure in people's homes, seeking to discover whether all exposure is good, or whether some is good and some not; and whether over-exposure of a presentable leader may lead to a decline in his and the party's popularity.

The government, for its part, must retain its existing majority and, whenever possible, extend it. While it has always the advantage of holding office and directing affairs, it also has the responsibility of exercising the initiative and of finding the remedies for the many ills that beset the country. The first essential is that it must get its measures through Parliament. Thus, while it must give the opposition ample opportunity for criticism, it must also be continually pressing Parliament for action. 'The Prime Minister is obliged,' said Mackenzie King on the radio in 1939, 'to keep constantly in mind two vital objectives: the one, to seek to provide opportunity for the fullest and frankest discussion of matters of public interest: the other, to see that sufficient time is provided for the full and proper discussion of the important business of government. It is a difficult and delicate task to hold the balance between the urgent demands of the government upon the time of Parliament, and a proper regard for the privileges, so essential to the sound functioning of a free community of the private members of Parliament.' From this flows the paradox that a government wants little verbal backing from its own supporters; what it needs is 'brute votes,' and while some parliamentary defenders are necessary to uphold its course on the floors of the House, every speaker over that minimum simply impedes the passage of government measures. Government backbenchers, indeed, do complain of having too little to do, and in 1969 Prime Minister Trudeau went to the unusual length of having a three-day conference with his parliamentary supporters, the main purpose of which was to improve relations between back and front benches, and enlarge the ordinary members' participation in policy formation and legislation. The proceedings involved a special session for the members' wives, who reportedly advised the prime minister fully and frankly of the domestic problems accompanying election to Parliament.[11] Late in 1969 the Liberal caucus established a formal system of committees for regular consultation with cabinet members.

The cabinet must avoid even the appearance of defeat or of weakness. This is the chief reason behind its stiff and unyielding attitude to many excellent suggestions coming from the opposition side. A few of these the cabinet may be able to accept with dignity and in a creditable display of open-mindedness; but let this become frequent, and the electorate will naturally conclude that the simpler solution would be to place in power the party which is so fertile in valuable ideas, rather than acquire them in this circuitous fashion. The same need explains the indirect influence of criticism, which has already been discussed. Criticism by the opposition casts its shadow before. How will the opposition attack this project? Will it be easier to defend next year than this? What will the farmers think of it? How will it affect the government vote in Ontario, or Quebec? What will be the attitude of the leading opposition newspapers? These will be anticipated as far as possible when the measure is being drafted, and the cabinet will then defend it ardently and refuse to accept any amendment of any consequence. If a serious flaw in the proposal is later discovered, the safest way of escape is to abandon it as unobtrusively as the circumstances (and the opposition) will allow.

Parliament concentrates and dramatizes the struggle for political power by bringing the political parties into immediate and continual conflict. Arguments are marshalled on one side and on the other, criticism and counter-proposals are made in full publicity, and the reputation of one side mounts as that of another falls away. Elections do not catch the voter by surprise or quite unprepared. The prestige of the government is frequently established or destroyed long before polling day, and even new issues find their place in an environment that is by no means unfamiliar. Moreover, there is always an alternative government near at hand – one that will pick up the work of its predecessor, make a few alterations here, develop certain things there, adapt old institutions to new ideas, and gradually advance a bit further the tentative experiment in human relations which is the business of government.

In government, as in most other spheres of life, man is journeying through a strange world. He is being pushed by forces which often he little appreciates or understands. At best, he is largely ignorant of much that will result, especially in the long run, from measures which he sponsors. Government is empirical. The statesman needs to be ready and quick to learn.

But no man is a ready critic of his own measures or quick to see their faults. It is eminently desirable, therefore, that in public affairs there should be an active body of critics, sharp to detect errors and persistent in pressing them home. Yet not captious, but responsible critics, who know that in due time they may have to stand by their criticism and take their place in the dock ...

These requirements are largely met by the party system ... It can easily be abused, and often is, and it may seem crude to the theorist. But given the right conditions, it has proved in practice a remarkably successful instrument for the journey through the uncharted seas of government.[12]

And those words were written over half a century ago, when government was much simpler than it is now.

8
The Senate

What's the matter,
That in these several places of the city,
You cry against the noble senate ...?
William Shakespeare, *Coriolanus*

The constitution has said since Confederation, in terms that could hardly be clearer, 'There shall be One Parliament for Canada, consisting of the Queen, an Upper House styled the Senate, and the House of Commons.' Manifestly the three parts of Parliament are not equal. Even Canadian dictionaries have omitted the queen in defining Parliament, although the institution could pass no legislation without the royal presence (almost always by proxy); and 'Upper House' is extremely misleading if it suggests that the Senate is superior to the Commons. (The term is all but archaic, but has roots that reach back to the House of Lords in the United Kingdom, which historically is of aristocratic origin, as distinct from the elected Commons.) The Senate, none the less, sporadically receives a great deal of attention, and writing about and discussing its reform is a firmly established Canadian tradition. The words, indeed, outnumber the actual reforms by astronomical proportions.

It is the peculiar fate of the Senate to be talked about as if its functions are less important than its usefulness as a pawn in larger games. In the 1860s the Senate received far more attention than the monarchy or the Commons, both of which were taken for granted as familiar and indispensable: the Senate was deliberately created as a new body for a special purpose. George Brown, a leading opponent of Sir John A. Macdonald who joined him to further the cause of Confederation, said in 1865 in the celebrated debates on the subject: 'The very essence of our compact is that the union shall be federal and not legislative. Our Lower Canada friends have agreed to give us representation by population in the Lower House, on the express condition that they shall have equality in the Upper House. On no other condition could we have advanced a step.' A similar sentiment still prevails; the Senate is still assumed to have a symbolic significance for the provinces and regions not shared by the House of Commons. The Senate of the 1980s, like that of the 1860s, continues to be seen as an almost mystical balance-wheel, and the myriad proposals for reforming the Senate have in common a general acceptance of that notion. Where proposals for improving the Commons lean heavily toward increasing the role and effectiveness of the individual MP, the Senate is viewed as a whole, the position of the individual senators a secondary consideration.

In one sense, that is paradoxical, for the Senate, in theory at least, was intended to be an independent legislative body, the senators exercising their judgment freely because they were free of the demands of the electorate and of the party alignments that dominate the Commons. It is a further paradox that when the Senate does act 'independently' of the Commons, as is sometimes the case when a new government has attained power and the opposition in the House of Commons retains a majority in the Senate, interest in changing the Senate, so that its independence will be reduced, invariably increases. This happened most recently in 1985 when the Liberals had a huge majority in the Senate to match the Conservatives' huge majority in the Commons, and the Senate delayed a major government bill until a particular condition was met. The condition, to add a third paradox, was a sensible one, predicated on the theory that a government ought not to seek to extend its plans for borrowing money into a future for which the same government's plans for spending money were not yet available to Parliament. But the resulting criticisms of the Senate for being so partisan and undemocratic far outweighed support for any parliamentary principles it may have raised. And once again, reform of the Senate was revived as an issue.

Clashes between the two houses were so inevitable from the start that it is difficult to believe that a politician as astute as Macdonald did not anticipate them. The BNA Act laid down that MPs were to be elected, and for a period not to exceed five years; senators were to be appointed by the crown (that is, the government of the day) for life. Inevitably a government in power for many consecutive years would load the Senate with its appointees, and equally inevitably a change of government would find the new cabinet facing a hostile majority in the upper house. In 1867 senators were appointed, for the first and only time, on a bi-partisan basis, as part of the Confederation coalition, and that may have postponed serious consideration of the possibility of deadlocks with the Commons. But as the original senators retired or died, the Senate became a part, and usually a useful part, of the prime minister's patronage pool.

Certainly at Confederation most of the talk about the Senate was remarkably high-minded. The constitution gave it the same powers as the House of

Commons, with one important exception: only the Commons could originate bills for the raising or spending of public money. But that proviso, combined with the Commons' political base in the electoral system, guaranteed from the start that the 'Upper House' would be in reality a lower one. The Senate was to protect the interests of the provinces, and to that end the three regions existing in 1867 (Ontario, Quebec, and the Maritimes) were given equal representation – twenty-four senators each. That basic rule has been departed from only rarely: (a) to give senatorial representation to the four western provinces, which were at first assigned two, three, or four senators somewhat arbitrarily but in 1915 were erected into another region with twenty-four senators, six each; (b) to recognize the admission of Newfoundland, which received six senators in 1949; and (c) to provide senators for the Yukon and Northwest Territories in 1976. The Senate's seats now total 104, giving it a growth rate substantially less than that of the Commons since 1867. Four or eight senators can be added (ostensibly to break possible deadlocks with the House), provided the regional balance is maintained, but the complex rules governing the additions have never been used. Each senator is appointed at large for his or her whole province except in Quebec, where each is appointed for one of the twenty-four electoral divisions that were the basis of Lower Canada's share of the pre-Confederation legislative council.

Representation in the Senate was not seen in the 1860s as one of the democratic elements in the constitution. One indication of this was shown in 1873 when Prince Edward Island entered Confederation: the complement of senators was not enlarged to accommodate the new province, but four senators were taken away from the other two maritime provinces to keep the regional total at twenty-four. Even before that, the Senate had been repeatedly spoken of as a necessary check on the potentially unruly democracy of the House of Commons. 'It must be an independent House,' Macdonald said of the Senate during the Confederation debates in 1865, 'having a free action of its own, for it is only valuable as being a regulating body, calmly considering the legislation initiated by the popular branch and preventing any hasty or ill-considered legislation which may come from that body, but it will never set itself in opposition against the deliberate and understood wishes of the people.' At the same time, the deliberate and understood wishes of the people were expected to be fairly conservative. Unlike the MPs, for whom even the modest and erratically observed property qualifications expected of them at the beginning were abolished in 1874,[1] each senator was (and is) required to own real property (within the province represented) with a net value of $4,000, and be worth $4,000 over and above all liabilities. Real property worth $4,000 in most of modern Canada would probably be little more than an ill-equipped cabin on a small lot, but in 1867 $4,000 was a sizable sum, nearly seven times the annual indemnity of an MP in the first Parliament. In addition, while an MP could be any age the electoral laws required, a senator constitutionally has to be a mature thirty.

Other constitutional provisions of varying importance can be itemized:

1 A senator may now, thanks to a landmark court case in 1930 (*Henrietta Muir Edwards* v. *Attorney General for Canada*), be either male or female. Although the monarch of 1867 was a queen, Houses of Parliament were exclusively male preserves until well on in this century, and even after women had been admitted to the electorate and the Commons, the Senate had no female members. In the 1920s a small group of energetic women took the initiative in challenging the all-male references to the qualifications of senators in the constitution. After losing a unanimous decision in the Supreme Court of Canada, this verdict was reversed on appeal to the Judicial Committee of the Privy Council in London, which until 1949 was the last court of appeal in Canadian cases. The Judicial Committee found that the constitutional phrase 'qualified Persons' included women.

2 A senator can vacate his or her seat by resigning, or by being absent for two consecutive sessions; by ceasing to be a citizen; by being adjudged bankrupt or insolvent; by being attainted of treason or convicted of 'felony or any infamous crime'; or by ceasing to qualify in respect of property or residence. He or she may of course reside in Ottawa holding an office under the government.

3 Unlike the Speaker of the House of Commons, the Speaker of the Senate is appointed by the governor general (always on the advice of the prime minister) and the same authority can remove a Speaker.

4 A quorum for doing business is fifteen, including the Speaker.

5 The most recent alteration in the Senate directly limited its powers for the first time since 1867. In 1982 new constitutional provisions, discussed in a later chapter, set a limit of 180 days on the time the Senate can hold up most proposed constitutional amendments favoured by the Commons if the Commons reasserts its position with a second vote. This change is significant in itself, but it has also given stimulus to other proposals for imposing more 'suspensive vetoes' on the Senate.

The dice were plainly loaded against the Senate from the start; and when one adds to the written constitution the convention that the cabinet is responsible only to the House of Commons, while the cabinet's power has grown enormously, the dice have become even more weighted. A more detailed consideration of parts of the Senate's constitution, and the uses made of them, will demonstrate how the Senate, whatever its inclinations, has not been able to avoid a minor role in parliamentary affairs.

APPOINTMENT

The first handicap placed on the Senate was the route all its members have to follow to get there. While the first senators represented all political groups, nobody had any illusions that subsequent appointments, made by a partisan executive, would be non-partisan. Senatorships have always been among the choicest plums in the patronage basket, and they have had since Confederation a quality demanded of few other appointments; for while a judge must have been trained in the law, and a high-ranking public servant or a director of a crown corporation is ordinarily expected to have some administrative judgment, literally anybody who meets the qualifications set out in the constitution can become a senator. Prime ministers have found the Senate a happily flexible instrument for party purposes, and while many have deplored the necessity, few have appointed opponents, or even those neutral politically, to the Senate. (The few exceptions are usually for personal reasons, such as friendship with a prime minister.) 'My hon. friend,' Sir Wilfrid Laurier told the House of Commons on 20 January 1908, 'would hardly expect me to submit to His Excellency the name of a man who represented us to be everything that was bad, who had nothing good to say of us, who declared that we were corrupt and wicked and guilty of all the sins in the calendar.' Besides, the Liberal leader added, if he were to nominate a lukewarm Conservative, perhaps more partisan Conservatives 'would be the very first to find fault with such an appointment.' He did not add, and did not need to, that any Liberal leader who appointed many Conservatives to the Senate (or vice versa), would speedily find himself in trouble with the partisans he needed most, those in his own party. Of recent prime ministers, Pierre Trudeau selected the most non-Liberals for the Senate, but even he chose only a half-dozen.

One result of the senatorial appointment system not fully grasped at Confederation was that partisan appointments could become not only convenient but imperative. The Fathers of Confederation could not have foreseen that a characteristic of Canadian politics was to be the long consecutive runs in office enjoyed by Conservatives and Liberals in turn, so that many incoming prime ministers saw no alternative to the results of partisan appointments to the Senate except more partisan appointments. Because of the general success of the Liberal party since 1896, every Conservative prime minister who assumed office in this century after winning an election has initially faced a Senate which he considered out of balance.

A second and more easily foreseen consequence of the appointment system was that faithful party service, either overtly through public activity or privately through financial or other support, has profoundly affected the nature of the Senate. Early in 1984, when eighty-six Senate seats were occupied, only four members called themselves Independent, and the Liberals outnumbered the Conservatives by sixty to twenty-two. Of the eighty-two partisans, forty had served in the House of Commons or provincial legislatures, or both, and the roster included several former provincial premiers. Of the remaining forty-two, several were defeated candidates, and an unknown number had been active behind the scenes as organizers and fundraisers. With the growth in importance of party organization in recent decades, senators without previous electoral experience are increasingly common. Larry Zolf reports in his irreverent *Survival of the Fattest* that of thirteen Liberal party presidents since 1935, eleven 'were or became senators.'[2] The Conservatives until recently have had fewer chances at appointing senators, but several well-known Conservative party workers have also made the grade without toiling in elected legislatures.

An astute prime minister can of course keep vacant senatorships dangling, filling them when the time is most advantageous, while postponing the disappointment or ingratitude of the unlucky as long as possible. Ordinarily few appointments to the Senate will be made in the year or two before a general election is anticipated; then vacancies will be rapidly filled just before the polling day. From 20 July to 14 October 1935 (election day), seventeen Conservative senators were created (ten of them MPs fleeing the expected disaster); and in the two months preceding the 1945 election eighteen Liberals (eleven of them from the Commons) joined the club. The Liberals in 1957, clearly overconfident, left sixteen vacancies for their grateful successors. The sixty Liberal senators of early 1984 had by 29 June become seventy-one, and Trudeau, the outgoing prime minister, accommodated his successor, John Turner, with a new twist. Turner, who became prime minister on 30 June, was concerned about the political impact of too many appointments emanating from an outgoing chief. Trudeau agreed to leave some vacancies (not all of them senatorial), provided his choices would be appointed by Turner before the next election.[3] Attempts to force governments to fill Senate vacancies within prescribed time limits have failed, and in the recent past individual seats have been left unfilled for as long as seven or eight years.

What kind of Senate results from this method of appointment? Generally the Senate includes a substantial number of able and industrious people who devote their time not just to the Senate but to special interests they represent. This would be fair enough if all major interests were fairly represented, but clearly they are not. Almost every modern observer who tries to report with some detachment on the Senate has concluded that, far from being merely harmless and ineffective as a legislative body, the Senate has been used, and uses itself, to entrench particular interests to the detriment of others. Colin Campbell, who published the first comprehensive critique of the Senate in 1978, observed that 'the Upper House serves mostly as a useful base of operations for legislators who employ technical

review and special studies mainly on behalf of Canada's business community.'
The fundamental bias thus perceived derives in part from the appointment system
and long tenure, and in part from the fact that senators 'very often hold leadership
positions in corporations, including directorships.' The last point can be readily
documented, and John McMenemy has updated Campbell's material to 1982. The
Senate's corporate sinews are not matched by equally strong labour and
agricultural muscle.[4] But then, as the qualifications for senators reveal, the Senate
was expected to protect the interest of property. Senators in 1984 designated their
professional interests (some listing more than one) as law (34 per cent), business
(29 per cent), education (10 per cent), public service (8 per cent), farming (6 per
cent), health professions (6 per cent), the media (5 per cent), and labour (2 per
cent).

The appointing power, in other words, has been used to produce a Senate in
which it is difficult for major segments of the population to have much confidence.
In recent years the segments have begun to include women's organizations, and in
1984–5 (at a time when the Senate included eleven women, the largest group since
Confederation) a case began whose purpose was to ask the Supreme Court to rule
on whether the failure to appoint equal numbers of men and women was not a
violation of Canada's acceptance of the United Nations Convention on the political
rights of women.

However, despite major flaws in Senate representation, it is only fair to add that
the appointing power has been used repeatedly to make minor adjustments to
recognize particular groups. Sporadic appointments of labour spokesmen have in
fact been made. In the past the Roman Catholic minority in Ontario and the
Protestant minority in Quebec have been overrepresented in the Senate, allegedly
to offset their inability to win a fair share of seats in the House of Commons.
'Similarly,' R.A. MacKay noted years ago, 'senators have been appointed as the
avowed representatives of the French in Ontario, of the Germans in Ontario, the
French in Western Canada, the Acadians in the Maritime Provinces, and more
recently of the Ukrainians, the Icelanders, the Indians and the Jews.'[5]

Such positive uses of the appointing power in a society as diverse as Canada's
can hardly be criticized as unsound, and yet more can be said of the Senate's uses.
Earlier chapters have stressed the importance of political parties to Canadian
government, and no observer of the Senate could deny its handiness as a lubricant
in the political machinery. Prime ministers have appointed elderly ministers to the
Senate to make room for younger blood and, especially before parliamentary
pensions were approved in 1952, Commons' seats wanted for other persons have
been created by pensioning off the incumbents with appointments to the upper
house. Conservative prime ministers in 1957 and 1979, acutely short of MPs from
Quebec, could if they wished have found some flexibility for their cabinets among

Conservatives in the Senate. Occasionally a prime minister has wanted a minister who has no seat in either house, and a useful expedient has been to induce an MP in a safe seat to resign in the expectation of receiving a senatorship in the near future, while the desired individual runs for the vacancy created in the Commons.

Useful as such devices have undoubtedly been, they do not together provide an adequate justification for maintaining a whole Upper House with over one hundred seats, nor can one overlook the fact that Senate vacancies are at the sole disposal of the party in power. The official opposition can at least await its turn, but the third parties have not yet had an opportunity to appoint a single senator.

TERM

A second great handicap imposed on the Senate at Confederation was the life term. The original purpose was, of course, to render the senators free to decide questions on their merits, without being unduly influenced by the pull of party motives and the fear of electoral defeat. Such advantages as these, however, were rendered nugatory by the partisan antecedents of the senators (which continued into their senatorial days), combined with the depressing consequences flowing from so secure and prolonged a tenure.

The life term inevitably led to senators remaining in the chamber long after they had passed the age of genuine usefulness. There were undoubted exceptions; but in the Senate, as in virtually all other positions, the rare meritorious case should not be allowed to establish the standard for the remainder. The great bulk of the over-age senators could not perform their duties with the same effectiveness as younger men. The House of Commons provides no parallel, for the process of election furnishes an automatic method of retirement which can discriminate between cases with merciless efficiency. Canada has had on at least two occasions the singular distinction of possessing the oldest legislator in the world, both centenarians; as this is written Canada has a ninety-five-year-old senator, appointed before the retirement age of seventy-five was set in 1965. The ages of senators whose years are known follow a consistent pattern (see Table 3). The ages at which senators are appointed in the first place follow a similar pattern. Most of them are over fifty when appointed, and at any given time the majority of them are over sixty.

What that means, in practical terms, is that most senators cannot consider themselves as being on the threshold of a promising career, but rather the opposite. The assurance of a security unrelated to performance and the constant association with others similarly situated have a deplorable but not surprising psychological effect, which militates against initiative and intensive effort. There will be those who may be largely unaffected, whose zeal for public service and whose habits of

TABLE 3
Ages of senators, selected years

Ages	1945	1953	1961	1969	1984
30–40	˙ 1	0	0	1	0
41–50	3	0	2	14	7
51–60	22	7	14	14	23
61–70	37	37	30	30	36
71–80	23	35	32	20	16
over 80	9	4	16	10	7
Total	95	83	94	89	89

SOURCES: *Parliamentary Guide*, 1946, 1953, 1961, 1969; *Canadian Parliamentary Handbook*, 1983–4

mind and training will have become so ingrained that they will toil unselfishly, unremittingly, and with conspicuous competence for years. An outstanding example of this in recent years has been Eugene Forsey, a constitutional expert who was a senator throughout the 1970s; but the Forseys are widely considered to be exceptional. For while the Senate may supply the opportunities, it does not supply the incentives for work. In most cases political ambition is dead; the needs of the future are guaranteed; and the salary is ample. Occasionally a senator takes an opportune moment to remind his fellows of the achievements in extreme old age of the Shaws who wrote plays, the Churchills who wrote books, and the Connie Macks who operated baseball teams – an exercise as revealing as it is touching.

It is not merely improbable, but inconceivable, that setting the senators' retirement age at seventy-five, with a pension beyond that, will by itself materially change the Senate. Senators are remunerated, incidentally, in much the same way as MPs, but their total package of emoluments adds up to roughly three-quarters that of the Commons. Senators have the usual office amenities, and a salary and tax-free allowance: in 1970 the salary was $12,000 and the allowance $3,000; in 1985 the figures were $54,000 and $8,800. Paying the senators such substantial incomes compared with MPs has often been criticized because they do not have the same responsibilities or demands on their time, and early in 1985 a commission on parliamentary salaries recommended freezing senatorial salaries until they became only 60 per cent of MPs'.

CABINET MINISTERS IN THE SENATE

The appointment system and the long years enjoyed by senators untouched by the demands of any electoral process have meant that the Senate, while undeniably useful in politics, has lacked a political base. And to its original handicaps others have been added. There has been a tendency, for example, for successive prime ministers to ignore its potentialities and give it an insufficient amount of work, which has been reflected in a diminished prestige. Senators have frequently been left out of party caucuses, not in order to encourage or maintain their independence of the party or of the Commons, but apparently because they were not wanted. But by far the most crippling blow dealt the Senate since Confederation is the modern practice of keeping the number of senators in the cabinet low. The first government after Confederation for a time contained five members of the upper house. The number varied in succeeding years and on the whole tended to diminish, although in the 1890s two prime ministers (J.J.C. Abbott and Sir Mackenzie Bowell) were senators. At one time or another every portfolio except Finance, Railways and Canals, Customs, and Secretary of State for the Provinces has been held by a senator. Borden introduced the custom of having no ministers in the Senate who were heads of government departments, and since 1921 this has become an accepted practice, though one occasionally broken under special circumstances. The primary reason given for this convention is that spending departments must have a minister in the House to defend departmental estimates, so that democratic control requires all these ministers to be in the representative body. After 1957 the cabinet included no representative from the Senate for five years, though the role of the government leader in the Senate was continued. (It is significant that Diefenbaker, though acutely short of MPs from Quebec in 1957, did not look for cabinet timber in the Senate, although Clark did in 1979; the Liberals, short of western MPs in 1980, had four western senators in the cabinet.) The leader of the government in the Senate now holds a full portfolio in his own right.

To a legislative chamber whose prestige was already badly battered, the decision to exclude its members from holding departmental portfolios was little short of catastrophic. For the cabinet, which has not since Confederation considered that it was responsible to the Senate, now possesses the best of all possible excuses for all but ignoring it. A minister will always wish to introduce his own measures into Parliament – 'to bring his own child,' as Senator Dandurand said, 'to the baptismal font' – and even if the government leader who sits in the Senate is also a minister, there will be few government bills introduced there. As a partial remedy for this condition the Senate in 1947 amended its rules so that it was able to give permission to a cabinet minister from the Commons to appear in the Senate chamber and speak on a measure which had originated there, but the experiment was not impressively successful.

The absence of ministers has another weakening influence on the effective participation of the upper chamber in the business of government. Information cannot readily be obtained through day-to-day inquiries or in the course of debate or other proceedings, and when finally secured after irritating delays it has become stale and uninteresting. A government leader with the best of intentions and the most extraordinary industry cannot be expected to have available at a few hours' notice all the relevant factual material that may be demanded by his inquiring fellow members. Though much has been done to improve the Senate's communications with the rest of the government, even today the government leader can be embarrassed by his inability to speak for the government with any assurance, and an amendment proposed in the Senate may have to be held over until the leader consults with the appropriate minister in order to ascertain whether it will be acceptable. While some Senate reformers apparently believe that 'strengthening' the upper house may once more include having government departments represented there, few observers in the 1980s consider it likely.

LEGISLATIVE ACTIVITY

In view of its given and acquired weaknesses, the Senate could hardly be expected to put on a dazzling performance unless, indeed, it was prepared to run the continual risk of appearing to undermine the democracy of the House of Commons and the party system. Most serious observers of the Senate have not denigrated its modest if inconspicuous contributions to the legislative process, even though its contributions reveal a particular bias. Part of the bias itself has been inconspicuous until revealed by recent studies, and part of the Senate's problem with its public image is directly related to the relatively unknown nature of much of its work.

Just as some of the Commons' activities are over-exposed in the media while others remain obscure, the senatorial activities that generally receive the most coverage have in common a capacity to make the Senate look weak. If the Senate has a daily sitting that lasts only a few minutes, or sits on only three days a week, those facts will almost certainly draw more attention than the equally relevant fact that no legislation may have been sent to it from the Commons. If a complex bill has been received, and the Senate passes it in two or three days, that will be observed more widely than the fact that a Senate committee has been giving detailed attention to the bill's subject-matter for two or three months or more. Eugene Forsey has recorded a striking instance that occupied wide public notice: 'In 1975, the Government introduced into the Commons an elaborate and comprehensive Bankruptcy Bill. The Senate promptly referred the subject matter to the Banking, Trade and Commerce Committee. The committee, after exhaustive hearings and minute examination, proposed 139 amendments. The bill died on the Commons order paper. When a new bill was introduced in 1978, 109 of the suggested amendments had been incorporated in substantially the form the

Senate committee had proposed, and 19 others adopted in part.' Dr Forsey agrees that 'it is pretty certain that the revising function will be exercised in a manner favourable to business,' although he is not so accusatory as Colin Campbell: 'Working primarily through the Banking, Trade and Commerce Committee, senators find ways to influence administrative decisions and the practical provisions of legislation which might affect the business and financial communities.'[6]

Senators have been showing increasing sensitivity in recent years to what are, in effect, charges of conflict of interest; but the main point to be made here is that, contrary to widespread belief, not all senators are idle all the time. It would be just as mistaken to assume that all senators apply themselves seriously to public business all the time, or that all Senate committees are as industrious as Banking, Trade and Commerce. The Senate's record varies considerably with the agenda of the House of Commons, as well as with its relations with the cabinet and the majority in the Commons. In the immediate postwar period, when Parliament was overhauling the bulk of Canadian statutes, the cabinet allowed the Senate to participate in this complex process, and its work was praised unreservedly by both sides in the Commons. Throughout those busy years the government was supported by a majority in both houses. But when in 1957 a new Conservative government faced a predominantly Liberal Senate, the number of government bills introduced in the upper house declined until it had earned the government's confidence. This was shaken twice in 1961 when the Senate insisted on one amendment which the Commons refused and recommended that another bill not be proceeded with; so the process of winning the cabinet's confidence had to begin again. It has been mentioned that the Mulroney government, with an enormous majority in the Commons and a large opposition in the Senate, had been in office only a few months when the Senate in 1985 delayed a financial bill, much against the cabinet's will, until some relevant information about how the government proposed to spend public money in the future was made available. The fact that in principle the Senate was right on that occasion did not prevent cross complaints about its stand, which the Conservatives, no doubt also correctly, saw as partisan.

The public outcry in the first few months of 1985 about the appointed Senate thwarting the elected Commons almost missed entirely the point that the Senate was not acting capriciously. The Senate has not, as a matter of record, in general behaved any more capriciously than the Commons, and has often saved the latter's time. For decades after Confederation, for example, divorce in Canada was available only by act of Parliament, and the burden of taking evidence and passing judgment in divorce cases was delegated to the Senate; gradually most provinces enabled the courts to hear divorce cases, but until they did the Senate sat on hundreds a year. Another Senate function, which has been modified although not eliminated, lies in the revision of badly or hastily drafted bills. All government measures have for years had to be approved by the Department of Justice's drafting section, but former senator Eugene Forsey has confirmed that on public bills 'the Senate has become primarily a revising Chamber,' because there is still a need to clarify them 'if they are not to be oppressive, or lead to much needless and costly litigation.'[7] The work is mainly done in committee, not on the floor of the House, so again the public rarely sees or hears about it.

Since the Senate's public troubles in recent decades have occurred when the Commons had a different majority than the Senate, it is easy to conclude that the Senate is naturally more active in all its partisan functions when that condition prevails. Several studies have shown that in the amendment of bills the Senate has historically always been active to about the same degree, regardless of party status.[8] In the delay or rejection of public bills, however, Senate activity, while sporadic, can be spectacular. Even a partisan action of the Senate, of course, may not be wholly partisan.

In 1961 the Diefenbaker government sought the resignation of James Coyne, the governor of the Bank of Canada, and when he declined to give it, introduced legislation to remove him. The bill passed the Commons, where the Conservatives had a large majority, but it was rejected by the Senate, where the Liberals held sway. The Senate's action was clearly partisan, but it also gave Mr Coyne an opportunity to be heard in his own defence, a right denied him by the Commons.

Recent decades have seen no cases of outright rejection of a whole government bill, although the Senate has delayed and amended proposed legislation. There are few precedents to establish a case, but the Senate has never claimed that it can reject or amend public bills regardless of public opinion. The chief instance to support that occurred in 1926–7, when the Senate first rejected an old age pension bill and then passed it because a party favouring it in its platform had been returned to office.

A special category of public bills is that related to the raising and spending of money. The constitution is clear enough about which House may initiate money bills, but it says nothing about whether the Senate can amend or delay them, and the point has frequently been challenged. The House of Commons, taking its cue from a British resolution of 1678, has since Confederation claimed a monopoly over all aspects of financial legislation. Standing order 87 now reads that 'All aids and supplies granted to the Sovereign by the Parliament of Canada are the sole gift of the House of Commons, and all bills for granting such aids and supplies ought to begin with the House, as it is the undoubted right of the House to direct, limit, and appoint in all such bills, the ends, purposes, considerations, conditions, limitations and qualifications of such grants, which are not alterable by the Senate.'

It is a fair statement that almost the only attention the Senate has given to this grand assertion is to ignore it. On the theoretical side the Senate has argued that if the constitution was intended to limit the Senate's power over money bills once initiated, it would say so. The Senate has insisted further that it could not discharge its functions as a guardian of provincial or regional rights if it had no power over money bills. What is more important is that the Senate has repeatedly amended bills that contained money clauses, and also bills that dealt exclusively with finance, including income tax bills. The Commons has accepted Senate amendments to money bills, usually adding a futile claim that its acquiescence must not be considered a precedent. The Senate could, if practice is any guide, amend a money bill out of all recognition, so that in effect the bill was rejected. Apart from specific legislative activity on money bills, the Senate's role in the broad field of parliamentary control of finance is not large.

The same cannot be said of another of the Senate's least conspicuous legislative activities, the consideration of private bills. A private bill is different from a public bill in that while it may deal with a matter of public interest, its immediate concern is with the individual rights or responsibilities of a person or persons. Bills to incorporate a company or charitable organization, or increase the capital stock of an existing company, are all private bills, and even with the elimination of divorce bills, the annual total of private bills remains large. When the parliamentary timetable was less crowded, members of Parliament often found gratification in presenting private bills on behalf of constituents. But with the growth in both government business and the size and number of private associations needing legislation, the main burden of handling private bills was shifted to the Senate by a simple device: in 1934 the fee for having private bills originate in the Commons was raised to $500, with extra fees for particular services (now detailed in standing order 133), while the Senate fee was left at $200. The Commons rules still provide an elaborate procedure for initiating private bills, but it would now be unusual for a private bill not to start in the Senate.

A private bill begins with a petition from its promoter asking for its passage. After the requisite fees are paid and all necessary information (which may include detailed maps) presented, all formalities are checked by the Senate's Committee on Standing Rules and Orders and, if all is well, the bill receives first and second reading like any other. Then the bill goes to the proper standing committee (like the House, the Senate has regular committees for the major fields of legislation, ranging alphabetically from Agriculture to Transport and Communications) and here something very like a court case ensues. The committee holds hearings at which opposition to the bill may be heard, with both sides represented by legal counsel, and the committee reaches a decision which is reported back to the Senate. Usually the Senate accepts each committee's recommendations, the bill is read a third time and sent to the Commons, where its passage is generally routine. It comes back to the Senate only to receive royal assent, also routine.

The work of Senate committees on private bills is readily taken for granted, but it can hardly be overestimated as an element in Canada's organized life. The procedure concerns not only business corporations but any charitable or other association that needs parliamentary sanction for its purposes. The Senate cannot of course make work of this kind; it can only deal with what comes to it, and some sessions are less busy than others. In recent years, in addition to dealing with incorporations and amendments to incorporations, private bills have variously concerned the Canadian Merchant Service Guild, the Royal Canadian Legion, the Order of Elks, and a church of the Byzantine Rite.

SOCIAL INVESTIGATIONS

The Senate's work on private bills takes place in the standing committees; most senators are assigned to from two to six of these, with the majority serving on three or four. But apart from the standing committees the Senate has in the past three decades found a new role in the investigation of social questions, and has in fact produced a small library of sound studies on such varied topics as land use, manpower and employment, the ageing of Canada's population, consumer credit and consumer prices, delegated legislation, poverty, and the mass media, to name but a few. Many of the studies are originally undertaken because of the interests of particular senators, but in many instances the resulting documents reflect credit on the whole Senate, if for no other reason than that it lets the investigations take place. Eugene Forsey has said: 'The report of a Health, Welfare and Science Committee sub-committee on childhood experiences as a cause of criminal behaviour is internationally recognized as a pioneering classic in this field.'

That particular committee happens to be a standing committee, but the quotation is typical of the reception given many reports of special committees. It is not true, as is commonly thought of the reports of royal commissions, that no action follows publication. Committees on the first four topics listed in the preceding paragraph, for example, led to the Agricultural and Rural Development Act, the Department of Manpower and Immigration, a reduction in the qualifying age for old age security, and the Department of Consumer and Corporate Affairs. Colin Campbell has found considerable value in the Senate's investigative role, although he adds: 'In reality senators' investigations are constrained not only by their own innate conservatism (senators, after all, continue to be drawn from the top socio-economic strata of Canadian society), but also by a consideration of what they feel a current government is likely to find acceptable.'[9] Both parts of the quotation are no doubt true, but anybody who has ever participated in the making of a report destined to go to a government or Parliament can testify that there is usually little point in recommending anything a government is likely to find unacceptable. The conservatism called into play, that is, is only partly the Senate's; and no sensitive reader can deny the value of the knowledge made available through most of the Senate's investigations.

THE PROTECTION OF RIGHTS

Since the original rationale for creating the Senate included a role for it as a protector of rights, it is pertinent to inquire how well it has performed. This is not easily determined. On the one hand the modern concept of rights embraces a far broader view than was the case in 1867, and it is hardly fair to assess the Senate's record in the 1980s without taking into account that it was established to deal with concepts of over a century ago. On the other hand the Senate, as in so many other areas, has been eclipsed by other protectors of rights. It would be an unusual citizen today who, with the alternative of taking his case to his MP, the nearest cabinet minister, a human rights commission, or (especially since the Charter of Rights was adopted) the courts, instead went first to a senator.

The Senate none the less has a record, uneven though it is, of protecting rights, and indeed frequently does so when sitting on private bills, most of which affect the rights of either individuals or organizations in one way or another. That kind of protection, paradoxically, was not made much of in the Senate of the 1860s; but the protection of property was, and it requires no great prophetic gifts to conclude that a legislative chamber full of business and professional people will be alert to threats to property. As for provincial rights, R.A. MacKay, the first scholar to study the Senate systematically, found that party lines generally overrode the interests of provinces when a decision had to be made. F.A. Kunz, the second analyst, made a serious attempt to document case by case the Senate's actions on rights generally, and found they generally met reasonable standards: 'The Senate has acted in the capacity of a sort of institutional Ombudsman in the Canadian parliamentary system.' The two most recent authors to dissect the Senate are less kindly: the subtitle of Colin Campbell's book, *A Lobby from Within*, tells its own tale, and Larry Zolf, specifically citing the Winnipeg general strike of 1919 and the treatment of Japanese Canadians during the Second World War, has written: 'in time of trouble the Senate was always the first to abandon those most in need.'[10]

All these conclusions are accurate, depending on how one looks at various parts of the Senate's history. Campbell's conclusions are quite consistent with the view that the Senate has been a zealous defender of minority rights, if one remembers that Sir John A. Macdonald pointed out at the start that the rich are always fewer in number than the poor. Male dominance of the Senate could be defended by the same kind of logic, since each census reveals that in the population at large men are in a minority.

REFORM

The preceding sentences offer a fitting entry into a discussion of Senate reform, partly because some of the proposals for reform (and they are legion) depend on a tenuous logic that at least appears to assume that the Senate can be altered without altering its relations with the cabinet or the House of Commons. So many schemes for a new Senate have emerged in recent years that it would be impossible – as well as profitless – to describe them all in detail in one book; and they enjoy so wide a scope that it would be difficult to think of a serious new proposal that has not already been touched on in those extant. By yet another of those paradoxes that have beset the Senate, many of the same people who have been so inventive in urging new Senates are the same people who helped entrench the existing model in the constitution in 1982. The Supreme Court held in 1980 that Parliament could neither alter nor abolish the basic constitution of the Senate on its own initiative, and in 1982 the Senate was listed in the new Constitution Act as one of those institutions that could be altered only by resolutions of both houses of Parliament and the consent of the legislative assemblies of at least two-thirds of the provinces, whose populations must total at least 50 per cent of the populations of all of them.[11] The Senate itself could hold up any such resolution for only 180 days, after which it could be bypassed if the House of Commons repassed the resolution; but no such limitation was placed on the provincial legislatures. For practical purposes that means that any four provinces could block Senate reform, even if the other six included all the largest.

Until the late 1960s talk of Senate reform ebbed and flowed with the size of the opposition in the upper house to the governing party in the Commons. Only the CCF and its successor, the NDP, have consistently favoured not reform but abolition; having never enjoyed a majority in either house, their position has remained untested. The Conservatives demanded reform before their victory of 1911, but in a development typical of the parties' attitudes to the Senate, found other priorities soon after. The Liberals favoured Senate reform in the early 1920s, and in 1925 the Commons passed (by a vote of 120 to 32) a resolution suggesting that something better than the existing Senate might be possible. A Dominion-provincial conference in 1927, summoned by the Liberal government, favoured a wide range of reforms, but nothing came of them. By the mid-1960s the only actual change that had taken place (apart from the adjustment of representation for the west cited earlier) was the replacement of the life term for new senators by a retiring age of seventy-five.

Prime Minister Trudeau took office in 1968 apparently more determined than most to improve the constitution, in the interests of a livelier federal system, and a booklet issued in his name in 1969, *The Constitution and the People of Canada*, outlined the form of a new Senate. The proposals included an altered system of representation; a fixed term for each senator (six years was cited as a possibility, as was eligibility for reappointment); a reduction in the Senate's power to hold up legislation indefinitely; the right of the provinces to participate in appointments; new powers for the Senate in relation to human rights (including language rights), and in ratifying the appointments of ambassadors, judges of the Supreme Court, and chairmanships of cultural agencies. The scheme was not presented as a final blueprint but as a working paper, and its significance lay in its comprehensiveness and its source. In any event, no immediate action followed.

The baton was then leisurely passed to a Special Joint Committee of the Senate and the House of Commons on the Constitution of Canada, which in 1971–2 travelled from coast to coast hearing hundreds of witnesses and receiving hundreds more submissions, producing a report containing 105 specific recommendations. Those for the Senate included enlargement to 130 members (mainly by doubling the representation west of Ontario); senators to continue to be appointed by the federal government, but half of them in each province from panels nominated by the provincial governments; retirement age to be lowered to seventy, with provision for those retired to continue to participate in senatorial activities without vote (or pay); a reduction in the Senate's power to hold up legislation indefinitely; and the qualifications for senators to be the same as an elector's, with residence in the province represented.

Some action followed, although not immediately. In June 1978 the government proposed a bill tentatively entitled The Constitutional Amendment Bill, whose senatorial suggestions included its replacement by 'The House of the Federation,' whose 118 members (again the increase to come mainly from the west) were to be selected in a decentralized appointment system through which one-half of each provincial delegation of senators were to be chosen by the House of Commons within thirty sitting days after each federal election, and one-half by each provincial legislature within thirty sitting days after a provincial election. The new House of the Federation was to have restricted powers in holding up or amending legislation, but special powers where language was concerned and in ratifying sundry appointments. The bill was referred to a joint committee of both houses and the committee raised the question of whether the federal Parliament could unilaterally alter the Senate in such a manner; and, as noted, when the Supreme Court was asked, it said no.

A subcommittee of the Senate's own Standing Committee on Legal and Constitutional Affairs produced in 1980 an excellent report on bicameralism in

Canada which included a survey of proposals for reform, and produced several of its own. The subcommittee considered and rejected the election of senators, and recommended that the appointing power be modified so that 'every second appointment should be made from a list of names submitted by the government of the province (or territory) concerned.' It also coolly appraised the Senate's operations and recommended a lowering of the retirement age; a fixed term of ten years; a strengthening of the role as a protector 'of regional interests and linguistic, minority and individual rights'; and a suspensive veto only over legislation.

The next action at the official level was indeed a series of major alterations in, and additions to, the Canadian constitution, but the opportunity to reform the Senate was not taken, except to reduce its power to delay a constitutional amendment. The Senate was widely discussed during the federal-provincial manoeuvring that led to the Constitution Act of 1982, with British Columbia at one point wanting to make Senate reform a condition of its acceptance of other proposals, and Saskatchewan (then led by an NDP government) also desiring at least reform, if not abolition. Other provinces were more or less satisfied with giving the Senate a low priority, and in the press of more important matters such as the Charter of Rights and a formula for amending the constitution, the Senate ended up with no priority at all. In a time of comprehensive constitutional reform, the institution whose reform has been most often discussed since 1867 remained all but unreformed.[12] But reform as a topic of discussion has survived. A Special Joint Committee on Senate Reform, instructed in 1983 to make 'recommendations concerning the method of selection, powers, length of term for Senators, distribution of seats and other matters that the Committee considers relevant,' produced in 1984 yet another comprehensive report. Its opening sentence was unequivocal: 'We have concluded that the Canadian Senate should be elected directly by the people of Canada.' The report went on to suggest a Senate of 144 members (all provinces and territories sharing the increase this time); a power to delay but not veto bills from the Commons; a double majority for bills affecting language ('an overall majority of all senators ... would have to include a majority of the francophone senators'); and a power to ratify appointments to federal agencies whose work has regional implications. That was in January 1984. Later in the year the government changed and by early 1985, as already mentioned, the Liberal Senate had irritated the Conservative cabinet, and talk of Senate reform assumed a more direct focus. On 7 June 1985, the minister of justice introduced a potential constitutional amendment which would allow the Senate to hold up money bills for only thirty days, others for forty-five; by 1987 it was sharing the fate of most attempts to reform the Senate – sitting still.

The preceding paragraphs have concentrated on official work at the federal level, but there are numerous semi-official and unofficial activities worthy of mention at other levels. In 1977 the federal government appointed a Task Force on Canadian Unity which in 1979 published a volume entitled *A Future Together*, in which the Senate was to be replaced by a Council of the Federation, a singular body of no more than sixty, 'composed of delegations representing the provincial governments and therefore acting under instruction.' The Constitutional Committee of the Quebec Liberal party in 1980 recommended tersely: 'The Senate should be abolished.' In May 1985 the legislature of Alberta, responding to a report from one of its committees which recommended a Senate without political parties, with each province having six senators, gave unanimous approval in principle to the election of senators.

As the foregoing sampler suggests, the problems of Senate reform do not depend on a shortage of notions. Rather, many a seriously proposed reform threatens to create as many problems as it would solve, and the more fundamental the reform the greater that danger seems to become. As its submission to the Joint Committee on Senate Reform of 1983–4, the Liberal minister of justice had prepared a document later published as a discussion paper, which surveys dispassionately most of the major alternatives in the topic, and a reader can hardly avoid being struck by both their quality and quantity. To take a single example, how to fill a Senate seat is assessed in a section which offers six different and mutually exclusive methods of performing that simple task: appointment by the federal government; appointment by both federal and provincial governments; appointment by provincial governments (a proposal pressed by British Columbia in 1978); indirect election (that is, election by members of provincial legislatures); proportional indirect election (that is, election by the legislatures and the Commons in proportion to the parties' strength in the last relevant provincial or federal election); direct election.[13] On each of those possibilities there are possible variations: for example, is appointment by the federal government to be a completely free choice, or limited to a panel of names chosen by some other body, such as the House of Commons or the provincial legislatures?

But filling Senate seats is but the beginning of the process. Once the senators are chosen, how long may they sit: until a fixed retirement age, or for a set term and, if so, how long a term? What is the fairest way to share Senate seats among the provinces; equal representation for all, or more seats for the larger provinces? And if the latter, should Ontario and Quebec, with unequal populations, have equal numbers of senators? Should the Senate have different powers than the Commons and, if so, in what way? If the Senate has either few powers, or large powers which circumstances rarely permit it to use, what real value will it have? If little, why bother to reform it? If the Senate is assigned important new powers, or is given a genuine political base through election, what are the implications for the cabinet's relations with Parliament, especially the Commons? Considering all the possibilities, would it not be simpler either to leave the Senate alone, risking an occasional clash with the Commons, or abolish it?

The quickening rhythms of debates on the Senate in recent years led Brian Mulroney's government in 1985 to plan yet another conference before 1988. That gives Canadians still more time to invent new ways for reforming the Senate.

9

The monarchy and the governor general

'Once,' said the Mock Turtle with a deep sigh, 'I was a real Turtle.'
Lewis Carroll, *Alice in Wonderland*

Two clauses in the Constitution Act of 1867 provide fundamental information about Canada as a monarchy. One (section 17) states: 'There shall be One Parliament for Canada, consisting of a Queen, an Upper House styled the Senate, and the House of Commons.' The other (section 9) says tersely that 'The Executive Government and Authority of and over Canada is hereby declared to continue and be vested in the Queen.'

Those admirably clear statements establish two positions. The monarch (and when the monarch is a king the word 'Queen' by constitutional alchemy becomes 'King') is the only part of Parliament who also holds executive power. The executive power through which Canada is governed from day to day, exercised almost entirely by or on the advice of the prime minister and his cabinet, derives from the queen. That position was stated forcefully in the House of Commons forty years ago by the acting prime minister at the time, J.L. Ilsley: 'The authority of the Government is not delegated by the House of Commons; the authority of the Government is received from the Crown ... His Majesty's advisers are sworn in as advisers to the Crown. The Government is responsible to Parliament ... but that is a different thing from the doctrine that the Government is a committee of the House of Commons or that it exercises authority delegated by the House of Commons. That is not so.'

Assertions like that may offend the sensibilities of super-democrats (as indeed they did in the debate just quoted), but the fact remains that governments in the Canadian parliamentary system do not lose their power when there is no House of Commons, as in the weeks between the dissolution of one parliament and the next general election. The executive power, to cite the constitution again, is 'vested in the Queen,' and, to cite Dr Forsey, 'The Government derives its authority from the Crown *and* is responsible to the House and the electorate.'[1] There is no conflict in that double conception; and the queen provides the constitutional bridge between Parliament and the executive.

The simplicity of the preceding statements is somewhat misleading, for there is much about the monarchy that is obscure and even mystifying to many Canadians. Why, for example, have a monarch at all when the governor general is empowered to discharge all the queen's duties in Canada? If a monarch is deemed indispensable why does Canada have to share its monarchy with several other Commonwealth countries? That in itself, combined with the residence of the monarch in just one of those countries, produces yet more confusion, for it is easy to conclude, as did the Constitutional Committee of the Quebec Liberal Party in 1980, that 'the Head of State of Canada is the monarch of another country.' (That quotation is interesting because, while technically correct, it is also true in reverse: the head of state in the United Kingdom is the monarch of another country, Canada – and Australia, and New Zealand ...) What are the real functions of any head of state if there is a prime minister and cabinet to look after all the real executive work? The answers to these questions cannot be found in the written constitution, which assigns the executive power to the queen without defining what it is. In a comment on one aspect of the executive power, the Special Committee on Reform of the House of Commons agreed in 1985 (*Third Report*, page 7) that when a prime minister requests a dissolution of Parliament, the governor general as a rule accepts the advice: 'In certain cases, however, the governor general is justified in refusing an immediate request for dissolution.' The 'certain cases' are not listed.

THE CONSTITUTIONAL ROLE OF THE GOVERNOR GENERAL

It is hardly surprising that when writers try to describe the role of the monarchy they use words such as 'elusive' to characterize the problems they encounter. Where much of the activity of the Commons and Senate is visible, the public manifestations of the monarchy appear confined to ceremonies, and old-fashioned ceremonies at that. The role of the monarch as head of the Commonwealth does not generally attract much public attention in Canada, even though Canada is seen by the Commonwealth secretariat in London as a basic model, embodying the concept of a union of people from different cultures.[2] The monarch's presence in Canada is occasional, invariably associated with public celebration. Several recent studies have found Canadians so divided over the monarchy that their authors can think of no realistic changes to suggest: the special joint committee of Parliament on the constitution that reported in 1972 frankly admitted that, adding 'As far as we are able to measure, Canadians are about equally divided between those who favour and those who oppose the Monarchy, with the proponents generally being older, and the opponents generally younger.' The committee, though its members were 'generally older,' said in its final report (page 29) that it 'prefers a Canadian as Head of State, and supports the evolutionary process by which the Governor General has been granted more functions as the Head of State.' The same paragraph raised the question of retaining or abolishing the monarchy some day; but a decade later the Constitution Act of 1982 put the monarchy on the list of subjects that could be altered only with the consent of both houses of Parliament and the legislatures of all ten provinces. Any hasty changes to the office of the queen or the governor general are thus extremely improbable, and evolution is the only course left available.

Evolution, as a matter of historical record, *is* the course the monarchy has followed, and not just in Canada, since Confederation. The governor general of Canada has followed the same path marked out generations earlier by the monarch across the sea, and he (or, as at present, she) now shares substantially the same disabilities, with some additional ones that come from *not* being the monarch. He is a legal survivor who has contrived to remain a political necessity – the once supreme chief whose powers have largely passed into other hands, yet who has nevertheless retained a substantial residue of his former ascendancy and importance. Authority has gradually been succeeded by influence; obvious and aggressive leadership has been replaced by the more subtle and intangible pressure of suggestion and persuasion. For the governor's influence on government is not negligible, although it rarely occurs through the exercise of his visible and more public functions. His talents find expression quietly and unobtrusively behind the scenes; and this is made possible and effective because the office itself carries an established tradition of integrity, unselfishness, and public service. This tradition and the atmosphere that surrounds the institution derive much of their potency from the influence that flows from the throne itself; for while Canadians in general do not look upon the monarchy with the same regard bestowed on it elsewhere, there is undoubtedly an emanation of a milder sort that makes itself felt across the Atlantic. The historical monarchy, in short, strengthens not only the modern monarch but her representative as well; the prestige, the dignity, the antiquity, the past record of the monarchy are all transferred in some measure and help substantially to maintain the repute and vitality of the office of the governor general. The contemporary monarchy, thanks to modern communications and transportation systems which have made the queen's voice and face so familiar, undoubtedly contributes to the same ends.

The development of representative and responsible government in the colonies of British North America meant that even before Confederation the power of the governors had begun to decline. The powers, originally autocratic but progressively diminishing with advances in self-government, were by the turn of this century beginning more and more to resemble those of the monarch, and the time was clearly not far distant when the identification would be virtually complete. Here and there the governor had been able to withstand the encroachments of the cabinet, notably in 1896, when Lord Aberdeen had refused to agree to appointments made by a defeated government. Thirty years later another refusal occurred when Lord Byng declined to grant a dissolution that had been requested by the prime minister. Canada has had no recent crisis involving gubernatorial powers, and never had one so dramatic as Australia did as recently as 1975, when a governor general dismissed the prime minister and called on the leader of the opposition to form the government.[3]

In the Byng dispute the governor general won but an empty victory, for the consequences were to the detriment of the long-run powers of his office. Not only did the prime minister, Mackenzie King, win the general election which almost immediately ensued; he was also free to interpret its results to support his own views, and a few months later went to the imperial conference in London determined to prevent any future recurrence of what he considered to be an undue interference with the constitutional powers of the prime minister. The result was the formal statement by the conference that the governor general of a dominion was the representative of the crown and not of any department of the British government, and that his position in relation to the administration of public affairs in the dominion was essentially the same as that of His Majesty the King in Great Britain. (This had, in fact, been the view taken by Lord Byng and Arthur Meighen throughout the Canadian crisis of 1926.)

This was a radical change, and directs attention to another important side of the governor's former activity. From earliest times he had been called upon to discharge a double task: he was not only the head of the colonial government, but also the representative and mouthpiece of the British authorities, in that he was charged with the duty of guarding the wider interests of the empire from colonial interference and encroachment. The former task had affected his relations with his cabinet and the Canadian people, and necessitated (at least in later years) the utmost neutrality in Canadian politics; the latter might compel him to take a stand which, while reflecting the desires of his principals in Britain, would nevertheless exacerbate his relations in Canada. In early days the British interests were carefully cherished, but as responsible government became more firmly rooted, local welfare tended to become the dominant consideration. This was partly owing to greater Canadian control over matters which had formerly been earmarked as of imperial concern and partly to a change of attitude and approach by the British government. Imperial considerations, in short, not only arose less frequently, but they became subjects for discussion and compromise rather than dictation and summary action. This general tendency was rapidly accelerated by the active Canadian participation in the First World War and the stimulating effects of the struggle on the growth of national sentiment.

The governor general's powers had thus by 1926 been assailed for almost sixty years by two forces moving in from opposite directions, yet both dominated by one common purpose – the desire of the Canadian people for more self-government. Canadians disliked an irresponsible official interfering in the country's political affairs and they were equally unwilling to permit their external affairs to remain outside their own control. The governor general as an active head of the local government, and as the guardian of imperial interests, stood in the way of both these worthy ambitions, although precedents had been steadily accumulating which made his old position more and more difficult to maintain. Thus by 1926 the besiegers had captured many of the outer works of the governor's citadel. It needed only one or two imperial conferences and the Statute of Westminster to complete the conquest, or at least to capture so much of the main stronghold that one or two small bastions could be generously and safely left in the hands of the defender.

The Constitution Act of 1867, as has been indicated, is curiously silent on the subject of the executive power in Canada. While this reticence may be explained in part by the influence of custom and precedent in the colonial governments of the Confederation period and the anticipated continuance of that influence in the government of the new dominion, it was also a logical consequence of the reliance placed on the common law as a vital interpreter of the unwritten portion of the constitution. The courts of England had for centuries interpreted the common (that is, customary) law, and used their power to define executive authority. It was therefore assumed in 1867 that both colonial and English courts would perform the same useful function in Canada.

The central institution exercising general executive authority was the crown, which may be described as that institution which is possessed of the sum total of executive rights and powers, exercised by the sovereign, by the individual or collective action of his or her ministers, or by subordinate officials. It is the supreme executive authority, which may become manifest through a number of outlets. Its nature and its profound importance in English government are best indicated by the fact that the greater part of English consitutional development for centuries was concerned with the changing conception of the crown and the shifting in the exercise of its powers. The long struggle in which Parliament tried to block and mitigate and direct the powers of the sovereign finally resulted in the former taking almost complete control, not, however, by checking the sovereign or openly seizing power, but indirectly and almost surreptitiously by gaining possession of and exercising his or her functions through the supplying of advice and the maintenance of the authority of the crown. The monarch is now able to do virtually nothing without the authorization of his or her constitutional advisers, the cabinet, who are, of course, always accountable to Parliament. Queen Elizabeth II today can do no wrong, simply because her advisers lift the responsibility from her shoulders and transfer it to their own. The crown has become an institution apart from the incumbent of the moment; kings and queens may come and go, but constitutionally and legally the crown goes on forever, relatively undisturbed by the impermanence of sovereigns.

The powers of the British crown are derived from two sources: statute and common law. The powers springing from the former are, of course, found in acts of Parliament; those derived from the common law are the survivors of the original powers possessed by the early English sovereigns before Parliament in the modern sense existed, and are generally described by the term 'prerogative.' The authority was originally extensive, and included the general powers vested in the monarch as supreme executive, lawgiver, judge, and warrior. But succeeding centuries have seen these reduced and limited by various contractual agreements (such as Magna Carta, 1215), by statutes (such as the Bill of Rights, 1689), and by simple disuse. The remainder is thus not so extensive as the original powers, but there is still a substantial residue which Parliament has permitted to remain under the control of the crown. This residue can, of course, be altered by Parliament.

Prerogative powers have the same legal validity as those conferred on the crown by statute, and while they are almost entirely exercisable on the responsibility of ministers, there is within this area a very small segment of independent authority. Statutory powers are fairly obvious and readily ascertained; but the prerogative, finding its origin in the misty past and interpreted by the courts only as the occasion has arisen, is uncertain. Statutory powers are constantly being increased and have, in fact, been expanded enormously in recent years. Prerogative powers, however, can shrink but not grow; for if a new executive power rests on valid precedent, it is no extension but merely a revival; and if it is given a new lease of life by act of Parliament, it becomes a statutory power.

Yet the prerogative is extremely important, and its significance may be readily appreciated by considering the part played in English government by the following, which are broadly prerogative powers, although they may have been affected by the enactment of statutes: the appointment and dismissal of public servants; the summoning, prorogation, and dissolution of Parliament; the creations of peers and conferring of titles of honour; the pardoning power; the power to do all acts of an international character, such as the declaration of war and neutrality, the conclusion of peace, the making or renouncing of treaties, and the establishment or termination of diplomatic relations.

Executive power in Canada is similarly vested in the crown, which manifests itself in both federal and provincial governments, but in each instance the crown naturally acts on the advice of a different cabinet. The powers of the crown in Canada spring from the same double origin of statute and prerogative, although both are one step further removed from their respective sources. The statutory powers come for the most part directly or indirectly from the Constitution Act, the great majority being found in acts of the Canadian Parliament. The prerogative powers are delegated by the queen on the advice of the Canadian cabinet to her representative, the governor general. The appointment of the latter and this delegation of power occur through what are known as the prerogative instruments: the Letters Patent, the Instructions, and the Commission. There is not merely a specific passing-on of the prerogative powers in these instruments. They also assume a continuing devolution by both statute and prerogative which is as great as may be necessary to enable the executive government to be effectively conducted. Prerogatives that affect Canada may be swept away by enactments of the Canadian Parliament, and prerogatives that have lapsed may on occasion be revived by executive authority if such revival is sustained by the courts.

A significant difference between the use of the prerogative power in Canada and Great Britain until 1978 was that substantial parts were not in practice exercised by the governor general, but remained in effect with the queen acting on the advice of the Canadian cabinet. Since 1978 Canadian ministers have advised the governor general on all relevant matters save one: the queen, on the advice of the prime minister, still appoints the governor general. Until 1967 the chief official honours were British honours conferred on Canadians through Canadian advice, but with the establishment that year of the Order of Canada, whose chancellor is the governor general, official honours (with a few minor exceptions) have been Canadianized too. Although (except for a brief flurry in the 1930s) knighthoods have not been available to Canadians for decades, the government has not acted to bar all acceptance by Canadians of honours bestowed by the queen.

An obvious and continuing difference between the monarch and the governor general lies in the way in which the two positions are filled, for there can be nothing in Canada to match the hereditary element that is so vital a part of the monarchy. The history of the choice of governors general in Canada presents one of the best examples of a constitutional development brought about through changes in custom and procedure, entirely apart from statute and formal amendment. The old method of appointment was by the sovereign on the advice of the colonial secretary with the approval, of course, of the British prime minister. After 1890 (following a protest from Queensland, Australia) the method was altered by consulting with the colonial government before the appointment was made, though this procedure, while common, was not invariably followed. In 1916 the Canadian prime minister was simply informed, without any preliminary consultation, that the Duke of Devonshire was to be the new governor. However, it is understood that on at least one occasion another member of the empire was sent a list of three or four names from which the cabinet was allowed to make its choice – a decided step in the direction of greater dominion participation.

The imperial conference of 1926 ushered in the modern period of appointment; for if the governor general 'is not the representative or agent of His Majesty's Government in Great Britain or of any Department of that Government,' the British cabinet obviously could not continue to make the choice. The prime minister of Canada recommends the appointment to the queen, and the latter acts on the advice so given; nevertheless, it seems to be customary to ascertain Her Majesty's wishes in the matter by previous consultation, inasmuch as the governor general is the sovereign's representative. Yet another consultation occurred on at least one occasion in Canada: Bennett stated in 1936 that when Lord Tweedsmuir's name was being considered, he, as prime minister in 1935, first discussed the matter with Mackenzie King, the leader of the opposition, so that the governor's appointment was in effect non-partisan inasmuch as it carried the approval of the leaders of both major parties. This precedent, however, did not establish a practice, and the latest governors have been appointed without consultation with the leader of the opposition.[4]

Parts of the Constitution Act of 1867 relating to the governor's position have been affected by evolutionary development, but they still remain on paper, and were not repealed when major additions to the constitution were effected in 1982. The governor has power (sections 55–7) to withhold his assent from a bill passed by the Canadian Parliament or to reserve a bill for the signification of the pleasure of the queen in Great Britain. Both these powers, although still legally extant, have been rendered obsolete by disuse and the declarations of the imperial and other conferences from 1926 to 1930. The explicit obligation imposed by the Constitution Act to keep the British government informed of the acts passed by the Canadian Parliament (to permit of possible disallowance) was faithfully observed until 1942 when it was quietly discontinued. This was followed in 1947 by the passage of an act amending the Canadian statute that had provided for transmission of copies of current acts to the governor general and to the British government.[5]

Past governors general have varied widely in quality. All have possessed the essential qualification of being what Queen Victoria called 'proper persons,' that is, of excellent social standing, although this has sometimes led to other more essential attributes being slurred over or ignored. It is difficult, for example, to avoid the feeling that the emphasis was somewhat misplaced when Queen Victoria approved the appointment of her son-in-law, the Marquess of Lorne, with the comment that the office would provide a 'distinction for Lorne' and a 'fine independent position for dear Louise.' When Lorne's term had expired the queen suggested the appointment for her son, Prince Leopold, but the British government preferred Lord Lansdowne.[6] Other members of the royal family, however, have occupied the position and have served with moderate distinction. Sir Robert Borden, who was by no means an unfriendly critic, has recorded that the Duke of Connaught 'laboured under the handicap of his position as a member of the Royal Family and he never fully realized the limitations of his position as Governor General,' an estimate which can scarcely be regarded as strengthening the argument for such appointments.[7]

A small but important group, of dubious merit in earlier years, was composed of professional soldiers whose inelastic minds, and experience and outlook far removed from the complexities and compromises of politics, sometimes proved an inadequate equipment for the trying role of constitutional monarch. A hundred years ago appointments of this nature were much more common than later, although the complaint of Joseph Howe regarding governors whose minds had become disciplined through years of military service 'into a contempt for civil business and fractious impatience of the opinions' of all of lower rank retains at least some of its force.[8] Lady Byng, for example, recorded in her memoirs that both she and her husband 'always shunned and detested politics,' an attitude which, whatever its justification, provided a strange equipment for the tasks awaiting them at Rideau Hall. But the above types include the dull governors and the failures; there have happily been others whose capacity was undoubted, whose interests were comprehensive, and whose talents won recognition not in Canada alone but in other countries as well. As long as governors general were chosen from royal or aristocratic personages, or professional soldiers, the choice of a female governor remained improbable, but in 1984 Jeanne Sauvé, who had already served as the first woman Speaker of the House of Commons, became governor general. In one more official area the male-only pattern was thus broken.

TENURE

The term and tenure of the governor general furnish futher illustrations of the impossibility of making the position simply a replica of that of the monarch in Great Britain. The term may be simply, if somewhat ambiguously, stated as being officially recognized as six years, customarily treated as five years, while on occasion it has been seven years. The office was formerly held at the pleasure of the British government, which made the governor virtually independent of any control by the colony, although a petition for recall would probably have been heeded by the Colonial Office. This situation has perforce changed since the imperial conferences of 1926 and 1930. The governor general may now be removed by the queen acting on advice tendered by the Canadian cabinet, and he can resign voluntarily. A governor is placed, potentially at least, at the mercy of his own cabinet, a subordination that makes assertions of independent opinions unlikely and any strong line of conduct impossible, and is apt to undermine the governor's influence and reputation for impartiality. For it must be assumed that the power of advising the queen to remove a governor is not merely nominal but real, and that the queen will act on advice so given.

The period of full dominion status in the Commonwealth had hardly begun when there occurred one decisive precedent on the fate of a governor who happened to incur the enmity of his cabinet. James McNeill, the governor general of the Irish Free State, was removed in this way in 1932 for the most trivial reasons and a successor was chosen who was more closely indentified with the De Valera government. Such drastic action, it need scarcely be added, was quite at variance with the tradition of the independence and party neutrality of the king's representative. The removal under these particular circumstances violated one aspect of this tenure; the new and partisan appointment violated another. The precedent thus established has not yet been called on in relation to Canadian practice; but it is worth recording that the importunities of the modern media in seeking interviews with those in the public eye may some day trap a governor general into some unintended but unforgivable utterance. Edward Schreyer, Madame Sauvé's predecessor, was severely criticized for speculating publicly about his post-gubernatorial career.[9]

The Constitution Act entitled a governor general to a salary of £10,000, which Parliament in 1970 changed to $48,666.63, a sum smaller than £10,000 would have been in 1867. Parliament can alter the governor's compensation, and as this is written the salary is under review; a retired governor's pension is one-third the salary. Canada's first governors general were wealthy men, but even they began to need extra money for living expenses, and today Rideau Hall is also supported by a budget of about $4 million for staff and other necessities.

FUNCTIONS

The functions of the governor general are many and varied, but they may be divided into two broad categories, depending on the manner in which the governor participates in their discharge. The first comprises those functions that are purely nominal and are performed automatically and inescapably on the advice of cabinet. These (which may spring from either prerogative or statute) need not be dealt with here, for they are more properly considered as functions of the cabinet, the governor's participation being that of giving consent as a matter of routine to the advice tendered. If the duties were confined to procedures of this nature, the post could most certainly be regarded as superfluous. There is, however, a second group of functions arising from both statutory and prerogative powers which, unlike some other powers of the same origin, has continued to be closely identified with the governor as a person and has not been brought under cabinet control. In these functions the governor as an individual takes an active part and their exercise will vary greatly with his or her special capacity and character. It is these which furnish the major justification for the simulacrum of kingship at Ottawa. The constitutional monarchy as it is known throughout the Commonwealth is far from being a useless survival which through inertia or kindness of heart has been allowed to linger on. It is an important office with useful and even vital duties to perform. Cabinet government, in short, presupposes some central, impartial figure at its head which at certain times and for certain purposes supplements and aids the other more active and partisan agencies of government.

Continuity of government
In the first place, the governor general is charged with the duty of seeing that there is always a prime minister and a responsible cabinet in office. One of the merits of cabinet government is its ready adjustment to change and particularly the speed and ease with which a new administration can step into the shoes of its predecessor. On most occasions this change of rulers is a purely mechanical operation, for it may happen that only one person will be in a position where he can accept the prime ministership with the assurance of receiving the indispensable parliamentary support. At such times the task of the governor is extremely simple and calls for nothing but a formal request to the obvious person to take the responsibility of constituting a new cabinet. Thus if a prime minister resigns after his party's defeat in a general election, the leader of the opposition or of the major opposition party must be the automatic choice; or, if the vacancy can be anticipated and if time permits, the majority party will select its leader and thus again make the governor's choice merely a formal one. In 1920, for example, when the retirement of Sir Robert Borden was imminent, the cabinet and the government party members held prolonged conferences and even took a ballot to ascertain the view of all the party supporters. Although a difference of opinion developed between the rank and file and the cabinet, agreement on Meighen was eventually reached, and three days before Sir Robert Borden resigned the governor requested Meighen to form a new government.[10]

There are other times when the choice is neither obvious nor simple. A sudden death or resignation or party dissension may cause the office of prime minister to fall unexpectedly vacant and someone must be charged with the duty of seeing that it is filled immediately and to the satisfaction of the Commons. It is the governor's task to take the initiative and pursue the matter unceasingly until a new prime minister is in office. This may involve consultation with those whom the governor feels can give sage advice, or it may necessitate preliminary negotiations with potential prime ministers to discover if they want the position, if they can form a cabinet, and if they are able to command the support of a majority in the House. In any event the responsibility for making the final choice rests with the governor, subject, of course, to the selection being sustained in the House of Commons. Thus Lord Aberdeen in 1894 called in Sir Frank Smith to advise him informally on a successor to Sir John Thompson, and in 1896, after first sounding out Sir Donald Smith, he asked Sir Charles Tupper to succeed Sir Mackenzie Bowell. Except for 1926 when Lord Byng, in a sense, selected Meighen as his prime minister by refusing King a dissolution, the governor general has not since 1896 had to use his own judgment in this regard; but there is no reason whatever to assume that the power has vanished in the interval. The conscription crisis in Canada in 1944 might easily have resulted in the governor being compelled to choose a successor to Mackenzie King.[11]

Mediation

A second duty of the governor general is to offer his services as a mediator and conciliator between the political party leaders when the occasion warrants. Intervention of this kind is usually of an emergency nature and will occur only in time of crisis. Thus the Duke of Devonshire in 1917 summoned Sir Robert Borden, Sir Wilfrid Laurier, and four others to a meeting at Government House to discuss the general political situation, involving coalition government, conscription, and the possible avoidance of a war election. Governors have sometimes intervened in a different kind of quarrel, that between the federal government and a province. Shortly after British Columbia's entrance into Confederation Lord Dufferin endeavoured to charm away the bitterness between that province and the Dominion, not always in a manner acceptable to the prime minister. Twenty years later Lord Aberdeen held a series of interviews with the premier and attorney general of Manitoba on the separate school issue. Efforts of this kind, however, rarely meet with more than a modicum of success, and there is always bound to be some doubt at what moment, if at all, intervention by the governor general should occur or whether matters should be allowed to take their normal though admittedly more troubled course. Canadians considered qualified to become governor general commonly have a record that is at least partly partisan, and while the prime minister who makes the recommendation may find it easy to accept his choice's intervention, an incoming former opponent may not.

Governors general have also been expected at times to act as quasi-diplomatic agents, formerly under instruction from the British government, latterly from that of Canada. This activity has in practice been confined to the paying of official visits to the United States. In early days these trips frequently had a definite and avowed diplomatic purpose, but today they are, on the surface at least, nothing more than gestures of goodwill and friendliness to a great neighbour. But, as President Roosevelt pointed out, there was nothing to prevent him and Lord Tweedsmuir from sitting on the same sofa and soliloquizing aloud; and if one overheard what the other said, that was unavoidable. It is probable that these social calls are still occasionally used to review unofficially and tentatively matters of common interest to the two nations. On another front, the governor general within Canada is involved in internal diplomacy in a way not formerly expected: the incumbent from now on will almost certainly have to be a bilingual Canadian, with the office alternating between those English- and French-speaking descent.

Social responsibilities
The governor is also the social head of the country and has always been supposed to exercise a moral leadership as well. This is, of course, a direct inheritance from England and one that received far greater prominence in Victorian times when the queen was a model of the social if not of all the constitutional properties. Greater emphasis is laid today upon leadership in various fields of worthy endeavour, the arts, social service, public health, youth movements, history, education, and all commendable phases of the national life come under the notice and patronage of the governor. But in voicing his views on any of these matters he must go warily lest he unwittingly trespass upon what some touchy person, political party, or organization considers to be a controversial issue on which officially and publicly he must have no opinion. A governor, for example, was once called to task for praising in the most general terms a distinguished Canadian statesman. Several recent incumbents have been both criticized and supported for suggesting a wider role for the governor. From the point of view of a governor general in the 1980s it is unfortunate that many of the public issues on which an experienced governor may well have views worth hearing (such as unemployment, disarmament, poverty in the Third World) have partisan aspects.

One side of the governor general's social activity is entertainment, and this is expected to include members of Parliament, the public service, the diplomatic corps, and any person of distinction who may be within reach. In earlier days, when nobles inhabited Rideau Hall, the entertainment often took the form of the routs and revels of upper-class British society; but with the proliferation of government activities and changes in the types of incumbent, entertaining today includes more practical matters: having the members of the Canada Council to dinner, for example, or holding a reception for new members of the Order of Canada. Closely associated with the governor's social activity are his duties as the ceremonial head of the government. She (or he) must, of course, open Parliament, receive foreign diplomatic agents, and perform similar routine functions; but she must also go on tour throughout the country once or twice a year and, en route, lay cornerstones, listen to innumerable addresses from municipal authorities, attend exhibitions, open museums and hospitals, and generally carry out all the wearisome tasks the monarch is expected to do in Britain.

The cynic may well question what purpose is served by many of these barnstorming performances. But there can be little doubt that even the most democratic countries desire this sort of thing, and the only real question to decide is what person is to spend time at it. The American president, who has no governor general to share his public appearances, is under enormous pressure to be seen publicly on every possible occasion, and since the advent of television coverage could not safely avoid it even if he wanted to. Public performances seem more than ever to be a necessary concomitant of democratic governments, and nations of the Commonwealth are fortunate in that they have accidentally at hand the means of satisfying these demands for display. The prime minister's time is usually too valuable to be consumed with relative trivialities, and the governor general relieves him of many ceremonial duties. Furthermore, the governor can do it in such a manner as to suggest the monarchical tie to those Canadians of royalist bent, without offending those of more republican tendencies, and in such a manner as to help make Canadians aware of their heritage; recent governors, for example, have made well-publicized trips to the far north.

To advise, to encourage, to warn

Another function of the governor general is that of adviser and consultant to the cabinet and more especially to the prime minister. Walter Bagehot, in discussing the English monarchy over a century ago, gave the classic definition of this function when he wrote: 'The sovereign has ... three rights – the right to be consulted, the right to encourage, the right to warn. And a King of great sense and sagacity would want no others.'[12] Queen Victoria, the sovereign at the time Bagehot's book was written, had her own peculiar ideas as to what this involved, and did not hesitate to favour one party or one prime minister when it suited her purposes to do so; but it is generally believed that her successors have had a greater regard for the niceties of the institution and have used these rights carefully and conscientiously. The Canadian governor general is expected to follow the same practice. Thus, while on all but the exceptional occasions the governor must follow the advice of his cabinet, he is not supposed to be blindly subservient to them. He must co-operate with them fully and in the last resort follow their counsel, but he is free – indeed it is his duty – to give his own opinions whenever he feels these opinions are worthy of consideration.

It is evident that the usefulness of this function and the extent to which it can be employed with profit will depend primarily on the character, capacity, and temperament of both governor general and prime minister and the confidence and good faith existing between them. Exceptional knowledge or the highest of motives is not in itself a sufficient guarantee of success. The governor must know when to interfere and when to abstain; and when he endeavours to give help and advice he must possess sufficient restraint, balance, and tact that he will persuade and not antagonize his cabinet. Lord Dufferin's attitude toward his chief advisers in Dominion negotiations with British Columbia, for example, has been described by Alexander Mackenzie's biographer as 'treacherous.' Lord Byng insisted on one occasion on receiving a delegation of strikers in an industrial dispute, despite the fact that several of his ministers told him that such action was both irregular and improper, and his stubbornness could scarcely have increased his influence with his constitutional advisers. The Duke of Connaught became much concerned in 1916 because the Canadian cabinet did not take certain steps which he considered desirable, and after lodging a number of unusually strong protests (which appear to have been singularly inappropriate) he added that he was remonstrating also because of his personal objections 'as Governor-General and a Field-Marshal in His Majesty's Forces, against the undoubted danger both to Canada and the Empire, which apparently the Canadian Government did not appreciate or entertain.' It would be painting the lily indeed to attempt to do more than quote verbatim a part of the reply of Sir Robert Borden:

I hope that my colleagues and I shall not be found wanting in respect or indeed in admiration for the wide military experience of Your Royal Highness and the high position which you hold as a Field-Marshal in His Majesty's Forces. It would appear to us that the matters under consideration do not call so much for the exercise of military skill or the application of military experience as the consideration of international law and the exercise of the common-place quality of common sense.[13]

Confidence between the governor and his prime minister is rarely present to the same degree as in the similar situation in Great Britain, a lack which may be attributed to many things, such as the mediocre talents of certain governors, the old functions of the governor as imperial officer and the consequent distrust of his attitude when national and empire issues clashed, and the fear of a revival or perpetuation of certain of the governor's former independent powers. Canadian cabinets, it seems, have not always kept the governor as well informed as they should of matters under consideration or even decisions made, and the wisest governor can do little or nothing if he is not apprised of cabinet business. The governor general has not since at least 1858 sat regularly in cabinet meetings, and thus has no way of acquiring knowledge except with the active assistance of the prime minister. Lord Dufferin's plea that while he had no desire 'to fidget with the administration of the country or to interfere in any way with the free action and official responsibility of my Ministers'[14] he was nevertheless worried about his growing separation from the business of the cabinet was an early indication of a difficulty which appears subsequently to have grown more acute. Thus the imperial conference of 1926, while providing for the new status of the governor, felt it necessary to add that 'a Governor-General should be supplied with copies of all documents of importance and in general should be kept as fully informed as is His Majesty the King in Great Britain of Cabinet business and public affairs.'

The extent to which the governor general is now used as a consultant by the Canadian cabinet and the influence which he exerts are both matters on which few can pronounce with certainty. The relations of the governor and the prime minister must in the nature of things remain generally unknown and the matters dealt with are even more deeply veiled by official secrecy. Only here and there are a few disclosures made, and these become public so long after the event that they often have little applicability to existing conditions. The following opinions, the first by Sir Wilfrid Laurier, the second by Sir Robert Borden, and the third by John Diefenbaker, indicate the value attached to this function of the governor general by those who came in direct contact with him:

The Canadian Governor General long ago ceased to determine policy, but he is by no means, or need not be, the mere figure-head the public imagine. He has the privilege of advising his advisers, and if he is a man of sense and experience, his advice is often taken.

It would be an absolute mistake to regard the Governor General [as the office was altered by the 1926 conference] as a mere figure-head, a mere rubber stamp. During nine years of Premiership I had the opportunity of realizing how helpful may be the advice and counsel of a Governor General in matters of delicacy and difficulty; in no case was consultation with regard to such matters ever withheld; and in many instances I obtained no little advantage and assistance therefrom.

During the time when I was prime minister there were two governors general ... and they were fully consulted as the representative of the Queen has a right to be. He also has the duty to give an opinion to the Prime Minister with regard to those things he believes necessary for Canada.[15]

In recent years there has been a general disinclination for the prime minister to use the governor general in this way: the necessary information is not always forthcoming, and consultation on matters of state has sometimes almost disappeared. This may, of course, vary with the personal elements in the situation. Thus a veteran prime minister such as Mackenzie King, while remaining on the friendliest terms with Lord Alexander, did not make a practice of consulting the famous soldier, presumably because he was confident that Alexander's advice on Canadian politics would be quite worthless. It is possible, however, that a different prime minister and a seasoned governor general of outstanding ability might conceivably lead to the establishment of a different relationship where the opinion of the governor might not only be sought but also be given the most careful consideration.

Reserve powers

Finally, the governor general has a reserve power in certain grave contingencies to act on his own initiative. The extent of this power is vague and the occasions on which it may be used are debatable and to some degree uncertain. But such a power most certainly exists, although its exercise must be regarded as justifiable only under the most exceptional circumstances. The broad rule, of course, still holds: the governor general will follow the advice given by his ministers, for they accept the responsibility and with it accept the praise or blame for the decision and its results. The advice given may be bad, it may be short-sighted, it may be foolish, it may be dangerous – all these considerations may induce the governor to remonstrate with his ministers and try to win them over to his point of view. But if they persist, his only course is to shrug his shoulders and acquiesce. The decision is not his but that of his government, and eventually the people and their representatives will deal with those who have proffered the advice. Should the governor set his will against that of his cabinet, his action at once tends to become a political issue and, whether he likes it or not, he will find himself a party leader in the opposition's interests.

At rare intervals a cabinet may pursue a policy that threatens to disrupt the proper and normal working of the constitution. This may sometimes be overcome by allowing matters to take their course or by the governor persuading his advisers to alter their policy and adopt a more seemly procedure than the one proposed. Such courses of action, however, may not prove feasible, and it may then become the thankless duty of the governor to intervene and insist on certain steps being taken more in accordance with the constitutional proprieties, even although this may necessitate – as it usually will – the virtual dismissal of his advisers and a search for another prime minister and cabinet to take their place. If, for example, a prime minister were shown beyond reasonable doubt to have accepted a bribe and refused to resign or to advise that Parliament be immediately summoned to deal with the matter, the governor would have an undoubted right to dismiss him from office. Or if a prime minister, having obtained a dissolution, was returned with a minority of members and promptly demanded another dissolution, the governor would have no real alternative but to refuse the advice and force the resignation of the cabinet. Mackenzie King was hardly celebrated as a champion of the powers of the governor general, but in 1926 he explicitly upheld the right of a governor not merely to refuse a prime minister a dissolution under certain circumstances, but also to dismiss him. 'I may say,' he asserted on 1 July 1926, 'that as Leader of His Majesty's loyal Opposition I am prepared to take responsibility for the dismissal of the hon. gentleman opposite.'

No exact rules can be laid down for the exercise of these reserve powers. Necessarily, they involve discretion (in both senses of the word); and threats to the constitution may be infinite in variety. There is even great divergence of informed opinion on certain recorded cases where governors acted on their own initiative. Two, already mentioned, have arisen in Canada in the last seventy years. Lord Aberdeen, in 1896, refused to make appointments on the advice of a government that had just been defeated at the polls. Lord Byng, in 1926, refused to grant a dissolution to a government that had had one only nine months before, that had been defeated in the House of Commons, and against whom a motion of censure was under debate. He insisted that a second election so soon after the first would be justified only if no alternative government in the existing Parliament was possible. Since the official opposition had 116 seats to the government's 101, there seemed a reasonable chance that an alternative government was possible. Arthur Meighen, the leader of the opposition who accepted office and responsibility for Lord Byng's action, added that no government was entitled to a dissolution that would prevent the House of Commons from pronouncing judgment on its conduct. Both these cases resulted in long and lively controversies.[16]

As recently as the spring of 1985 a relevant case arose in Ontario, when the province's Conservative party, in power for over four decades, was defeated in an election that gave the combined opposition parties, the Liberals and the NDP, a majority in the legislature. Without forming a coalition, the two agreed to defeat the government and support the Liberal leader as premier. Had the Conservative leader, who had advised the lieutenant-governor on the dissolution which produced his defeat, requested a second dissolution when an alternative government was clearly available, the governor would have had a constitutional duty to refuse. In two other notable occasions (involving Lord Dufferin in 1873 and Lord Lorne in 1878–9), a governor general accepting his prime minister's advice profoundly aggravated the opposition.

While admittedly occasions warranting the use of the reserve power are impossible to define, two conditions ought to be present. The constitutional procedures set in motion by the cabinet in the matter in question must be such that they would not simply involve some temporary inconvenience – they would have to perpetuate for some time a state of affairs which was plainly intolerable and a violation of the spirit and intent of the constitution. Further, there should be no reasonable doubt of the essential wisdom and justice of the governor's intervention; if any such doubt is present, it constitutes prima facie evidence that he should hold his hand. For if the governor moves on his own responsibility, he must at once obtain other advisers and will thus sooner or later be compelled indirectly through his new cabinet to seek justification at the polls for the use of his emergency power. In short, he must be so sure of the inherent righteousness of his intervention and his popular vindication that he is willing to stake both his reputation and his office on its general acceptance. If it be objected that the above two conditions are seldom found and hence any assertion of the reserve power will be extraordinary indeed, the argument is not weakened but confirmed; for the great justification of the retention of this prerogative is that it *is* an emergency device invoked to re-establish genuine democratic control at a time when the normal constitutional procedures have faltered and are in danger of being improperly and unscrupulously employed. The mere existence of the power will, in fact, tend to prevent the need for its exercise arising.

A review of these functions of the governor general will immediately reveal that a successful governor must possess certain qualities above all others; in particular, he (or she) must be able to maintain the most conscientious disinterestedness and impartiality toward Canadian political affairs. If he is to be allowed to choose a new prime minister, if he is to be of any service as a mediator between conflicting parties, if his advice is to carry weight, if in emergencies he is to act as the guardian of the constitution, and, to a less degree, if he is to provide social and cultural leadership, his political opinions and prejudices must be above criticism and he must enjoy sufficient security to speak and act both honestly and fearlessly.

Recent constitutional changes have actually made it more difficult for the governor general to remain impartial and aloof, to discuss public matters frankly with the prime minister, and to give advice and to take action without fear of immediate consequences. The governor's dependence on the federal government has, since 1930, become complete: to it he owes his appointment, his salary and allowances, and his tenure of office. The imperial conference of 1926, which ingenuously asserted the similarity of the positions of monarch and governor, took in fact the first steps which would destroy much of that cherished similarity. The conference cut the governor loose from British control; but in so doing, it brought him in Canada under the control of the federal government, and the latter status was as unlike that of the British sovereign as the former. (This was of course as true for the members of the Commonwealth which were not federations.) For while it is true that the sovereign holds office in Great Britain at the will of the British Parliament (that is, the monarchy in the United Kingdom is hereditary because Parliament wishes it, and the same is true of Canada), it is no less true that the traditions and prestige of the office and the present monarch's unique position in the history of Britain and in the affections of the people give her a bulwark of defence which is built deep into the national life. The governor will always be at a disadvantage in any comparison with the monarch, for not only does the position by comparison lack tradition and prestige, but the term of office is temporary and the governor's detachment and neutrality are by no means so firmly established. Indeed, with the growing popularity of royal tours, so exhaustively covered by radio and television, a governor general may sometimes appear to be overshadowed even in his own country.

But although it is impossible to create any exact copy of the original institution in Canada, certain safeguards can be erected which will materially increase the prestige and security of the governor's position and enable her (or him) to be a more useful member of the government. Appointment on the advice of the Canadian government must be retained, although this could be purged of any partisan implications by prior consultation with the other major party leaders. The precarious term and tenure of the governor as it exists today could be changed to a fixed term of five years, tenable during good behaviour, with removal only by joint address of the two houses of Parliament. The salary could be explicitly guaranteed for the governor's entire term. Such (or similar) measures would give him an independent position approximately equal to that enjoyed by the sovereign and enable him to act more effectively and usefully than under existing conditions.

These changes, however, would have little merit and might even prove dangerous if they were not reinforced by the selection of suitable people who would be both able and politically impartial at the time of their appointment. Such a demand, in former days, frequently raised a question which has since been answered, namely, the desirability of appointing a native Canadian. Vincent Massey became the first Canadian governor general in 1952; he was succeeded in 1959 by Major General Georges Vanier; and in 1967 Roland Michener, a former Speaker of the House of Commons, assumed the office. Since then the office has been held by a distinguished diplomat, Jules Leger; a former premier of Manitoba, Edward Schreyer; and Madame Sauvé, who was in turn an MP, a cabinet minister, and Speaker of the House.

At the time of Vincent Massey's appointment (he too had been a cabinet minister and his party's president), grave doubts were expressed in many quarters; for although Massey had a distinguished record of public service in many fields, he was also unmistakenly identified with the political party whose leader selected him in 1952. As the careers of Vincent Massey and his successors have demonstrated, it is no more dangerous to appoint Canadians to Rideau Hall than it is to appoint them to the Supreme Court, the Canada Council, or any other federal body. Certainly, as the history of the office of lieutenant-governor has amply shown,[17] there will always be risks in partisan appointments. But these could be lessened, if not entirely removed, by the simple process of consulting the opposition. Far from being, as Sir Wilfrid Laurier once put it, 'a laudable but misguided expression of national pride,' the first Canadian appointments have been successes, so much so that there is no pressure whatever to return to selections from the United Kingdom or (as has often been suggested in the past) to appoint governors from other Commonwealth countries. In any event, should Canadian appointments become unsatisfactory, there is nothing to prevent the choice of future governors general from other countries, including the United Kingdom – a potential development which would no doubt be hailed as one more of the nebulous ties that bind crown and Commonwealth together.

Whatever the nationality of the governor general, it remains true, as Professor MacKinnon wrote:

The monarchy therefore serves democracy. It keeps the ministers in second place as servants of the state – electable, responsible, accountable, criticizable, and defeatable – a position necessary to the operation of parliamentary government. The people and their parliament can control the head of government because he cannot identify himself with the state or confuse loyalty to himself with allegiance to the state and criticism with treason. He is discouraged from the common tendency of officials, whether elected or not, to regard and make themselves indispensable, to entrench themselves in expanding power structures, to resent accountability and criticism, and to scoff at the effects of prolonged tenure of office or advancing years. Moreover, such control avoids the charges of treason, executions, assassinations, revolutions, and miscellaneous other expensive upheavals which so often accompany attempts to control and change governments that take themselves too seriously.[18]

All that is so; and yet with an absentee monarch it remains difficult to maintain the mystique of the monarchy in Canada. On 23 February 1965, Prime Minister Pearson, responding to a resolution in favour of abolishing the monarchy passed by a group of young Liberals, assured the House of Commons that it was his government's policy 'to maintain the monarchy as a cherished, strong and important part of our constitution which has earned and will receive our loyalty and our respect.' Pierre Elliott Trudeau, no doubt reflecting his Quebec background, appeared less enthusiastic about the monarchy, and it was his government that produced the Constitutional Amendment Bill of 1978, which proposed (section 43): 'The executive government of and over Canada shall be vested in the Governor General of Canada, on behalf and in the name of the Queen.' That proposal, along with similar suggestions that arose during the events leading to the Constitution Act of 1982, produced much opposition. It was also the Trudeau government that took the initiative in creating that act, which entrenches the monarchy in the strongest constitutional position it has yet had. Canadian attitudes toward the monarchy have always varied, not only between the older and the younger generations, but between provinces and regions. The constitutional status of the monarchy could hardly be clearer. The offices of monarch and governor general will undoubtedly continue to evolve, but for the calculable future both are here to stay.

10
The prime minister and the cabinet

'The first essential for a Prime Minister is to be a good butcher,' said Mr. Asquith, and then added, 'there are several who must be pole-axed now.'
Winston Churchill, *Great Contemporaries*

If a political system can be said to have a centre of gravity, it is, in a country governed like Canada, the cabinet. Yet its general activities, thought indispensable, receive scant attention in the written constitution or the statutes. The constitution has a few provisions which mention the Privy Council, the chief of these stating that 'There shall be a Council to aid and advise in the Government of Canada, to be styled the Queen's Privy Council for Canada; and the Persons who are to be Members of that Council shall be from Time to Time chosen and summoned by the Governor General and sworn in as Privy Councillors, and Members thereof may be from Time to Time removed by the Governor General.' Yet this Council is not the cabinet, although by custom the cabinet constitutes the active part of the Council. Acts of Parliament have created the government departments and individual ministerships, but again it is through custom that the ministers who occupy these positions are in the cabinet. The prime minister and the cabinet undoubtedly exercise extensive power, but this power is not explicitly given them by the law, and they exercise it formally through some other body in accordance with the custom of the constitution. The really vital things about the cabinet rest on the constitutional conventions. When should a cabinet resign? How does it obtain office? What are its powers? What is the relation between a prime minister and his cabinet, between one cabinet minister and the others? How many should there be in the cabinet? How is a prime minister chosen? One may search the law books in vain for answers to these questions.

MEMBERSHIP OF CABINET

The cabinet and the ministry have usually been treated in Canada as though they were the same body, and during a large part of Canadian history they have in fact been identical. But from time to time one or two members would appear in the ministry (that is, those chosen by the prime minister to be his advisers) who were not in the cabinet; and since the Second World War a fairly large penumbral group of parliamentary secretaries – members of Parliament who are attached to the cabinet yet not formally considered as part of either the cabinet or the ministry – has appeared. The number of parliamentary secretaries cannot exceed the number of ministers whose salaries are provided for in the Salaries Act, and prime ministers tend to rotate them so that during the ordinary four or five sessions of any one Parliament a large number of MPs may have an opportunity to serve a minister as an assistant. Custom decrees that the retirement of the cabinet will always involve the retirement of the parliamentary secretaries as well.

Whether a salaried parliamentarian employed as a member of the executive is in or out of the cabinet depends not on the political nature of his position, but on whether he has been invited by the prime minister to join the select circle of colleagues who meet together from time to time to decide matters of high policy. To this extent the line between a member who is within and one who is without the cabinet is potentially an arbitrary and variable one; but in practice the great bulk of the members of the cabinet are there ex officio. The headship of a government department, for example, is held to entitle its occupant to a seat in the cabinet.

Members of the cabinet (sometimes the executive, as well as the ministry) are thus by no means alike in status; there are, indeed, several different types of positions to be distinguished. The first of these, in a class by himself, is the prime minister, who has both powers and a position not shared by his colleagues. He alone is his party's leader, and as such his influence is enormous, particularly if he has recently led the party in an electoral victory. He alone is asked by the governor general to form a government, and he selects all his ministers. He also has attached to his position the equivalent of a small department, the Prime Minister's Office. He alone, by resigning, can carry with him the resignation of all other ministers. He alone advises the governor general on a variety of crucial matters, including major appointments and the dissolution of Parliament. He receives the lion's share of media coverage, for while most ministers are constantly making statements relevant to their duties, only the prime minister can speak for the whole government. It is small wonder that a recent incumbent publicly said that he regarded the power in the office as 'excessive.'[1]

But the prime minister, powerful though he may be (and the use of the powers, of course, depends on how the prime minister interprets them), cannot become a dictator. To remain in office, he needs the support of his cabinet, as well as that of a majority of MPs, and the ministers around him are associates, not subjects. In recent years the nature of that association has been changing, as will be described in more detail in a later chapter. For the moment it is necessary to note that the cabinet has an internal hierarchy, and the rung next to the prime minister is occupied by the ministers who are political heads of departments. Some of the departments, such as Finance and the Treasury Board, have duties that affect all other departments, while others, of which Energy, Mines and Resources, or Science and Technology, are among the most conspicuous, have duties that coordinate vast activities essential to the nation's economy. Some departments serve only specific elements in Canadian society, such as Labour or Agriculture. The importance of the different portfolios varies, in relation to both the country as a whole and the strengths and weaknesses of the party in power, and the individual ministers thus vary in importance too. It is widely believed that to move a minister from a lesser to a major department is a promotion, even though all ministers get the same pay.

Separate from the political heads are ministers who are in the cabinet but not heads of full departments. Before 1971 these ministers were called ministers without portfolios, and they were assigned specific tasks, for reasons that ranged from aiding an overworked minister to supporting a minister who, though old or incompetent, was still desired in the cabinet because of seniority, or because he added needed regional or some other desirable element to the cabinet. Since 1971 such ministers have held an august title, minister of state, with a subtitle such as External Relations or Finance. There are full ministers for those departments, so that the minister of state for finance, for example, is a form of assistant to a minister with his own portfolio. Other ministers of state are not attached to other departments, but have their own duties in, for example, a branch called Fitness and Amateur Sport. As this is written, there are forty ministers in the cabinet, twelve of them ministers of state.

Both those totals are subject to change, as the prerogatives of the prime minister include deciding on the size of his cabinet and determining who holds what post. A similar right of historical interest turns on a few offices whose holders were recognized as being members of the ministry they served, but not the cabinet. One office in a modern cabinet, the solicitor general, was not a cabinet minister for over twenty years after its creation in 1892, and moved in and out more than once before becoming an apparent fixture in 1945. Two other political officers, controllers of Customs and Inland Revenue, had similar histories but did not survive to cabinet rank, their duties being absorbed into new departments whose heads are now cabinet ministers. The parliamentary secretaries mentioned above are of course also political officers, and any doubt about their rank was settled in 1959 when it was made explicitly clear that they are not junior or quasi-ministers.

Another essential distinction has already been lightly touched upon: the distinction between the Privy Council and the cabinet. The Privy Council, as the constitution states, is composed of those chosen by the governer general, and they are, by custom, always recommended by the prime minister. All cabinet ministers must first be made members of the Privy Council, although it may contain other persons of distinction, such as a Prince of Wales, a British prime minister, and a Canadian high commissioner in London, all of whom have been members. In 1953 the chief justice of Canada, the Speakers of the House of Commons and the Senate, and the leader of the opposition were all made members of the Privy Council before they left for the coronation where they formed a part of Canada's official delegation; and in 1967 the ten provincial premiers were admitted as part of the centennial celebrations. Those appointed to the Privy Council remain members for life, and hence it will include not only ministers from the present cabinet, but also all surviving ministers of past cabinets as well. The Privy Council would therefore, if active, be a large and politically cumbersome body (at any given time it may number over one hundred) with members continually at cross-purposes with one another. It has saved itself from this embarrassment by the simple device of holding almost no meetings of the whole council. The Privy Council as such does meet, however: a meeting was called in 1947 to receive the formal announcement by the king of his consent to the marriage of Princess Elizabeth, and the queen herself chaired meetings in 1957 in Ottawa and in 1959 in Halifax. Quite apart from such ceremonial occasions, 'routine meetings are considered to take place every time the Governor General participates by approving an Order in Council ... In this century the Council has met formally at least nine times, three times since 1945. On two of these occasions non-ministers attended, and at some of the meetings Government business was discussed.'[2]

It remains true, none the less, that the truly operative part of the Privy Council is the cabinet. And the cabinet, lacking any legal status of its own, masquerades as the Privy Council when it desires to assume formal powers; then it speaks and acts in the name of the entire Council. The governor-in-council is therefore the governor acting on the formal advice of ministers of the cabinet, and the instrument of such formal decisions becomes an order or a minute of Council. The cabinet, even when it acts informally, will consider itself to be functioning as the Council (and enforce, for example, the Council's oath of secrecy upon its members) but, for the most part, in the conduct of its discussions and in its settlement of policies it is simply a group of the leading members of the majority party. The prime minister and cabinet as such thus exercise no formal powers; they decide rather how some regularly constituted authority – the governor general, the governor-in-council, a particular minister – is to discharge functions with which that authority is legally entrusted and concerning which it will, as a matter of custom and convenience, accept direction from the prime minister and the cabinet.

The governor general is not president of the Council; orders and minutes of Council are ordinarily passed by the cabinet and then forwarded to the governor for his approval.

The principle that the members of the cabinet must not only have seats in one of the houses of Parliament but that they are at all times responsible to the House of Commons lies at the very roots of Canadian politics, and it was the acceptance of this convention that over a century ago transformed representative into responsible government. A minister, even the prime minister, may of course be without a parliamentary seat for a brief period. If a party convincingly won a general election, for example, but its leader failed to carry his own constituency, the party would not have to seek a new leader, but merely a new seat for the leader; or a minister may be brought into the cabinet from outside Parliament, and be without a seat until one is found for him. (In 1944–5 General A.G.L. McNaughton was minister of national defence for over nine months, during which he failed twice to be elected; so he was relieved of his ministerial duties.)

SUPPORT OF PARLIAMENT

Whether or not all its members have parliamentary seats, it cannot be emphasized too strongly that a cabinet cannot continue in office if a majority of the Commons will not support it. Though for some years after Confederation practices were more flexible, if nowadays the House of Commons withdraws its confidence from the cabinet, one of two consequences must ensue; either the cabinet must be changed so that the Commons can obtain an executive to give it the leadership it will accept, or the Commons must itself be changed to provide the cabinet with the support it must have if it is to remain in office. One of two courses of action is thus ordinarily available following a cabinet's defeat: the resignation of the cabinet, or the dissolution of the House. The one gives the House a new cabinet, the other gives the cabinet a new House. The second alternative, of course, may not be decisive in the way expected. If the electorate chooses a House that will support the cabinet, harmony has once more been restored. If, however, the electorate elects a majority of members opposed to the prime minister who advised the dissolution, the result would be a new administration in which the House would have confidence. A government defeated at the polls is not obliged to resign until it meets defeat at the hands of the House, although there is a well-established body of precedents favouring immediate resignation under such circumstances. If the result of the election is such that there is any doubt of what the outcome will be when the House assembles, then the cabinet is justified in awaiting the verdict of the people's representatives. Thus when the 1925 election deprived the Liberal government of a majority of seats and gave a larger number (though not a majority) to the

Conservatives, the former was entitled to stay in office until the House had cleared up the ambiguous situation. In 1957, none the less, another Liberal cabinet in an analogous situation resigned promptly after an election in which no party won a majority; and in 1962 a Conservative cabinet with minority support remained in office until two weeks after the election of 8 April 1963, when, again failing to get a majority, it resigned without meeting the House.

As was pointed out earlier, the House's withdrawal of confidence is not necessarily proved by a single defeat of a government measure. The most recent proposals for reform of the Commons recommended more formal recognition of the circumstances under which MPs would be freer to vote against a cabinet without running the risk, in effect, of really defeating it, but the House standing orders were not amended to include provisions for more 'free votes.'

Even if they had been, the cohesion within political organizations means that there will be little danger of cabinets rising and falling every few weeks or months, for in Canada the prime minister, the cabinet, and the majority supporting them generally belong to the same party. As was mentioned earlier, that is not always the case, and so-called minority governments, in which the executive must draw support from at least one other group, are not rare: sometimes such cabinets have short lives, as in 1925–6, 1957–8, 1962–3, 1972–4, and 1979–80, and sometimes long, as in 1921–5 and 1963–8. Even executives drawn from a majority party are not immune; disgruntled MPs from a governing party need not vote against their leaders to topple them. For example, Macdonald won the election of 1872 by 103 seats to 97, but abstentions led to his departure from office in 1873.

Coalition governments, based on a union of two or more parties, have not been uncommon in the provinces, but at the federal level Canada has seen only two examples, both brought about by issues considered of greater importance than party differences. Confederation was brought about by a coalition and, while the bulk of the coalescing took place before 1867, some of its results, such as the initial membership of the Senate, were projected into the Confederation period. A post-Confederation case of coalition occurred in 1917, when Borden's Conservatives were joined by many Liberals to form the Union government in the pursuit of the war effort. That coalition worked smoothly at first, and Borden repeatedly paid tribute to the sincere and cordial co-operation he received from those Liberal ministers who had been his former opponents, although some of Sir Robert's party found the novel association most distasteful. But the war had scarcely been concluded when disintegration set in, and the Liberal supporters of the government began gradually to slip back to their former allegiance. In a few months' time the strain was increased when the Liberals held their convention to choose a new leader, and a little later the illness of Borden forced his resignation as prime minister. The Unionists tried repeatedly to avert the collapse of the coalition, but to little avail. The necessity for compromise and the spirit of conciliation had vanished and the Liberals, who appeared to know what they were about, were returned to power in 1921.[3]

RESPONSIBILITIES

Whatever the basis of their support, the members of the Canadian cabinet acknowledge three separate and distinct responsibilities: a responsibility, through the governor general, to the monarch, which is now rarely invoked; a responsibility to the prime minister and to one another, which produces what is called the 'solidarity' of the cabinet; and a responsibility, both individual and collective, to the House of Commons. And beyond the Commons, of course, is the electorate.

Responsibility to the crown

The responsibility to the governor general is, of course, the survival of the original responsibility which the royal advisers owed to their principle and which, in Canada, was owing in the early days to the colonial governors. Its essence is stated in a constitutional provision already quoted: 'The Executive Government and Authority of and over Canada is hereby declared to continue and be vested in the Queen.' It is by virtue of this authority that the members of the cabinet become the advisers of the crown, the governor is entitled to be taken into the full confidence of the cabinet (which, in fact, rarely occurs), and the ministers act in the name of and for the crown. It was this relationship which the minister of finance had in mind in 1945 when he stated that 'the authority of the Government is not delegated by the House of Commons; the authority of the Government is received from the Crown.' The responsibility to the governor general is, it is true, largely inactive and is rarely invoked against the cabinet, because democratic controls have for the most part rendered it unnecessary. The Canadian House of Commons has taken upon itself the duty of ensuring that the cabinet follows virtuous paths, and this surveillance is normally quite sufficient and far preferable to scrutiny or punishment from any other source. But, as earlier pages have indicated, there may be certain contingencies which would make it desirable for the governor to intervene and invoke the latent responsibility to the head of the state. To that degree and only to that degree can the responsibility to the governor be invoked as an active or punitive measure. The fact remains that constitutionally the cabinet must have the confidence of the governor, just as it does the confidence of the Commons.

Responsibility to the prime minister

The members of the cabinet are responsible to one another, and particularly to the prime minister. It is an essential cabinet convention – dictated by convenience, the need for a united policy, and fear of the opposition – that all members must openly agree on all important public questions, and apparent contradictions among ministers must be explained away. Ministers can and do fight in private, but in public they stand as one so convincingly that journalists can score a coup by discovering (or perhaps inventing) evidence of differences in the cabinet. It follows that all members of a cabinet must consider the views of one another in making any important announcement or in taking a decision that might be considered as involving government policy, and this leads in practice to prior consultation and discussion in cabinet, or, at least, with the prime minister. This done, if the minister secures agreement on his proposal, the cabinet will support it to a man; failing such agreement, the dissenting member must acquiesce in the rejection of his ideas or tender his resignation. A prime minister can demand that a dissenting minister depart, as Laurier did in 1902 when rejecting Israel Tarte's advocacy of a higher tariff than the cabinet favoured; and King in 1944 performed the unusual feat of getting rid of two ministers, one for favouring conscription for overseas service and one for opposing it.[4]

Responsibility to the House of Commons
The responsibility of the cabinet to the House of Commons has been the key to the control of the executive power in Canada as in Britain. The powers of the crown have remained for the most part intact or have even been increased, but the exercise of those powers has come under the cabinet and this body in turn under the general scrutiny of Parliament. This is the central fact of parliamentary democracy; for it is this practice which keeps the system both efficient and constantly amenable to popular control. Like many another central fact in political life, this one has been changing. The traditional view is that the minister at the head of every department is responsible for everything that is done within that department, and inasmuch as he will expect praise or assume blame for all the acts of his subordinates, he must have the final word in any important decision that is taken. Only if the minister can clearly demonstrate his initial ignorance of the offending act and convince the House of the prompt and thorough manner in which he has attempted to remedy the abuse can he hope to be absolved from at least opposition censure. Even when that theory was in full flower, if a majority of the Commons supported a cabinet in a clear evasion of responsibility, as is not unknown, neither the opposition nor the electorate has an effective instrument to enforce responsibility before the next election.

With the enormous growth in government activities in recent decades, another view of ministerial responsibility has appeared which holds, at its simplest, that modern government is too complex for a minister to be held responsible for every minute detail under his jurisdiction. Many members of the cabinet, with headquarters in Ottawa, none the less preside over departments with branches from coast to coast, and the ministers, if they are to concentrate on their main jobs, cannot possibly be kept informed about the activities of every coastguard sailor or every employee in district taxation offices. And if a minister cannot know, how can he in any realistic sense be responsible? Besides, a whole second public service, housed in crown corporations and other non-departmental agencies, has been created, many of its sections deliberately set up to remove them from political control. While crown corporations usually have a minister who speaks for them in Parliament, no single minister is usually considered responsible for their activities; in the departments themselves responsibility can no longer mean what it did when each department had only a few employees. (The Department of Labour, which had 10 employees at its creation in 1901, and only 303 in 1940, had reached 10,731 by 1959; yet throughout its history it has had one minister at its head.) The general theory that ministers are responsible still thrives, although the theory of what responsibility means is changing. It can take new and sudden departures. For instance, if a confidential cabinet document is leaked and the culprit is discovered, who should leave – the employee who leaked it, or the minister (or the cabinet) whose security was so poor that the leak happened in the first place? There are no longer clear and simple rules, and each individual case involving ministerial or cabinet responsibility is settled according to its own circumstances, which usually include the government's majority in the Commons.

Another element in cabinet solidarity is the custom that the entire cabinet will normally accept responsibility for the acts of any of its members, so that the censure of one will become the censure of all. The members of a cabinet therefore resign office simultaneously. It is not impossible, however, for the House to censure one member or to allow a cabinet to throw an offending minister to the wolves, and to accept such drastic action as offering sufficient amends for wrong-doing, provided, of course, the cabinet clearly does not countenance the objectionable act and that the purge is made with promptitude and without equivocation. Such charity cannot be expected as a matter of course, and again it must depend both on the mitigating circumstances and on the way in which the House chooses to regard the whole incident.

CABINET-MAKING

The most notable characteristic of the Canadian cabinet is the representative nature of its membership. The cabinet is to a unique degree the grand co-ordinating body for the divergent provincial, sectional, religious, racial, and other interests throughout the nation, and the same characteristics are now extended to committees of the cabinet. Cabinets in other countries frequently exhibit similar tendencies, but not over as wide a field or in compliance with the same strict requirements. The inevitable consequence is that the choice of the prime minister is seriously restricted and he is often compelled to push merit to one side in making some of his selections. Cabinet positions will undoubtedly be available for the ablest of the government's supporters, but the balance may be filled from the ranks of the party for reasons as varied as they are unconnected with parliamentary and administrative efficiency. Paul Bilkey, a sympathetic observer of the formation of the Borden cabinet, recorded his reflections thus:

Those who have not witnessed the making of a Government have reason to be happier than those who have. It is a thoroughly unpleasant and discreditable business in which merit is disregarded, loyal service is without value, influence is the most important factor and geography and religion are important supplementary considerations.

The Borden Ministry was composed under standard conditions and was not, therefore, nearly as able, as honest, or as industrious an administrative aggregation as could have been had from the material available. Industrial and other magnates were present during the process of gestation, not, of course, in the public interest but in their own, which was quite a different thing. There were some broken hearts – in one instance, literally. In others, philosophy came to the rescue, but the pills were large and the swallowing was bitter.[5]

Those words are mirrored in other reminiscences by journalists and politicians about other cabinets, and there is no sign that drawing a cabinet of 40 mainly from a Commons of nearly 300 MPs is any easier than finding 20 among 220 or so. Brian Mulroney, forming the largest cabinet in Canadian history in 1984, had at least the advantage of having supporters in every province and territory; for the first requisite in cabinet-building is that every area must, if possible, have a minister, a rule accepted by Macdonald in 1867. There have had to be exceptions (Prince Edward Island, for example, has had no minister for years at a time), for as Canada grew not all victorious political parties always had MPs in every region; but the general rule of broad representation has never been rejected. The cabinet has, in fact, taken over the allotted role of the Senate as the protector of the rights of the provinces and it has done an incomparably better job. Any province today would relinquish all its senators without the slightest compunction if by so doing it could double its representation in the cabinet.

The importance of provincial representation, which is now a rigid convention of the constitution, has been illustrated many times, sometimes with revealing by-products. At the start, two of Macdonald's ablest supporters were not on his list of ministers, one because he would have made one Irish Catholic too many, the other because other politicians from his province had more appealing claims on the prime minister. As has been mentioned, a Conservative leader short of MPs from Quebec, and a Liberal similarly situated in the west, have turned to the Senate for regional ministers. Alberta twice gave King trouble. Its citizens elected no Liberals in 1921; but King, after some inquiry, found an available Liberal ex-premier of the province and got a seat for him – in Quebec. In 1935 Alberta elected only one Liberal, who had no great claims on King; he became a minister without portfolio.

The convention that each province should have at least one representative in the cabinet makes another convention almost mandatory, namely, that the large provinces must each be given more than one representative. 'Each of the Maritime Provinces having received representatives,' Macdonald had explained in 1868, 'the least that could be given to Quebec, with a due regard to population, was four, while the least that could be given to Ontario, the largest Province of the Confederation, was five.' The actual pattern followed by successive prime ministers in forming their cabinets has naturally varied with their individual judgments and their various strengths in the provinces, but the rule enunciated by Macdonald has never been abandoned. Ontario's quota of ministers has been as low as three, but never two; and Quebec has been down to two, but never one. At the same time, the smaller provinces have found that their right to a minimum of one has tended also to become a maximum. There are enough exceptions to make generalizations difficult, and the exceptions are also due to special circumstances. For example, Saskatchewan, with seventeen MPs, had two Conservative ministers after 1957, but one was the prime minister and the other a veteran provincial leader of the party, a combination which had also existed in the Liberals before 1945, when the province had twenty-one seats. In the 1957 case, interestingly enough, the two ministers comprised two-thirds of the seats won by the party. The general rule that cabinet representation is related to a province's size, and the victorious party's strength in it, is still accepted as a standard followed by prime ministers.

Numbers alone do not tell the whole story. Quebec adds another element, for Quebec's representation in the cabinet has to be divided between French- and English-speaking members, with the former outnumbering the latter; thus (although again there is no set rule), French-speaking Roman Catholics have generally held from three to six or more posts, with the English-speaking Protestants holding fewer, and occasionally none. Ontario obviously cannot be outdone, so that province may commonly expect to have a more or less guaranteed minimum number of ministers that bears some relation to the total allocated to Quebec, although here, as with Quebec, the total number of government supporters from the province in the House is an important factor. Within these two provinces divergent loyalties and interests have given this representation a local territorial basis as well. Thus the French-speaking constituencies in Quebec have tended to fall into two groups, one centring on Quebec, the other on Montreal, while the English-speaking constituencies (formerly most of the Eastern Townships) have historically formed another unit. (It is too soon to tell whether Mulroney's strength in Quebec, and his obvious hope to make of the province a Conservative fortress, will alter these informal arrangements.) Ontario has not been so clearly divided, although both northern and western Ontario have claims that are usually recognized; and in the past Toronto has been know to complain because its special views have had no advocate in the cabinet councils, while both the Pearson and Trudeau cabinets were criticized for being top-heavy with urban members.

Provincial representation has frequently been further elaborated in that a few portfolios, for prolonged periods, have been recognized as the special preserve of certain areas. The Department of the Interior was early headed by an Ontario member most of the time; but as western Canada developed, the portfolio drifted in the direction of the major interest. Agriculture (with one break occasioned by a shortage of personnel) went to the prairie provinces for much of the department's history. For many years there was a tendency to give the French Canadians (usually from Quebec) either Public Works or the Post Office and to choose the minister of justice from Quebec. In recent years, however, prime ministers have shown more flexibility in the allotment of portfolios, the most significant development probably being the assignment to Quebec of more economic portfolios. The mere names of those portfolios above reveal another element worth noting: Interior is now gone, Fisheries has become Fisheries and Oceans, and the Post Office is no longer a department but a crown corporation.

The federal character of the cabinet is emphasized further in the ways in which ministers discharge their functions as provincial representatives. Each minister is constantly concerned with the widely scattered interests of his special province and he acts, and is supposed to act, as its spokesman, advocate, dispenser of patronage, and possibly electoral organizer.[6] In cabinet councils he will be expected to advise, not only on matters within his particular department, but also on any topic whenever it concerns his province; and his opinion, by virtue of superior knowledge of that locality, will merit exceptional consideration. An interesting illustration occurred in 1947 when the Dominion government held up its proposal for Newfoundland's entry in the federation until there was a New Brunswick representative in the cabinet. St Laurent, soon to be prime minister, said that the admission of the tenth province was an issue of particular importance to the maritimes, adding revealingly: 'no final decision will be attempted by an incomplete cabinet.'[7]

When a provincial government is controlled by the same political party as that in power in Ottawa, the province will commonly expect its federal cabinet minister to use his good offices to promote the requests the provincial government may make. Consultations and negotiations will proceed through the normal channels of the appropriate federal and provincial departments, but these will often be supplemented by the more informal proceedings through the province's representative in the cabinet. The latter may, indeed, show some resentment if the province ignores him and approaches another minister for intervention on behalf of the area which he feels to be peculiarly his own. Appointments in a particular province (when not made by the Public Service Commission) are thus made on the formal recommendation of the minister in whose department the office lies, but he will normally consult the minister representing the province concerned before making his recommendation. An unusual variation on this pattern occurred in Saskatchewan in 1935–45 when the province's senior minister was the prime minister, Mackenzie King, who on both counts would make final decisions; but the junior minister, who knew provincial politics intimately, was James Gardiner, who had previously served two decades in the provincial legislature as member, minister, premier, and leader of the opposition.[8] Some elements of federal-provincial affairs became more formalized with the creation of a cabinet secretariat for federal-provincial relations in 1974, but the political element remains; and will.

The possibilities of sectionalism in the cabinet have not been exhausted by giving special representation to provincial interests alone. Ethnic origins and relation are also carefully considered, although they are to some degree taken into account in determining the provincial quota. The majority of French Canadians from Quebec are always Roman Catholic, the English Canadians often Protestant. But almost invariably the cabinet will contain an Irish Roman Catholic, usually from outside Quebec, and the Acadian French or the French-speaking from Ontario or the west may also be given a special representative. Brian Mulroney added new weights to these delicate balances in 1984 by *being* an Irish Catholic from Quebec, as well as his party's first successful leader from the province. Formal recognition of the leading Protestant denominations, while still considered sometimes, is not as important as it used to be. It is unlikely that any modern prime minister will show the pride with which Alexander Mackenzie drew attention to his cabinet of 1873–8 with its complement of five Catholics, three Anglicans, three Presbyterians, two Methodists, one Congregationalist, and one Baptist.

Many other interests and claims go into cabinet-making. John Diefenbaker was the first prime minister to choose a minister of Ukrainian descent, and he also selected the first female minister, who served in one of the lesser portfolios. The Mulroney cabinet of 1984, reflecting, as the cabinet often does, major changes in the mood of the electorate, included six women, some in major portfolios. The recognition of women's claims to cabinet posts is not only here to stay, but will undoubtedly grow more important if more local constituency associations nominate women as candidates, a crucial factor in this sort of development. In the past other more transient interests, such as the Orange Lodge, have demanded consideration, while dominant economic groups such as farmers, financiers, unionized workers, and businessmen will always be in a prime minister's mind as he ponders his cabinet. Mulroney's cabinet was unique apart from its wider recognition of women MPs: political parties have been choosing fewer lawyers as candidates since the 1960s, and the Conservative ministry of 1984, for the first time in many decades, had only one-quarter of its members drawn from law. Usually lawyers comprise half or more of the ministers but, as John Courtney has shown, their place seems to have been taken at least temporarily by that category of citizen somewhat misleadingly known as 'small businessmen.'[9] Ex-cabinet ministers, if they are still around in Parliament, constitute another group with claims to re-appointment, and it is significant that while Mulroney's 'shadow cabinet' of thirty-three MPs prior to the election of 1984 contained twenty survivors of Joe Clark's short-lived government of 1979–80, there were more new faces in the cabinet actually formed.

The roster of demands is thus a long one, and the pressure to increase the size of the cabinet in order to meet all these demands is tremendous. The number of prizes has been appreciably increased in recent years by the growth in size of the cabinet, and by the institution of parliamentary secretaryships, for these have opened up new possibilities in meeting demands for sectional representation. The temptation to turn the assistantships to good advantage and produce the finer shades of sectional representation has in fact proved irresistible, and a modern roster of parliamentary assistants often reads like a miniature cabinet. It is easy, of course, to decry the practice of forming a cabinet in the Canadian way, for excellent men do get passed over and mediocrities take their places, and every cabinet within living memory has contained examples which prove only too well the validity of the argument. But some consideration must be given to the divergent views and interests which are an inescapable condition of such a large and varied country, and ethnic, religious, and cultural differences add to the difficulty. A practice that selects cabinet ministers even partly on grounds of religious beliefs may seem generally reprehensible (and possibly, if a case could ever be proved, a violation of the Charter of Rights); but from a wider aspect, it is simply an acknowledgment of the fact that men's confidence in one another is based in part at least upon qualities of this kind, and that efficient government in its broadest sense is unobtainable if these human limitations are ignored. In short, a regrettable practice may have to be accepted because the alternative will be even worse. The real problem here is one of degree: the cabinet must be constructed with an eye to the representative character of its members, but these factors cannot be permitted to displace all the highest qualities of mind and character which a cabinet must contain if it is to function effectively.

Conflicting interests which are so clearly defined might appear to be a shaky foundation on which to build cabinet unity and a common policy. But it would be wrong to underestimate what cabinet ministers share: the intangible ties of party membership, which may invoke a long history of past struggles, shared antipathies, similar habits of thought, loyalty to the party leader, the desire to defeat the enemy at all costs and the allied determination to stay in office. These are reinforced by the conventional insistence on the solidarity of the cabinet in public and the joint responsibility of its members in Parliament. Two other characteristics of the cabinet also assist this unifying process: the secrecy of its deliberations and the pre-eminence of the prime minister.

SECRECY

The secrecy considered here is not peculiar to cabinet government, although for a cabinet, secrecy has particular implications. Few delicate negotiations of any kind can be carried on entirely in public, whether they concern relations between sovereign countries, or between a corporation and its unionized employees, or among academics considering the promotion or hiring of other academics. Cabinet secrecy is an essential element in the life of a government, requiring ministers in public to be loyal to each other and to their chief; their only alternative, if they cannot do that, is to leave. The same alternative faces a growing number of public servants who, with the growth in the cabinet's internal organization made necessary by the increasing burdens on ministers, have had to be admitted to proceedings formerly known only to ministers. At the same time, a general conviction that secrecy is indispensable can lead to keeping secret, facts and documents whose disclosure would in fact cause no harm, and in several countries in recent years there has been pressure to enact access to information laws through the application of which any citizen, including journalists and members of the opposition, can obtain copies of material that would otherwise not be available. In Canada Donald C. Rowat has given an academic lead to the pressure for access laws, and in 1984–5 the arguments in their favour received a rather bizarre boost when the auditor general found it necessary to sue the government for access to documents he considered important to the discharge of his lawful duties.[10] At the time of writing his appeal has been turned down by the Federal Court, but the Supreme Court has yet to render what could be a momentous decision. How far access to public documents is compatible with the demands of cabinet government remains to be seen, but there seems little doubt that public documents will become increasingly available throughout governments in Canada. There is no doubt either that total access to all information will never be possible as long as cabinet government survives.

The rule of cabinet secrecy is customarily somewhat relaxed on those occasions when a minister's resignation makes it desirable that the reasons for his disagreement with his colleagues should be made known, and at such times the permission of the governor general (through the prime minister) is first obtained. In any event, if a debate develops on the minister's explanation, the general tenor of the discussions in council is almost inevitably revealed. In November 1944, for example, the disclosures in regard to the essential facts preceding the resignation of J.L. Ralston were so complete that he was led to remark in the House that 'in this debate and especially in the Prime Minister's speech the other night the doors of the Privy Council have been pretty well opened, and there is not very much that has taken place there, which one recollects, that has not been revealed to the House and to the public.'

THE PRIME MINISTER

The pre-eminence of the prime minister was cited early in this chapter and the chapter will repeat, for emphasis, some points already made: it is hardly possible to exaggerate the importance of the prime minister in a government like Canada's. It is often said that a prime minister is the first among equals, but that is untrue because he has no equals. The idea does contain some truth; it calls attention to one important aspect of this relationship, namely, that the other ministers are the colleagues of their chief and not his obedient and unquestioning subordinates. Their position bears little resemblance to that of the members of the federal cabinet in the United States, whom the president may appoint or dismiss, instruct or forbid, consult or ignore, as he may see fit and without any great fear of the consequences. A prime minister who tried to issue orders to his ministers or interfere persistently in their departmental work might find that before long he was out of office; for if at any time the ministers chose to rebel, their combined influence in the party and in the House could, and in all likelihood would, bring about his speedy downfall. Seven ministers did rebel against Prime Minister Bowell in 1896, and he had to agree to their conditions. A smaller and less spectacular revolt played a part in Diefenbaker's defeat in the Commons in January 1963. All members of the cabinet acknowledge the leadership of the prime minister, and will usually bow to his decisions, but they can never completely surrender their individual judgment or responsibility. Sir Winston Churchill, in *Their Finest Hour*, dramatically illuminated a prime minister's position:

Power in a national crisis, when a man believes he knows what orders should be given, is a blessing. In any sphere of action there can be no comparison between the positions of number one and number two, three or four. The duties and the problems of all persons other than number one are quite different and in many ways more difficult. It is always a misfortune when number two or three has to initiate a dominant plan or policy. He has to consider not only the merits of the policy, but the mind of his chief; not only what to advise, but what it is proper for him in his station to advise; not only what to do, but how to get it agreed, and how to get it done. Moreover, number two or three will have to reckon with numbers four, five and six, or may be some bright outsider, number twenty. Ambition, not so much for vulgar ends, but for fame, glints in every mind. There are always several points of view which may be right, and many which are plausible ...

At the top there are great simplifications. An accepted leader has only to be sure of what it is best to do, or at least to have made up his mind about it. The loyalties which centre upon number one are enormous. If he trips he must be sustained. If he makes mistakes, they must be covered. It he sleeps, he must not be wantonly disturbed. If he is no good he must be pole-axed. But this last extreme process cannot be carried out every day; and certainly not in the days just after he has been chosen.

The powers of the prime minister spring from his position of primacy in the government reinforced by his leadership of the majority party, which usually owes its majority to his leadership during the last election. To these must be added the extensive legal authority of Parliament which in large measure he indirectly controls. He is the directing force in both cabinet and Parliament, and he thus presides over the one and guides the deliberations of the other. He determines the cabinet's agenda and is the major influence in helping it arrive at decisions; he leads the Commons, answers many of its questions, with its consent apportions its time, and submits the measures of his government for its approval. He must be consulted on important decisions by all cabinet ministers and he can if necessary advise the governor to dismiss a minister. He serves as the one great co-ordinator of executive policies. In addition to his normal duties, he has a special interest in and responsibility for foreign affairs.

The prime minister is the link between governor general and cabinet, and is in a special sense an adviser to the former. He recommends all important appointments to the Privy Council. He also has the responsibility for advising the governor when Parliament should be convened and when it should be dissolved – a power that adds greatly to his strength, not only in the House of Commons, but in the cabinet as well. Like some other powers, the power to advise dissolution may appear to lie dormant for prolonged periods, the prime minister not having to threaten to use it precisely because his colleagues all know it is there; and of course its strength dwindles as the time approaches when another election has to be held because the constitution says so.

In many matters the prime minister is able to obtain substantial aid from the members of his cabinet, and this is particularly true when a decision touches upon their respective departments or the special interest or area which they individually represent and on which they speak with exceptional authority. The successful prime minister is one who can merge the many diverse talents and interests of his cabinet so that they form a united team, working in good spirit for the benefit of all. Party ties and association will not only create trust and confidence, they will also make it easier for the members of the cabinet to criticize freely and yet maintain their friendly relations intact. When the goodwill breaks down and the tension mounts, or when a dispute between ministers of departments develops, the prime minister is usually the diplomat who is able by resorting to persuasion, threats, appeals to party and personal loyalty, to bring about reconciliations and keep the cabinet together. As Mackenzie King's diaries reveal, he frequently reinforced his own leadership by the ingenious device of offering to abandon it.

The degree to which the prime minister will use his colleagues to advise and assist him will depend on many factors, the chief of which used to be purely personal, now reinforced by changes in the cabinet's own organization. The personal attributes include ability and loyalty. In every cabinet there are likely to be ministers who cannot perform their own departmental duties effectively, or are of little use as consultants in the wider field of general government policy. Others may not have the full confidence of the prime minister or the respect and unreserved approval of their colleagues. Thus there usually arises within the cabinet a small group of four or five ministers who, because of ability of various kinds, exceptional local and sectional confidence, personal qualities or character, will be highly regarded by the prime minister and will be consulted by him on all matters of importance. Occasionally the prime minister may have a special colleague whose intimacy makes him a friend and almost a partner in the office. Ernest Lapointe, for example, was for many years a great friend and counsellor to King, and there can be no doubt that King derived no small assistance, particularly in all matters involving French Canada, from his colleague; St Laurent, a French-Canadian prime minister, similarly relied heavily on his redoubtable colleague from Ontario, C.D. Howe; Diefenbaker appeared to have a special colleague in Howard Green, and Pearson, for a time at least, in Walter Gordon. Trudeau at first appeared to be a loner, but as the consultations preceding the constitutional changes of 1982 developed, his confidence in Jean Chrétien also became apparent. Clark and Turner hardly had time to reveal their special allies and Mulroney has as yet made no conspicuous selection. Special relationships are not common (or not revealed if they are), for the position of prime minister does not encourage intimacies and friendships. These are apt to create jealousies and antagonisms and may also expose him to exploitation by selfish interests, so that he finds his greatest protection lies in partial seclusion and a withdrawal from many norman human relationships. He may, indeed, have closer contacts with a selected group of civil servants and members of his personal staff than with some of his political associates.

The prime minister may also be compelled to preserve his aloofness for a more selfish reason: to defend his own position against attack from within the cabinet. It is a rare prime minister who will be so sure of his invulnerability that he will be prepared to run the risk of developing the capacity and building up the reputation of other ministers to a point where they might become powerful enough to challenge his primacy. If such a threat should arise, the prime minister's powers and prestige in both party and government are usually so enormous that the would-be crown prince disappears from the political scene. The leader of the pack, so long as he maintains his vigour, will tolerate no rival, and he possesses both the will and the means to enforce his supremacy. Thus King, when he had persuaded J.L. Ralston to enter his cabinet in 1939, jubilantly confided to his diary: 'If I were designating tomorrow the man for Prime Minister, I would select Ralston without a moment's hesitation. Years ago, I felt the same way about him. He is the most unselfish man, I think, that I have met.' Yet when tomorrow came, and it appeared that in fact Ralston might be an acceptable leader to conscriptionist forces in the Liberal party, King felt very differently: 'The truth is he just wants to have his own way and is prepared to sacrifice me or the party to have it; justifying no doubt his conscience in that this is a war where men are being slain and that conscription is necessary for victory.' In the event, Ralston resigned, and King adopted his policy and stayed in office.[11]

The dominance of the prime minister in cabinet and Parliament inevitably accentuates his importance in the country as well, although some of the ministers will have a local or restricted prestige that within a smaller sphere may be the equal of his own. The position and person of a prime minister are so eagerly dramatized by press, platform, television, and radio that he has difficulty in securing his personal privacy. His merits are extolled and exaggerated by his friends, his faults are described and exaggerated by his enemies. In an election campaign, the issues will be in large measure formulated and selected by the party leaders, and it is therefore the prime minister who will determine the emphasis to be given to the different policies of the government, although in this he must clearly respect the opinion of the party. Thus while Bennett did not hesitate on the eve of an election to announce a new and radical reform program, a large section of his party did not approve of it, and were thus forced to choose between an acceptance of the platform and the repudiation of the prime minister – an unhappy dilemma that certainly did not improve the party's position in the election which followed. Mackenzie King on a number of occasions announced that, while he had accepted the party platform, he nevertheless regarded it as no more than a statement of policy of a very general kind which he would implement at his own discretion. Diefenbaker campaigned in part in 1962, not on the basis of his adherence to his party's platform, but the promises he had himself made and kept.

The qualities of leadership which any prime minister worthy of the name is bound to possess and the opportunities for leadership which are an inescapable accompaniment of the office thus combine to exert a steady pressure toward autocratic methods and decisions. The successful prime minister is one who can be both the unchallenged master of his administration and yet at the same time avoid the faults and dangers of absolutism. For he must always strive to have it both ways. Even a casual student of the lives of Macdonald, Laurier, Borden, and King cannot fail to be impressed with the rigorous authority that frequently marked their political relations; and when some cabinet discord or internal dispute gave an occasion for action, firm and even ruthless decision was the unfailing response. The development of autocratic characteristics in the prime minister is, however, always restrained by at least two major checks. He must retain the confidence of his party, and the latter's chief and most reliable spokesmen are usually the cabinet; and given the searching eye of the television camera, he cannot *appear* too often to be autocratic. (Journalists of the Trudeau era often wrote of the prime minister's arrogance and single-mindedness, but he frequently appeared on the screen to be ingratiating and good-humoured.) Ministers, while generally acquiescent, may feel it necessary to oppose the prime minister if they believe that he has gone too far, or is damaging their own careers by his public performances. They are bound to keep him in touch with opinion in their own regions, particularly if that opinion is out of step with the endless polls that reach a modern leader. They are in close contact with the party supporters in Parliament and throughout the nation; their political lives, like his, are forfeit if wrong decisions are taken, and they dare not permit unwelcome proposals to pass unchallenged. There is, moreover, the potent sanction that always lies behind all their representations, protests, and expressions of opinion – that in the last resort they can not only criticize but dethrone him.

It is here that any parallel between the democratic ruler and his totalitarian counterpart breaks down. The prime minister may have enormous powers, but the basic conditions under which he governs compel him to wield his authority strictly on sufferance. He moves in an atmosphere of friendliness, tolerance, and suspended judgment in his own party, in one of constant criticism, suspicion, and outspoken condemnation elsewhere. His retention of office is thus continually under attack; he can never ignore incipient dissatisfaction and revolt among his own supporters, and he must soothe the ruffled feelings and anticipate the indignant outbreaks before they reach the acute stage. He can never lose sight of the paramount necessity of retaining the confidence of the House and, behind the House, of the electorate. No matter how lofty his position, he can always be defeated and displaced. The war for political supremacy is unending, and a victorious engagement today may be speedily followed by disastrous defeat tomorrow, as the confident Liberal party of 1956 discovered in 1957–8, or the Conservatives of 1958, with the largest majority in Canadian history until then, discovered in 1962–3. The most any prime minister can hope for is a temporary success, which will give him time and opportunity to consolidate his position and prepare his defence for the next encounter.

11
The cabinet: functions

Nothing has impressed me so much in the course of my inquiry as the almost intolerable burden which the present system of transacting business imposes on Ministers themselves. Sir George Murray, *Report on the Public Service of Canada*

A cabinet's majority in the House of Commons can hardly be expected to include a quota of people whose personal expertise in agriculture, labour, or fisheries can be matched up with portfolios named Agriculture, Labour, and Fisheries; nor should it. It is a popular misconception in Canada, and one which surfaces frequently, that a political head of a department should be an expert in the subject-matter of his portfolio, when what is really needed is an expert who can explain and defend his department's work in Parliament or outside, see that the work is in fact in the hands of responsible professionals, and hold his own on their behalf with his cabinet colleagues. A modern department is in any event so large and varied that no single individual could possibly be an expert in all its work. A minister need no more be an expert in subject-matter than the president of an automobile factory needs to know how to manufacture and fit together every part of a car, or a university president needs to be able to teach every course in the calendar.

The ideal minister is an intelligent, alert executive of unquestionable integrity, as aware of the democratic foundations of his position as he is of the ramifications of his portfolio. If he really is an expert (simultaneously an agriculturalist, say, and minister of agriculture), he may lack the very qualities most needed in a minister. Experts are indispensable, and they are often energetic and imaginative, both qualities desirable in a minister. But an expert's enthusiasm for his subject-matter may lead him to interfere in areas where his own specialty, though relevant, is of limited application; or where his own knowledge, because of the time he must give to his parliamentary and other political chores, may become rapidly out of date. Sometimes a minister may appear to have an expert's qualifications for his portfolio: James Gardiner, minister of agriculture for twenty-two years, was also a good farmer, but he was a canny enough politician to know that his abilities as a prairie grain grower did not necessarily extend to growing hay on the salt marshes of the maritimes, or to the products of Canada's fruit belts. It is true that lawyers are appointed to legal portfolios such as Justice or Solicitor General, but it is not their understanding of the law alone that is needed; lawyers are also appointed to many other portfolios, and most of Canada's prime ministers have been lawyers. One genuine exception to these generalizations is Lester Pearson, who served as an expert in External Affairs for two decades before he became its minister, and as its minister he earned the Nobel Peace Prize shortly before he was elected leader of the Liberal party.

A successful minister is indeed an expert, and what he is expert at is being a minister. A new prime minister, until he has developed some expertise himself in choosing ministers, will probably consult widely within his party over each individual selection, but the time at his disposal is limited. Undoubtedly the formation of every new cabinet includes a certain amount of hopeful guesswork on the part of the prime minister; but he can be cheered by the knowledge that if he guesses wrong the inadequate minister can be disposed of in a variety of ways, ranging from outright dismissal, through a shift to another portfolio where the offender may be able to do less harm, to a patronage appointment that removes the delinquent from the scene, to retirement because of ill health. (Ill health, in politics, often appears easy to arrange.) The turnover of ministers is in fact high, sometimes almost phenomenally so: in King's cabinet of 1935–48, thirty cabinet posts saw ninety-one occupants, most of them migrants travelling from portfolio to portfolio.

INTERNAL ORGANIZATION

It may seem odd to list its own organization as a function of the cabinet, but it could not discharge its other functions if it were not itself organized. It may seem odd, too, to record that for several decades after Confederation the cabinet was not organized; except for its remarkably casual meetings around a table, there was rarely an orderly agenda. It is true that the cabinet itself is a committee of the Privy Council, but even as a committee of a larger body the cabinet for decades gave little thought to its own structure. There were a number of understandable reasons for this. The cabinet was small, holding at twelve to fifteen portfolios until nearly the turn of the century. Government business was also small: the annual federal expenditure after Confederation would not now support a modest university campus or a small city. Government was also simple: before the invention of income tax necessitated by the demands of the First World War, Ottawa had few techniques for raising specific sums of money at will, but relied almost entirely on revenues based on the ebb and flow of commerce which yielded money from customs and excise taxes. Before the days of massive expenditures on defence, or social policies such as family allowances and old age pensions, successive governments in effect simply spent what came in.

Borden's cabinet of 1917–20 was the first to have more than twenty portfolios (which did not mean that there were always that many ministers), and the cabinet's size ranged in the twenties until relatively recently. Prime Minister King made a valiant effort after 1935 to reduce the cabinet, mainly by combining portfolios, producing in the process possibly the first 'super-ministry' in the Department of Transport, which assumed jurisdiction over the work of two former departments and a branch of a third. King managed for a time to hold his cabinet at sixteen, the rock-bottom size of a body that must represent Canada's major regions. But the pressures of the Second World War made a larger cabinet inevitable, and the cabinet has been swelling since. Diefenbaker had twenty-three ministers in 1960, Trudeau thirty in 1970, and Mulroney broke all records with forty in 1984.

It is a truism that there are few policies that can even be adequately discussed by thirty or forty opinionated people in one room, let alone settled by wise decisions, even assuming that the members had nothing else to do. Ministers have a great deal to do besides attend cabinet meetings, and prime ministers since at least King have devoted considerable thought to improving the cabinet's capacity to reach decisions while at the same time lifting some ministerial burdens. Given the immeasurable increase in the scope of government activities in this century, there is a special poignancy in the headnote to this chapter. It was written virtually before the modern Canadian political and administrative apparatus had been thought of, in 1912.

A prime minister who wishes to do something positive about the intolerable burdens on ministers has several options open to him.

1. He can permit the ministry to become substantially larger, while keeping the cabinet itself small. As already noted, Canada has on occasion had a few political executives who were not cabinet ministers. But any large use of ministers outside the cabinet has a built-in danger: some regions or major elements in Canadian society might feel slighted if their representative were to be assigned a junior rank.

2. He can keep the cabinet small but resort to a larger use of parliamentary secretaries. This has the same general disadvantage as 1, and also one of its own: parliamentary secretaries are not even ministers.

3. He can rely more heavily on non-political advisers, such as committees of public servants, and advisory groups drawn at least partly from the public. Such committees do exist, many of them valuable additions to the governmental structure, sometimes pointed to as admirable examples of how democracy works;

but their most obvious limitation lies in being 'non-political.' Cabinets are political, and it is political responsibility that is the essence of a properly functioning cabinet.

4. He can create more super-ministries which combine two or more governmental topics into one, as railways, ships, and airplanes were brought into Transport. There are other such departments (consider the staggering implications in a title like Energy, Mines and Resources, or Science and Technology), and more will undoubtedly be formed from time to time. Again there are limits; lightening the burdens of the whole cabinet by increasing those of particular ministers does not necessarily solve anything, particularly if the ministers holding the great umbrellas need extra support from ministers of state or ministers without portfolios assigned to the department. Making a cabinet smaller by creating conditions that may in the long run make it larger poses a kind of dilemma not uncommon in politics, but it can hardly be called a lasting solution.

5. He can invent more non-departmental agencies outside the direct jurisdiction of individual ministers. Recourse to these devices has in fact been had on a grand scale, and in 1979 the Royal Commission on Financial Management and Accountability counted nearly four hundred of them, varying in almost every imaginable way in size, importance, origins, and duties. Important though they are, the non-departmental crown agencies have also added to, without solving, some problems of cabinet organization.

6. Finally, he can organize the cabinet into a series of sub-cabinets, to which powers are delegated in ways that do not diminish the responsibility of the whole cabinet.

While all of the options listed here have at least been experimented with, the sixth is the most promising, and has produced a quiet revolution of its own in recent years.

The Canadian cabinet now has a formally recognized group of committees, almost all of them larger than Sir John A. Macdonald's whole cabinet in 1867, and all of them showing the same broad regional representation that he and his successors have found indispensable. How the present cabinet system evolved to its present status is a story in itself, but one whose broad outline can be shown summarily. The cabinet's internal organization has gone from almost none; through special arrangements necessitated by the two wars, when far-reaching decisions often had to be made more quickly than a whole cabinet could do it; then through ad hoc committees to standing committees; to standing committees with secretariats supplied by the Privy Council Office, which is also the secretariat to the full cabinet. The present committees are so clearly defined that they have taken on the kind of distinction that separates major portfolios from minor; the Priorities and Planning Committee, for example, has more prestige than the Security and

Intelligence Committee, though both are at this writing chaired by the prime minister. An individual minister's place in the pecking order can now be seen partly from the committee or committees he or she serves on.

That brief recapitulation of a complicated chronicle omits many significant highlights. It is important, for example, not only that the cabinet had to be temporarily altered to meet the exigencies of war, but was twice able to do so. In the war of 1914–18 the cabinet was divided into two committees of ten each, one on war, the other on reconstruction and development, with the prime minister as the common chairman. In 1939–45 a small inner war committee under the prime minister was struck. Neither of the war organizations survived the cessation of hostilities for long, but it was only six years after 1945 that another committee began to burgeon, the Treasury Board. The board, a committee of the Privy Council almost moribund for much of its history, grew in importance in the 1940s, and in 1951 emerged as a kind of war committee empowered to deal with almost anything except war. It made itself so useful that in 1966 its chairman, originally the minister of finance, received his own portfolio as president of the Treasury Board, charged with, among other things, 'general administrative policy ... financial management ... personnel management in the public service.' In 1973 one of Canada's most astute observers of government, J.E. Hodgetts, wrote in *The Canadian Public Service* of 'the brooding presence of this omnicompetent arm of central management.' In any political structure an omnicompetent management is likely to attract, if not create, rivals, and by 1979 there were four departments and agencies responsible for central management: the Treasury Board (which now has two secretariats of its own), the Department of Finance, the Privy Council Office, and the Public Service Commission.

The necessity for the modern shape of the cabinet, with its named and staffed committees, was first perceived clearly by Trudeau, who expressed concern over the roles of his ministers, so nearly overwhelmed by the flow of work with its accompaniment of massive flows of information. The structure he began was continued in form by Clark in 1979–80, though in that period the term 'inner cabinet' was often substituted for the Priorities and Planning Committee. When Trudeau regained power he returned to the development of the committee system, which Turner had little opportunity to alter in 1984. Mulroney's initial cabinet was organized into nine committees, the chief among them again Priorities and Planning, whose fifteen members included all the major ministers, seven of them from the west, three each from Ontario and Quebec, and two from the Atlantic provinces. The other main committees included the Treasury Board, of course, economic and regional development, social development, and government operations. (All five existed under Trudeau, three under the same names.) Other committees deal with security and intelligence, the public service, legislation and

House planning, and a special committee deals with necessary routine matters. In 1985 another committee of the Trudeau era, that on external affairs and defence, was revived.

Since so much about cabinet government is secret (not even the names of ministerial committee members were made public at first), it is not easy to assess the effectiveness of the cabinet's modern organization, but there is little doubt that the committees are becoming, if they have not already become, the decision-making branch of the government, with the cabinet acting in the main as the ratifier of committee recommendations. The 'spending committees' (the main five above) receive what are in effect mini-budgets. Following a practice that had been evolving before the Clark government gave them more formal status (and concurrently approved by the Royal Commission on Financial Management and Accountability), these mini-budgets put 'ceilings on expenditures for specified functions of government' and the committees are early charged with allocating monies to programs within the ceilings. The social development committee, for example, would be told that a total of x dollars was available for specified social policies, and would share the money among the policies up to the total. The total sums with their documentation are popularly called 'envelopes,' and each envelope contains what each committee can spend.

Or, more accurately, what recommendations on expenditure they can make; for the final responsibility is still the cabinet's. The PCO provides the secretariat for each committee (there are occasional exceptions, the most enduring being the Treasury Board, whose secretariats are in that department) and that means that the PCO has itself emerged as a major department of government. While once major only in the sense that it was the office which made and kept crucial records, the PCO is now seen as one of the nerve centres of the public service. It must be distinguished from the Prime Minister's Office. The PMO, which has also flowered in the past two decades, is the prime minister's political arm, whereas the PCO is permanent and administrative. Until at least John Diefenbaker the PMO was small, consisting of the prime minister's personal staff, augmented when necessary by people seconded from the staffs of various departments. Trudeau again took a particular initiative in attaching an advisory staff to his own office, and the PMO is now so well established as part of the upper establishment that journalists vie with each other in sniffing out evidence of rivalry between it and the PCO. If some observers are to be believed, the PMO and the PCO (though their respective functions are clearly different) are as competitive as teams in the CFL.[1]

There is no doubt some truth in such reports, for Ottawa has always had departments and ministers considered, at least by themselves, as some sort of elite. Wars put the defence and related departments into a special category. Finance has always been a dominant department, *the* dominant department until the Treasury

Board emerged in the 1950s as a powerful competitor for attention. External Affairs was for years set apart, partly because the prime minister himself kept the portfolio; but apart from that, External Affairs had an esprit de corps that exasperated some public servants in other departments, since it included a claim on the best young recruits passing civil service examinations. Significantly less about External Affairs has caught the media's attention since the emergence of the modern PMO and PCO.

It is too early to do more than indicate how the cabinet's committee structure will affect Ottawa's gossipy rivalries, but there can be no doubt that it will. Powerful committees not only mean new work for ministers, in reading vast amounts of documents pertinent to their committee work; they also mean different alignments of ministerial strength. James Gillies, an experienced minister himself, prepared a report for the Committee on the Reform of the Commons in 1984 in which he said that Trudeau, building on foundations laid by Pearson, decided that 'nothing could come to Cabinet, except under special circumstances, which was not first vetted through a cabinet committee. With this change, the era of the independent, strong all-powerful cabinet minister, and of the great influence of the traditional line-department deputy-minister ended.'

But cabinets are among the most elastic bodies conceivable, and any prime minister may some day decide he needs 'all-powerful cabinet ministers.' If he (or she) does, the cabinet structure will change again.

LEGISLATIVE FUNCTIONS OF THE CABINET

The relations between the cabinet and the House of Commons have already been described from the point of view of the Commons, and it would be idle to pretend that the same phenomena cannot also involve the point of view of the cabinet. The enormous influence of the cabinet over the Commons, through its actual powers, party and caucus ties, and the promise of patronage to come – perhaps ministerial rank itself – needs no further exposition here. However the cabinet is organized internally, these legislative powers remain.

1. The basic legislative power of the cabinet is the *general control* it exercises over the House of Commons at all times: for it is through this control that the other powers become effective. The prime minister, assisted by the cabinet, leads and directs the House in virtually everything it attempts to do. He writes the speech from the throne for the governor general to deliver to Parliament indicating the chief measures to be considered during the session. Until 1986 the House chose his nominee for its Speaker. The prime minister and the cabinet will determine the daily order of business and the time to be devoted to different matters, and the rules of the House are designed to facilitate the legislative work of the cabinet. This

program is, of course, always subject to interruptions by the opposition, which may avail itself of those opportunities for inquiry and criticism provided by the rules, although there is a tacit understanding that government affairs must have first claim on the time of Parliament and enjoy a general preference. The underlying control of the cabinet is perhaps best exemplified by its power to take a stand on any question and enforce that stand on its party followers.

2. The cabinet *dominates all legislation*. Public bills may be introduced by any member, but if he is of the ministry or a parliamentary assistant, they become 'government' bills. The great bulk of pending legislation falls in the category of government bills, which take up on average at least four-fifths of the time of the House.

The public bills fostered by private members do not often reach the statute books, though a patient member who annually brings up a pet project may live to see its merits finally recognized by the government. The time for the consideration of public bills of this type is limited, and the general practice is for the cabinet to remain indifferent or opposed to the public bills it has not fathered; it is usually indifferent, too, to private bills, those quite different measures which deal with the much more restricted interests of individuals and corporations. The public bills fostered by the cabinet are, in contrast, its chief concern. They represent the cabinet's legislative plans for the future and may vary from proposals of first-rate importance to those for the simplification of departmental procedures; from the most comprehensive reforms to those that are intimately related to and arise out of the day-by-day administration in the departments.

The cabinet is extremely sensitive about the general excellence of its own measures; and while it may at times consider and even accept suggested amendments, the overwhelming tendency is to refuse to make any important revisions in the bill as originally introduced. Governments, like other mortals, hate to admit they are wrong, and it is not hard to believe that a government that continually admitted to error would have a difficult time in the next election. Even a backing down, therefore, is likely to be accompanied by a face-saving explanation. But governments do back down: in 1985 the Mulroney cabinet abandoned a budgetary proposal to cease allowing old age pensions to be tied to the cost-of-living index; in 1969 the Liberals altered the original draft of the Official Languages Act. In both these instances, revealingly, strong opposition came from outside Parliament, and in the 1969 instance the opposition parties in the House were actually on the government's side.

3. The cabinet *controls all financial legislation*. The cabinet, by constitutional decree, custom, and the rules of the House, must introduce and sponsor all measures to spend or to raise money; and as any proposed amendment which would endeavour to diminish a tax or an expenditure contrary to the cabinet's

wishes would almost certainly be treated as a vote of lack of confidence, its control over finance is not likely to be seriously threatened. Admittedly this places enormous powers in the hands of a very small group, even though these powers will be exercised under constant scrutiny and criticism. The system has, however, undoubted advantages. The cabinet is in the best position to judge the purposes to which public money should be directed as well as the productivity and incidence of possible measures of taxation, and the fact that those who spend the funds are likewise charged with the task of devising ways and means to raise them places a restraint on expenditure whose mere existence may come as a surprise to some.

4. The cabinet, acting as the governor-in-council, *enacts subordinate legislation* under the authority delegated to it by acts of the Canadian Parliament. Its legislative output may be known as minutes or orders-in-council, the distinction being largely one of form and apparently of little consequence. The subject-matter of this delegated legislation may range from questions of purely departmental routine to those of first-rate importance with far-reaching consequences, from the approval of a contract or the amendment of a minor regulation to the establishment of a nation-wide system of price control in time of war.

The number of these orders and minutes is very large even in ordinary times, while in time of war they naturally increase greatly with the additional cabinet responsibilities and the need for immediate executive decision and action. Thus from 25 August 1939 to 2 September 1945, the governor-in-council disposed of 92,350 items of business, a tremendous total, although not so impressive as it appears at first glance. A very large part of these orders and minutes were concerned with routine matters, and not more than 4 or 5 per cent of the total represented action which was legislative in any real sense of the term. Even so, the numbers give a good idea of the cabinet's enormously important function in supplementing the legislative activity of Parliament.

From time to time some MPs and outside observers become exercised over a practice by which Parliament lays down in legislation little more than general principles, within which the cabinet or a minister (or a crown agency, discussed in a later chapter) is empowered to apply the principles in detail through making orders. Indeed, the overseeing of delegated legislation, like improving the authority of MPs and parliamentary committees, or the reform of the Senate, is a recurring topic of discussion. Nobody, in fact, has yet produced a better technique for adapting principles of law-making to the detailed complexity of the modern state, and parliamentary procedures accept that. The problem remains of keeping everybody, including MPs, informed, and trying to ensure that the delegated powers are not abused.

5. The cabinet still has, on paper at least, a *negative authority in the provincial field* which was used sporadically in the past, usually against smaller and

unfriendly provincial governments. Any act of a provincial legislature, within a year of its receipt in Ottawa, can be disallowed by order-in-council. The federal executive may also be called upon to give or refuse its consent to a provincial bill which the lieutenant-governor of the province has not signed but has 'reserved' for its consideration. For one government to have the power to disallow an act emanating from another legislature may seem an eccentric provision in a constitution, but it must be remembered that in 1867 Canada was a colony of Great Britain, and the imperial cabinet had similar powers over Canada itself; it seemed ordinary common sense to give Canada's national government the same powers of the legislatures of the provinces. The proposed Constitutional Amendment Bill of 1978 would have eliminated the powers of disallowance and reservation (the British power over Canada, unused after 1873, disappeared in 1926), but it was not proceeded with, and the powers remain. One might have expected them to be a topic of discussion in the years preceding the constitutional additions of 1982, and for a period they were. But in the final negotiations they received so low a priority relative to other matters that few accounts of the pre-1982 negotiations even mention them.

A fundamental reason for this is that by the 1970s the powers had lain dormant for many years, and were no longer an issue. They never were used much: out of the thousands of acts passed by provincial legislatures, only 112 were disallowed, although there were other cases where a province modified its course to avoid disallowance. Even fewer provincial bills were reserved: in round numbers, seventy, and of those, fourteen were approved by the federal authority. Neither disallowance nor reservation, that is, has been a persistent drain on provincial energies, and both in modern times have fallen into disuse. When in 1961 the lieutenant-governor of Saskatchewan, on his own initiative, reserved a bill for the national goverment's consideration, the bill not only received assent, but there were suggestions that perhaps the lieutenant-governor should be rebuked, if not dismissed, for daring to use his constitutional powers.

In the times when the powers were used, a clear pattern of attitudes emerged. Ottawa at first obviously used them to interfere in provincial affairs: from Confederation to 1896, sixty-six provincial laws were disallowed, for reasons that varied with the national government's view of why any particular law should be struck down. A province had exceeded its powers, or threatened private rights by being discriminatory or unjust, or bypassed 'sound principles of legislation.' The provinces naturally objected to federal supervision of their affairs, and at a conference in 1887 condemned the federal use of its powers. Their protest caused no formal change, but it is significant that from 1887 to 1896 there were only seven disallowances. The disallowance power (with which reservation can be coupled) was fading.

The fading continued into the next period (1896–1920), during which the provinces' jurisdictional powers grew, as the courts enhanced provincial legislative powers in a series of major decisions. The disallowance power remained, but of the thirty times it was used in this period, nineteen were more or less the same disallowance: British Columbia was trying to place legal restraints on the activities of aliens and Ottawa, mindful of the implications of these provincial laws with regard to international policy, disallowed them all.

After 1921 only sixteen acts were disallowed, twelve of them Alberta's, whose Social Credit government had fiscal and monetary notions which, whatever their merits, came under federal, not provincial, constitutional powers. There has been no disallowance since 1934, and it seems unlikely at this writing that the power will be used again. The box score by provinces will indicate one reason for being sceptical of many of its uses in the past: only 16 of the total 112 disallowances concerned the two largest provinces (Quebec 6, Ontario 10), while the smaller provinces suffered 43 (British Columbia), 12 (Alberta), 3 (Saskatchewan), 28 (Manitoba), 1 (New Brunswick), 9 (Nova Scotia), and none for Prince Edward Island and Newfoundland. Nevertheless, it should not be concluded that the two largest passed fewer undesirable acts; one of the most notorious provincial statutes in Canadian history, known as the Padlock Law, was Quebec's, and it was not disallowed. It was in due course struck down by the Supreme Court, and the availability of the courts is now one of the reasons for the fading of disallowance. Even before the adoption of the Charter of Rights in 1982, successive federal governments had come to accept the assumption that the provinces, except in extreme cases, were entitled to make their own way, including mistakes, with aggrieved individuals free to challenge the province in the courts. Some of the main reasons that might have been adduced to activate the disallowance power before 1982 seem to have been largely dissipated by the charter; but the disallowance and reservation powers are still in the constitution.[2]

EXECUTIVE FUNCTIONS OF THE CABINET

Whereas a cabinet's use of disallowance can be counted accurately, even though one has to speculate about the reasons for its use, its executive functions are less easy to describe precisely. The phrase 'executive functions' in its broadest sense covers everything the cabinet does, and in discussing its organization and legislative functions this chapter has already discussed executive functions. A summary is none the less essential, and some repetition, for emphasis, is also necessary.

1. The outstanding duty of the cabinet is to furnish initiative and leadership: to provide the country and Parliament with a national policy, and to devise means for

coping with present emergencies and future needs. On minor matters this is the concern of only the department affected; but as the importance or scope of the issue increases, it becomes more and more a matter for the prime minister and the whole cabinet who, after much consideration and discussion, will decide what is known as 'government policy.' The process of deciding may admittedly be a long one, for as both Sir John A. Macdonald ('Old Tomorrow') and Mackenzie King demonstrated, leadership in a country as diverse as Canada, in the interests of national unity, can sometimes take the form of appearing to provide none at all. As King confided more than once in his diary, *preventing* something from happening can involve statesmanship of a high order.

Despite their overall responsibility, ministers do not necessarily start all legislation. The initial inspiration or impulse will often originate with an individual minister or the cabinet, and a rash minister may sometimes make public commitments without consultation with his staff or even with his colleagues. But this is only a beginning. The proposal must be examined, criticized, appraised in the light of past experience, adapted, and recast many times before it is ready for trial or for incorporation in a government bill; and at all stages in this proving process the practical knowledge and information of the public servants are of inestimable value. However, the process may be reversed, for an enormous number of new and modified policies grow out of the administration of existing statutes and regulations. These policies will almost invariably originate with the public servants themselves who alone are in a position to draw upon the experience and wealth of data which have been built up through many years of administrative practice. Any significant change of this kind must receive the endorsement of the minister, and the proposal now has to get through a cabinet committee, all of whose members will be sensitive to the political aspects of a change.

The pressures of modern government require a cabinet to assimilate enormous amounts of information. A great deal of it comes from the public service, from the party's own organization, or from the pressure groups that surround all governments. Sometimes, to accommodate particular lobbies, consultative groups are set up. More information comes from parliamentary committees, many of which are established specifically to conduct inquiries. The research branch of the Library of Parliament is always producing studies. But all these sources are not enough, and for reasons that vary with each instance, governments in Canada resort to several devices, most of them familiar to anyone who follows political news.

The best known is the royal commission, which usually has members chosen both for their expertise and for their prestige, so that there will be no reason to doubt the seriousness of any conclusions they may reach. A royal commission can be set up for any purpose, and many of them – usually one-man inquiries set up to investigate some untoward event, such as a series of unexplained leaks of minor but confidential information – may attract little attention. Major royal commissions, however, add an element of pageantry to the daily round as they travel from coast to coast, hold public hearings for the convenience of everybody with anything to say, and produce reports full of recommendations that give everybody another opportunity. The simple letting off of steam is indeed a valuable function of many royal commissions on controversial topics.

That is not their only function. A cabinet may be genuinely unsure of what course it should take on an issue, and sets up a commission to get help. A cabinet may also not want to make a hasty decision on a subject, or perhaps any decision at all, and a royal commission given a complex assignment may take months or even years to complete its work. A government may be willing to accept, as a recommendation from a commission, a policy which it was reluctant to adopt solely on its own: after an inquiry, which may itself help create a public opinion in favour of a particular move, the government can gracefully agree with the commission's learned finding. A cabinet, when selecting members of a royal commission, will naturally try to avoid loading the dice against itself, and the report of a commission to the government that appointed it carries a kind of moral authority to which the opposition is happy to refer if it agrees with the commission. Royal commissions are remarkably independent once set up (the whole purpose, after all, is an inquiry as impartial as the proceedings of a court), and its members are free to recommend whatever they wish within their terms of reference. If, before a commission reports, a general election results in a change of government, the new cabinet may not feel obliged to take too seriously the work of a body created by its opponents; but the new opposition may find the report of a commission it set up a handy source of criticism if the government does nothing. Every decade produces one or two outstanding royal commissions, and among the notable postwar studies are those on Arts, Science and Letters; Health Care; Bilingualism and Biculturalism; Government Organization; and Financial Management and Accountability.

Not all commissions of inquiry are designated 'royal,' although as far as the nature of the work is concerned the distinction between a royal or other commission is largely technical. But a cabinet can set up any kind of inquiry it wishes, and since Lester Pearson's time the term 'task force' has become the designation used for many unroyal investigations. A task force lacks the prestige of a royal commission, but it is also a more flexible device, and usually considered less expensive. A task force may bring together public servants and outsiders, or federal and provincial officials, in a less formal way than a royal commission, but also in a way less independent of the government. A royal commission for its own purposes has almost the status of a high court, whereas a task force is an ad hoc group, and again one set up for any information-gathering the cabinet wants. In recent years there have been task forces on Canadian Unity; Housing; and Major Capital Projects in Canada until the Year 2000. The Committee on Election Expenses which worked in the mid-1960s was not then called a task force, but probably would be today. The total number of commissions of inquiry of all kinds since Confederation would be difficult to determine, but an educated guess would be close to two thousand.

Intimidating as that figure may sound, the amassing of information in the electronic age continues at an increasing rate, and no political executive can afford not to keep up with whatever is relevant. The growing use of polling may to some extent offset this, on the general grounds that no matter how much is known, the crucial information is always what the electors think, or say they think. But even the best polls cannot predict what the electors will think *after* a cabinet has announced what it considers a necessary policy, as the Mulroney cabinet discovered after the presentation of its first budget in 1985. Nor can polls assist a government on those occasions when, on the basis of information received, it feels that it must adopt a particular policy regardless of what the electors think, simply because the ministers are convinced that it the best policy. An unyielding attitude by a government on a complex question raises a presumption that it may well be right, for underneath its decision is almost certainly the conviction that time and a wider knowledge will vindicate the wisdom of its policy. 'There are times,' one of Canada's most experienced politicians, Chubby Power, wrote in his memoirs, 'when unpopularity will be found necessary in the interests of the country, and risks must be taken.'

2. Each member of the cabinet is individually charged with the responsibility of exercising a general supervision over the work of his particular department. These broad departmental divisions will change somewhat in number and character in accordance with the fluctuating demands and needs of the nation, and any unusual event such as a war will see very marked alterations in response to the exceptional conditions. A number of minor activities may be grouped for reasons of convenience under one political head, and it is thus not uncommon to find a minister in charge of two or more departments or divisions. The following were the portfolios in Canada in 1986, the nature of their activities being broadly indicated by the titles: deputy prime minister; external affairs; finance, justice; state; agriculture; health and welfare; veterans' affairs; national defence; labour; fisheries and oceans; transport, energy, mines and resources; national revenue; public works; employment and immigration; Indian affairs and northern development; solicitor general; treasury board; regional industrial expansion; consumer and corporate affairs; supply and services; presidency of Privy Council; leader of the government in the Senate; science and technology; international trade;

environment; and communications. Several of those titles did not exist in 1970, and to them must be added the ministers of state already mentioned.

The two critical tests to which most acts of Parliament are daily subjected are their administrative practicability and the extent to which they meet the need for which they were designed. Acts of Parliament are being continually amended as their shortcomings under these two tests become apparent. The task of a minister is not only to secure the desired amendments and thus obtain a legal framework within which departmental administration can function, but also to familiarize the members of the House with the problems involved and convince them that the proposed changes are both desirable and necessary to achieve the ends which the House has in mind.

3. While the minister is almost always technically ignorant of the special activities of his department, he need not and should not for that reason be nothing more than a useless ornament at the top of the administrative pyramid. (French-Canadian ministers, it should be noted, have on occasion had to overcome the additional handicap of being a French-speaking executive marooned at the top of a predominantly English-speaking department that was, furthermore, established in accordance with English and American concepts of organization.) The public servants under him know infinitely more about the inner workings of the department and the minutiae of the varied tasks on which they are engaged than he can ever hope to know himself; but his own contribution, although made along quite different lines, is no less valuable. While the public servant must supply the technical knowledge, the minister will add much to the drive and vigour in the department and will endeavour to keep the aims and efforts of his assistants in proper focus. Public servants are apt to be too much concerned about their immediate task and their own official convenience; their expert knowledge acts as a screen obscuring their view of other departments, interfering with other contacts and relationships, and cutting them off from public opinion. Furthermore, the bias of their profession may distort their outlook and make them distrust new and unfamiliar ideas; precedents and well-worn methods may become inviolable, and the road to the goal may be regarded of at least equal importance as the goal itself.

The amateur minister, if intelligent, enters this oppressive atmosphere like a fresh breeze from the sea. He possesses few predilections, and those he has are of an entirely different kind from those of his subordinates, a fact that makes him far more useful to the department than if he were simply one more expert among many. He can ask an infinite number of questions and can demand exact and exhaustive answers; he can, when he desires, bluntly refuse to follow a suggested policy; he can shake up the lethargic and transfer the bunglers to a place where they can do little harm. He poses problems for solution. When future departmental plans are being formulated, he is the one who can gauge the views of the public and can insist that all sides of a question be carefully considered before final action is taken. And he must persuade the relevant cabinet committee that he is right.

The minister is in the nature of things bound to act throughout in constant consultation with his expert public servants, and his own ideas, whether valuable or useless, are necessarily tempered by the advice he will receive; his highest-ranking advisers, he may find, will have policies of their own. His reforming zeal is certain to suffer many defeats, and properly so, for the departmental methods and policies which he may criticize will frequently prove to be right. But the mere fact that the bureaucrat knows that his proposals must be able to satisfy a curious and perhaps sceptical minister, bound by no professional prejudices, has in itself a wholesome effect and tends to produce wiser proposals. The minister can never afford to forget that he will be expected to defend and justify his department's policies before Parliament and the country. Yet at the same time he realizes that those policies must be technically and administratively sound if they are to meet the need which has called them into being.

Inasmuch as the minister is politically responsible for his department, he is given supreme authority, and he therefore has the power to overrule any of his public servants at any time. They, for their part, give the best advice they can, and if the minister persists in disregarding it – as he has a perfect right to do – they must then acquiesce, and bend all their energies to the problem of making the best of what they are convinced is a mistaken policy. The minister has the privilege of overruling his bureaucrats even although it involves the making of blunders in Parliament and suffering, if need be, for them.

The necessity of maintaining democratic control and the necessity of securing technical efficiency are thus two principles that can be reconciled: the one is a complement and corrective of the other. The two combine to produce the administrative paradox that the best person to wield final authority is one whose major interest has been largely outside the specialized field with which his particular department is primarily concerned.

This is not to suggest that all ministers will measure up to all the opportunities which await them in their departments. They will not. Too many find it much easier to swing with the tide, to accept methods and procedures with little or no question, to refuse to take the trouble of trying to grasp the real functions and aims of their departments, to be led off by some things they can readily understand and neglect those which are difficult or bothersome and hence demand genuine concentrated effort, to become absorbed in some of the trifling questions that are immediately in front of them while ignoring the more remote and intangible problems which can be postponed for a month, six months, or five years. Even some of the best ministers may have trouble in extricating themselves from the morass of detailed administration; for Canadian tradition and practice –

maintained in no small measure by the ministers themselves – have done little to set the cabinet free from such impediments and restraints. One of Trudeau's goals in having little come to cabinet unless a cabinet committee had considered it was to help free ministers of duties that interfered with policy-making, and the success of the committee system in this regard must vary with each minister and prime minister. Even some of the best ministers, it must be added, may find themselves distracted from all their duties if the prime minister is about to step down, and several of his colleagues wish to step up.

4. Another of the executive functions is co-ordination, and that is also one of the aims of the modern committee system. A cabinet can co-ordinate only if it is organized, and enough has been said earlier to show how far the cabinet has come from the days when ministers were bogged down in departmental detail. Ministers will no doubt always have the kinds of problems that a group of forty people engaged in seeking the same ends will have. But there can be no doubt that the cabinet's capacities as a co-ordinator have been enormously enlarged since the 1960s.

5. Finally, the cabinet performs collectively a wide variety of explicit executive acts, usually in the name of the governor-in-council and on the immediate initiative of the prime minister. A number of the more important of these acts, some already cited, are summarized here:

(a) The making of appointments, which may range from comparatively minor positions to ambassadors, high commissioners, privy councillors, judges, and senators.

(b) The removal or dismissal of public officials. Some hold office at pleasure and may thus be removed with few formalities. Others may hold office legally at pleasure, but in practice during good behaviour, and the removal is then 'for cause,' usually after an inquiry. Some public officers, such as county court judges, enjoy a legal tenure during good behaviour and can be removed only after a formal investigation. A limited number, such as the judges of the Supreme Court and the auditor general, can be removed by the governor-in-council only after a joint address asking for removal has been passed by both Houses of Parliament. In these last cases, the function of the governor-in-council is almost if not entirely automatic.

(c) The summoning, prorogation, and dissolution of Parliament. The summoning of Parliament is simply its convocation whenever a meeting is deemed to be necessary; it must meet 'once at least in every year.' Prorogation is the act of terminating a parliamentary session. Dissolution terminates a Parliament, and a general election must then be held to select a new House of Commons. The summoning and dissolution of Parliament is done on the advice of the prime minister.

(d) The participation in international affairs by the appointment of plenipotentiaries, the issuing of instructions to those plenipotentiaries, the ratification of international agreements and treaties, and so on. Parliament may be consulted and even asked to approve international agreements and treaties, but this is largely a matter of convenience and political strategy; the actual ratification is purely an executive act.

(e) The power of clemency, that is, the issuing of a reprieve or pardon to offenders against federal laws, notably for criminal offences. This may be applied to individuals or, a more unusual example, to a group, such as the general amnesty given to offenders under the Military Service Act after the First World War.

(f) The decision of certain matters relating to the provinces. The cabinet appoints the lieutenant-governor in each province, gives him general instructions and from time to time supplementary instructions, and may remove him if he proves unsatisfactory. (Two have in fact been removed, one in Quebec in 1879, one in British Columbia in 1900.) Several of these constitutional powers have been long unused, as has the authority to hear appeals from certain sectarian minorities in the provinces on educational matters.

(g) The hearing of appeals from decisions of federal regulatory bodies has often been a duty allocated to the cabinet in the statute setting up the regulatory body. Its use has varied considerably over time.

These discussions of the cabinet's functions cannot be left without a reminder that they are but general descriptions of extremely complex institutions which are continually undergoing changes. An institution like the cabinet may look much the same under a Trudeau, a Clark, a Turner, or a Mulroney: but all those prime ministers have seen their offices differently, and have had different approaches to their colleagues, their parties, the public, and the media. The system of powerful standing committees is well established, and in some form or other will certainly last for an indefinite period. But one of those committees, led by energetic ministers, could conceivably emerge as a leader as individual departments headed by adroit ministers used to do. Since its creation the Priorities and Planning Committee, chaired by the prime minister, has been the leader, but a change in emphasis that put social programs, or any other broad range of policies, in the forefront, could change the emphasis within the committee structure. Any committee the prime minister decides to chair is a committee deserving close attention. A description of the cabinet can portray the cabinet at a moment in time, but the changes in the cabinet in just the last few years offer grounds for concluding that change will continue.

12
The public service

When he went around to the teeth office to pick up his share of the welfare state, he was asked to sign a receipt for the teeth after trying them on. He was understood to say that in order to get the teeth he had already filled out more forms than ought to exist in any single country, and now he had them had no intention of signing any more forms, ever.
Norman Ward, *Mice in the Beer*

THE DEPARTMENTAL SERVICE

The public service is by far the largest part of the government of Canada, and partly for that reason a large portion of its activities are not familiar to the general public. The chief actors featured in the preceding chapters of this book, even if one included all constituency executives, MPs, senators, and ministers' political staffs, would number only a few thousand; but the federal public service, including the armed forces and the RCMP, and those who work full time in departments and in other agencies, totals in round numbers about 580,000 people. The precise number at any moment is impossible to determine, for public servants, like other employees, come and go; also at any moment an unknown number of 'temporaries' are on the payroll. Of the total, only approximately 40 per cent are under jurisdiction of the Public Service Commission. Even excluding the RCMP and the armed forces, those working under crown corporations and other agencies outnumber those in departments under ministers, so that what used to be called the second public service has become the first in terms of numbers. The public service 'proper' is for many purposes under unified control; the rest are denizens of what Professor Hodgetts called in 1973 'a veritable jungle of quasi-departmental agencies.'[1]

The ministerial departments might be added to the jungle, for they too take an impressive variety of forms. The basic reason for that is a sound one: any branch of a government serving the public has to adapt itself to those it serves, and an organization suited to assisting agriculturalists would not necessarily work in the operation of a publicly owned railway. The words 'publicly owned railway' reveal an additional consideration fundamental to an understanding of the Canadian public service: the vast expanses of the country coupled with its small population have meant that many enterprises seen as essential could only be undertaken, in part or in whole, through governments. One of the endless debates that goes on in Canada is about how much, if at all, governments should be engaged in participating in the private sector of the economy. But from the first day it has been doing so. Section 145 of the original Constitution Act of 1867 declared that a railway was essential to consolidate Confederation, and 'it shall be the Duty of the Government and Parliament of Canada to provide for the Commencement, within Six Months after the Union, of a Railway connecting the River St. Lawrence with the City of Halifax.' The eastbound tracks, that is, were part of Canada's constitution, and in due course a westbound railway, now paradoxically sometimes held to represent private enterprise at its best, was secured through generous subsidies and grants of land from the federal government.

Those last sentences are not phrased to take sides in the continuing debate over public versus private enterprise, but merely to indicate one aspect of the importance of the federal public service in contributing to Canadian affairs. The adapting of a large administration to a changing variety of perceived needs has presented, and will continue to present, serious challenges to the organizational skills of politicians and administrators, many of them unlike those faced by parties and Parliament. Much of the work of the parties in Parliament, indeed, faces the political segments of the government away from the administrative. Where politicians of necessity seek publicity for a great deal of what they do, the day-to-day routine of governing (which can be seen in any urban telephone book to range through the alphabet from agricultural inspections to youth programs) are rarely considered newsworthy as long as they run into no trouble. They none the less require continual attention from those in charge, for any large organization, however efficient, keeps creating its own internal dilemmas. The popular word that denotes the general activities and problems of the public service is bureaucracy, a word sometimes used as if it applied to government alone; but any perceptive consumer of the late twentieth century knows that governments are no more bureaucratic than large private corporations.

The coexistence of public and private sectors that must work together, as in Canada, poses continuing questions about the public service. Should a public service be operated as if it were amenable to the same kind of executive direction as a private company? If airports are needed for private airlines, as highways are needed for trucking outfits, and only governments have the authority and capacity to construct airports and highways, should they be expected to do so at a profit? Nobody expects a public school system to show a profit, but if provincial educational policies, instead of being administered by ministers of education, were to be turned over to crown corporations, should they then become a source of revenue, and if so, how? Should a single service such as the post office, which provides essential services whether it is a department or a crown corporation, be expected to pay for itself because it charges fees? Should control of the public service be as centralized as possible, to facilitate clear lines of accountability that can be more readily examined by auditors or parliamentarians, or should there be a maximum decentralization, to encourage local initiatives by the managers of the service's myriad branches? If decentralization is employed, can accountability be enforced by uniform rules that apply throughout the service, or should the rules in a public service be different from agency to agency? How representative of the general population should the public service be? The electoral system can be relied on to produce MPs from the major elements in the population, although it continues to produce far more males than females. But how does one organize a service of appointed persons to be adequately representative of women at all levels of management, or of French-speaking Canadians? That sample of questions includes several whose answers do not come from the public. 'Regrettably,' Wallace and Fletcher report in *Canadian Politics through Press Reports* (page 50), 'most reporters choose to describe only the defects of bureaucracy or, more accurately, the symptoms of modern government.'

The organization of the public service is one of the preoccupations of the cabinet and a handful of key departments, sporadically aided by royal commissions whose reports reach the public through a recurring theme: something in the public service is breaking down, if it hasn't already. The fact that the same royal commissions, like the auditor general, often find much that is good is not the stuff of headlines. An organization set up to meet conditions of, say, postwar reconstruction, may be at least partly obsolete when the reconstruction has ended. Managerial techniques suited to an economy enjoying high employment may falter when recession comes. The conclusions reached by observers change too, and theories of organization considered the best at one time also become obsolete. For example, departments under ministers once comprised most of the government of Canada; in modern times recourse to non-departmental agencies has become essential, if only to avoid a ministry so vast that even a large majority in Parliament would be insufficient to give the prime minister the needed manpower.

Before the rise of the non-departmental segments of government, prevailing theories of public administration looked at government departments, and in due course the other agencies, as organizations to which work was allotted in a variety of distinguishable ways. The chief of these, *function*, is revealed in names:

Justice, Agriculture, Health and Welfare, and so on. Under such titles in each case are gathered most of the relevant governmental activities suggested by the names. Some departments combine several allied functions, as National Defence covers the armed forces on land, sea, and in the air, and Transport covers civilian aviation, railways, and water transportation in navigable waters, including canals. The crown agencies have equally revealing names: National Museums of Canada; Unemployment Insurance Commission; Canadian Broadcasting Corporation; Canadian National Railways. (The distinction between Transport and the CNR is that the latter actually operates a railway.)

Function as used above is not the only principle of grouping activities that has been employed. *Work process*, the gathering together of services that would otherwise be scattered though a number of departments but can be more efficiently performed by one, describes the work of Supply and Services, which is responsible for large amounts of the government's printing, distribution of publications, collecting of statistics, issuing of cheques, and purchasing of materials. Another service agency of vital importance in a bilingual state is the Translation Bureau, which translates the words spoken in Parliament into the official language in which they were not uttered, and does the same for written words emanating from Parliament and the public service. *Clientele*, which is a basis of organization for dealing with groups for special reasons, provides part of the rationale for departments with names such as Veterans' Affairs, or Indian and Northern Affairs. *Territory* is also a basis for organizing departmental work, and a good example is Agriculture, which has many scattered research stations and experimental farms for work on Canada's many varied crops and types of soil.

The fact that Agriculture is mentioned above under both function and territory, and would with equal validity have been cited under clientele, suggests that a classification of departments based on such terminology cannot be precise, and the use of the key words, as Professor Hodgetts notes in *The Canadian Public Service* (page 112), can in real situations be 'difficult and sometimes unproductive.' Hodgetts proposes, in effect, abandoning such terms as useful analytical tools, by grouping at least the ministerial departments into four categories:

1 Departments with one primary purpose or function which can best be performed by a centralized headquarter's staff. Under this category are listed ten departments from which it is convenient to select the Treasury Board. The board, at the latest count, had just under 1,000 employees working in its two secretariats in Ottawa, approximately 30 per cent of whom are French-speaking, and 40 per cent women.

2 Departments with more than one major function for which a centralized organization is also required. The most relevant of these for our purposes is the

Secretary of State, through which office several services report to Parliament. Its employees number just over 3,000 in Ottawa, nearly 70 per cent French-speaking, 65 per cent women.

3 Departments with one primary function that is best performed by means of a dispersed staff and organization. Hodgetts found eight in this category, the largest, Transport, having 21,000 on staff in Ottawa and across Canada, barely 22 per cent of them French-speaking, and slightly fewer than that women.

4 Departments with more than one major function in which dispersed operations are essential. Of the half-dozen in this classification the largest, well known to every Canadian who pays customs or excise duties, or income tax, is National Revenue, with over 25,000 employees in Ottawa and elsewhere, over 26 per cent French-speaking, 46 per cent women.

The cabinet was appreciably smaller in 1971 when Hodgetts devised his useful divisions than it is now, but it was as true then as now that the functions of the ministerial departments above require several kinds of organizations. Nevertheless, every department has a hierarchical structure which can be described in general terms; and every department has some dealings with a handful of other branches of the government, particularly the auditor general, the Privy Council Office, and most notably the Treasury Board.

The Treasury Board can here add to its many functions by serving as an example of how a department is organized. It has two separate secretariats, and since they have a similar structure only one need be described. That one is the part of the department under the secretary of the Treasury Board, the highest-ranking public servant of his section of the department. (The other part is under the comptroller general.) The importance of the board in the government of Canada can be seen from the opening paragraph of one of its own publications, *Role of the Treasury Board Secretariat and the Office of the Comptroller General*:

The Treasury Board Secretariat examines the proposed spending programs of all government ministries, departments and agencies and keeps under constant review the development of approved programs to ensure effective expenditure management. It recommends Public Service personnel management policy to the Board in the areas of human resource utilization, compensation, pensions and insurance, and staff relations. As well, it negotiates the terms of collective agreements with the various bargaining agents. It is concerned with the development of effective managerial practices and efficient administration throughout the government.

In a word, if the government of Canada can be said to have a general manager, it is the Treasury Board, a fact which the Royal Commission on Financial Management recognized by recommending that it be renamed the Board of Management. In many relevant areas of government, the board is designated as 'the employer.'

The hierarchy employed by the board to manage is like that of most ministerial departments. At the top is the minister, the only political executive in it; his title is president of the Treasury Board. Immediately below the minister is the secretary, already mentioned; the secretary's office has attached to it a communications division and an office of legal services, both with directors. Reporting to the secretary, and through him to the minister, are six main branches, each with its own head variously named deputy secretary, director, or director general. (The following is adapted from the document quoted above.)

1 The *Administrative Policy Branch* has four main sections, for planning and evaluation, policy development and revision, policy implementation and review, and co-ordinator of regulatory reform.
2 The *Program Branch*, apart from several assistant secretaries (one of whom has particular duties involving crown corporations), has several directorates variously dealing with (a) external affairs, defence, science and environment; (b) industry, transportation, and natural resources; (c) social, employment, housing, and culture; (d) general government services; (e) budget co-ordination, which has three sub-branches of its own dealing with estimates, expenditure analysis, and management information systems.
3 The *Personnel Policy Branch* has five main sections dealing with personnel management, organization and classification, staff relations and compensation, developmental personnel policies, and evaluation of programs.
4 The *Official Languages Branch* has three sections dealing with the application of the Official Languages Act within departments and agencies, an activity returned to below.
5 The *Administration Branch* has five sections, each with a director, dealing with administrative, financial, personnel, language, and security services.
6 The *Executive Service Branch*, not surprisingly, covers executive services.

It must not be thought that when the board's organization shows a division charged with, say, external affairs or defence, it means that the board makes Canada's foreign or military policy. What it does, in effect, is try to see that the departments charged with those responsibilities are so organized and financed as to be able to discharge them adequately. The board's description of its Program Branch's role says at the start that it is 'in the context of agreed policies and priorities, to analyze and evaluate departmental and agency program and project proposals, and to recommend to the Treasury Board the best means of achieving program objectives in the light of available financial and manpower resources and their optimum allocation against competing demands.' A similar role is performed when proposals for new policies are made.

In the discharge of these functions the Treasury Board naturally has to consult with other parts of the government. To take an example of increasing importance in recent decades, the official languages, the relevant branch of the board's secretariat 'maintains close liaison with the other branches of the Secretariat, particularly Personnel Policy and Program Branches, and with the Public Service Commission, the Office of the Commissioner of Official Languages, the department of the Secretary of State, all federal departments and agencies, and many other bodies.' An administrative landscape of such scope might well intimidate the most adventurous explorer, but the description itself makes clear that it is talking about an expedition of considerable size. The Office of the Language Commissioner, for example, who reports directly to Parliament, has its own set of duties applying the Official Languages Act in federal departments and agencies, and therefore its own bureaucracy, and its own set of publications. The Public Service Commission, which also reports to Parliament, has a set of duties relevant to the staffing of the public service, including its language requirements.

It is difficult to be precise about all the differences between the duties of the Treasury Board and the Public Service Commission, and there were periods in the past when the two seemed to be competing with each other over the management of the public service. It is clear now that the board, working under the cabinet and its committees, is the manager; and the commission, in a similar sense, is the personnel office, in charge of screening and hiring staff. The demands on such an office, acquiring staff to be paid out of the public purse, and subject to parliamentary and other criticisms few private employers need worry about, must receive attention here.

One of the fundamental facts of the public service is, of course, that it is public, not private. For several decades after Confederation this was taken to mean that ministers were responsible for their departments, which further meant that vacancies were filled by patronage. Canada never experienced a full spoils system in which a change of government was followed by a substantial turnover of the population of Ottawa and elsewhere, with nominations for the public service coming not just from ministers and MPs, but even from the defeated candidates of the victorious party. Those three categories of citizens, however, had the ruling influence on the filling of vacancies, many of which they created by charging that incumbent civil servants, the appointments of their opponents, had been guilty of active participation in the last election campaign – as indeed they often had. The results of such a method of staffing the departments was inevitable. As early as 1880 a royal commission reported:

To this baneful influence [patronage], we believe, may be traced nearly all that demands change. It is responsible for the admission to the service of those who are too old to be efficient; of those whose impaired health and enfeebled constitutions forbid the hope that they can ever become useful public servants; of those whose personal habits are an equally fatal objection; of those whose lack of education should disqualify them; and of those whose mental qualities are of an order that has made it impossible for them to succeed in private business. It is responsible too for the appointment of those who desire to lead an easy and, what they deem, a genteel life.

Since the royal commission was following up on a House of Commons committee of 1877 that reached similar conclusions, it may seem surprising that the first Civil Service Act, passed in 1882, was almost as feeble as the persons described in the quotation. It provided for tests so elementary that the ministers were still free to appoint anybody except perhaps the subnormal and illiterate.

As government grew in scope, the burdens on the ministers also grew, and the distribution of patronage became increasingly time-consuming. Partly for that reason, but partly also because the need for efficiency in the civil service was becoming increasingly apparent, the chances of reform improved in the first decade of the century, particularly after another royal commission reported in 1907 that the service was getting not better, but worse. The Civil Service Act of 1908 provided genuine improvements: it created an independent commission under whose aegis competitive examinations were to be held, with those getting the highest marks earning the right to fill vacancies as they arose. The chief weakness of the act was that it applied only to the 'inside' service, in Ottawa, and not all of that. The entire service, with some exceptions, was placed under the Civil Service Commission in 1918. The commission itself has had a chequered history, much of it attributable to the desire of each governing party in turn to exempt more and more of the public service from its non-partisan jurisdiction. It has been studied by itself, by parliamentary committees, and by yet more royal commissions; and in 1967 it was succeeded by the Public Service Commission and relieved of some of its predecessor's responsiblities, which went to the Treasury Board.

Long before 1967 it had become clear that many aspects of organization and personnel management in the public service were properly executive functions, and not those of an independent commission reporting directly to Parliament. The historical causes that brought about the gradual acceptance of that development had their roots in the Second World War and the subsequent creation of 'the administrative state,' with its multiplicity of defence, social, and industrial policies, all of which required more central control than was possible in more leisurely times when government was smaller and responded more slowly to whatever problems the public perceived. It is none the less still useful to consider briefly what earlier civil service commissions had to cope with, chiefly because the main problems of creating and maintaining a public service persist no matter what agency is in charge.

In the beginning the Commission had an essentially negative assignment: to prevent, or at least minimize, the use of patronage in staffing the service. Until 1908 the commission was handicapped by the absence of feet which it could use to take even faltering steps, but once the merit system was accepted it proved workable, and the latest reports of the Public Service Commission still declare that 'merit is, and must remain, the fundamental principle of staffing in the Public Service.' The acceptance of merit still leaves it to be defined and applied; and while merit can be readily defined as the meeting of clear standards based on knowledge and ability, its application has required the working out of many details, the chief of which can be outlined in a series of queries and comments.

Entrance
A sound entry into the public service means through some other gateway than patronage. For many types of employment, merit can be assessed through set examinations, earned certificates or degrees, years of experience in a particular occupation, or a combination of these. For others, the determination of merit can be extremely difficult – for example, how does one examine people for cleaning offices or washing windows? However it is done, a necessary element in any entrance policy must be fairness: the public service must be open to all citizens, wherever they live. At the same time, one can justify giving special concessions to certain groups for particular reasons. The oldest example of this is the preference given under stated conditions to veterans of the armed forces, which meant, for example, that after public service examinations a veteran could be placed on a selective list ahead of non-veterans who had earned higher marks.

Tenure and removal
Tenure in the public service is at pleasure – in other words, a civil servant, at least in theory, can always be dismissed. By custom, tenure now depends on good behaviour, nowadays modified by the terms of collective bargaining agreements allowing for grievance procedures, and by a dismissed or demoted employee's right to appeal. Considering the size of the service there are surprisingly few appeals (a total of 2,400 of all kinds in 1983, for example, only 69 per cent of which concerned recommendations to demote or release). Until 1966 political activity was generally considered misbehaviour (especially if it was in the interests of the wrong party) and it is still in individual cases a source of controversy. But in general public servants may now attend political meetings, contribute to a

candidate or party, and obtain leave of absence without pay to enter a contest. Every election now sees a few civil servants seeking, and sometimes winning, public office. The Charter of Rights will undoubtedly enlarge the political opportunities for public servants, since it asserts unequivocally that every citizen has the right 'to be qualified for membership' in the House of Commons or a provincial legislature.

Gradation

Even before the advent of collective agreements which included detailed job descriptions to ensure that public servants doing the same work received the same pay, the Canadian service recognized that the grading of personnel was important, as was the system of promotion between grades. At first the problems of classification were treated in a casual and indeed haphazard manner, but gradually (and influenced in turn by English and American experiences) the need for systematic gradation began to be perceived at the opening of this century, and in turn it was refined to take into account the requirements of different levels of the service. One general admission scheme for every citizen, for example, would not necessarily attract or produce well-trained university graduates for technical or managerial positions, and these became increasingly demanded by the service as government grew. Until the Treasury Board became the general manager of the service, the classification system seemed at times almost out of hand: the standard category of positions numbered 1,729 at the start, 2,400 by 1939, and 3,700 by 1946. In the latter year a Royal Commission on Administrative Classifications in the Civil Service grappled with the problem of finding and developing managerial skills, and found the postwar service failing both in the recruitment of enough able people and in using them properly once they were in. 'Many persons of ability and promise,' the commission reported darkly (pages 13–15), 'are lost in blind alleys or emerge from them too late in life.'

Forty years later there are no doubt individuals of whom that statement would still be true, as there would be in any large organization. But the assignment to the Treasury Board in 1967 of 'personnel management in the public service, including the determination of terms and conditions of employment of persons employed therein,' has made marked changes in the service. The Treasury Board, by its very nature as manager and employer, will never be the most popular of departments, but there is now much less doubt than used to exist about who is in charge of the public service, or about the status of the citizens who work in it.

Gradation also involves promotion between grades, and the Treasury Board lays down the broad personnel policies within which each department is operated, while the Public Service Commission is in charge of the mechanics of individual cases. In recent years the departments have been delegated larger powers over internal administration, but the Public Service Commission conducts audits of the use of delegated powers, and where promotions are concerned, individuals have a right of appeal. The bulk of the appeals cited previously concerned 'selection processes.'

Staff relations

The Treasury Board, as already noted, is the bargaining agent representing the government of Canada in negotiations with unions, and its role here is unequivocally clear. The old Civil Service Commission had an interest in staff relations and in its later years paid increasing attention to the associations that became the Public Service Alliance of Canada. The Civil Service Act of 1961 permitted consultations with staff associations; the Public Service Staff Relations Act of 1966 established full collective bargaining, but not with the Public Service Commission as the federal agent.

By 1966 many employees in specific parts of the public service, such as Canadian National Railways, were already members of unions, so that the extension of collective bargaining throughout the service was hardly a revolutionary development. What has followed is the establishment of the usual necessary bureaucratic apparatus to deal with bargaining, such as the Public Service Staff Relations Board, whose chairman and vice-chairman can be removed only by a joint address of the Senate and House of Commons. The impact of collective bargaining on the service, and therefore the public, has varied greatly with the unions themselves. Some have chosen to forgo their right to strike in return for acceptable rights to arbitration. Others, more militantly led, have already gone out on strike, and a few seem to be regularly threatening to do so. As this is written, serious attempts to organize the employees of Parliament are being made, which raise questions of unusual interest: would a strike that crippled or even threatened a sovereign Parliament be a breach of parliamentary privilege? As with so many questions in politics, nobody will know for sure until something happens.

What kind of public service results from the circumstances described so far? Keeping in mind that government departments and agencies are beset by the same frailties found in any large organization, the short answer is: a good one. While the media will always delight in publicizing 'horror stories' turned up by the auditor general and other inquirers, and it is in the interest of many lobbies to exploit myths of governmental inefficiency, Canada is in fact a well-governed democracy. That can be seen by anybody who takes the trouble to read, for example, the entire text of an auditor general's report, or the annual reports of departments and agencies, or the reports of parliamentary committees, all readily available documents. Government organizations are no more noted than any other for self-criticism, and their reports, with rare exceptions, are based on a philosophy of 'best foot forward'; most of them nowadays have public relations branches, euphemistically designated as communications services. But they all also have observant critics: the auditor general, the parliamentary opposition, the media, and members of the general public. Each governmental department or agency has its own particular audience to satisfy. The service as a whole, viewed dispassionately, can be seen to have adapted itself, sometimes awkwardly and even painfully, to changing Canadian problems. Certainly, in the area of representativeness, it is currently trying, to quote the Treasury Board, 'to ensure that the Public Service is as representative of the Canadian population as possible and that women, Natives and handicapped and other designated groups have access to jobs and opportunities for advancement.'

Progress in any organization as large as the public service, whose members and directors have differing views, can rarely be both rapid and democratic, and the statistics published annually in the reports of the Public Service Commission show how far from being representative in significant areas the service remains. At this writing, for example, the tables showed that 60 per cent of the entire service under the commission consisted of males, with the female numbers of federal employees across the country ranging from a low 26 per cent in Newfoundland to a high of 53 per cent in the Yukon. The range varied enormously throughout the individual departments, with several having substantial majorities of female employees (e.g., over 60 per cent in Employment and Immigration, National Health and Welfare), and others operating with as few as 20 to 30 per cent (Transport, Public Works, Environment). In one sense those figures may be truly representative, reflecting the degree to which particular occupations and professions in the country at large attract women. But there are other categories of which that cannot be said: of those earning less than $20,000 a year, women comprised 68 per cent, while of those earning $60,000 and over, 96 per cent were men. The commission publishes statistics on public servants by their type of employment: management, scientific and professional, administrative and foreign service, technical, administrative support, and operational. Women comprised 6 per cent of management, 23 per cent of scientific and professional, and 12 per cent technical. In all officer categories women contributed 25 per cent of the total; but in administrative support they attained 82 per cent. If a greater measure of equality between the sexes in the public service is the goal, there is plainly work to be done; nevertheless, there are other categories of citizens that are worse off. Perhaps they can all take heart from the fact that the public service not so long ago was, with a few exceptions, also an English-speaking enclave, but the position of the French-speaking has improved vastly in recent decades. (The supplying of the statistics cited above, incidentally, is one of the services performed for the Public Service Commission by Supply and Services.)

THE OTHER SERVICE

The public service discussed in the last section can of course be no better than the people who make it work, and the same is true of the non-departmental parts of the service which require more systematic attention than this chapter has so far given them. As has already been noted, they vary enormously in size, purpose, and organization, so much so that the Royal Commission on Government Organization reported in 1966 (Volume 5, page 68) that 'whatever meaning the term "Crown Corporation" may have had originally, it has none today.' And the non-departmental agencies are not even all crown corporations.

Many attempts, both official and unofficial, have been made to classify all the agencies of government, the official ones to tidy up procedures for financial accountability (first done in the Financial Administration Act of 1951), the unofficial ones usually to clarify their status for analytical reasons. In between lie the reports of royal commissions, official bodies which have no control over the acceptance or rejection of their recommendations; the latest of these on this subject, that on Financial Management and Accountability, produced as part of its report an unusually detailed and useful set of criteria for classifying departments and agencies. After remarking that 'the listing of many agencies in a particular category is a judgement call,' the commission produced four categories based on the susceptibility of the bodies to 'direction from government with respect to policy and management.'

Category I contains those 'susceptible to direction with respect to both policy and management.' These include the ministerial departments already discussed, and those branches of government which, while not whole departments with their own ministers, are designated legally as departments under the ministers of related departments. The best known of these is probably the Royal Canadian Mounted Police, whose minister is the solicitor general, but the list includes, among others, the National Library, the Public Archives (both under the secretary of state), and the Office of the Governor General's Secretary (the prime minister). In addition, the list includes bodies only partly qualified to be in this category, because while they are designated as departments under one relevant statute, they are not so designated under another, the Public Service Employment Act.

Moving still deeper into category I one finds the parliamentary departments, which are designated as departments but which are set up to be independent of ministerial control. For convenience they report to Parliament through a minister. Several of these have already been referred to: the auditor general, the chief electoral officer, the Public Service Commission. The Canadian Human Rights Commission and the commissioner of official languages also belong here. And finally the category includes temporary special status departments that disband when their work is done, such as the Task Force on Canadian Unity and royal commissions. Their numbers fluctuate and cannot be listed in a table, but all the others in category I when the commission reported totalled fifty-six.

Category II, those 'susceptible to direction with the respect to management,' enjoy at least some autonomy in the interpretation of policy. These the commission labelled as independent deciding and advisory bodies, further subdivided into bodies that regulate other things, those that make decisions to settle cases or disputes, those that make grants, and those that can merely offer advice. The commission's list of these numbers thirty, and twenty-eight of them do not meet all the criteria set down for category II.

The regulatory bodies include well-known agencies often in the news, such as the Canadian Radio-Television and Telecommunications Commission and the Tariff Board, as well as others more rarely heard of, such as the Anti-Dumping Tribunal and the Restrictive Trade Practices Commission.

The deciding bodies include such varied agencies as the Canadian Pension Commission, the National Parole Board, and War Veterans' Allowance Board. Institutions such as these often sit almost like courts, hearing applications and appeals and ruling, in effect, on who gets what, if anything.

The granting group contains several bodies that are of particular significance to students: the Social Sciences and Humanities Research Council, the Natural Sciences and Engineering Research Council, the Medical Research Council, the Canada Council. Patronage of the arts and scholarships used to come from popes and kings, but in a democracy committees of one sort or another are the inevitable devices, and all these organizations depend primarily, although not always exclusively, on money given them from the federal treasury. In all cases the fundamental purpose of using independent boards is to minimize the chances of partisan intervention in what are essentially creative enterprises, whether the enterprise is one political scientist or a symphony orchestra, a medical research worker or a theatrical company. Overt political interference is regarded as a violation of what is popularly called the 'arm's-length principle,' but it can happen.

The advisory bodies are often heard from. They include the Advisory Council on the Status of Women, the Economic Council of Canada, the Law Reform Commission, and the Science Council of Canada.

Category III consists of those bodies popularly regarded as crown corporations: they enjoy autonomy in management but are subject to a general direction where policy is involved. Since each is set up for its own purposes, the group is difficult to break up into sub-groups, as each is to some degree in a category by itself.

Some crown corporations are well known. For example, the Canadian Broadcasting Corporation reflects the policies of successive governments over nearly half a century to have a public broadcasting system, but internally the CBC operates itself. Similar statements can be made of Air Canada, Canadian National Railways, and the National Film Board. All of those mentioned (and there are many others) reflect the view that in the provision of necessary services to a large country with a small population located in one long belt from east to west, governmental participation is essential. Other crown corporations rarely make news except in their special environments: the Canada Deposit Insurance Corporation, the harbour commissions (as a group, probably the oldest crown corporations in existence), the Royal Canadian Mint, the St Lawrence Seaway Authority. Another group, whose members the Royal Commission on Financial Management and Accountability found particularly difficult to classify because they combine marketing and regulatory or advisory functions, deal generally with foodstuffs. The list includes, among others, the Canadian Dairy Commission, the Canadian Saltfish Corporation, the Canadian Wheat Board.

Category IV, shared enterprises, consists of non-departmental organizations that enjoy autonomy in both management and policy interpretation: in essence, they are enterprises in which the government of Canada is a shareholder along with other interests. In several, of which Canadian Arctic Producers Limited or Abenaki Motel Limited are representative, the other interests are native peoples' organizations. In others, provincial governments are involved, as in the Saint John Harbour Bridge Authority; and in yet others, including international bridges, the partner is the government of the United States. Private investors often participate, as in the Footwear and Leather Institute of Canada. To this general category the Lambert Commission adds corporations sponsored by governments in a way that is not the same as those entities just referred to: for example, Hockey Canada or the Vanier Institute of the Family.

The complex classification above is necessary to emphasize the remarkable scope of the public service of Canada, not just in the sense of what it does, but in the extraordinary number of forms its organizations take. The forms are continually changing and while some, such as the Privy Council Office and a few other departments, have been around since Confederation, others are of recent origin and, far from enjoying permanent status, are sometimes talked of as candidates for 'privatization,' that is, being sold off. The creation of any new government enterprise, particularly a crown corporation, usually sets off arguments about 'one more' extension of bureaucracy, while at the other end the prospect of selling one off raises the question of why an enterprise commercially attractive to private buyers should not be kept for the benefit of all taxpayers.

This second service has always been with us (harbour commissions, for example, pre-date Confederation), but it is only in the past few decades that it has surpassed in size the departmental organizations. Non-departmental agencies are a handy device for a cabinet, for they can keep burdens on ministers from overwhelming them, and they can make it possible to hold down the size of the cabinet, which is smaller than it would have to be if cabinet ministers were directly responsible for everything. The devices are also flexible, since a particular organization can be constructed to cope with each new area seen to need governing, and it is for the same reason that they vary in form. Some, as noted, are aimed at reducing possible political interference in a service. Some were established to attract into government businessmen who are reluctant to become civil servants: a sturdy entrepreneur who would not dream of becoming an assistant deputy minister might not object to becoming a member of a board of directors, a form he is already familiar with. The non-departmental agencies that have boards (and not all of them enjoy such amenities) have boards of different sizes, with the individual members serving for terms of different lengths, with the terms both renewable and non-renewable, and with relationships with a minister or the cabinet ranging from almost none to close direction. Parliament takes a differing interest in the agencies; those present in many districts (such as the Canadian Broadcasting Corporation or the Canadian National Railway), and thus providing jobs and service to electors, generally receiving far more attention than those that do not. Obviously, the generalizations that can be made about the non-departmental branches of government are few in number.

There is one that has been made increasingly in recent years: holding them accountable, to Parliament or the public, can be difficult, a discovery made almost annually by a parliamentary committee, a royal commission, or an auditor general. One auditor general once referred to the crown corporations as resembling 'enormous icebergs floating lazily in the foggy Atlantic, silent, majestic, awesome'; and since it was an iceberg that sank the *Titanic*, governments over the years have kept trying to invent ways to hold non-departmental agencies accountable. Over all of them there is always some control, of course, for apart from the cabinet's collective responsibility there is the undoubted fact that ministers initiate any legislation creating a crown corporation, and ministers appoint the heads of them; and there is always a watchful parliamentary opposition.

The most systematic attempt to exert more control over non-departmental agencies came in 1984 when Parliament, urged on over the years by its own Public Accounts Committee supported by the auditor general, enacted major amendments to the Financial Administration Act which do, in fact, add to the responsibilities of the crown corporations, especially, for being accountable. The amendments, which rewrite major parts of the act, do not go as far as the committee desired: it had recommended a super-ministry to control all crown corporations. That would have enlarged on a practice already in use, for some crown agencies do have subsidiaries, and at least one, the Canadian Development Investment Corporation, oversees other corporations. Nor did the amendments to the act go as far as several auditors general have proposed, and subject them all to the same auditing procedures as the departments. But the auditor general does audit some corporations listed in the act, while some have auditors appointed otherwise, in time-honoured devices which give successive governments some patronage in the accounting trades.

What the new statutory provisions do (and since they came into force only on 1 September 1984, it is too soon to judge how well they do it[2]) is add substantially to Treasury Board influences on the crown corporations, while at the same time bringing them closer to the auditor general. The board's description of its role already cited anticipated its changing responsibilities, and lists as one of the duties of its crown corporations division 'the development of policy (and periodically legislation) on matters of general applicability to crown corporations such as control by and accountability to government, methods and frequency of reporting, etc.' When on 15 March 1984, the president of the Treasury Board introduced a long series of amendments to the Financial Administration Act, it appeared at first that his zealous department had gone too far, since the bill would have damaged, if it did not destroy, the arm's-length principle considered desirable for such cultural agencies as the Canada Council and the CBC. But on its way through the House of Commons, an amendment was added to make clear that the new rules did not apply to them.

For the rest, the act which emerged (32–33 Elizabeth II, chap. 31) may mean a new way of life. The statute is a lengthy one of over 150 clauses, some of them in themselves also long and complicated, but a sample of its salient points suggests that the day of the free-floating iceberg may be ending. The act adds 'the control of Crown Corporations' to the descriptive subtitle of the Financial Administration Act. Each corporation is given an 'appropriate minister.' The act asserts that 'Each Crown Corporation is ultimately accountable, through the appropriate Minister, to Parliament for the conduct of its affairs.' The government is empowered to give directives 'to any parent Crown Corporation' – that is, one that can spawn subsidiaries; and 'each parent Crown Corporation shall annually submit a corporate plan for the approval of the Governor in Council.' That part of the act also spells out what the corporate plan must contain, and authorizes the Treasury Board to prescribe the form in which the annual audit or other report is to be presented. As of January 1989 the auditor general will become the auditor or joint auditor of a list of named corporations, and as of the passage of the act in 1984 any other auditor is obliged to consult the auditor general on any matter that the auditor thinks should be brought to Parliament's attention. Parliament's opportunities to review any given corporation were enhanced in a number of ways, not the least of which is that it will itself have a voice in the creation of any new bodies; in the past corporations came into being in several haphazard ways, at the will of a minister or the cabinet.

It is appropriate to end a chapter on the public service by returning to a topic of fundamental importance to both departments and non-departmental agencies – delegated legislation. A potential problem in the new rules for crown corporations is that those already existing will presumably continue under their current constitutions, at least until the Treasury Board finds good reasons for recommending changes. Many branches of the government, including departments and non-departmental agencies, have the authority to make regulations which have the force of law and, as J.R. Mallory has written, some regulations are issued under powers that are themselves 'wide and ill-defined'; so that, in effect, a bad or foolish regulation may yet be legal. In a timely essay (revealingly entitled 'Curtailing "Divine Right": The Control of Delegated Legislation in Canada'[3]) Mallory traces the history of attempts to impose Parliament's influence on regulations passed under laws passed by Parliament, leading to the Statutory Instruments Act of 1971, which was followed by the creation of a Joint Standing Committee on Regulations and Other Statutory Instruments. The committee, starting strongly with the redoubtable Eugene Forsey as the co-chairman from the Senate, found itself engaged 'in a series of battles with departments and agencies which persist in drafting regulations which are sloppy, lacking in apparent statutory authority, or are in other ways defective.' The committee has tried to improve itself and its own instruments, owing a good deal to the energies of its senatorial component; but scrutinizing delegated legislation is not politically exciting (or even necessarily politically valuable), 'so the Statutory Instruments Committee labours bravely on in almost total obscurity.'

The committee, and the Statutory Instruments Act, are among the most recent developments in a long history of attempts to enhance Parliament's contribution to the day-to-day business of government. It is to be noted that in 1971 they were hailed as great steps forward in improving parliamentary control over the executive; and the same is true of the 1984 act addressed to the administrative and financial accountability of crown corporations. In 1984 the bill was amended to meet strenuous objections, and finally passed with the support of an agreement among all parties in the Commons; it passed in a Commons in which the Liberals had a majority, and came into force just days before the Progressive Conservatives took over. The act of 1971 also had a rough passage, but the value of its purpose was not challenged.

The control of delegated legislation and of crown corporations has another characteristic in common worthy of a reminder: they deal with large fields of complex activity. This chapter has attempted to outline some of the complexity in departmental and non-departmental tasks and forms, and there is a parallel element in delegated legislation. A regulation can be a simple order to do or refrain from doing something, or it can be a detailed decision which raises profound questions of individual rights apart from the actual subject-matter. If a body has the power to make decisions in a way designed to save the time and expense of going to court, should an aggrieved individual have a right to appeal? And if so, to whom, the courts, or the cabinet? Or should the acts of any public servant be subject to appeal to another independent public servant, an ombudsman, for investigation and report? Since Canada has no federal ombudsman, his duties cannot be described here. The provinces use such an official, and for particular areas there are federal servants whose duties involve a function that resembles an ombudsman's – the Commission of Official Languages, for example, or the Canadian Human Rights Commission. But the only general ombudsman is Parliament itself.

Whether Canada will create a federal ombudsman is unknown, but given the evidence of a growing interest in the accountability of the executive branch, it seems likely. Accountability has become the current preoccupation of analysts of the public service. Where at the beginning reform of the public service meant the gradual reduction of patronage, it now means the development and co-ordination of managerial skills in a way that somehow balances the needs for centralized control and better reporting to Parliament, with the needs of the managers who need freedom to manage. There is no simple or single solution, but a variety of solutions pointing in the same direction. Parliament enacts statutes which severally spell out the duties of ministers and their departments. Executive action supplements parliamentary, to subject the departments and now the crown corporations to the influence of the Treasury Board. Parliament and cabinet arrange for the scrutiny of delegated legislation enlarging its scope in recent years by conflict of interest guidelines and provisions for access to information. The auditor general is a servant of Parliament, not the ministry.

The centralized character of the whole process is one reason why, indeed, the largest branch of the government of Canada can be dealt with in a single chapter. Most of the departments and non-departmental agencies would each merit a book in themselves if their work were to be appraised adequately; many of them now publish annually a book-length report, and many of them are publicly criticized and analysed in Parliament. The body of independent studies, largely by academics, has reached impressive proportions, and professional students of public administration support learned periodicals. The amount of readily available information about government enterprises of all kinds is truly staggering. But different though they are, collectively they can be summarized under a one overall principle: collectively they comprise the public service, and as the public service they must be accountable. The words are straightforward enough, but making accountability real, as this chapter has attempted to show, takes continuing effort.

13
Judges and courts

As it turned out I was one of [Magistrate Bassett's] last customers, for a couple of weeks later he inherited a pot of money from a distant relative and retired to the country. That, at least was the story that had been put about. My own view was that he had got the stuff by sticking like glue to the fines. Five quid here, five quid there – you can see how it would mount up over a period of years.
P.G. Wodehouse, *The Code of the Woosters*

Accountability has different dimensions when it is expected of the judges who interpret the law. Members of Parliament and the parties behind them, as previous chapters have shown, are subject to a variety of restraints, ranging from the electoral law, which at its most forceful may be used to reject a party's candidates entirely, to the rules and procedures governing how the victorious candidates are expected to behave after an election. Public servants work under the administration of cabinet ministers – who also have restraints on them – or under the Public Service Commission and other institutions, or under the directors and managers of non-departmental agencies; they are always subject to guidelines covering conflict of interest and the ultimate checks of the auditor general or some other auditing process. Judges and the courts exist substantially outside the systems containing those who make and administer the laws. Judges are not treated as public servants, and the courts are directly managed by no minister, even though judges are paid from the public purse and the same source supports the courts. Judges do not carry out the policy of any government, and indeed may decide that a government has failed to prove its case when it appears as a litigant. Yet a court decision may have profound political repercussions: as when, for example, the highest court held in 1930 that women were persons qualified to sit in the Senate; or when, in more recent times, courts have held that an individual's compulsory retirement from employment at a fixed age is discriminatory and thus a violation of constitutional rights.

A clearer view of the judiciary's position in the governmental structure, and the reasons that justify it, can be seen from the perspective of the functions of judges and courts. If the reactions of writers in newspapers, magazines, and books for over a century (and the responses of electronic media in more recent decades) can be taken as reliable, the aspects of law that most interest the public are those dealing with crime – offences which if left unchecked would threaten the community, such as murder, theft, or dealing in dangerous substances. If two neighbours disagree over the precise location of a fence dividing their property, for example, the public is assumed to have little interest so long as they approach their problem through surveyors and lawyers. If, however, one neighbour decides to settle the problem by inserting the other head-first into a post hole and incorporating him into the fence, the police will intervene and the media will have a story; and the more prominent the persons involved, the more newsworthy it will be. For that kind of reason, the public is more familiar with allegations and prosecutions, and the trials of accused, than with the less theatrical activities of court cases not concerned with crime. Although the criminal law is obviously of vast significance, and some lawyers specialize in it, the day-to-day functions of judges and courts are generally not exciting.

A committee of the Canadian Bar Association reporting on the independence of the judiciary in 1985 began its comments with a summary of basic types of conflict that can develop in a society such as Canada's:

(1) *Disputes between individuals*
An individual in such a dispute is commonly a citizen or a group of citizens, but the term includes other kinds of legal individuals such as corporations.
(2) *Disputes between individuals and governments*
Governments are treated as individuals by the courts. As a result, it is especially important that governments not be able to influence a judge, i.e., that his independence from governmental pressure or control be assured.
(3) *Disputes between governments*
Canada being a federal state has rules determining the areas in which the federal and provincial governments may legislate. These rules are as clearly stated as possible, but it is not realistic to expect that all ambiguities and conflicts will be avoided.[1]

More details about the provisions that can lead to disputes between governments are presented in later chapters. In the mean time it is important to note that all three categories of disputes listed above can arise only where individuals are free to create them, and that the fair settlement of any of the categories cannot be left either to one of the parties in a dispute or to those who make or administer the laws whose application is being contested. There must be a group of arbitrators, independent of legislators and public administrators; and it follows that selecting and appointing the arbitrators, and protecting them from improper influence after they are appointed, are major tasks in any democratic government. The tasks are not made easier by the changing nature of modern society. A single new invention such as the automobile or the airplane or the computer, which from hesitant starts soon assumes a monopoly over important aspects of human mobility and communication, requires whole new bodies of law that can develop during the careers of individual judges, requiring of them a capacity to adapt to new conditions. Powerful social changes have demanded similar adaptations. Industrialization has produced an impressive variety of new laws covering everything from safety in work places to the rights of individuals to absent themselves from work altogether. Urbanization, which crowds humanity in unprecedented quantities in small areas, or the growing recognition of women's rights, has been reflected in legislation. Every significant change in the way human beings behave will have significant repercussions for the law, and thus for the judges who interpret it.

A reader who has glimpsed the myriad ways in which the modern state has established administrative devices will not be surprised to learn that the law and the courts also exhibit considerable variety in form and substance. Historically the roots of Canadian law, except in Quebec, can be traced to a remarkably influential English creation called the common law, whose strength rested not only on its usefulness in Britain, but on the theory which held that when Englishmen left home to colonize other parts of the world, they took their common law with them. Today most of the English-speaking countries of the world owe much to the common law. It is none the less not easy to describe. A fundamental element in it is that the common law, in a phrase beloved of jurists and legal commentators, is 'judge-made law,' a term which in the late twentieth century may not sound even vaguely democratic. But the term is accurate. In the days before Parliament had emerged as a law-making body, and before Parliament had created administrative agencies empowered to issue regulations having the force of law, the king's judges travelled about settling disputes by the local customs, and settling later disputes on the basis of the principles applied in earlier similar cases; in other words, they accepted precedents as trustworthy guides in maintaining the king's peace in his realm. 'In time,' Chief Justice Brian Dickson wrote in 1982, 'that body of law supported a full complement of legal principles, given shape and cohesion by the application of like principles in alike circumstances.'[2] Serious lawyers rejoice in the common law, and celebrate its pragmatism, in a characteristic phrase, as 'marked by a delight in robust common sense.'[3]

In the days before Parliament had become a deliberate maker of laws, the judge-made principles of the common law were the major sources of law. They were supplemented early by another body of law known as equity. Suitors disappointed in the common law courts learned to petition the monarch for relief, and the king referred such petitions to his chancellor, who was expected to determine what was equitable: the chancellor, in effect, provided a means of appeal. The dual system of institutions applying the common law and doctrines of equity has long since been replaced, but the two sets of interpretation have remained, and provincial courts will sometimes designate a particular individual as a judge in equity.

Both systems have been overtaken by laws passed by Parliament, which has expressed most basic principles of law in statutory terms, thus replacing the older forms. The same is true of the other main root of Canadian law, the civil law that prevails in Quebec – an importation, not surprisingly, from France, whose Code Napoléon was based on ancient Roman law. The right of French-speaking North Americans to retain their legal system was laid down in the Quebec Act of 1774, and confirmed in a section of the Constitution Act of 1867 which allocated 'property and civil rights in the province' to provincial jurisdictions. That provision perpetuated relevant principles of the common law in the other provinces, but in Quebec it meant that matters concerning personal, family, and property relations were to be governed under different rules. As with the common law, historical principles of the civil law have been embodied in statutes, and since Canada is a federal state with both national and provincial governments, it is important to note that the federal jurisdiction also covers topics which might sound like 'property and civil rights.' The criminal law is Parliament's responsibility, and so are many items essential to the nation's commercial life: bills of exchange, banks, navigation, and patents and copyrights, among others.

The burden of interpretation laid on the courts by tradition and statute is a complex one, and what was said earlier about the courts' basic role in settling disputes must be supplemented by mention of further duties. A court does not usually intervene until an actual case comes before it, but there are categories of judicial activity that are different from the hearing of disputes. There are, for example, provisions which allow a court in some circumstances to intervene if it can be convinced that the commission of a legal wrong is contemplated but has not yet taken place. A court may also act in an administrative or supervisory capacity as, for example, when it deals with a deceased's estate or a declared bankrupt's property. Most important of all in the 'non-dispute' functions of the higher courts is the obligation to give opinions on legal questions referred to them by governments. Parliament and most of the provincial legislatures have passed laws authorizing their respective governments, in effect, to ask the highest court in each jurisdiction for statements on the interpretation of the constitution, or the constitutionality of real or proposed legislation. After considerable grumbling on the part of Supreme Court justices who objected to the practice, that court itself, when asked (in a reference) if such references were valid, agreed that they were.

Reference cases, after a slow start, have become a major portion of judicial decisions in Canada. The advantages to a government of getting an advance opinion from a high court on a potentially controversial issue are obvious, but so are the dangers to the courts. The temptation for a government to bypass an awkward decision by referring the subject to the courts, thus using the judicial process for political purposes, is always present, and there can be no doubt that the abuse of references would threaten the courts' independence. Justices have traditionally comforted themselves with the assurance that reference opinions are only opinions, not legally binding like a formal decision. Nevertheless, it is not easy for lower courts to ignore the opinions of high courts, legally binding or not.[4]

THE SYSTEM OF COURTS

Given the variety of matters in which courts can become involved, it is clear courts could be organized in a variety of ways. They could, for example, in some civil cases be separated according to the amount of money involved in a dispute, with the lowest level confined to amounts not exceeding (for example) two or three thousand dollars, and intermediate and higher courts dealing progressively with larger amounts. Criminal courts could be similarly stratified according to the seriousness of offences as defined in the law. Courts could be divided by topics, into family, commercial, criminal, and constitutional courts. The trouble with all such appealing systems of organization is that they are too simplistic: a family matter could easily have commercial aspects, possibly criminal implications, and even raise constitutional points if fundamental rights are a factor. Classifying crimes by their weight raises similar problems for several reasons: all crimes are serious, and to the individual a criminal record is a criminal record which can follow him or her forever. Consider the problems of categorizing theft. Is cattle-rustling in western ranchlands the same kind of offence as the well-organized stealing of automobiles in a metropolitan area? Is an individual disguised by a ski mask holding up a corner grocery the same kind of criminal as an unmasked computer expert who uses his skills to deplete a pension fund?

The Canadian system of courts tries to recognize differences in legal matters through a hierarchy which accommodates them all, and in general (there are exceptions) allows for the appealing of decisions from lower to higher courts. The system requires the co-operation of both the federal and provincial governments. The constitution empowers Parliament to create a general court of appeal (the

Supreme Court of Canada), and 'any additional courts for the better administration of the laws of Canada.' The provincial legislatures have jurisdiction over 'the administration of justice in the province, including the constitution, maintenance, and organization of provincial courts, both of civil and criminal jurisdiction, and including procedure in civil matters in those courts.' That means, among other things, that federal laws are enforced in courts under provincial jurisdiction; and while Parliament has control over procedure in criminal matters, it means further that some parts of criminal law may not be evenly enforced across the country because provincial attorneys general may have differing views about particular subjects. All the courts at the lowest level of the hierarchy – that is, the local courts most familiar to the average citizen – are the creations of the provinces. A typical case that is to travel through the hierarchy to the top may start in a provincial court – for example, a French-speaking citizen residing outside Quebec wants to determine if he has to pay a parking ticket issued in English only – and be appealed by either side to a higher provincial court, and then (since a constitutional point is at stake) go to the Supreme Court.

The hierarchy varies from province to province, but in every instance appears much the same; and the word 'appears' is important, for the hierarchy in any one province is not the only element in the structure of the courts, since courts are divided according to not only rank but also to some extent the subjects they deal with. The hierarchy is none the less there, and while in many cases an appeal from a lower court may be made to a higher, the reverse is not true. And improbable as it may seem to some of those called upon to appear before a court, the system in general includes as one of its purposes the convenient availability of justice to as many people as possible.

MINOR PROVINCIAL COURTS

These courts in each province are entirely under provincial control, from the nature of their organization to the appointment and payment of the judges, and naturally vary from province to province. They are the 'local' courts, and their number varies with the number of localities seen by the province to need them. Ontario, the most populous province, has nearly two hundred communities served by provincial appointees, and Prince Edward Island fewer than half a dozen. The provinces with the most thinly settled areas need to serve a disproportionately large number of centres considering their total populations, and each of the three prairie provinces has, in round numbers, a hundred or more. The most important of the local courts are now generally called provincial courts and are presided over by judges; they used to be familiarly known as magistrate's courts. The judges, although they usually have 'home courts,' commonly have jurisdiction throughout the province, and they are authorized by both federal and provincial laws to hear a wide variety of cases, including some criminal matters. They hear a large number of cases, far more than the higher courts; depending on the province, the lowest courts see the start of 80 or 90 per cent of all cases.

Each province also has a set of specialized courts established to deal with particular matters, and their judges are often also members of other courts. Judges of the provincial courts described above are commonly also justices of the peace, who serve a number of purposes, often in areas where the facilities of a full court are not readily available. There are courts designed to deal with particular family subjects apart from divorce, and juvenile matters. Most provinces have surrogate courts which deal with problems arising over the estates of deceased persons and the interpretation of wills. There are also small claims courts which are concerned with sums of money not large enough to justify the expense of a full-scale court hearing with attendant legal costs. In general, if there is a field of human activity that generates recurring problems under the law, there is likely to be a provincial judicial arrangement to deal with it. One of those frequently in the news is the coroner's court, which investigates many deaths from other than natural causes.

County and district courts
Not all provinces are organized into counties, which historically served as judicial districts, but those without counties can still be organized into judicial centres. Only four of the provinces now have county or district courts, although at one time they all did. The county and district courts are presided over by judges appointed and paid by the federal not the provincial authority, but the province is responsible for the courts' organization and maintenance. It is common for county and district court judges to have jurisdiction beyond their local boundaries. In Saskatchewan until 1980, for example, the judicial district was the whole province, with judicial centres located in the major towns and cities, and a judge could be assigned by the provincial chief justice to preside over cases in any of them. Saskatchewan's district court system, like that in several other provinces, has been absorbed into a higher level. Where they exist, the county and district courts have much the same kind of general jurisdiction as that conferred on provincial courts, and their judges are usually empowered to sit as if they were in fact also judges of provincial courts. The county and district courts sometimes hear cases dealing with larger amounts of money than can be dealt with in the lower courts, and appeals from the lower courts to a higher level are permitted under the terms of the relevant provincial legislation.

Superior courts in the provinces
Each province has a high court which, unlike the courts already mentioned, has

headquarters in the provincial capital. The judges of superior courts may travel to hear cases in other centres, but their courts are generally identified with a specific building recognized as the province's senior courthouse. The names of provincial superior courts take several forms (Supreme Court, High Court of Justice, Court of Queen's Bench, and even Superior Court), but they are essentially the same courts, enjoying comprehensive and unlimited jurisdiction, and the power to reach decisions that can be appealed only to the highest national tribunals. The superior courts themselves can of course be appealed to from the lower courts already described. Under many circumstances defined in law, a party to an action before a superior court may request a jury, although the request is not necessarily granted automatically. Expert lawyers have argued that the abolition of trial by jury in civil cases would save valuable time and money. But the right of an accused person in criminal cases to be judged by his peers is not in danger; with clearly stated exceptions, it is enshrined in the Charter of Rights and Freedoms.

Since the superior trial courts are the highest in each province, and their judges are appointed and paid under federal authority, it is not uncommon (especially when Parliament and the provincial legislature support executives drawn from different political parties) for tensions to arise between governments. A province may provide for more judges than is considered necessary by the federal authority, even though members of Parliament frequently urge that their provinces need more judges. In the period 1982–4 the Conservative government of Saskatchewan, dissatisfied with the lack of consultations they had enjoyed with the federal Liberal government about judicial appointments in the province, moved in the opposite direction to reduce the number of available judgeships. 'The resulting impasse,' a committee of the Canadian Bar Association reported laconically in 1985, 'persisted until the federal Progressive Conservatives were elected in September 1984.'[5] From which one can deduce a relevant lesson: while judges on the bench are expected to be impartial, the process by which they reached there may be different.

Courts of appeal in the provinces

All provinces have provincial courts of appeal, in some cases a designated part of the province's superior court, in others a separate court. In Saskatchewan the Court of Appeal is separate from the Court of Queen's Bench (the court to which the province's former district courts were added), of which the appellate judges are nonetheless *ex officio* members; the Court of Appeal is presided over by the chief justice of the province. In Ontario the appeal court is part of the Supreme Court of Ontario. Judges of appeal courts are among those federally appointed, with the provinces again responsible for the courts' organization and maintenance.

Appeal courts have a general jurisdiction in civil and criminal cases, and are rare among high courts in that their names actually indicate what they do: they hear appeals. Within each province there is no higher judicial authority, the appeal courts having the last judicial word within their province's boundaries.

Courts created by Parliament

Parliament, as has been noted, has a comprehensive power to create 'a General Court of Appeal for Canada' (the Supreme Court of Canada) and 'any additional courts for the better administration of the laws of Canada.' Some of the courts established under the federal authority are well known; others serve relatively narrow and specialized purposes and receive little public attention. To the individuals served, however, they are of great significance. There are citizenship courts, which do not deal with disputes in the ordinary way but are charged with determining the qualifications of applicants for Canadian citizenship, and then admitting the qualified. There is a Court Martial Appeal Court, comprising designated judges from other courts, which hears appeals from military tribunals; its decisions can be appealed to the Supreme Court. In 1983 an administrative tribunal known as the Tax Review Board was elevated into the Tax Court. Other federal tribunals such as the National Energy Board are courts of record: that is, while their decisions are subject to review by a higher court, their documents are accepted as authentic and relevant evidence, and do not have to be taken again.

There are, in short, numerous kinds of federal courts, and Parliament may add more by statute when a need is perceived. Three courts deserve more specific description. The first (and this often surprises citizens) is Parliament itself. Parliament historically developed out of a court, and the House of Commons still retains what are clearly judicial functions. (The Senate's status in this regard is less clear, and in any event of less account.) The Commons is the sole judge of who may sit in it, and whether they were properly elected; the most famous member rejected was Louis Riel, who earned the distinction twice. The House may also summon witnesses, and once imprisoned an unco-operative visitor who had been summoned. The legislative assembly of Saskatchewan, exerting its ancient privileges, twice seated the runner-up in an election in preference to the winner. Parliamentary bodies exercising their judicial capacities can plainly enjoy rich lives.[6]

Other national courts do too, but more sedately. The main federal tribunal apart from the Supreme Court is called the Federal Court of Canada, a name which reveals nothing of its functions. The Federal Court was preceded by the Exchequer Court, which originally had the same members as the Supreme Court: the Exchequer division was a court of first instance, the other was for appeals. The Exchequer Court became separate in 1887, and survived until 1971. The modern Federal Court exercises a wider jurisdiction than its predecessor.

The Exchequer Court, as its name at least suggests, dealt with financial matters: cases involving the revenues of the crown, suits against the crown in federal affairs, disputes arising from the expropriation of property, and related matters. The court also heard cases arising from maritime law, and the laws governing patents, copyrights, and trademarks. The Federal Court inherited all those duties, and more. As succinctly described in *The Canadian Encyclopedia*'s first edition, the Federal Court 'also has a supervisory jurisdiction in relation to decisions of tribunals and inferior bodies established by federal law. It is divided into a Trial Division and a Court of Appeal. Generally, matters originate in the Trial Division, but some appeals from, and some actions to set aside decisions of, inferior tribunals proceed directly to the Federal Court of Appeal. An appeal lies from the Court of Appeal to the Supreme Court of Canada with leave of either court. The main office of the court is in Ottawa but it regularly sits throughout Canada according to the circumstances of the action and to suit the convenience of the parties.'

THE SUPREME COURT

One of the chief uses of the Federal Court of Appeal has been to reduce the workload of its superior, the Supreme Court of Canada. That court, established by federal statute in 1875, has had a more chequered career than any similar institution in the country. From the start some of the Fathers of Confederation favoured a national appeals court, but there was apparently insufficient agreement among them for it to be provided for in the constitution. Macdonald thought it at least 'wise and expedient' to empower the new Parliament to establish a court if it saw fit, but several French-Canadian speakers in the Confederation Debates of 1865 saw dangers to Quebec's unique civil law in a tribunal whose judges would come largely from other provinces. The Supreme Court's creation in 1875 was followed by several serious attempts to abolish it. It was agreed that Canada, as a British colony, had no need of a national court superior to the provincial courts: the colonists had taken to North America not only the common law but also the right of any subject of the crown to appeal to the foot of the throne for redress of grievances. Such appeals were dealt with by the Judicial Committee of the Privy Council, which sat in London.

From 1875 to 1949, in fact, the Supreme Court of Canada was a supreme court in name only. Technically the Judicial Committee of the Privy Council is an advisory body, rather than a court giving judgment, but its advice had all the force of law, and even after 1949 the influence of its advice, as is natural in any system that relies so much on precedents, remained considerable. It may seem odd that a nation would rely on a court outside its own borders, but Canada was not fully independent until the Statute of Westminster of 1931 created the modern

Commonwealth. As early as 1888 Canada had attempted to abolish appeals to the Judicial Committee in criminal cases, and the committee found that to be ultra vires (that is, outside the powers of Parliament) in 1926. With the passage of the Statute of Westminster Canada had the power to abolish all appeals, and did so for criminal cases in 1935. The lingering retention of appeals in civil cases depended partly on doubts about the powers of the provinces in regard to their abolition. But in 1947 the Judicial Committee held that Parliament could abolish all appeals to it, and in 1949 that was accomplished by a statute which made the Supreme Court of Canada the final court for all cases begun after its passage. True to ancient principles governing legal rights, cases begun before the act's passage could still go to the Judicial Committee, and a few years passed before the last of them was disposed of.

From 1949 the Supreme Court assumed a new role, not just as a settler of disputes, but as the final interpreter of the Canadian constitution, a role which caused some uneasiness among provincial governments well aware that the federal authority appointed all the high court judges. Since this chapter is concerned with the courts as institutions in the Canadian polity, the particular activity of reviewing the meaning of the constitution is reserved for a later chapter. For the moment, it is important to note that for nearly four decades the Supreme Court has been handing down decisions which have created little unrest. Inevitably its new significance raised questions about how representative of the provinces it should or must be, and serious suggestions that it should be reformed by allowing the provinces to participate in the selection of its judges.

Such questions were of less moment before 1949, since appeals directly from provincial superior courts to the Judicial Committee in London, bypassing the Supreme Court of Canada, had been not only possible but common. The Supreme Court in 1875 was established with a chief justice and five judges, two of whom had to come from Quebec because of Quebec's different civil laws; when the court was enlarged to a total of seven in 1927, and then nine in 1949, Quebec's share of the court was guaranteed, and is currently set at three. The mere existence of such a provision naturally helped other provinces to believe that they too were entitled to a share of the court, and while only Quebec has a legal guarantee, the principle of sectional representation has become firmly if unofficially accepted by custom. In 1985 the court consisted of one justice from the Atlantic region, four from Quebec, three from Ontario, and one (the chief justice) from Manitoba. One of the three from Ontario is the court's first female justice, appointed in 1982.

The Supreme Court's jurisdiction has changed in ways other than that involved in becoming the court of last resort for Canadians. Its mandate was from the start a broad one, obliging it to hear appeals from a variety of lesser bodies. When its workload began to increase after 1949, there began talk about lightening its burdens and thus shortening the long delays that could occur between the start of an appeal and its actual hearing. In what the Supreme Court's chroniclers have called 'one of the most significant developments in the history of the Court's jurisdiction,' the federal government in the 1970s moved to limit the grounds on which appeals were permissible. For example, any civil case that involved more than $10,000 could be appealed automatically; in 1975 the monetary consideration was removed and 'the justices were given authority to grant leave to appeal on the basis of whether in their judgment the case involved an issue of public importance or of a legal significance.' The court still had to accept the reference cases already mentioned, and criminal cases where there had been a judicial dissent below; but in general it was given substantial control over its own timetable. However, it continues to hear a large number of cases, the total of appeals running to well over one hundred in an average year.[7]

The court's workload has been affected again, and possibly in a momentous way, by the constitutional changes of 1982. Those changes added to the constitution the Charter of Rights and Freedoms, and made clear that the Supreme Court would have the final word in deciding what the charter meant. The court itself, for the first time, was imbedded in the constitution: its composition can be changed only by a resolution that is passed both by Parliament and all the provincial assemblies, and other aspects of it can be altered only by a parliamentary resolution and two-thirds of the assemblies representing at least half the provinces' total populations. The constitution now declares that 'the Constitution of Canada is the supreme law of Canada, and any law that is inconsistent with the provisions of the Constitution is, to the extent of the inconsistency, of no force or effect.' Only the Supreme Court can finally determine consistency or inconsistency, and the role thus thrust on it is potentially of incalculable magnitude. The court has always interpreted the constitution, but until 1982 the constitution did not include a bill of rights. (John Diefenbaker's bill of rights was an ordinary act of Parliament.) How the court interprets the charter may profoundly alter the powers of Parliament and the provincial legislatures.

As this is written, the impact of the court's view of the charter is not clear. One of Canada's most eminent legal authorities, Dr W.R. Lederman, has suggested that the impact may not in the event prove to be drastic: 'In general, my opinion is that the direct impact of the Charter standards is on legal arrangements and legal relations only, and by no means all of them at that.'[8] Judging by the public utterances of both politicians and judges, there is some kind of unofficial hope that the courts will use self-imposed restraints in deciding what the charter means. A similar restraint, however, did not appear on the part of all litigants who have invoked the charter on their own behalf during its early years.

A few questions, most of them based on cases begun in lower courts, can illustrate the point. If, as the charter says, 'every citizen has the right to vote,' and discrimination based on age is unlawful, where does that leave individuals who are not allowed to vote because they are not yet eighteen? If discrimination based on religion is forbidden, what of Sunday observance laws which require various shop owners to remain closed regardless of their beliefs? If 'everyone has ... freedom of thought, belief, opinion and expression,' what of those whose doctrines, however sincerely held, are considered harmful to others? If 'English and French are the official languages of Canada,' and another part of the constitution assigns the criminal law to Parliament's jurisdiction, does a French-speaking person accused of a crime in a province that is not itself bilingual have the right to be tried in French? Does a person suspected of driving while impaired have the right to refuse to take a breathalizer test until he has consulted his lawyer? If 'everyone has the right to life, liberty and security of the person,' what of those who object to the testing of cruise missiles above their heads – or, for that matter, the flying of airplanes over any inhabited area? Those queries represent a minuscule sample of the hundreds of charter cases now before the courts, only a baker's dozen of which, as this is written, have reached the Supreme Court.

They all give point to an observation made in 1985 by the Canadian Bar Association committee on the appointment of judges: 'With the proclamation of the Charter in 1982, the constitutional work of Canadian courts took on a revolutionary new dimension.' The courts, whose main constitutional preoccupations before that date had been with the division of powers between federal and provincial legislatures, must now consider whether the charter puts some kinds of legislation beyond the reach of *any* elected law-making body. Not one of the judges who must take over the 'revolutionary new dimensions' is elected: all are appointed, and together they constitute a small minority of the people empowered to make major decisions on behalf of Canadians.

It is pertinent further to inquire into the circumstances governing the selection of judges, and how they are treated after selection.

THE POSITION OF THE JUDICIARY

Appointment and promotion

The process of selecting people for high office has a unique aspect where judges are concerned; they are expected to fulfil unique functions in unique ways, yet they still depend on the public purse. There are, after all, only a handful of ways of filling public offices, and two of them, military conquest and heredity, can have only limited, if any, application in a liberal democracy. Election is of course indispensable, but the broad sweep of the party and representative system, admirable though it is, emphasizes among other things some of the characteristics least desirable in a judiciary: the taking of sides in political issues, for example, and the seeking of personal or partisan popularity in the interests of re-election. There remains the selecting of judges by merit, as large numbers of public servants are chosen, or patronage – that is, appointment by somebody. There are countries, of which France is probably the best-known example, in which young people trained in the law choose a judicial career, which they enter at the bottom after graduation from established courses, and thereafter work their way upwards much like other professional public servants. In Canada judges have always been taken from the practising bar, most of them entering at the rank they will hold for the rest of their working lives. Except for those lower court judges appointed under provincial authority, they are selected and appointed by the federal executive, by the same official instruments that create senators and members of federal boards.

Judicial appointments, that is, fall into the category covered by the catch-all term 'patronage.' At its crudest, that means that the best general route a lawyer with judicial ambitions can follow involves being in favour with a successful political party. When one party is so successful that it stays in power for prolonged periods, as the Conservatives did for twenty-four of the first twenty-nine years after Confederation, or the Liberals did from 1935 to 1957, lawyers in the 'other' party, however able, are all but excluded from appointment. Members of third parties, none of which have held power at the federal level, have with occasional exceptions been permanently cut off from the bench. And yet, if judges are to be appointed, what sounder appointing body could be found than the country's duly constituted government, which is responsible for so many other crucial decisions?

While it is easy to criticize judicial appointments, it is fair to add that judgeships have never been created with the same partisan abandon as have senatorships. 'I have always laid down with respect to the judiciary,' Canada's first prime minister wrote, 'the principle that no amount of political pressure shall induce me to appoint an incompetent or unworthy judge'; and while with some exceptions Macdonald and his successors managed to find competence and worthiness in their own parties, the parties were sufficiently supplied with able lawyers that a high level for judges' qualifications could generally be maintained. As Canada grew so did the amount of judicial patronage, and by the late 1970s the federal government, not counting federal courts themselves, had jurisdiction over 602 of 1,470 judgeships in Canada, the other 868 being provincial responsibilities. One study of Quebec revealed that over the province's judicial history to the 1970s, 54 per cent of the judges on the Court of Appeal and 34 per cent of those on the Superior Court had been elected politicians at the national or provincial levels. The same study showed that in recent years a considerable drop in such appointments had taken place.[9]

A large part of the credit for the decline in the use of overt political patronage for the bench belongs to the legal profession, for in recent decades it has taken an increasing interest in appointments, generally finding sympathetic ears in Ottawa because most prime ministers (and of course ministers of justice) had legal training. The liaison between the government and the profession took on more formality beginning apparently in the late 1960s, when both Pierre Trudeau and John Turner, as ministers of justice, told the Commons that they had consulted the president of the Canadian Bar Association, and through him a committee on judicial nominations, before appointing a judge. By the 1980s the consultation had been institutionalized, and in a letter to the *Globe and Mail* (on 1 September 1984) the president of the Bar Association described the process:

[The Association's] national Judicial Appointments Committee has operated successfully by way of agreement with the federal Government since 1967. The purpose of this committee is to screen on a confidential basis names supplied by the Minister of Justice. To suggest names would detract from its effective, independent and valued advice to the minister. The agreement is that if a proposed name is found to be unqualified, such person is struck from the list.

The appointing power remained with the federal government, but the profession's influence, as reported by the association in 1985, is reflected in the fact that 'in one recent three-year period, the Committee reviewed 382 names, 64 of which were rated as not qualified.'

Since all kinds of citizens appear in courts, a doctrinaire democrat might challenge the influence of a single small profession over the appointment of judges, even though the actual appointments remain with the political executive. (In any event it is relevant that all kinds of citizens appear also in hospitals and universities, and both doctors and professors, though usually in less conspicuous ways, exercise considerable influence in selecting high-ranking members of their respective trades, many of whom draw salaries provided by the taxpayers.) There are, however, limitations in the consultative process for selecting judges. Not all appointments are included, for there is rarely consultation about the promotion of judges already appointed to a superior court; yet that is of particular interest because many recent elevations to the Supreme Court of Canada have been promotions from other courts. Because of varying practices in provincial bar associations, or variations in provincial court structures, inconsistencies can arise over the assessment, or the assignment, of particular individuals. Partly because the procedures involved must be confidential, the public's knowledge of how judges are appointed is not great. There are other problems, but the most important single weakness was made dramatically plain in 1984, when in the transition of the prime ministership from Trudeau to Turner, the entire consultative process was bypassed. The nature of the bypassing was revealingly commented on by a committee of the Canadian Bar Association: 'it is inappropriate for cabinet ministers to be appointed directly to the bench ... The committee therefore recommends that no such candidate be considered for appointment for at least two years after resigning from the cabinet.'

The committee also offered twenty-four other pertinent conclusions, all dealing with the single matter of appointment. But assuming all judges are properly appointed, after so exhaustive an assessment of character, training, and experience that previous political affiliations become irrelevant, there would still remain to be considered how a nation keeps its judges true to the criteria by which they were chosen. Attention must therefore be given to the devices that come into operation after appointment is effected.

Working conditions after appointment
If there is one word that epitomizes a sound judiciary, it is independence: independence from previous business, professional, or political connections that might affect a judge's impartiality; from insecurity and want; from distracting administrative burdens; and even from criticism to which a judge is not free to respond. The work of a judge demands wisdom as well as knowledge, conscience as well as insight, a sense of balance and proportion, and if not an absolute freedom from prejudices, at least the ability to detect – or suspect – such failings. The paragon who displays such qualities and earns the remarkable degree of independence that is accorded a judge is not easy to find, and once found may discover that a judge has to live an isolated social life. Judges have been known to resign not because they did not like the work, but because they did not like the loneliness.

Judicial independence cannot be guaranteed by repeated statements that it is indispensable and therefore exists. Statements which more or less assume that, frequently heard in Parliament and elsewhere since Confederation, are common, and received a reiteration in 1985 from a learned committee of the Canadian Bar Association. But the principle of independence, like many another in the political world, has to be supported by practice and actions, the chief of which are summarized below.

1. *Tenure*. The foundation of judicial independence is security of tenure. In modern society secure tenure is considered necessary in many professions: scientists cannot be free to do research if unpopular findings may lead to their dismissal, and teachers of all kinds cannot do their work properly if unpopular opinions produce the same result. Almost alone, however, the members of the judiciary, and especially those of the higher courts, are close to irremovable except

for deliberate wrong-doing. Governments put judges in office, but they do not thereafter remove them for stupidity, error, laziness, irascibility, and other endearing human traits. It is ordinarily considered a lesser evil to leave a difficult judge on the bench, than to endanger the security and peace of mind of the entire judiciary. 'Judge x is utterly incompetent,' a nameless lawyer once averred, 'and it's often a great advantage. If I lose, there's usually grounds for appeal.'

Parliament has recognized that age may lessen a judge's efficiency, and in 1927 set a retirement age of seventy-five for the Supreme Court; age limits were later extended to provincial superior courts. (Such restrictions, it should be noted, may also be violations of the Charter of Rights and Freedoms.) Parliament has tried other tactics: for example, a provision for judges to retire on generous pensions, regardless of age, after fifteen years on the bench. Parliament has also provided a more drastic measure, the cessation of salary payments, after careful investigation by his peers, to a judge incapacitated by age and infirmity. These devices generally involved initiatives by the federal minister of justice, and thus bore the unwelcome suggestion (usually unfairly) that politics was becoming mixed up in the administration of justice.

There is now a Canadian Judicial Council, enshrined in the Judges' Act, which is charged with promoting 'the quality of judicial service' for federally appointed judges serving in courts administered by the provinces. At the request of the federal minister or any of his provincial equivalents, the council may investigate the capacity of a judge and if necessary recommend his removal. Several of the provinces also have judicial councils whose functions include seeking the names of individuals who are considered worthy of judicial appointment in the first place.

2. *Removal*. The power of removal is of course closely related to tenure, and it cannot be emphasized too strongly that as long as a judge of a higher court observes the canons of 'good behaviour' (a legal term given a generous interpretation since Confederation) removal is extremely difficult. Judges of the lower courts staffed by federal appointment can be removed by order-in-council after a judicial inquiry; and judges appointed to provincial courts by provincial governments, while cases are rare, are similarly exposed. In 1984–5, indeed, queries and challenges in several provinces raised the question of whether a provincial court judge, appointed by the same attorney general who may argue a case in the provincial court, and may also advise a judge's removal, is truly capable of holding the kind of independent hearing guaranteed by the Charter of Rights. The principle involved went for decision to the Supreme Court of Canada, and on 19 December 1985, that court, in a major decision applying specifically to Ontario but likely to have general acceptance, held that provincially appointed judges were indeed independent.

The process of removal for federal and superior court judges is a joint address of both houses of Parliament, followed by actual dismissal by the governor-in-council. The whole process is complicated, and nowadays for federally appointed judges in provincially administered courts involves the Canadian Judicial Council, which may recommend removal on several grounds, including age, infirmity, misconduct, or conduct that places a judge 'in a position incompatible with the due execution in his office.' A parliamentary address for removal must pass the Commons and Senate separately, and while the process has on occasion actually begun, no federal or superior court judge has yet been removed. The case that came closest to removal, in 1966–7, is instructive for its detail, and not least because the judge concerned, Mr Justice Leo Landreville, was not accused of any misbehaviour on the bench, but of allegedly improper involvement in transactions that took place before he was appointed. Nevertheless, he was investigated by the provincial bar association of Ontario, then by a royal commission whose report was referred to a joint parliamentary committee, which in turn found the judge 'unfit for the proper exercise of his judicial functions' and recommended the commencement of a parliamentary address. The judge unsuccessfully petitioned to be heard at the bar of the House of Commons, the address started on its way, and the judge resigned. More recently Mr Justice Thomas Berger, of the British Columbia Supreme Court, was rebuked by the Judicial Council for 'indiscreet' public comments about the treatment accorded Canada's aboriginal peoples in the constitutional negotiations of the early 1980s. The prime minister voiced his objections, and a judge of the Federal Court laid an official complaint about his fellow justice, after which the Judicial Council was censorious but found no basis for recommending Judge Berger's removal. The judge was perhaps merely unfortunate in the timing of his critical remarks on a political issue, for other judges have expressed both supporting and critical views on such varied topics as nuclear disarmament and publicly supported medicare plans without being investigated. But this episode demonstrates that it is still a highly prized tenet in the theory of judicial behaviour that judges ought not to express public opinions on controversial matters.

3. *Extra-judicial duties*. It may seem paradoxical, therefore, that judges are often called upon officially to indeed express their opinions on controversial matters. In one sense, the impartiality of judges provides the very reason why high court judges are often selected to serve as royal commissioners, or as other inquirers into difficult subjects affecting the common weal. But that same impartiality can be called into question if a judge, however judiciously, reaches findings about which non-judges hold lively partisan opinions. Neither judges nor lawyers officially support the use of judges outside the courtroom, and the committee of the

Canadian Bar Association which reported on the independence of the judiciary in 1985 endorsed the view that 'a judge should restrict his public comments to three subjects – the law, the legal system, and the administration of justice.' The committee was speaking of public comments in general, but Chief Justice Brian Dickson, speaking to the convention that received the committee's report, was more explicit: 'In particular, I think we must approach with reluctance judicial participation in royal commissions and inquiries. Such involvement may suggest to the public not only that judicial time is not sufficiently occupied by the primary task of deciding cases ... but also, as is in fact the case, that judges are embroiled in politically contentious disputes.'

Immediately before, during, and after the time in which the chief justice spoke, Canadian high court judges were inquiring into the deaths under mysterious circumstances of babies at Toronto's Hospital for Sick Children, the Canadian record in handling Nazi war criminals, and the spectacular collapse of two parts of the banking system. These were all high-profile contentious matters, which furthermore took judges away from their courts at a time when both the legal profession and members of the public were expressing increasing concern about the backlog of cases in the courts. Neither the extra-judicial use of judges nor the heavy workload of the high courts can be dismissed as temporary aberrations. Complaints about delays in court hearings and decisions have been chronic in Canada. The historians of the Supreme Court of Canada, Professors Snell and Vaughan, found it advisable to include a chapter about the court entitled 'An Instrument of Politics, 1918–1933,' and in it to chronicle the non-court activities of several justices in that period. The chapter includes this remarkable assertion: 'As well, the Supreme Court justices continued to offer political and legal advice to the political executive. Some of this was solicited.'[10] On 21 June 1946, the minister of justice told the Commons that 'there are at present about fifteen judges who are doing some work that is outside the performance of their ordinary duties.' A statement like that could be made in almost any year.

If such use of judges is a Canadian tradition, yet so frequently criticized by able observers, why does it continue? Judges can refuse extra work, and many have; others, perhaps lonely in their isolation on the bench, seem to have welcomed it, sometimes justifying it on the grounds that judges are eminently suited to conduct inquiries that are clearly in the public interest. That last point is clearly valid, for nobody could realistically claim that judges serving off the bench perform badly. On the contrary, their work is generally thorough and comprehensive, their reports a gold-mine of useful information on an impressive variety of subjects. At the other extreme, there occasionally arises a suspicion that some judges, at least, have used extra-judicial work to augment their incomes; although a judge under the Judges' Act may not accept extra pay for extra work, living and expense allowances have on occasion been generous.

4. *Salaries*. This chapter has said a good deal about the real and assumed high-mindedness of judges, and it may sound anticlimactic to end with a brief discussion of how much they are paid. Yet the pay of judges (using the term in its broadest sense to include expense allowances and pensions) is a crucial element in their recruitment and retention, and thus plays an integral part in their independence. A commission on judges' salaries and benefits whose chairman was a former minister of justice reported in 1983 that it 'accepts the principle that the salaries of the judiciary should be adequate to preserve the role, dignity and quality of Canada's judges, and to enable them to provide their families with a standard of living commensurate with their position in Canadian society.'

Judges' remuneration can be formally tied to their independence in a number of ways. They are expected, for example, to refrain from business transactions that would be ordinary for anybody else, such as investing in tax shelters. What they are paid is embodied in a statute that frees them from having their remuneration voted on annually in Parliament. The statute can naturally be amended, but both the law and tradition protect the judges from having their incomes interfered with capriciously by an executive backed by a parliamentary majority. When during the drought and depression of the 1930s the salaries of public servants were cut, those of judges were not (although they were subjected to a matching income tax). Devices such as these help preserve both the reality and the myths of judicial independence, but they do not settle one of the most difficult of the relevant problems: philosophical considerations aside, how much in cold fact should judges get?

There is general agreement among lawyers and politicians that any lawyer competent to be a judge can earn large amounts of money. That in itself gives few clear indications of how to make judicial salaries attractive to successful lawyers, partly because a brilliant trial advocate, for example, or a wealthy corporate expert, may by his very background have raised grave doubts about his ability to be impartial. Judicial salaries that are either too high or too low could attract the wrong kind of practitioner to the bench. But a high court judgeship carries with it enormous prestige and comfortable security; to many people, not all of them lawyers, a judgeship is the pinnacle of achievement in the legal profession, and for position some sacrifice in income is not unreasonable.

In the event, judges' salaries are set by democratic compromise. There has been an understandable reluctance to make judges' remuneration equal to that of particular ranks in the public service, lest it create the impression that judges are civil servants like the rest; but as a benchmark by which to assess judges' pay, the remuneration of top civil servants has become increasingly respectable. The Canadian Bar Association's committee on judicial independence recommended in 1985 'that the salary level of Superior Court judges should be not less than that of senior deputy ministers in the federal government. This guarantee would be included in the Constitution and the salary paid to senior deputy ministers would become the floor for discussions with the Treasury Board.' A parallel recommendation was made for provincially appointed judges.

It is not easy, at a time when fiscal restraint is part of general public policy, to persuade responsible ministers that a specific salary guarantee to anybody should be enshrined in the constitution. The federal government's response to the recommendation of the commission on judges' salaries mentioned above, delayed by a succession of prime ministers and a general election in 1984, fell somewhat short of the ideas of both the 1983 inquiry and the Bar Association's committee report of 1985. The association itself, in its annual meeting of 1985, passed a unanimous resolution condemning the government's inaction on judges' emoluments, and in October of that year the minister of justice introduced a bill to raise them by 12 to 15 per cent, depending on the court. The recommendations fell considerably short of the Bar Association's hopes, but it still raised the chief justice's basic pay from $117,800 to $135,000, and that of other Supreme Court justices from $108,400 to $124,200. Provincial superior court judges received slightly smaller increases, but the bill put all high court judges over the $100,000 mark.

REFORM OF THE COURTS

Judges and courts in the 1970s and 1980s, like other major Canadian institutions, have become the object of many proposals for reform. The constitutional discussions of the period, indeed, included such a variety of notions that, as with the Senate, it would be difficult for an interested observer to produce a wholly new one. At the same time, it would be idle to pretend that the reform of the courts, and especially the Supreme Court of Canada, has spawned a literature as voluminous as that on the Senate. The proposals have several main sources: the legal profession, which generally wants the Supreme Court entrenched in the constitution, with or without changes in its size or the nature of its personnel; provincial governments, which generally want a voice in the choice and appointment of the judges who would have a deciding voice in matters dear to provincial hearts; provincially appointed judges who seek status similar to their federally appointed brothers; and federal ministers who seem prepared to consider any proposal, even if only as one card in the endless federal-provincial game.

Since the constitutional amendments of 1982 entrenched the Supreme Court without making other changes, only an indication of the nature of the proposed reforms need be given here, and these are limited to the Supreme Court. A joint parliamentary committee of 1972, following the constitutional discussions of 1971 that created the document known as the Victoria Charter, recommended among other changes that the federal and relevant provincial attorneys general should agree on the appointment of Supreme Court justices. The recommendation also included an elaborate procedure to be followed when the two could not agree. The Ontario Advisory Committee on Confederation recommended in 1978 that federal nominations to the court should need the approval of the House of the Provinces, a body that was to replace the Senate. The federal Constitutional Amendment Bill of 1978 followed the nomination process of the Victoria Charter, with ratification by the proposed new House of the Federation necessary for each appointment. In the same year the Canadian Bar Association recommended that the federal govern-ment retain the appointing power, subject to the consent of a judiciary committee that was to be part of yet another reconstituted upper house. British Columbia and Alberta each produced its own scheme in the late 1970s, both featuring an enlarged provincial role in Supreme Court affairs, and the Task Force on Canadian Unity in 1979 offered similar proposals. Some proposals favoured enlarging the court to eleven members, and some a new separate constitutional court. As negotiations quickened towards the constitutional changes of 1982, the Supreme Court continued to provide a lively issue, but in the end, apart from entrenchment of changes in the court (about which there seems to have been little disagreement), the federal government gave up no constitutional authority over the appointing power. As this is written, discussions have arisen over having the appointment of judges reviewed (but not necessarily ratified) by a committee of the House of Commons.[11]

The Supreme Court remains, as it has been since 1949, supreme; and with its new responsibilities as the final interpreter of the Charter of Rights and Freedoms, supremacy, and thus accountability, are taking on new dimensions. Another new dimension appeared on 1 May 1987, when the federal government agreed to fill future vacancies on the Supreme Court from lists proposed by the provinces – provided, of course, that any appointee be acceptable to the federal government. The Canadian Bar Association's role was not mentioned in the agreement.

14

The roots of the constitution

Historically, French Canadians have not really believed in democracy for themselves; and English Canadians have not really wanted it for others. Such are the foundations upon which our two ethnic groups have absurdly pretended to be building democratic forms of government.

Pierre Elliott Trudeau, *Federalism and the French Canadians*

So far this book has concentrated on the main groups of performers on the public stage: the party faithful, candidates and parliamentarians, ministers, public servants, and judges, all of them indispensable to the workings of Canadian government as we know it. They are all seen on their several stages, some, like the judges, generally available to the masses only within the circumscribed limits of a courtroom and others, like any gifted performer, creating their own stages wherever they go. An analogy with the theatre cannot be pushed too far, for true professional actors rarely see themselves as carrying out public duties that further the operations of any government. But for good or ill, modern electronics have made actors of most people in public life, and while some may perform amateurishly, and others reluctantly, few can rely on remaining permanently out of range of the camera's eye. The shyest of public servants, regardless of the area of work, may suddenly be catapulted into national notice, possibly for reasons that have little or nothing to do with his or her occupation. In that regard government is not necessarily now different from other professions: long before television, for example, stimulating teachers and persuasive courtroom lawyers were also performers.

It is time now to look away from the contemporary political performers to pay more attention to the stages. A good deal has already been said about some of these, for one cannot write about elected politicians without a word about the electoral system and Parliament, or about judges without describing courts. But behind and surrounding every established stage is a theatre, parts of which may never be seen or even considered by theatre patrons; yet those same parts may be of ancient lineage, indispensable contributors to what politicians and civil servants and judges do today. If people in public life are actors, the theatre in which they perform is generally summed up as 'the constitution.'

REPRESENTATIVE AND RESPONSIBLE GOVERNMENT

In Canada, whose basic constitution was written in the 1860s, the political institutions may not seem to derive from antiquity, even though, as the constitutions of the modern world go, Canada's belongs among the older. But even in the 1860s the Fathers of Confederation were not only creating a new country, whose government for the first time would combine parliamentary institutions with a federal state; they were also dealing with older ideas so familiar that they hardly needed to discuss them. It is a striking feature of the debates that preceded Confederation that of the three parts of Parliament only the Senate received much detailed attention. The monarchy, derived from one of the oldest known forms of government, could hardly be assessed seriously at all without arousing suspicions of disloyalty; it was the republic to the south, not the British monarchy, that was receiving poor notices in the 1860s. The House of Commons as such was not discussed in detail because no discussion was needed: everybody knew what a Commons was, and how it worked, and Canada could not be expected to get along without one. Before a line of the first draft of the British North America Act of 1867 was set on paper, the House of Commons existed in people's minds. It got there as a conception of European origin, for none of the major North American attempts to adapt government to the continent took much notice of the governments, some of them patently successful, already effected by native peoples. Like the languages brought to North America, government was imported.

Yet in the decades immediately preceding Confederation there were plenty of relevant topics to study and to discuss. The colonies that were to become Canada, as part of the British Empire, shared from the start the same assumptions that governed other British settlements in North America: wherever they migrated, the British took the common law and related institutions with them, and the first permanent English-speaking settlement on the continent, established in 1607, had a representative assembly by 1619. (Colonies acquired by conquest had no such rights, but practical politics dictated that in the long run Quebec, as a province of Canada or in its previous existences as Lower Canada and Canada East, could not be permanently treated as being all that different from the others.) Nova Scotia had an elected assembly in 1758, the first of the potential Canadian provinces to be so treated; Prince Edward Island was next, in 1773. When the American Revolution drove large numbers of Loyalists north they added North American ideas about self-government to the English strain, which itself in turn owed much to the Norman French. All these, translated into the North America of the nineteenth century, contributed significantly to demands for further developments for representative government in the colonies that became Canada.

As in the more southern colonies, tensions inevitably developed between locally elected legislative members and governors sent out and instructed from Europe, and in the days when a simple message going in either direction could take weeks to cross the Atlantic, they were not easily dealt with. The chronicle of the struggle between assemblies and governors was nowhere quite the same, some colonies having the good luck to have for a period sensible governors sensitive to local needs, other assemblies frustrated because an indifferent governor had access to public revenues that did not depend on taxes granted by the legislators. In Upper and Lower Canada before the 1840s influential small groups disparagingly called the Family Compact and the Château Clique gathered around the governor. Their loyal (and profitable) support of gubernatorial as against assembly power led to dissatisfaction so deep as to provoke the abortive revolutions led by William Lyon Mackenzie and Louis-Joseph Papineau in 1837. Those uprisings were failures as revolutions, but they seem to have convinced those in power in London that they had possibly been in error in concluding that a root cause of the American Revolution had been the excessive powers of elected assemblies. So in 1838 the British government appointed Lord Durham, well known as a moderate in political matters, governor-in-chief of the British North American colonies, and charged him particularly with assessing public affairs in the Province of Canada.

His report, one of the great documents of both Canadian and British colonial history, broadly supported critics of the existing system. In Upper Canada, Durham found, power rested with 'a petty, corrupt, insolent Tory clique,' and the situation was not dissimilar in the other colonies. In Lower Canada, the clash between English- and French-speaking elements, divided not only by language but by religion, added a special dimension. 'I expected to find a contest between a government and a people,' wrote Durham in a famous passage, 'I found two nations warring in the bosom of a single state: I found a struggle, not of principles, but of races; and I perceived that it would be idle to attempt any amelioration of laws or institutions until we could first succeed in terminating the deadly animosity that now separates the inhabitants of Lower Canada into the hostile divisions of French and English.'

Durham found that the governor had never been free to follow his own judgment, for he was hampered by his advisers in the colony and tied down by instructions from, and constant supervision by, a British secretary of state for the colonies and British civil servants. But neither minister, Parliament, nor civil servant had sufficient knowledge of local conditions, and, as a result of this ignorance, neither Parliament nor the British people had ever been able to maintain any more than a sporadic interest in colonial affairs. The governments in the colonies had become confused and increasingly incompetent. The governor was the central figure, but there were no heads to the important departments, and the members of the executive council took an equal part in all matters that came before them. This council, with no special legal qualifications, also sat in each colony as a court of appeal. Municipal institutions either did not exist at all or were ineffective, and nowhere was there an adequate system of municipal taxes. A large part of each government's revenue and expenditure was not dependent on the annual vote of the legislature but was administered under executive and not legislative control. The fundamental weakness common to all the governments was their failure to meet the elementary political needs of their communities for the control of their own affairs through the subordination of the executive to the legislative authority.

Durham, in a word, favoured the immediate grant of responsible government, and for Upper and Lower Canada he recommended their reunion into one province, in the clear expectation that the British element in the two would then be able to absorb the French. He wrote, in words that today sound eccentric, of 'a complete amalgamation of peoples, races, languages and laws.' The joining of the central colonies was effected in the Union Act of 1840, which provided for an elected assembly of eighty-four in which Canada West and Canada East would have forty-two members, an appointed legislative council, and a single governor over the whole. English was to be the language of record, but the exclusion of French proved unworkable and in 1848 the languages were placed on an equal footing for all official purposes. Durham foresaw in these changes the groundwork for a wider union of all the colonies – Confederation – but in 1838–9 he thought the time not yet ripe. His masters in Britain thought the same of responsible government, and it was not achieved by any of the colonies either by the Union Act or any instrument.

Durham's view was that responsible government needed no such legislation: a simple instruction from London could require each governor to accept into his executive only those who had the support of a majority in the assembly. He saw no difficulty (although some of the governors did) in a governor subject both to the wishes of local representatives and to imperial superiors. The solution was a division of subjects: the governor would follow the advice of his local executive council in matters of local concern, and as an agent of the British government he would protect from local encroachment the subjects seen as of imperial significance, so that the local cabinet and assembly would not trespass on the field of his principal.

Whether Durham's list of subjects would have proved workable was not overtly tested in the early 1840s, but covertly the British Colonial Office was placing an increasing emphasis on the desirability of governors in British North America paying more attention to advisers who were acceptable to the inhabitants of the colonies; and while this was by no means the same as responsible government, it helped create a favourable climate. A change in government in Britain in 1846 produced in the Colonial Office a minister, Lord Grey, who was prepared to give Durham's whole scheme a fair trial, and he was aided by two able and liberally minded governors appointed to the colonies. One, Sir John Harvey, was sent to Nova Scotia before Grey took office, and in 1846 Lord Elgin (Durham's son-in-law) was sent to the Province of Canada. Grey guided his governors on how to move toward responsible government, and while the transition was not easy, it did take place. On 25 January 1848, following a general election, the first direct vote of want of confidence in an executive was passed by the assembly of Nova Scotia, and the government was changed.

It was the first effective vote of its kind to be taken outside Great Britain. The other British North American colonies, each in their own way, soon exercised the same principle, and as new provinces became Canadian after 1867 their governments were set up to recognize responsible government. In no instance, including Parliament itself, was responsible government given statutory recognition; it began, and has remained, a convention of the constitution. Its lack of legal definition owes something to the fact that the meaning of responsible government has had to be flexible to accommodate differing views. Certainly from the start a great principle was involved: the responsibility of the executive to the legislature. But also at the start the principle was related to such mundane matters as control over patronage, for the legislators wanted for their own use powers that had belonged to governors. The first prime minister, Sir John A. Macdonald, made clear after 1867 that he considered proper constitutional government and control over patronage to be two sides of the same coin. New meanings for responsible government were added when governments began to learn ways of controlling through taxation their annual incomes, instead of relying on customs duties that depended on the whims of commerce; and more were invented when crown corporations, with no ministers at the head, began to rival departments as instruments of government. New elements again became important with the rise of agencies that are neither crown corporations nor ministerial departments, such as the chief electoral officer and the auditor general.

Like most constitutional achievements, that is, responsible government has continued to change since the start. In the pre-Confederation period it involved changes essential to the developing British Empire, out of which emerged the modern Commonwealth whose members are fully independent countries. In North America, responsible government led to the creation of Canada, for it was colonial statesmen, not British, who used the system to push through the plans for Confederation. It is important to add that by the 1860s they were men aware not only of representative and responsible government, but of the need to work them in ways that, for the period, recognized considerable tolerance of religious and linguistic differences.[1]

THE ACHIEVING OF CONFEDERATION

Equipped with a growing experience of representative and responsible government, the politicians of the pre-Confederation period not only were more able to consider a union of the British North American colonies, but were obliged to. They were receiving valuable training in self-government at the same time as Britain was, in effect, reorganizing its empire so as to force more self-reliance on the colonies; a preferential tariff on colonial exports, for example, was abandoned just as responsible government was being won. The colonies were subjected to quite different pressures from the United States, particularly after the outbreak of the Civil War in 1861, which gave the colonies a large bellicose neighbour immediately to the south. Apart from political developments beyond the colonies' control, technological changes were producing yet additional impacts. The colonies, largely dependent on economies that used water power for energy, coaches and canals for much of their internal movements of passengers and goods, and sailing ships on open waters, were finding it difficult and expensive to convert to steam power, railways, and ships with engines.

Each of the colonies had its own internal problems too. Probably the worst case was that in the Province of Canada, where the union created in 1840, far from solving all major political problems, produced new and larger ones. A constitution of two disparate communities, yet with equal representation in the legislature, could only result in various kinds of deadlocks, and it did. The ingenious attempts of men such as Macdonald to find their way out of a series of impasses make a fascinating chronicle in its own right, as two pertinent statistics can attest: between 1841 and 1867 the colony had eighteen cabinets; after 1867, Canada's eighteenth cabinet was not reached for ninety years. Equal representation was irksome to Canada West in another way, for the province that would become Ontario was wealthier than its down-river partner, Quebec, and hence paid more taxes into the common pot. It also had a larger and more rapidly growing population, which make a demand for increased representation sound not only realistic but a matter of high principle. For their part the Maritimes, particularly affected by the troubles of an industry using wooden sailing ships, felt the isolation from their inland British cousins, and their politicians for years had been seeking a rail link to the St Lawrence basin, which was confidently expected to open up new inland markets.

Almost everything, in short, pointed to a union of the colonies as a way out of political, economic, and military dilemmas.

Once the movement toward Confederation started, it proceeded with remarkable speed, and it is noteworthy that despite the difficulties of communications and transportation in the 1860s, the actual negotiations for Confederation did not take as long as those that culminated in the constitutional amendments and additions of 1982. There were fewer participants in the 1860s, of course, and a greater sense of urgency, which in turn made solutions easier to accept. None the less, the small group destined to earn immortality as the Fathers of Confederation proceeded with despatch, and once again it was Nova Scotia, the cradle of representative and responsible government, that took the initiative. Its premier in 1864, Charles Tupper, introduced a resolution in the provincial legislature proposing a conference with representatives of New Brunswick and Prince Edward Island to discuss the union of the three under one government, and similar resolutions carried in the other two. A meeting was arranged for Charlottetown in September; the government of the Province of Canada asked if it could attend to discuss a wider union, and the request was granted. The subsequent Charlottetown Conference was by no means the first interprovincial meeting, for others had been held to talk about specific matters of common concern such as postal services, tariffs, and railway lines. What was different about the conference of 1864 was its scope, and the fact that many public leaders in the Maritimes and the Province of Canada met for the first time; to meet in the east at all, indeed, they had either to travel down the St Lawrence by ship or, as they chose to do, to go by railway through the United States. After a summer devoted by the central representatives to what would now be called a fact-finding tour of the Maritimes, enough facts were found to give impetus to plans for a general union. The conference itself was small (five each from the three Maritime provinces, eight from Canada), but it represented a variety of political views, and the delegates from the centre drew particular strength because they could, as representatives of a coalition government, speak with one voice. In the event, they took over the conference's agenda, a general union being given precedence over the Maritimes' original but more limited idea. And in due course the conference carried its deliberations to Halifax, Saint John, and Fredericton. All the sessions were secret, a necessary precaution which aroused natural suspicions among some observers, and their chief known result was a decision to reassemble in Quebec in October 1864, with a delegation from Newfoundland added.

The Charlottetown Conference had no authority to make decisions, but it did explore and reach tentative agreement on several fundamental considerations. What remained for the Quebec Conference was not the question of whether a federation should be formed, but precisely how, and who were to be its members.

The Quebec meeting was moderately larger than that at Charlottetown, with only Nova Scotia again sending five delegates; the other two Maritime provinces sent seven, and Newfoundland two, while the Province of Canada shrewdly sent its entire cabinent of twelve. Again the major political parties were represented, although the nature of the colonial governments gave the whole conference a Conservative edge; but there is little evidence of voting on partisan lines. Each colony had one vote except for the Province of Canada, which had one each for its two divisions; apparently the two did not split once, and there is only one known instance of the Atlantic group outvoting Canada four to two. (Prince Edward Island, interestingly enough, voted against all the others in half of the known votes.) Since the Quebec Conference was also secret, such statistics are incomplete, and depend on careful historical reconstruction pieced together from many sources.

What was not secret was the result: the Quebec Resolutions can rightly be seen as the first informal draft of the bill that was to create the Dominion of Canada, a federation which, unlike its southern neighbour, would have a strong centralist bias. To that end, the proposed Canadian constitution included these characteristics:

1 The provincial legislatures were granted a moderate list of powers, all of them, in the 1860s, of a local or private nature. Several powers which in the United States belonged to the individual states, such as some pertaining to criminal law, were to be federal for the new Canada.
2 The provinces were given a limited power of taxation, Canada a general power.
3 The federal government was granted all powers not explicitly given to the provinces. The federal grant of power was illustrated by a long list of topics placed explicitly under federal jurisdiction. 'We have given the General Legislature,' to quote Macdonald, 'all the great subjects of legislation. We have conferred on them, not only specifically and in detail, all the powers which are incident to sovereignty, but we have expressly declared that all subjects of general interest not distinctly and exclusively conferred upon the local governments and local legislatures, shall be conferred upon the General Government and Legislature.'
4 The federal government was to have the power of appointing and removing the provincial lieutenant-governors (styled superintendents in the initial draft of the final act), thereby placing the Canadian government in the position held until that time by the British government in relation to its colonies. The federal government would then have in each province an agent and spokesman who could refuse assent to, or reserve, bills of the provincial legislature; and there can be little doubt that the expectation was that the lieutenant-governor's

influence would be real. The federal appointment powers also covered all judges of provincial courts above the lowest rank, and senators who, in theory at least, were to represent the people of their provinces in Parliament.

5 The federal government was given the right to disallow any provincial law within a year of its passage – another reflection of the authority Britain held over its colonies.

The structure outlined in the Resolutions was clearly not a pure federal system in which the component parts would be of equal or co-ordinate rank with the central government. The central government in Canada was to have powers which were not only withheld from, but in some instances could be exercised over, the provinces; the latter were not given, either individually or collectively, any similar powers over the central authority.

The Quebec Resolutions thus were centralist, as was repeatedly attested to by the leading politicians of the 1860s. That conclusion can of course be challenged, and it has been. What is more important is that subsequent events profoundly altered their apparent meaning anyway. The courts, as a later chapter outlines, gave broad interpretations to provincial jurisdiction over property and civil rights (a term which, viewed objectively in the 1980s, appears to cover most of the things modern governments do), and took a narrow view of the federal government's residual power. Central appointment of lieutenant-governors and senators did not turn out to be an instrument that strengthened the federal authority in any significant way; and disallowance, after some initial use, also petered out. In contrast, provincial powers over their own natural resources and education, both regarded as almost trifling matters in the 1860s, grew enormously in significance. It is difficult today to gauge the attitude taken toward resources before modern technologies made them so important, but it is on record that in the 1860s Quebec Resolution 66 offered Newfoundland an annual federal payment of $150,000 in return for 'all its rights in Mines and Minerals, and of all the ungranted and unoccupied Lands of the Crown'; and some statesmen of the period considered the offer needlessly generous.

Future developments aside, the politicians toiling toward Confederation spent much time on the details involved in converting resolutions into legislation. Some of these, such as the composition of Parliament and federal jurisdiction over federal elections, have already been described. Considering later developments, it is striking that the division of powers between Ottawa and the provinces seemed to cause few difficulties when they were being worked out, but financial considerations did. The new provinces would have certain limited powers, but the major sources of income would go to the central government, so that the provinces would be dependent on federal subsidies for major portions of their incomes. The assignment of executive power to the queen, to 'be administered according to the well understood principles of the British Constitution,' bothered nobody, nor did agreement on the respective divisions of authority over law and the judiciary. The Maritimes were satisfied with the provisions proposed for an intercolonial railway. The Quebec Conference, in short, thanks in part to careful advance work particularly by Macdonald and his colleagues, lasted only three weeks, and its two failures seemed relatively minor: the conference was as far as Newfoundland and Prince Edward Island were ready to go, and they did not join Confederation in 1867.

The Quebec Resolutions, once settled upon, were in some danger of entering a state of limbo. No colonial legislature had formally authorized the conference (although that of the Province of Canada had been told of the government's federal intentions), and the delegates in 1864 were reluctant to test the proposals in elections: that expedient, they felt, leaned too much toward American as against British practices. Only the Province of Canada, in a celebrated debate early in 1865, gave legislative approval to the Quebec Resolutions and requested that the imperial Parliament implement them. The premier of New Brunswick did hold an election on them, and was soundly defeated. The premier of Nova Scotia, eyeing the results in New Brunswick, went back to square one by sidestepping the Quebec Resolutions and securing approval of the original proposal for Maritime union. By any normal assessment of these procedures, the Resolutions received only one affirmative vote out of a possible five.

The Canadian cabinet, undaunted, sent a delegation to England to discuss, among other topics, federation, and the colonial ministers found a sympathetic ear. The chronicle of how New Brunswick and Nova Scotia were led to change their minds tells a devious tale, but too long even for summary. In the event both Maritime colonies, without openly accepting the Quebec Resolutions, gave legislative approval to a reconsideration of the idea of a federation, and the Resolutions became the basis for the reconsideration. The London Conference of 1866 produced new resolutions which included changes from the Quebec Conference, but a comparison of the final British North America Act (it went through seven drafts) with the Quebec Resolutions cannot fail to reveal, at the very least, a common ancestor. There were substantial changes made in many areas, but both wedded the parliamentary system to a federal system, one in which the central government began with large powers. Since it has often been argued that Confederation was the result of a compact between the provinces (or, in recent years, between two peoples, the English and the French in Canada) it must be added that nothing in the 1860s seemed influenced by such theories. Ontario and Quebec, as separate provinces respectively dominated by the two language groups, were in fact created in the same act of Parliament that created Canada and could not have been part of a compact before that.

That act, to the considerable chagrin of Canadian observers in London, passed the imperial Parliament routinely: it received royal assent on 29 March 1867, was proclaimed on 22 May, and came into effect on 1 July. To the end it remained without the support of a general consensus among the participants from British North America, as expressed either through their political leaders or in general elections. Some people in Nova Scotia, indeed, were so dissatisfied that they greeted 1 July 1867 with streets draped in black, and in the first federal election in that year the electors returned eighteen out of nineteen MPs pledged to repeal the act. But the same election confirmed the selection as prime minister of one of Confederation's greatest champions, John A. Macdonald; and he, not Maritime MPs, was to dominate the formative years of the new country.

Canada's political institutions, as set up in 1867, clearly reflected their British origins, as their creators intended. The cabinet, and Parliament and its practices, are the most obvious examples, even down to the nomenclature adopted: Her Majesty's Privy Council for Canada, the House of Commons, and, if Macdonald and others had had their way, the Kingdom of Canada – but that title was considered too provocative to please Canada's large neighbour. But 'Senate' is the name of an American institution, and the influence from south of the border showed clearly. The United States was the closest model of a federal state, and Macdonald said of its constitution in 1865 that he believed 'it is one of the most skilful works which human intelligence ever created.' But among its perceived weaknesses was an inordinate emphasis on the authority of the individual states as against the central authority; and just as the Americans nearly a century earlier had sought to adapt parliamentary government to a new American republic by correcting weaknesses in the British constitution, Macdonald and his colleagues sought to adapt the federal system to Canada through avoiding weaknesses seen in the American one.[2]

To the British and American influence so plain in the 1860s can be added another equally plainly Canadian: the guarantee that both English and French could be used in Parliament, federal courts, and the legislature and courts of Quebec – provisions that had their counterparts in Manitoba, when it was admitted in 1870, and in the Northwest Territories when their government was organized. The other areas admitted as provinces (British Columbia in 1871, Prince Edward Island in 1873, Alberta and Saskatchewan, created out of the Territories in 1905, and Newfoundland in 1949) were not made officially bilingual. New Brunswick is put on the same basis as Quebec by the Constitution Act of 1982, which also expressly declares English and French to be Canada's official languages. Under the Official Languages Act of 1969, a by-product of the Royal Commission on

Bilingualism and Biculturalism appointed in 1963, bilingual districts can be set up anywhere in Canada where either English- or French-speaking persons, though in a minority, constitute at least 10 per cent of the population. Not many countries in the world have to deal with languages at the constitutional level, and recent cabinets have included a member whose portfolio may portend a new dimension, a minister of multiculturalism.

DOMINION AND NATION

Canada is declared to be a dominion in the opening lines of the act which created it: 'Whereas the Provinces of Canada, Nova Scotia and New Brunswick have expressed their Desire to be federally united into one Dominion ...' The term has been used in other official documents several hundred times, most notably for our purposes here in the Statute of Westminster of 1931, the legal foundation of the modern Commonwealth, which says in part: 'In this Act the expression "Dominion" means any of the following Dominions ...' and listed are Canada, Australia, New Zealand, South Africa, the Irish Free State, and Newfoundland. In Canada in recent years, Dominion as a term has been fighting for survival and seems to have lost. It has no equivalent in French, and the closest approximation to a translation conveys an entirely different idea. So the old Dominion Bureau of Statistics, known to generations of Canadians as DBS, has become Statistics Canada, and our national holiday has gone from Dominion Day to Canada Day.

The progression from dominion to nation has taken even longer than the arguing about nomenclature, but it has rarely been quarrelsome. By 1867 several indispensable steps had been taken toward colonial autonomy, and Confederation itself, partly because of the sheer size of the new federation, provided for one large voice where formerly there had been several lesser ones. The list of topics regarded separately as of imperial and colonial concern was flexible from the start, and adjustments in relations between London and Ottawa could thus usually be made by day-to-day discussions and negotiations rather than confrontations and crises. Confederation itself offered a classic example of that: colonials drew up their own terms for uniting, and the government at London offered primarily advice and guidance. The original BNA Act was the first, and greatest, of a sequence of agreements and settlements that culminated in the Constitution Act of 1982, which removed the last vestiges of even technical legalities about Canada's constitution that affected relations with the United Kingdom.

Even before Confederation, British North America was on the path to autonomy. In 1859, for example, a protest from English manufacturers about a law in the Province of Canada that imposed a tariff on British goods rose to the official level and raised the possibility that the Canadian statute might be disallowed by

Britain. The Canadian minister of finance, Alexander Galt, took a firm no-nonsense line which depended in part on his view of responsible self-government. 'The Government of Canada,' Galt wrote, 'acting for its legislature and people cannot, through those feelings of deference which they owe to the Imperial authorities, in any manner waive or diminish the right of the people of Canada to decide for themselves both as to the mode and extent to which taxation shall be imposed ... Her Majesty cannot be advised to disallow such acts, unless her advisers are prepared to assume the administration of the affairs of the Colony irrespective of the views of its inhabitants.' In other contexts those could have been fighting words, but in the mid-nineteenth century in British-Canadian relations they merely set the tone for a lot more of the same, and in regard to a lot more than taxation.

After Confederation the road to autonomy split in three, although the separate routes met together at the end: they traversed control over Canada's internal affairs; over external affairs generally; and over specific relations within the empire, and ultimately the Commonwealth. The shortest was probably the first, the longest the last. But in all cases the restraining power was the British government, which had its own special concerns, often pressed by British economic interests, which favoured postponing the attainment of complete independence by the colonies. Although there were detours and distractions, the direction remained the same: the removal of all restrictions on colonial governments, and their emergence as separate though still related countries.

The watershed all three routes crossed was the war of 1914–18. In British North America's internal affairs by 1867, intervention by British authorities had been reduced to minor matters, generally through the governor general, whose powers as an agent of the imperial government were at first uncertain, and certainly not clarified by the routine instructions each governor received. Canadian cabinets after 1867 naturally took the same view that Galt had in 1859: any exercise of the governor's powers, either on his own or on guidance from his home government, was to be resisted if he was not acting also on the advice of his Canadian executive. As late as 1876 Lord Dufferin was to urge upon his prime minister, Alexander Mackenzie, that 'within the walls of the Privy Council I have as much right to contend for my opinions as any of my Ministers'; but he had picked a target that could respond. In 1878 Edward Blake, Mackenzie's minister of justice, secured major changes in the Commissions and Instructions issued to the governor, basing his case on the premise that Canada was not a small colonial dependency and could not be treated as such. Canada was, Blake wrote in 1876, 'a Dominion composed of an aggregate of seven large provinces united under an Imperial Charter, which expressly recites that her constitution is to be similar in principle to that of the United Kingdom.' Since that charter was a statute of the imperial Parliament,

Blake's argument was not an easy one to discount. Although there were still to be rumblings over the governor's powers to disallow provincial legislation, to dismiss a lieutenant-governor, to make public statements on matters of policy, to exercise the prerogative of mercy, to refuse a dissolution of Parliament, to reject appointments recommended by the prime minister, the trend was toward acceptance by the governor of the advice of his Canadian government. That goal was met, it is to be noted, not through following the exact wording of the act of 1867, or through its frequent amendment, but through negotiated developments and reliance on precedents. The result was that by 1914 Canadian practices virtually coincided with British, and the reality of Canadian autonomy in internal affairs was accepted.

But this was not true of Canada's external relations. The direction was the same, but progress much slower; in fact, in some aspects of foreign relations it was all but non-existent. In commerical and political treaties of immediate concern Canada had made some advances, and there was some recognition of Canada's place in a few international conferences. But when war broke out in 1914 Canada did not have the power to decide whether it would participate: the scope of participation was Canada's to decide, but the fact of participation was decided by the British declaration of war.

Commercially, the development of Canadian autonomy followed the route indicated by Galt in 1859. Before Confederation the colonies had been allowed to send representatives abroad for informal discussions. More formally, Canadian agents began to be accepted as associates of British negotiations in an advisory capacity, although they did not sign any resulting agreements. Then Canadians assumed part of the role of the negotiators, through a convenient fiction which saw Canadians chosen as part of British delegations. In 1892–3 (and in this development the redoubtable Charles Tupper played a leading part) a Canadian actually signed a treaty jointly with a British ambassador, and then that position was reversed: a British ambassador signed jointly in a treaty which Canadians negotiated. Soon the British role was cut out, the Canadians informally negotiating agreements which could be implemented by the passing of reciprocal legislation internally. The course was not as smooth as that summary may suggest, but the changes did occur, and the recognition grew that Canada, unless the Canadian government wished, was not to be bound by new trade agreements made by the British government.

Politically, progress was well behind Canada's moves into commercial autonomy. Commercial agreements specifically affecting Canada were one thing; political deals that affected Canada as part of a larger empire were something else. Canada did make some advances, setting up with the United States in 1909 (for example) an international joint commission on boundary waters and related matters, a body manned by Canadians nominated by Ottawa, but formally appointed on British responsibility. That was seen as a Canadian matter. But just a few years earlier, the Canadian government had been profoundly irritated when the Alaska boundary dispute was settled in favour of the Americans, a British high court judge voting with three Americans against two Canadians. Sir Wilfrid Laurier then deplored Canada's lack of power to make treaties. Nevertheless, before 1914 Canada did sign two agreements resulting from international conferences, the British delegates signing for the remainder of the empire. But where in commercial matters Canada's progress towards autonomy was slow but steady, that in political affairs was uncertain and subject to genuine setbacks.

Internal imperial relations offered yet another story, again one marked mainly, though not entirely, by a recourse to talking rather than formal enactments. As early as 1879 Alexander Galt became Canada's first high commissioner to London; the post was below ambassadorial rank but it none the less provided a handily placed spokesman for Canada. Eight years later the first general colonial conference was held, an informal colloquy attended by prime ministers and selected colleagues who could not bind their respective governments by firm decisions, but who were able to use the conference for increasingly important discussions of relevant topics. The colonial conference, meeting roughly every four or five years, developed into an imperial conference, and the talks progressed through general political topics to imperial defence and imperial foreign policy, the outlying members – Canada especially – showing a reluctance to take part in a centralized imperial policy. By 1914, in short, it was clear that Canada and the other dominions were completely self-governing in internal affairs, while held at the discussion level in imperial foreign policy, which included such vital matters as declaring war and making peace.

The First World War was to change all that. Having had no part in the diplomatic failures that led to its outbreak, Canada (and in varying degrees the other dominions) found in a gallant and conspicuous contribution to the Allied cause the basis of a sturdy new nationalism, which contributed further to a conviction that sacrifice justified a greater say in events. In 1917 the dominion prime ministers were summoned to meet with the British War Cabinet as an empire cabinet. In the following months their discussions were acted upon, so well that the dominions took part in the postwar peace conference, signed the peace treaties, and joined the League of Nations as participating members. The first years of peace saw other major constitutional changes, with Canada usually leading the way in establishing the determination of its government to be master in all its affairs, even if – or perhaps especially if – it meant abandoning diplomatic unity within the empire. An imperial conference in 1926, the most celebrated in this particular history, produced a resolution that kept the dominions loyal to a common monarch, but on terms that left each member of the Commonwealth to run its own affairs. The conference spoke of the relationship between Britain and the others in these terms:

Their position and mutual relation may be readily defined. They are autonomous Communities within the British Empire, equal in status, in no way subordinate one to another in any aspect of their domestic or external affairs, though united by a common allegiance to the Crown, and freely associated as members of the British Commonwealth of nations ...

It is an essential consequence of the equality of status ... that the Governor-General of a Dominion is the representative of the Crown, holding in all essential respects the same position in relation to the administration of public affairs in the Dominion as is held by His Majesty the King of Great Britain, and that he is not the representative or regent of His Majesty's Government in Great Britain or of any Department of that Government.

The conference discussed a number of the implications of these statements: for example, disallowance of dominion legislation by Britain was declared to be obsolete; the retention of judicial appeals to the Judicial Committee of the Privy Council was left to each dominion; each should possess the power to make treaties, acting through the sovereign on the advice of its own cabinet; no member, including Britain, could be committed in foreign affairs without the explicit assent of its own government. And there were other declarations, generally covering co-operation and consultation between members of the Commonwealth. One result was plain: diplomatic unity in foreign affairs was abandoned, and the monarch could follow several contradictory policies depending on advice received from the relevant governments.

These declarations were only that, not law, and in subsequent conferences in 1929 and 1930 more concrete advances towards a comprehensive statute were made until in 1931 the Parliament of the United Kingdom passed the Statute of Westminster. That document made clear the genuine independence that now accompanied dominion status, variously relieving the dominions of British laws passed in colonial days, and providing that no imperial act was to apply to a dominion unless the latter requested it. It left the dominions free to amend their own constitutions, but for Canada an interesting exception was made: the Statute of Westminster was not to affect the British North America Act of 1867 and its amendments, chiefly because federal and provincial politicians had not yet agreed on an amendment process. The delay in reaching agreement was not the fault of any other member of the Commonwealth, but had exclusively, and peculiarly, Canadian roots.

The Statute of Westminster was responsible for an instructive series of events in

1939. When the United Kingdom went to war against Germany, Australia and New Zealand considered that the British declaration included them. But the monarch of South Africa was advised to go to war three days later, and in his Canadian capacity the king went to war four days after that, while for Eire he remained neutral for the duration. After the war, as after that of 1914–18, the members of the Commonwealth asserted themselves by taking part in various international organizations, such as the United Nations, the North Atlantic Treaty Organization, the Colombo Plan, and the North American Air Defense Agreement.

Precisely what the Commonwealth means to each of its members is not easy to summarize, for each case is different. Since its creation it has revealed an almost startling flexibility, losing members (South Africa by invitation) and gaining new associates who may be republics, not monarchies, as is India, or even having a monarch who is not the queen. In 1952 the contemporary monarchies decided on a new title – rather a series of titles –for the newly crowned Queen Elizabeth, each settling on 'a form of title which suits its own particular circumstances, but retains a substantial element which is common to all.' The most substantial single element is the queen herself, who on any given day may find herself at war with the Falkland Islands in one capacity, but otherwise at peace; or opening, as Queen of Canada, the St Lawrence Seaway, a project of no apparent interest to her as Queen of New Zealand. Grenada may find the United States intervening in its domestic affairs, with the rest of the Commonwealth conspicuously not rallying to the cause, on either side. The Commonwealth, like the monarchy, is not an easy institution to explain to outsiders.

The same can be said of the Commonwealth in Canada, where the electorate's attitude ranges from total unawareness to a lively interest, although some of the interest has itself been based on a misconception of Canada as a country with continuing colonial ties to Britain. The Commonwealth, from its birth as a sort of gentlemen's club of white and English-speaking nations, has become predominantly non-white and non-English-speaking, comprising nearly fifty countries and a quarter of the world's population. It seems clear, none the less, that the Canadian electorate accepts membership in the Commonwealth, for there has never been a significant political group whose platform included opposing membership, while at the same time Commonwealth affairs receive frequent, if erratic, coverage in the media. In 1985 the Commonwealth Parliamentary Association held a series of successful meetings in Canada, and its Canadian branch publishes an informative journal.

Membership in the Commonwealth is in truth in Canada a difficult thing to oppose, or even raise as an issue, since the constant and almost invariably friendly communication between its members has such an attractive positive side, while at the same time committing nobody to anything. The United Kingdom may join the European Common Market and the Canadian prime minister speak critically of it; or the Canadian prime minister may undertake a private peace mission of his own, and no member of the Commonwealth can legitimately object. And the Commonwealth is also concerned with external relations which, at their clearest, remain vague; the government of Canada, like that in every country, must always give high priority to pressing, and changing, domestic matters. For the rest of the Commonwealth, what does the discovery of oil in the high Arctic, possibly affecting Canadian sovereignty, mean? Does Canada, or the nearest province, own offshore natural resources; and if the province, how is compensation paid to the two provinces that have no offshore? Is Canada one nation or two? If two, do both attend relevant conferences on external matters? If only one, what of the other groups of Canadians whose mother tongue is neither English nor French? What are other Commonwealth members to do, or think, about Canada's unique position as the only country in the world whose territory is stretched between the current super-powers? Or about its status as one of the two thin pieces of bread sandwiching the United States? Every member of the Commonwealth could produce a list of such questions, each list different, and each list that of an independent country. Canada's list concerns Canadians; and many Canadians, returning from seeing the poverty and hunger in other Commonwealth countries, have observed that as domestic problems go, Canada doesn't really have many.

Thus the backdrop of Canada's developing constitution; the rest of this book will take closer looks at some of the details. From the representative government first achieved in 1758, to responsible government in 1848, from the combining of responsible government with a federal system in 1867, and the subsequent extension of that until it occupied half a continent, Canada's government has continued to experience profound structural changes which still go on. Externally the original colonies, all of them tiny settlements at the start, have gone from complete political subservience to an external power, to an independence so generally accepted that it is sometimes hard for Canadians to appreciate that the struggle for economic independence, as distinct from political, may have only begun.

15
The nature of the constitution

I have found that the best analogy to use when describing the constitution to an Inuit audience is the backbone of a whale.
Robert G. Williamson, University of Saskatchewan

A LAYERED WEAVING

Previous chapters have indicated the varied nature of the elements that make up the Canadian constitution, and the purpose of the present section is to lend to that variety a more systematic summary, which will necessitate some repetition of points already made. The variety is such that differing schools of thought have developed not only about what the constitution means, but about what it was intended to mean. At one extreme the centralists of the 1860s frequently referred to the future Parliament in such terms as 'the real Legislature of the country, whilst the local assemblies were to be allowed to sink to the position of mere municipalities.' Since large parts of the future provinces then had no municipal organizations, there was a vacuum to be filled, and those words (Alexander Galt's) made sense. But not to those who saw the future provinces as the real sources of governing power, with the federal government restrained, and confined to matters of general interest. The impetus for a strong central government came mainly from the spokesmen for what was to be Ontario, and partly for that reason those from the projected Quebec saw in a federal union an escape from English and Protestant manipulations of local affairs. The Maritimers, for other considerations, found it difficult to take seriously the notion that their familiar local governments were to be reduced to 'mere municipalities,' with political power over them resting several hundred miles to the west.

A written constitution
The nature of the constitution in the 1860s, as seen from communities far apart in

more than the geographical sense, can be argued about endlessly, just as it has been in the last years of the twentieth century. There is less room for disagreement about the nature of several basic elements that make up the constitution. It is a fact, for example, that the act of 1867 emerged as a written document, although that does not mean that Canada has a written, as distinguished from an unwritten, constitution. The United States can fairly be said to have a written constitution, for its fundamental document describes in remarkable detail the fundamental parts of government and the legal relations between them. Great Britain has no such single instrument, and its constitution in that sense is unwritten. Canada falls between the two: there is a document which creates the country, but it is not only incomplete, but often misleading. Any outsider reading the original British North America Act could justly conclude that Canada was governed by a powerful monarch, assisted within the country by a governor general who is in turn assisted by a council of the governor's choice. After all, the act says that the governor general appoints all the members of one part of Parliament, and decides when to call together the elected members of the House of Commons, and when to send them home. Except in their narrow legal aspect, not one of those conclusions is sound, but all are solemnly enshrined in the constitution. The act does not say anything about the cabinet, or who really chooses its members; nor does it mention that the cabinet is not the council described, but only a small part of it. The act does not say that virtually everything of legal significance the monarch or the governor general does is on the advice of that unmentioned cabinet. The written parts of the constitution, in other words, are dependent on officially unwritten understandings about what they mean. The understandings can unofficially be written about in books such as this; they may also be assessed in part, as one has been in recent years in a landmark decision by the Supreme Court. But the written and most obvious part of the Canadian constitution cannot be relied on as a guide to the nature of the country's government. It is one thread in a rich fabric, part of the backdrop described in the preceding chapter.

It is pertinent now to look at other parts. Not all of them can be appraised in a single volume, for the whole is too complex for even a complex summary. The Canadian House of Commons, for example, is often hailed as one of many praiseworthy heirs of a glorious British parliamentary tradition, and rightly so; but that British tradition owes much to institutions of Norman France. The earliest parliaments, history tells us, were derived directly from the councils of the Norman kings; and Simon de Montfort, who in the thirteenth century championed a limited monarchy ruling through elected advisers, was born and educated in France. How much of that can be traced down to Canada? For one, the word Parliament: it comes from *parlement*, a parley; and Commons is *commune*.

Apart from antique words, the House of Commons can be used in other ways to illustrate constitutional variety. The Commons is provided for in the written part of the constitution, which prescribes the first system of representation to be used. It is also empowered to make its own laws about who gets into it, so that the Canada Elections Act, while itself at any moment a part of the Canadian constitution, is also amendable like any other statute. Once members are elected, another segment of the constitution, the written rules of procedure (which are also amendable), allows the House to decide who can sit in it, for any duly elected member can also be suspended or expelled. Another part of the constitution allows the House to decide what cabinet it will support. The House seen on television in the 1980s, that is, consists of elements centuries old, on the one hand, and such things as Speaker's rulings which can be viewed as they are made today, on the other.

There is much more. A familiar illustration like the House leaves untouched numerous other relevant parts of the Canadian constitution. An earlier chapter described the impact of English common law on Canadian legal and judicial practices, and cited also the particular case of Quebec, whose use of French civil law was confirmed as early as 1774. No conceivable amount of constitutional change, whether directly connected with Canada's attainment of complete political independence or not, could lessen the enduring importance of these two sets of legal principles as parts of the constitution. Since Canada began life as a British colony, many British statutes applied to Canada as part of the empire, and some (of which the British North America Act of 1867 is the most conspicuous example) applied only to Canada. The Statute of Westminster applied to all the newly defined dominions and stated clearly that certain British statutes were to have no further force in any of them. But the Statute of Westminster was itself British, and it applied to the dominions. The loosening of imperial legal influence over the separate dominions has had to be effected with care, for a general declaration that British statutes were after a given date to cease to apply to, say, Canada could have included the act which created the country.

The Constitution Act of 1982 clears up any doubts about the surviving application of British statutes to Canada, and does the same for British orders-in-council, a few of which are of particular interest because they created new provinces. Exactly how many British statutes survived down to 1982 is impossible to say without a more technical exploration than would be justified here (some, for example, dealt with the slave trade) but it is safe to say that there were probably well over a hundred, only a few of which, such as the BNA Act and its amendments, have been significant in modern times. The same is broadly true of British orders-in-council which became part of the Canadian constitution the day they were issued.

The Constitution Act of 1982 tidied up this interesting British-Canadian axis in two ways: it declared that no future act of the United Kingdom Parliament 'shall extend to Canada as part of its law'; and it repealed all existing British instruments and made them, where they were still applicable, the law of Canada. There are thirty instruments cited in the schedule to the act entitled 'Modernization of the Constitution,' four of them British orders-in-council, eighteen British statutes, and eight Canadian statutes, five of the last passed after Parliament attained power to amend the constitution in certain ways in 1949. (The other three deal with the creation of the three prairie provinces.) The twenty-two statutes of British legal origin are dealt with in a manner best shown by illustration:

No. 1. British North America Act, 1867: four sections are wholly or partially repealed, and in one repeal the act is renamed the Constitution Act, 1867. Most of the act still stands.

No. 4. Order of Her Majesty's Council admitting British Columbia into the Union, 16 May 1871; without alteration, the order is renamed British Columbia Terms of Union.

No. 20. British North America Act, 1943; repealed in its entirety (so are five others).

Starting with the original BNA Act of 1867, and ending with the act of 1982, there are now fourteen enactments named Constitution Act; those of British origin now have Canadian titles.

Of the statutes just mentioned three enjoy an additional distinction as part of the constitution: they are statutes of the Parliament of Canada which, once enacted, cannot be amended by it because at the moment of their passing they became provincial constitutions and could thereafter be amended only by the relevant provincial legislature. These statutes created Manitoba, Alberta, and Saskatchewan, and the only possible source of federal legislation touching them would be alterations in provincial boundaries, and even they would require provincial consent. (Manitoba's boundaries have in fact been enlarged, but not those of the other two.)[1]

Apart from statutes that become provincial constitutions, a considerable variety of both federal and provincial acts also qualify as constitutional because of their subject-matter, even though in form they are ordinary statutes. The creation of the Supreme Court of Canada, changes in the electoral system including the franchise, the adjustment of federal grants to the provinces, the establishment of new departments or crown corporations, and many other statutes altering the structure of government in Canada may not at first sight appear to be parts of the constitution because they are not commonly referred to as such. But they are obviously different from laws and regulations covering such specifics as the taxes on tobacco or initial payments to be made to farmers each year on the forthcoming wheat crop.

Not among the 'organic' laws cited above, curiously enough, are the treaties covering many Canadian Indians. Although they have involved such fundamental matters as transfers of territory and guarantees of certain hunting and fishing rights, the treaties have not been regarded by non-Indian authorities as part of the constitution, but as documents that place no limits on the legislative powers of Parliament. In the events leading up to the Constitution Act of 1982, Indian spokesmen lobbied energetically in both Ottawa and London in search of clearer statements on the constitutional status of native peoples, even taking their case to court in the United Kingdom. They received a fair hearing, but lost, and while British parliamentarians debating the 1982 act expressed a considerable interest in their cause, the text of the constitutional additions of 1982 remained, inevitably, in the words agreed on in Canada. Part II of the act defines 'aboriginal peoples of Canada' to include Indian, Inuit, and Métis in Canada, and declares: 'The existing aboriginal and treaty rights of the aboriginal peoples of Canada are hereby recognized and affirmed.' Since the rights depend in turn on federal legislation, it is not yet clear whether since 1982 they are now to be taken as part of the constitution, or if they are, what that will mean in practice.[2]

Judicial decision has already been cited as a source of constitutional creation, and a more detailed sample follows later; the courts' interpretation of the Charter of Rights, as mentioned, holds vast and unknown implications for more judicial creativity. Other institutions add to the constitution. The parliamentary rules and forms by which the Senate and House of Commons conduct their business are clearly essential to a democratic institution, and they are not all written down in the Constitution Act of 1867 or in the printed rules of either House. On paper, for example, English and French are legal equals in Parliament, but until relatively recently English was the day-to-day working language simply because, while most French-speaking MPs could also speak English, few English speakers could perform in French. Many an MP whose mother tongue was French has in the past complained that he was obliged to speak English in his own Parliament in order to be understood. The simultaneous translation system introduced when John Diefenbaker was prime minister has altered that, but of at least equal significance is the acceptance by the political parties of the necessity for their leading members to be bilingual. As this is written all three party leaders in the Commons use both languages, in startling contrast to the practices of twenty years or so ago, when it was considered normal for leaders to speak only English. The impact on the constitution of such a change may be imponderable, but it is also undeniable; because of it, Parliament works differently.

The parties apart from their leaders also add to the constitution. Until recent years political organization as such in Canada worked entirely outside the law, despite the fact that the parties, and they alone, brought forth the people who became prime minister or leader of the opposition. Increasingly Parliament has found it necessary to recognize the existence of parties for varied purposes: paying a needed stipend to leaders of minor parties; regulating political finances so as to make the parties accountable for both the raising and spending of funds; and granting funds to parties for research. Parties used to be known in the election laws merely as 'political interests,' but now their indispensability is no longer seriously disputed. Institutions as necessary as parties can hardly be ignored as contributors to the workings of the constitution, even though, again much of what they do is not prescribed in written documents.

Constitutional convention
This chapter so far has been moving away from recognizable constitutional documents toward a broader acceptance of practices and customs as part of the constitution, and it is necessary now to pay more systematic attention to the elusive concept known as the constitutional convention. The significance of convention has already been referred to in foregoing discussions of responsible government, and of the transition from colony to independent nation, but more remains to be said. For one thing, it is not easy to define precisely what is or is not a convention. It is well understood that a cabinet in Canada, although no law says so, must have the support of a majority of the members in the elected part of a legislature. But when an installed cabinet, possibly backed by almost a whole legislature, then refrains from suppressing all criticism of itself, and does not abolish the opposition parties or send their supporters to concentration camps, is that in response to a recognized convention, or is it just a good idea? The Charter of Rights added to the constitution in 1982 has probably changed the answer to that question, although that is not clear beyond doubt. Although the charter guarantees freedom of expression, and each citizen's right to qualify as an MP, it does not say that the House of Commons cannot exercise its ancient right to expel unwanted members. Before 1982 the charter did not exist, but ministerial self-restraint did. Was that a constitutional convention?

There is not much help to be found in judicial decision, for the other reason that makes conventions hard to define is that they are rarely legally enforceable, and until 1981 in Canada were rarely even mentioned by courts. A judge can look at a written law or order, or read the precedents of common law, and interpret them; but who can interpret a concept that defies simple definition? Therein lies one of the major sources of constitutional flexibility, for while written instruments can be themselves rigid, and be rigidly interpreted, the same has not been true of conventions. The real sanction behind conventions is their acceptance, and the consequences that can follow from breaking them. If a cabinet is defeated once on a snap vote in the House of Commons, for example, it does not follow that the House has withdrawn its support. But if a cabinet stayed in office in the face of repeated defeats it would legally run into difficulties because Parliament grants it funds, and a government cannot be run without money. And it would run political risks in hanging on to office when the House of Commons was repeatedly making plain that it wanted a change. Conventions may not have the force of written law, but breaking them may produce results as unwelcome as those that follow law-breaking.

That proposition was raised indirectly in a curious way in a celebrated constitutional case that came to the Supreme Court of Canada in 1981, *Attorney General of Manitoba et al* v. *Attorney General of Canada et al*. The court was obliged to ponder the differences between conventions and laws, and to do that the judges had to consider what a convention was, and whether, in the matters referred to it, a convention existed at all. The case had its immediate origin in an attempt by the federal government, under Prime Minister Trudeau, to hasten the process of securing a new constitution act through unilateral action in Parliament. After prolonged negotiations, which ended in a failed conference of government leaders in 1980, the federal authorities decided, in a popular phrase, to go it alone. When Trudeau refused to refer his proposals to the Supreme Court for a ruling on their constitutionality, three of the eight dissenting provinces (only Ontario and New Brunswick supported the federal position) referred questions of their own to their provincial high courts; Manitoba and Newfoundland presented similar questions, and Quebec used different wording to raise the same principles.

The central question on convention referred to the courts appeared in the original Manitoba and Newfoundland submission in these words:

Is it a constitutional convention that the House of Commons and Senate of Canada will not request Her Majesty the Queen to lay before the Parliament of the United Kingdom of Great Britain and Northern Ireland a measure to amend the Constitution of Canada affecting federal-provincial relationships or the powers, rights or privileges granted or secured by the Constitution of Canada to the provinces, their legislatures or governments without first obtaining the agreement of the provinces?

The question is straightforward enough on the surface, although it leaves room for disagreement about its last five words: are 'the provinces' all the provinces, or a simple majority of the ten, or a majority that includes a minimum percentage of the total population?

There is a larger question. Since the conventions of the constitution include a variety of understandings, precedents, and working accommodations, but rarely law, in what sense are they the business of the courts? The majority decision of the Supreme Court, in answering yes to the quoted question, none the less includes this statement: 'Perhaps the main reason why conventional rules cannot be enforced by the courts is that they are generally in conflict with the legal rules which they postulate and the courts are bound to enforce the legal rules.' Lawyers arguing for the federal government and for Ontario urged that the Supreme Court should not answer at all the questions about whether the convention referred to existed, on the ground that no 'justiciable issue' was raised, and the matter was therefore 'not appropriate for a court.' The vote answering the provinces' question was six to three in favour, and the justices were careful to point out that they were not enforcing a convention, but merely answering a question about whether or not a particular convention existed. Even the dissenting justices (including the chief justice) noted that 'no legal question is raised' by the queries about convention referred to the court, but that 'Courts, however, may recognize the existence of conventions ...' On the basis of a valuable and comprehensive view of relevant practices and writings, that is, six justices of the Supreme Court said there was here a convention of the constitution, and three said there was not. The same court, with a different internal division, voted seven to two that the federal government was legally empowered to proceed with its proposals – but, by six to three, 'not according to convention.'

As parts of the constitution of Canada, where does that leave the conventions? Since, in the light of the court's answers, the federal government decided not to use its legal powers to go ahead, but to bow to the convention now acknowledged, will the Supreme Court's action in 1981 mean that in future there will be a trend toward conventions becoming hardened into statements of legal force, through appeals to the courts about whether or not each particular convention exists? The courts have dealt with conventions before, particularly those dealing with the developing nationhood of the parts of the British Empire, consistently taking variants of the line that the sanctions behind conventions are political, not legal, so that conventions cannot be enforced as laws. But in this case, without the Supreme Court departing from that course, a government chose to attach less significance to its legal powers than to a convention said by the court to exist. That recognition had a highly political result: the aftermath altered the direction of constitutional developments sought by the federal government and the provinces, the former affected by the court's answers on the convention, the latter by the court's view that Parliament had the legal power to do what the executive wanted. The court's answers, it will be recalled, were supported by a majority only; and the lay reader of the record can hardly fail to be struck by the cogency of both the majority and dissenting judicial views.

The case, in any event, was an impressive demonstration of the importance of judicial decisions as a part of the constitution. The convention itself, dealing as it does with the right of the provinces to be consulted about certain constitutional amendments, is no longer of more than academic interest, since the Constitution Act of 1982 included several tolerably clear sections on how to amend the constitution in the future. The constitution now says in part VII of the 1982 additions: 'The Constitution of Canada is the supreme law of Canada, and any law that is inconsistent with the provisions of the Constitution is, to the extent of the inconsistency, of no force or effect.' Since the Supreme Court will make the final decisions about what is inconsistent, its role as the interpreter of constitutional correctness can only grow. The court's performance in its role is not readily predictable, but it is fair to add that the courts can only deal with what is sent to them, in disputes or references, and the Canadian judiciary has a reassuring tradition for eschewing irresponsibility.

More predictable is the rigidity which the constitution of Canada had placed on it in 1982. While the uncertainties of the processes for amending the constitution before 1982 were often unsatisfactory to the point of exasperation, they at least allowed for some flexibility; the new rules are far more precise, and therefore more inflexible. They give new meaning to the statement that there are two basic sets of law-making authorities: the constitution-amending authority, and those bodies which, under the constitution, make all other laws, through Parliament and the provincial legislatures. The legislatures which make 'all other laws' may, as was shown earlier, create subordinate bodies, including crown corporations, regulatory bodies, and particular servants of Parliament like the auditor general. Of course, all of them must also be set up within the rules of the constitution, as must any orders-in-council passed at the federal or provincial level. Oddly enough, the governments closest to most citizens, the rural and urban municipal councils, have no constitutional status, but are subordinate bodies assigned to provincial jurisdiction. The actions of all the law-making authorities are of course subject to judicial review, also under the constitution.

The practice of leaving final decisions about the constitution in the hands of non-elected officials was well understood by the Fathers of Confederation, for in the setting up of a federal structure with two separate levels of government, neither level could be left free to determine the powers of the other. From the start, it was accepted that the courts would not only interpret the terms of the constitution, but set aside enactments which were repugnant to those terms. In Canada until 1982 the power of the courts to declare acts ultra vires (literally, outside the powers) was never as important as the same power in the United States, for the American courts had an additional duty of deciding if acts of Congress or the individual states involved matters outside the jurisdiction of *any* government. Until 1982 the Canadian constitution, apart from a few specific guarantees covering education and language, and the general guarantees implied in such provisions as those creating elected legislative bodies, was presumed to divide all powers between the federal and provincial governments. John Diefenbaker's celebrated Bill of Rights of 1960 was itself an ordinary act of Parliament; and as such it applied only to topics under the jurisdiction of Parliament, which could itself amend the act like any other. Before that, it must be confessed, there had been some notable violations of human rights at both federal and provincial hands, and the Bill of Rights, however well intended, did not materially add a great deal to the protection of citizens, partly because the courts, unused to applying a Bill of Rights to other laws enjoying exactly the same parliamentary sanction, showed no lasting enthusiasm for it. A few cases reached the Supreme Court, and they stand out precisely because they were not merely important, but exceptional.[3]

The new Charter of Rights and Freedoms is part of the constitution, and applies to federal and provincial governments. Just as people have in the past expressed doubts about the wisdom of wedding the cabinet system to a federal structure in Canada, there are now those who are sceptical of reconciling the parliamentary system with a constitutional Bill of Rights that limits all governments. Since the first marriage is well into its second century, there may be hopes for the second.

THE DISTRIBUTION OF POWERS

To abstract the constitution of a federal state from the society in which it lives can be misleading if one forgets that governments are not the only federalized institutions in a federal state. Many, if not most, national organizations use federal structures, and the obvious examples to point to here are the political parties: they are not mentioned in the written constitution, but they all maintain federal and provincial wings, or are constantly seeking to create them if they do not. Apart from politics, many other activities use federal structures: there are federations of labour, of native peoples, and of artists, and professional and business interests frequently organize themselves into provincial bodies, with a national office at the top. (A few, of which the lawyers' associations are probably the outstanding example, impose a kind of interprovincial tariff on their members, so that a person qualified at the bar of one province cannot practise in another without joining another bar.) Amateur sports organizations are often so constructed that provincial or regional leagues play internally for most of their seasons, but the best teams among them vie for a national title. The federal principle, that is, is everywhere, and cannot be considered an exclusively governmental property.

The dangers of considering it governmental only are compounded when one refines its study to isolate for comment such specific activities as the distribution of legal powers between governments, or federal-provincial financial relations. A distribution of powers, as has already been emphasized, is essential to any federal system. Yet ordinary citizens are rarely directly involved in what the distribution means, even though their lives may be affected every day by the fact that radio and television broadcasting, to take one well-known example, is under federal and not provincial jurisdiction. Since education in each province is under provincial jurisdiction, the use of broadcasting for educational purposes can clearly be a matter for discussion and perhaps dispute, but such disputes do not often create political issues of general interest. Every day in Canada there are dozens of committees of civil servants meeting to talk about federal and provincial responsibilities in each relevant area of governmental activity. Whatever the subject, the participants are aware that responsibilities mean costs, and costs mean taxes; and when there are two levels of government, each is likely to take an unkindly view of raising money for whose spending the other can get credit. When disputes cannot be settled by public servants, they tend to gravitate to the political arena and then do become public issues to such an extent that observers wonder why Canadians, acting through their governments, can appear to be less united than they are as citizens.

It is time to look more closely at the legal statements from which governments derive their power. The original distribution between federal and provincial legislatures (and most of the basic provisions refer to Parliament and the legislatures rather than to executive authority) was in part a 'start-up' arrangement, but it was also expected to be lasting. Few clauses in the act of 1867 even implied what sections 41, 47, 130, and 131 asserted, that 'Until the Parliament of Canada otherwise provides,' certain practices were to continue: section 130, for example, is hardly even heard of now, but in 1867 it provided for the first federal public service, making 'Officers of Canada' out of all former provincial officers not now needed for continuing provincial duties. Once used, the section was, in legal terminology, spent. As already noted, there are also spelled out in the original act a few fundamental guarantees; sections 17 to 20, for example, ensure an elected Commons with recognized parliamentary privileges, and the following sections ensure the provinces' places in the Senate; other sections establish elected legislatures for the new provinces. Section 133 puts the use of French and English in Parliament and the legislature of Quebec, and in federal and Quebec courts, beyond the reach of any ordinary law-making authority. Section 145 (in what is, for a constitutional document, an odd provision) binds the new Canada to start building a railway from the St Lawrence River to Halifax 'with all practicable Speed.'

The limits and commitments outlined above (and there are others) are normal elements in a new constitution, and apart from them the great bulk of law-making powers, necessary to the day-to-day carrying on of government, are shared by Parliament and the provincial legislatures. The basic sharing is as follows.

1. Parliament was given in section 91 a comprehensive grant to 'make laws for the peace, order, and good government of Canada' in relation to matters not specifically assigned to the provincial legislatures. 'For greater certainty, but not so as to restrict the generality' of the comprehensive grant, a list of specific subjects is given in detail. The whole is one grant of power: a comprehensive statement followed by a list of examples.

An additional federal power which grew in significance as Canadian nationhood developed was that needed to make treaties. The original treaty clause (section 132) was plain enough for its time: 'The Parliament and Government of Canada shall have all powers necessary or proper for performing the obligations of Canada or of any province thereof, as part of the British Empire, towards foreign countries, arising under treaties between the Empire and such foreign countries.' The passage of time raised several questions about that clause, ranging from general queries concerning Canada's treaty obligations, not 'as part of the British Empire' but as an independent member of the Commonwealth, to specific inquiries about whether Canada, through the treaty power, could invade areas under provincial jurisdiction. The post-Confederation inventions of the technology necessary to flying and broadcasting, for example, clearly involved somebody's 'property and civil rights,' a provincial matter. But judicial interpretation gave the federal authorities control over aeronautics and broadcasting, in part by the treaty route, since both had international ramifications. Other judicial decisions made clear that it was legally possible for the federal government to negotiate a treaty whose implementation was then left to the provinces, because of the subject-matter. The provinces cannot themselves, except as agents or delegates of the government of Canada, negotiate treaties with foreign governments; none the less they come close to it when they make commercial agreements with jurisdictions outside Canada. The language issue in recent years has seen Quebec receiving particular recognition in some international conferences involving foreign French-speaking jurisdictions.

2. The provincial legislatures receive their main powers in section 92, a list of subjects on which they could make laws. The topics are quite specific: for example, direct taxation within the province, public lands belonging to the province, municipal institutions, the administration of justice, 'shop, saloon, tavern, auctioneer, and other licences.' There is no general grant of power to compare with that given to Parliament in section 91, but one provincial topic, 'property and civil rights in the province,' has grown vastly in scope since 1867, partly because of new kinds of property, and new meanings for 'civil rights.' All the topics listed in section 92 were expected by the Fathers of Confederation to

have limited applications, and this is borne out by the last item: 'generally all matters of a merely local or private nature in the province.'

The Constitution Act of 1982 augmented provincial powers by an amendment which inserted a new section, 92A. While reserving Parliament's primacy where it is relevant, the section gives each legislature exclusive jurisdiction over exploration and development of non-renewable and forest resources and electrical energy in the province, and empowers the province to export to other parts of Canada the products, provided no price discrimination is allowed in supplying other parts. The provinces are also given an enlarged power to raise 'money by any mode or system of taxation' in the resources cited.

3. Concurrent powers over immigration and agriculture are given to both levels of government in section 95, again with federal primacy preserved. While some overlapping would seem inevitable with two governments sharing the same power, federal and provincial authorities have generally been successful in agreeing on how to divide their responsibilities in the same fields. In agriculture, for example, grades and standards (indispensable elements when products flow into national and international trade) are generally of federal determination, while the actual production of goods to meet the standards is governed by the provinces. A third concurrent power was added in 1951 (and clarified in 1964), when a new section 94A empowered Parliament to enact laws in relation to old age pensions, until then a provincial field; in this case the primacy of provincial legislation was preserved. In 1982, as already noted, a fourth concurrent power was augmented when the provinces were given a limited power to share in Parliament's capacity to raise money by any system of taxation. The two had always been able to raise money by direct taxes, and the 1982 amendment enlarges the provinces' capacity to tax. The taxing power differs from jurisdiction over specific fields of legislation such as agriculture (since tax money, once collected, can be spent on any topic the constitution allows) but it qualifies now as a concurrent power, of limited application in each province.

4. Education (in the sense of an organized system of public and high schools and universities) is assigned by section 93 to the provinces, subject to safeguards which permit aggrieved minorities to appeal to the governor-in-council; although the latter may act on its own initiative to order remedial measures. By the time Newfoundland entered Confederation in 1949, the courts had become the most convenient guardians of sectarian rights in education, and no provision was made for Newfoundlanders to appeal to federal authorities. In practice that route of appeal has become generally obsolete, although it remains on paper.

The foregoing itemization of major elements in the distribution of power between federal and provincial levels of government makes the whole sound far simpler than it is. While the founders may have had clear ideas about what they meant in 1867, they could not possibly have foreseen, for example, that the most lucrative form of direct taxation available to both sets of government would not be such simple matters as customs duties or levies on property, but income taxes imposed on individuals and corporations. They could not have known that new technologies and new devices for spending money (such as credit cards) would enlarge beyond recognition the significance of banking, bills of exchange, promissory notes, patents, and copyrights, which were all placed under federal jurisdiction, even though many of the devices involved would also come under the provincial power over property and civil rights. These apparent anomalies have one by one been taken to courts, along with hundreds of other cases arising from the written words of the constitution, and succeeding generations of judges have invented a fascinating series of doctrines for interpreting the words.

The whole subject of the distribution of powers requires more space than could be justified in a general survey such as this, but a further sampling of problems and decisions will serve to illustrate the scope of the legal side of the constitution. Nobody in 1867 was greatly exercised about fuel oil, although it did exist for uses other than those we now consider usual: the courts decided that a provincial tax on a person who purchased fuel oil at the time of its first sale in the province was an indirect tax because the purchaser would probably pass the tax on to somebody else, and it was not within the province's capacity to levy direct taxes. When Alberta attempted to levy a tax on certain funds of banks doing business in the province, the courts held that the real intent was not to raise revenue but to interfere in banking, which is under federal jurisdiction. The courts, that is, have looked to 'the pith and substance' of statutes, not only to prevent legal invasions, but also to decide that the same topic may for some purposes be in the federal field and for others in the provincial. A familiar illustration from our judicial history is legislation to regulate the sale of alcoholic beverages, which in one aspect may deal with public safety and be federal, and in another concern only local licensing policy and be provincial. Such distinctions are not necessarily permanent either, because changing circumstances may lead to changing judicial opinions. 'The life of the law has not been logic,' one of America's greatest jurists once wrote, 'it has been experience.' When Oliver Wendell Holmes wrote that, the constitution of Canada was in its teens.

Canada's experience with judicial interpretations of the distribution of powers has sometimes raised the suspicion that more than logic was at work. Not all constitutional decisions concern the distribution of powers alone, for there have been major cases on such matters as regulation of trade, provincial authority in relation to municipal institutions, and civil liberties, which have not been confined to issues between federal and provincial governments. The courts' views on sections 91 and 92, however, have always held great interest for Canadian observers, not just because until 1949 the last word on their meaning lay outside Canada, with the Judicial Committee of the Privy Council, but because the committee's views for long periods seemed to run counter to the plain meaning of the original British North America Act. What Sir John A. Macdonald and his colleagues thought they were doing in the 1860s was expressed by him in the Confederation Debates on 3 February 1865: 'We thereby ... make the Confederation one people and one government, instead of five peoples and five governments ... one united province, with the local governments and legislatures subordinate to the General Government and Legislature.' In less than three decades Lord Watson, rendering the decision in *Liquidators of the Maritime Bank of Canada* v. *Receiver General of New Brunswick* in 1892, said of the original Constitution Act: 'The object of the Act was neither to weld the provinces into one, nor to subordinate provincial governments to a central authority.' Half a century later W.P.M. Kennedy, a distinguished Canadian scholar of the law and a leading advocate of the centralist theory of Confederation, felt impelled to write: 'Seldom have statesmen more deliberately striven to write their purposes into law, and seldom have they more signally failed before the judicial technique of statutory interpretation.'

When Canadian observers talk like that, they are usually referring to the opening part of section 91, already cited, which endows Parliament with the power to 'make laws for the peace, order, and good government of Canada, in relation to all matters not coming within the classes of subjects by this Act assigned exclusively to the legislatures of the provinces; and for greater certainty, but not so as to restrict the generality of the foregoing terms of this Section, it is hereby declared that (notwithstanding anything in this Act) the exclusive legislative authority of the Parliament of Canada extends to all matters coming within the classes of subjects next hereafter enumerated.' If the act of 1867 had not added the list put in 'for greater certainty,' its interpretation by the courts might have been different, for the very list, which was 'not so as to restrict the generality of the foregoing terms,' in effect turned out to do just that.

What happens when a single document is interpreted over the decades by succeeding generations of judges who pay a good deal of attention to the words of their predecessors can perhaps be envisaged through a homely analogy. If one takes a hundred numbered sheets of white paper, leaves the first as it is and paints the other ninety-nine with a pale shade of paint, then leaves the second with a single coat of paint but covers again the other ninety-eight, leaves the third with two coats but covers the other ninety-seven, and so on, no two consecutive pieces will differ sharply from each other, but the hundredth will be considerably different from the first. And so with judicial interpretations of the old British North

America Act: the paint analogy is not wholly valid, for it is both a smoother process, and a more deliberate one, than courts follow. Judges did not deliberately set out to alter the meaning of the act, but applying their talents successively, and listening to each other, they did. And what they did has been both harshly criticized and lauded as correct, the judge-watchers' opinions ranging from scholarly objectivity to frank advocacy of stronger federal or stronger provincial powers. When in recent years several leading cases went in favour of the federal authority, it naturally encouraged talk of reforming the Supreme Court; before the Supreme Court became the final arbiter in 1949, there was less talk of reforming the Judicial Committee of the Privy Council because there was no practical way Canadians could do it.

The leading cases in the interpretation of Canada's constitution have been ably collected and commented on by several scholars,[4] and the chronicle is too long and complicated to receive more than short summary here. It is also so varied a chronicle that summary can be misleading: the itemized statements below refer specifically to the meanings attached to the peace, order, and good government clause quoted above. Often they include, directly or by implication, a consideration of the provincial topic, property and civil rights; for once that phrase was opened up to go beyond matters of purely provincial and local interest, it could be taken to mean that if a subject fell under the topic it was therefore provincial, unless something else in the act asserted the contrary. Since property and civil rights covers a remarkable range of human activity, the phrase could in fact be so interpreted as to take strength away from the federal powers over peace, order, and good government.

– For several years after 1867 the Judicial Committee followed the literal text of the act. In a case destined to be quoted nostalgically for decades by federalists (*Russell* v. *The Queen*), it was held that a federal local option law concerning liquor regulation was of general or national importance related to public order. The committee considered whether the same law did not come under the provincial 'property and civil rights,' and observed: 'Few, if any, laws could be made by Parliament for the peace, order, and good government of Canada which did not in some incidental way affect property and civil rights; and it could not have been intended, when assuring to the provinces exclusive legislative authority on the subjects of property and civil rights, to exclude the Parliament from the exercise of this general power whenever any such incidental interference would result from it.'

– The committee soon abandoned that view. It began by dividing the federal grant of power in section 91 into two parts, general and enumerated: the general grant then became not the governing part of Parliament's power, but a grant 'in supplement of its enumerated powers'; the enumerated part became of greater consequence in interpretations than the general grant it illustrated 'for greater certainty.'

– The federal list in section 91 was taken to override the provincial powers listed in section 92, while section 92 was taken to override the general power of Parliament for peace, order, and good government. In the competition between the two lists the provinces enjoyed an advantage, largely because of the elastic capacities of property and civil rights.

– The general power of Parliament for peace, order, and good government remained in the act and had to be accounted for; the courts decided that in it lurked an emergency power which could be invoked in time of dire necessity. (The two world wars qualified as emergencies; the world-wide depression of the 1930s apparently did not.)

– In 1946 the Judicial Committee challenged its own invention of the emergency doctrine. The decision in *Attorney General of Ontario* v. *Canada Temperance Federation* included this: if the subject-matter of a law 'is such that it goes beyond local or provincial concern or interests and must from its inherent nature be the concern of the Dominion as a whole ... then it will fall within the competence of the Dominion Parliament as a matter affecting the peace, order, and good government of Canada.'

– The disappearance of the emergency doctrine was temporary, and it was reasserted as early as 1947. Its course in recent decades is difficult to characterize, for while constitutional cases have been settled without it, the Supreme Court in 1976, in *Reference re Anti-Inflation Act*, revived a version of it to decide that the federal government could establish a program of wage and price controls. The court rendered its decision by a seven-to-two majority, and the majority opinion was expressed in two judgments, respectively signed by four and three justices. But on the specific point of whether combatting inflation could be justified under Parliament's power to make laws for peace, order, and good government, the clearest judgment was rendered by one of the dissenters, and on the point four other judges agreed. A majority, that is, felt that the national dimensions of a problem were not alone enough to make it a matter for 'p. o. and g. g.'; there had to be an emergency to justify Parliament's action. It was, one observer has noted, 'the first time that the judiciary invoked the emergency doctrine as the constitutional basis for peacetime economic regulation.'[5]

Winning a case for what at the time struck many as the wrong reason does not mean that Parliament is powerless in economic matters, for the list in section 91 numbers several economic topics. Land beyond a province's boundaries can hardly be under a province's jurisdiction, and when British Columbia sought to claim mineral rights under the waters off British Columbia, the Supreme Court found in favour of federal jurisdiction. (*Reference re Offshore Mineral Rights of British Columbia*, 1967, did not silence provinces' claims about their offshore areas, and the dispute has continued to this day.) Other natural resources clearly under provincial jurisdiction have none the less led to decisions favourable to federal authority. For example, Saskatchewan, supported by several provinces, but opposed by Ottawa, failed to secure a particular payment from oil producers because the court held that the procedures followed involved an indirect tax, and thus one that was not then within provincial jurisdiction (*Canadian Industrial Gas and Oil Ltd.* v. *Government of Saskatchewan*, 1978). Saskatchewan lost again in the following year when a policy it adopted in regard to potash was found by the court to take the province beyond its undoubted power over natural resources within its boundaries into marketing the products outside them, and that was a federal matter (*Central Canada Potash Co. Ltd. and Attorney General of Canada* v. *Government of Saskatchewan*, 1979).

These cursory summaries of complicated court decisions must not be taken as a substitute for the full documents. But they do illustrate why judicial setbacks on important matters of principle are taken seriously by the provinces, and can lead to lingering dissatisfaction with the Supreme Court and the federal monopoly over the appointment of its judges. It contributes to a 'box-score' view of the court's work in disputes over federal as against provincial powers, the won-lost ratio of cases sometimes becoming a news item. Furthermore, when the federal government has failed to get its way, as in its reference about Parliament's authority to mend or end the Senate in 1980, or its unilateral attempt to seek constitutional amendments in the following year, the issues have been considerably more abstract than those the provinces raise about specific natural resources like oil and potash. Generalization about judicial decisions is no doubt unwise in many respects, but it is a fact that federal acts in recent years have fared better before the Supreme Court than provincial ones. A provincial government may point to that as proof of bias, while Ottawa regards the same fact merely as proof that federal governments do their homework better. If the positions were reversed, it would still be a normal part of federal-provincial relations in Canada. Meanwhile, as statutes and references pass solemnly under the eyes of the Supreme Court, the text of the constitution remains innocent of even a mention of 'emergency' in connection with Parliament's power to make laws for the peace, order, and good government of Canada.

FINANCING FEDERALISM

Disputes over the distribution of powers in Canada have always had a known source of settlement: whatever one may think of a court decision, or a series of them, a pronouncement from the highest judicial body always settled something. Financial problems rarely reach the end of the line so easily; each settlement commonly lays the groundwork for the next dispute, and some of the disputes are themselves by-products of clear judicial decisions interpreting the distribution of powers.

At the start everything looked simple. Since the federal authority was to be paramount, with the provinces 'subordinate bodies,' the provinces were not expected to need large incomes. The federal government was taking on the major public functions, as well as assuming existing provincial public debts. It made sense therefore that the federal government should also assume the chief source of former provincial revenue, customs and excise duties. In each of the Province of Canada, New Brunswick, and Nova Scotia, the two taxes in the 1860s (although their individual importance varied from one colony to another) brought in well over half the province's revenue. Their transfer to Parliament left the provinces, on average, with 17 per cent of pre-Confederation income, not enough to meet their post-Confederation responsibilities, small though these were thought to be. On the financial front, Confederation began with a series of arrangements that made the new provinces at least partially dependent on the federal government.

The details are a striking tribute to the ingenuity of the Fathers of Confederation. Faced with the necessity of trying to treat as equals provinces that were in fact unequal, not only in size, population, and wealth, but in the relative burdens of public debt they bore before 1 July 1867 and their relative dependence on the sources of revenue they were losing, the draftsmen of the constitution devised a scheme which aimed at equal treatment by recognizing the relevant inequalities. The federal authority, as noted, took over the provinces' debts, and also most of the public works for which the debts had been incurred. An elaborate formula was worked out that created a bookkeeping allowance for public debt of approximately twenty-five dollars per head of population in each province: if any province's actual debt was less than its allowance, it received annual interest on the difference (5 per cent); if greater, the province paid interest to the federal government. In the event, New Brunswick broke even on this arrangement, Nova Scotia received interest, and Ontario and Quebec were to pay interest out. From the beginning the debt allowance was manipulated to increase payments to the provinces, sometimes in bizarre ways. Ontario and Quebec, for example, had their allowance raised to cover their original joint debts, and succeeded further in getting a refund of the interest they had in the meantime paid, with interest on the interest. The prairie provinces entered Confederation with no debt, but still received debt allowances, and Manitoba, when its population according to the 1881 census was 62,260, was assumed to have 125,000.

The original financial provisions, seen in the 1860s as major settlements for the provinces, have now diminished sharply as a fraction of each province's income, and it is of historical interest that the first subsidies were declared to be 'in full settlement of all future Demands on Canada.'[6] They included specific annual sums ranging from $50,000 to $80,000 for the support of each provincial legislature, and unconditional annual subsidies of eighty cents per head of population. Both became manipulable, the first by law from the start, the per capita grants raised by the invention of fictitious populations for new provinces. In 1907 a general revision of the original arrangements was enacted, and by that time it was apparent that the forty-year-old financial terms were inadequate. Even in 1867 an annual extra sum had been awarded New Brunswick, on the excellent ground that the money was needed; that precedent made more special grants hard to resist. Special grants became common, and by the time the federal and provincial governments had reached the 1970s and begun to talk seriously of making significant changes in many parts of the constitution generally, the specific financial arrangements had already survived over two dozen alterations; some of them even echoed the financial spirit of the 1860s, and were characterized as 'final and unalterable,' a Canadian euphemism for 'until the next one.'

A final and unalterable settlement in a federal system embodies almost a contradiction in terms, for the scope of government activity at both federal and provincial levels changes constantly, and in recent decades at accelerating rates. Judicial interpretation of the distribution of powers in Canada helped contribute to the flexibility of the financial terms of Confederation, for the provinces' need for money might have been less had the courts' interpretation of Parliament's power over peace, order, and good government not become so narrow. But apart from that, the provinces' responsibilities, like that of the federal government, have grown enormously with changing technologies and changing conceptions of the role of the state in the twentieth century. The cost to the provinces of education, to take one example, was a few million dollars in 1867, and about the same number of billions in the 1980s: judicial interpretation had almost nothing to do with that. When one adds to that the provinces' assigned jurisdiction over 'Local Works and Undertakings' (in terms of cost, mainly roads and highways), and new functions, virtually unknown in the 1860s, concerning public health, old age pensions, or labour legislation, it is not difficult to accept the conclusion that the provinces have always needed more money than they could easily raise with limited powers of taxation. Yet another factor came from the vast differences in the provinces themselves: Ontario and Prince Edward Island have identical jurisdictions over education, but if a wealthy industrialized province can spend far more per child on modern well-equipped schools than a small Atlantic island, is that to be accepted as reasonable? If, as citizens of Canada, Maritimers and central Canadians are to have equal educational rights, who pays the costs, and how?

In education, and in countless other fields, Canada and the provinces have worked out an impressive system of what can properly be called deals, some ad hoc but most of them enjoying long lives, and most of them requiring not just transfers of money but the establishment of administrative arrangements to manage each transfer. These can be simple, consisting of a small committee of federal and provincial officials from one or two provinces, or huge, involving departments in Ottawa and all ten provincial capitals. A parliamentary committee studying fiscal affairs in 1981 listed over two hundred federal-provincial agreements, their subjects ranging from those frequently in the news, such as health insurance and post-secondary education, to unfamiliar dealings over rabies indemnification, handicapped refugees, native court workers, and harbours for small craft. It should come as no surprise that the study of intergovernmental relations has become a recognized academic discipline.[7]

Behind such developments lie those already cited: a massive growth in governmental expenditure at all levels since Confederation, based largely on changing perceptions of public functions; growing disparities among the provinces, which in turn have meant changes in the nature of provincial needs for federal assistance; and an accelerating need for co-ordination in policies. A few statistics can pinpoint the precise meanings of these facts and illuminate some of their implications for federal finances in Canada. Even before the impact of the costs of the Second World War and the subsequent emergence of many new social policies, the Royal Commission on Dominion-Provincial Relations (the Rowell-Sirois Commission, which reported in 1940) had shown that from just after Confederation to 1937, annual federal expenditures had grown from $20 million to $478 million; provincial from $7 million to $258 million; municipal from $8 million to $282 million. Within those totals are revealing details: in the pre-1937 period provincial expenditures on education multiplied (in round numbers) twenty-five times, municipal education costs nearly fifty times. Federal expenditures on public welfare in the period, leaving out the incidence of unemployment relief during the depression of the 1930s, multiplied nearly ninety times. Revenue from sources used at Confederation also changed vastly: down to the First World War the federal government made no significant use of its power to levy direct taxes, and today direct taxes on personal and corporate incomes are its major sources of income. The Second World War made its own contributions to federal financing in Canada: budgetary expenditures on defence and mutual aid, for example, multiplied over thirty times from 1939 to 1943, the peak year, and in the postwar period expenditures on social services burgeoned, those for health, family allowances, and old age benefits rising from almost nothing in 1939 to hundreds of millions annually after 1945. Much of the postwar rise in the expenditures of all governments concerned matters under provincial jurisdiction, and the largest proportion was demanded of provincial and municipal jurisdictions.

All levels of government in the current decade have annual budgets running far beyond the first expectations. The minister of finance, in his budget speech on 26 February 1986, observed in part, 'The Government of Canada will spend $53 billion this year on social programs ... $12.6 billion in cash is transferred to the provinces for health, education and welfare. The total contribution, which also includes tax transfers, is about $20 billion.' Therein lies the significance for this chapter of huge expenditures: they not only tax the energies (and patience) of taxpayers, but demand of federal-provincial administrators the invention of methods for the satisfactory transfer of larger and larger sums raised by one government to the spending powers of another. The recipient provinces, like the federal government, have of course had to exploit all the taxation powers the constitution provides.

Sharing revenues and costs
Apart from the devices already described for the increasing of federal payments to the provinces, added administrative inventions must be cited. Beginning in 1912, the dominion began to provide grants to provinces for matters under provincial jurisdiction which the federal government nevertheless wishes to see developed, and the principle followed was simple: the federal government provided money for each participating province to spend, subject to specified conditions. These conditional grants were the forerunners of modern shared-cost agreements, and their history was erratic. A province, offered assistance for an agricultural college it could not itself afford, might find that after the federal grant expired the province had to maintain a college. Divided jurisdictions created other problems. Can the federal granting authority insist on the auditing of expenditures made by officials under provincial jurisdiction? Can it prescribe the standards to be followed by provincial administrators? Can it withhold payments if it feels that further increments have not been earned? The answers to these questions varied from topic to topic, and from province to province, and party politics often became a factor. The conditional grants included some genuine achievements, but the parliamentary task force of the early 1980s found them to be 'an inherently unsatisfactory device ... [we doubt] whether joint administration of activities by the Dominion and a province is ever a satisfactory way of surmounting constitutional difficulties.'

What then? The parliamentary committee just quoted went on to explore the device called revenue-sharing, which was succinctly referred to by the prime minister on 4 November 1968: 'it is our intention to get out of a lot of these areas of social services and let the provinces assume them. We will give them the tax room which goes along with these expenditures.' What he meant has turned out to be complicated in practice (and naturally it has meant a lot of jargon about tax abatements and tax points) but the essence is simple: Parliament may use its power, say, to tax citizens in a particular income bracket at 40 per cent, but instead it collects for its own treasury only 30 per cent, leaving the other 10 per cent to the province. By yet another device, the federal government will actually collect the entire 40 per cent, and for each individual taxpayer pay the 10 per cent to his province; so the citizen fills out only one return, and the province is spared the trouble of establishing its own income tax collection system.

That over-simplified description of a basic modern tool of government in Canada omits much detail about the ongoing fiscal arrangements (which are now rearranged every five years), and obscures what the money is used for once collected. A statistical reminder of one of the roots of fiscal federalism in Canada is in order. The following figures for 1980–1, which show federal transfers as a percentage of provincial incomes, reveal the varying extent to which the provinces depend on federal money:

Newfoundland	51%	Ontario	25%
Prince Edward Island	56%	Manitoba	41%
Nova Scotia	53%	Saskatchewan	21%
New Brunswick	51%	Alberta	12%
Quebec	35%	British Columbia	24%

Those figures naturally vary from year to year, for a province heavily dependent on one or two resources of international importance can find good and bad years occurring with startling frequency. The least dependent province above, Alberta, as this is written has been suffering severely from a drop in world oil prices.

What the figures demonstrate for any year is the use of fiscal devices to even out the disparities between provinces, and this is now done by two accepted policies, equalization and stabilization. Equalization as a necessity was recognized explicitly for the first time by the Royal Commission on Dominion-Provincial Relations in 1940. Prior to that, the frequent adjustments in subsidies had been based on the fictitious assumption that the provinces were as jurisdictions essentially equal, so that adjustments were to meet special needs in exceptional cases. (The adjustments were sometimes sought so blatantly by needy provinces that contemporary observers referred to them as 'raids' on the federal treasury.) The commission's Report, while still speaking of special grants, referred to them now as instruments 'designed to make it possible for every province to provide for its people services of average Canadian standards.' Each province was to be able, 'without resort to heavier taxation than the Canadian average, to provide adequate social, educational, and developmental services.'

The specific proposals of the commission were opposed by several provinces and shelved during wartime, but their influence was immense. The heavy taxation necessitated by the demands of war compelled the provinces to enter agreements through which they relinquished certain productive taxes in return for federal guarantees and payments so that, among other things, provincial governments became accustomed to comprehensive financial arrangements with Ottawa. Canada's experience after 1945, shared by men with long memories of the depression and the war, heightened an awareness of the importance of financial policies as tools in economic and social welfare; co-operation among governments whose taxable capacities varied became taken for granted.

Equalization as a systematic corrective of provincial disparities was not immediately accepted after the war. At a meeting that convened intermittently from August 1945 to May 1946, the two levels of government worked at sorting out their several responsibilities and sources of money, the federal spokesmen hoping for an extension into peace of its wartime financial hegemony, and expressing willingness in return to accept wide responsibilities for, among other things, pensions, unemployment assistance, and health insurance. The meeting, like its predecessor on the Rowell-Sirois Report, failed in the immediate sense; but it led to new federal proposals known as tax rental agreements which were accepted by all but the two largest provinces. Beginning in 1947 the agreements, with changes, were renegotiated every five years (Ontario signed in 1952), and equalization in its modern form began in 1957. The form was initially simple, although as usual the details were more involved. In essence, the first equalization payments were based on a formula which ensured that all the provinces would have their incomes brought up to the level of the yields per capita of three 'standard taxes' in the two wealthiest provinces in each year; the bases cited were specific rates on personal and corporate income taxes, and succession duties. The formula has changed (for 1987–92 the basic taxes will consist of a list of over thirty, not three), but its essence has not: the federal government, in effect, is used as a leveller that shifts money from the wealthier parts of Canada to the poorer. In 1982–3 the six provinces entitled to receive equalization payments under the existing formula received a total of $4,476.1 million, ranging from $123.2 million for Prince Edward Island to $2,435.8 million for Quebec. The provinces receiving none that year were Ontario, Saskatchewan, Alberta, and British Columbia.[8]

Equalization moved from the statute-books into the constitution in 1982. Part III of the Constitution Act provides that, without altering the rights or responsibilities of Parliament and the legislatures, they are (with their respective executives) committed to '(a) promoting equal opportunities for the well-being of Canadians;

(b) furthering economic development to reduce disparity in opportunities; and (c) providing essential public services of reasonable quality to all Canadians.' Those clauses leave much undefined, but part III also specifically commits Parliament and the government of Canada 'to the principle of making equalization payments,' so that provinces 'have sufficient revenues to provide reasonably comparable levels of public services at reasonably comparable levels of taxation.' The constitution omits mention of stabilization payments, although they may well fall within that splendid phrase 'reasonably comparable.' A stabilization payment is just that: in bold terms, it protects provinces from sudden fluctuations in their annual incomes by guaranteeing that next year's will be at least 95 per cent of this year's. That formula, too, has varied, but not in principle.

One other major device of federal-provincial financial arrangements must be described, Established Programs Financing, or EPF, which is a combined refinement and consolidation for particular purposes of other devices, so framed as to permit individual provinces either to participate in, or opt out of, the programs involved. In a sense, EPF has been based on the assumption that, among the many fundamental programs essential to Canadian federalism, some are more fundamental than others. In the words of the parliamentary task force on fiscal federalism in 1981; 'The expression "established" was applied to programs that had achieved a certain level of "maturity" – that is to say, programs that had been in effect long enough and that commanded sufficient public support to justify the presumption that they would not be discontinued by the province.' Since they were as permanent as any democratic program is likely to be, and dealt with topics into which some of the provinces were loathe to countenance a continuing federal intrusion by way of shared-cost financing, the federal government began in the 1960s to offer to withdraw from the programs, substituting tax abatements for conditional grants. The first specific field chosen was hospital insurance, and some related welfare plans, and EPF now provides for both federal and provincial governments to participate in paying for the basic policies in hospital insurance, medicare, and post-secondary education as permanent commitments, but on terms that leave the provinces free to set their own priorities, within financing that guarantees each of their minimum revenues. The words, again, disguise formulas and accounting concepts all but unintelligible to an ordinary citizen.

These are the basic forms of fiscal federalism. In the 1980s the federal government transfers money to other governments under many headings, some of them as old as Confederation, others newly invented. To call the entire structure complex would itself be a gross over-simplification, but it would be foolhardy to dismiss it because of that. Parts of it, such as sections of EPF, treat the provinces, on a per capita basis, with a rigid equality; others, like equalization, abandon that rigidity in the interests of equality, so that some provinces get nothing, others several hundred dollars a year for each citizen. Nobody at any level of government is ever totally satisfied with every aspect of it, and complaints (especially during provincial elections when the governing party in Ottawa is different from that nearest home) are so common as to be predictable. But no major problem in federal-provincial financial relations that comes under the constitution has yet been found insoluble. The Rowell-Sirois Commission observed in 1940: 'In the course of our work we have come to appreciate as never before the achievements of the Fathers of Confederation.' The work of the Parliamentary Task Force on Federal-Provincial Fiscal Arrangements in 1981 confirms that the founders had able successors.

CONCLUSION

It is important to repeat here an earlier warning: the isolation from the whole of the distribution of powers, and financial relations, should not be taken as more than an indication of their importance to the constitution. They are not the whole, and it is possible for a citizen to live a satisfactory life in Canada with little or no direct knowledge of either of them. There are major parts of Canadian society, such as those dealing with the arts and public support of them through governments, which are rarely thought of in constitutional terms, but which are no less significant because of that. Sometimes an issue, such as those concerned in abortion, or day care, or minorities, or the status of women, may seem for years to have no constitutional aspect; and then suddenly it becomes necessary to discover which level of government is responsible for it, and who pays for it. Then a new aspect of the distribution of powers and federal-provincial financial relations is likely to be discovered too. Even then it will receive the most attention from a relatively few activists, not the entire electorate. The subject-matters in this chapter provide parts of the stage on which political actors of all kinds perform, but the whole is much larger.

Countries that do not enjoy either a federal distribution of powers, or the complicated financial dealings that go with them, nevertheless share with countries such as Canada the same aggravating problems. In the 1980s these include high rates of unemployment and soaring deficits, and each country has in turn its own unique difficulties. Canada's share of the last would include at the top of the list those that have arisen from displacing the original nomadic peoples who populated the territory by peoples from elsewhere who take increasing industrialization and urbanization for granted; no Canadian government, or political party, has yet produced a constitutional solution for Indian and Inuit claims to land, or more self-government. The continuing negotiations around federal constitutional and financial matters have left almost untouched many equally challenging issues.

It is true, notwithstanding, that Canadian federalism has built into it a trait not foreseen by the Fathers of Confederation: each level of government always has an adversary it can blame for partial or complete failures, a truth borne out by the history of almost every major issue. Of course, clever private interests are often able to exploit for their own ends differences between governments.[9] High oil prices are good for provinces that produce oil, but not for central Canada, which consumes vast quantities of it. Low grain prices are hard on the prairies, but good for consumers who want low food prices. In both these familiar situations, any governmental policy that suits all parties is impossible. The usual course is then to seek some kind of compensation, sometimes elaborately disguised, for the victims. As this is written, the federal government is seeking to cut, not the actual payments made under segments of EPF, but projected *increases* in the payments, hoping to save the federal treasury around $6 billion by 1991. The provinces, according to well-understood rituals, resist.

16
The growth of the constitution

In French-English relations, Quebec-Ottawa relations, and federal-provincial relations more generally, there is no resting place, no end to tensions and frustrations. There are no constitutional utopias. We have to be satisfied with the stumbling efforts of imperfect men to keep our problems at bay.
Alan Cairns, *And No One Cheered*

The growth of the constitution and the growth of government, although necessarily related, are not the same. Important elements in the growth of government may not be known to the written constitution, or even the law, except in so far as they are subsumed under the same laws that apply to everybody else. Probably the most important single example to this, at least until 1987, has been the rise of pressure groups, those organizations which use their rights of free speech and freedom of association to lobby governments on every conceivable topic. Pressure groups have always existed in Canada; in the years following Confederation, journalists often commented on how the opening of every parliamentary session brought to Ottawa swarms of people described in 1875 as 'vampires many of them, come to fatten upon the public thing.' The growing complexity of the state inevitably brought with it new kinds of lobbies, and finally in January 1987 a House of Commons committee recommended legislation that would require lobbyists and their principals to make public their attempts to influence legislative and administrative action. If the committee's recommendations are adopted, pressure groups will be brought within the law in a manner that recognizes their importance in government, but they will remain outside the constitution.

There are other major examples of the differences in the growth of government and the growth of the constitution. The development of the welfare state in the twentieth century was accompanied by few changes in the constitution, and the same is true of Canada's roles in international affairs, as a member of such alliances as the United Nations, the North Atlantic Treaty Organization, and the North American Air Defense Command. Domestically, some of the fundamental differences between changes in the constitution and in government can be seen in the provinces. With a few exceptions in specific areas, all ten (and the territories) come under the umbrella of the same national constitution, yet all of them are different. Quebec is often perceived to be the most different, and that is, of course, true in many ways. But it would be a gross error to conclude that, although Quebec is undeniably different, all the others are the same, or are affected in essentially the same ways by constitutional changes.

Not all change may be considered growth, for change in one part of the constitution may produce a diminution in another. The courts' addition of the emergency clause to their interpretation of 'peace, order, and good government' provides a classic example, for while the meaning of section 91 grew, few federalists considered it a productive extension. Parts of a constitution can simultaneously change at differing speeds. While the extension of the franchise to women during and after the First World War meant a dramatic (and in 1916-17, an abrupt) change in the direction of Canadian democracy, the basic institutions within which the change took effect – the electoral system and the House of Commons – themselves remained much the same. Parts of a constitution can be flexible, easily adapted to changing needs, while others are more rigid and difficult to alter easily. This chapter deals with the development of the Canadian constitution since Confederation, moving in general from the more flexible to the more rigid components. Two of the more flexible, conventions and judicial decisions, have already been dealt with in some detail, for elements in the nature of the constitution naturally play roles in its change.

THE MORE FLEXIBLE COMPONENTS

Conventions
Conventions are flexible in a different sense from judicial decisions, for the latter deal with deliberate interpretations of law while conventions adapt laws, and adapt to laws, often without overtly interpreting them at all. Judicial interpretations are flexible in that they keep parts of the constitution in continual motion; but they also have a rigidity not found in conventions, for once the Supreme Court has spoken its word is final. With conventions there is nearly always room to manoeuvre. Conventions can none the less be loosely classified according to their relationship with law – from none whatever to close contact with statutes and the written parts of the constitution.

The first category is that of pure custom, in which the constitution develops with no immediate connection with any law. The custom underlying responsible government, which requires an executive to resign when the House of Commons withdraws its support, has been supplemented by a second custom, which sees a government clearly defeated in a general election resign before the new House even meets – that is, *before* the House has withdrawn support in a formal way. When an election is unclear, producing a minority situation, the resignation of the incumbent government depends on the government: in 1929, for example, the premier of Saskatchewan, J.G. Gardiner, though his party had not won, insisted on calling the legislature to see if its members would indeed deprive him of office; they did. But when in 1957 a federal Liberal government under St Laurent failed to win a new majority, the same Jimmy Gardiner, now federal minister of agriculture, was unable to persuade the prime minister to meet the House to make John Diefenbaker's supporters defeat the government; St Laurent insisted on resigning at once. Another familiar custom was then resorted to: when a prime minister resigns because he has lost an election, the governor general summons the leader of the opposition to form a government. Within Parliament itself the day-to-day uses of English and French depend partly on custom, regardless of the law.

Conventional usages also operate in fields that *are* covered by legislation. Ordinarily an amendment to a statute may provide the simplest route toward change, but there are laws which fall short of producing a structure that is complete in all essentials. It is law, for example, which creates a new government department and the office and salary of the minister who heads it; but it is custom which puts the minister in the cabinet. And the composition of the cabinet itself, determined by the prime minister so as to give the broadest possible representation to Canada's major groups and regions, is one of convention. Laws which open up wholly new areas of activity, such as that permitting collective bargaining in most of the public service, create new fields for convention, while other conventions develop where collective bargaining is not allowed, as in the support staff serving Parliament itself. As with statutes, conventions also develop in relation to the written constitution, and are so powerful that the written words have sometimes had their meaning not only altered, but nullified. The best-known example, already cited, is the whole relationship of the governor general to other major institutions of the government, which is not what the Constitution Act of 1867 says, but is governed by convention.

Judicial decision

The previous chapter said enough about judicial interpretation to make clear the role played by the courts in the development of the constitution, and the general point needs no further exposition. Judicial review in a federal system is plainly inescapable, since neither level of government could be expected to trust the other to define its own powers; and if those levels of government with elected components cannot be expected to make final interpretations of a constitution, the courts are equally plainly the most reliable institution to which to turn. It is important to note that for each issue a Supreme Court interpretation is final in two senses: it is not only the last word (unless subsequently altered by a differing decision of a formal constitution amendment), but also the end of a process. Every day politicians and public servants have to interpret relevant parts of the constitution to carry on their work, and their interpretations may be accepted for years. It is only when a challenge is issued (and it may be a challenge initiated by private citizens) that the courts have an opportunity to render a decision; judges do not roam the statute-books at will, seeking laws to interpret.

It is pertinent to ask if judicial interpretation of a constitution should be based on different premises from those relied on for ordinary statutes. The Judicial Committee of the Privy Council, a British judicial body interpreting a law passed by a sovereign British Parliament, said of the British North America Act as early as 1887 (in *Bank of Toronto* v. *Lambe*) that the courts 'must treat the provisions of the Act in question by the same methods of construction and exposition which they apply to other statutes.' For that reason the committee could not accept as evidence the unmistakable words of the Quebec Resolutions, or the speeches made by influential Canadians in the Confederation Debates of 1865. The Privy Council occasionally did depart from its own rigid rules, observing in 1930, as an instance (in *Edwards* v. *Attorney General for Canada*), that 'there are statutes and statutes; and the strict construction deemed proper in the case, for example, of a penal or taxing statute or one passed to regulate the affairs of an English parish, would be often subversive of Parliament's real intent if applied to an Act passed to ensure the peace, order, and good government of a British colony.' These are comforting words to a federalist, but many Privy Council decisions do not read like interpretations of a living constitution or, to use an image employed in the case just quoted, 'a living tree capable of growth and expansion within its natural limits.' The Supreme Court of Canada, arbiter since 1949, has of course always been manned by justices aware of a constitution; and its leading decisions, whether one agrees with them or not, invariably reveal at least an attempt to understand its federal nature.

Judicial review, therefore, remains a fundamental element in the development of the constitution. Anyone concerned about the principles involved in letting nine appointed judges have the final say about laws passed by elected legislatures should find comfort in observations from one of Canada's great public servants, O.D. Skelton. Speaking to a special committee of the Senate which in 1935 reviewed judicial interpretations of the British North American Acts (and issued a highly critical report), Dr Skelton said: 'Courts may modify, they cannot replace.

They can revise earlier interpretations, as new arguments, new points of view are presented; they can shift the dividing line in marginal cases; but there are barriers they cannot pass, definite assignments of power they cannot reallocate.'

Other forms of change
Among the more flexible parts of the constitution must be listed some ordinary statutes and orders-in-council, and also legal amendments authorized by the constitution itself which by their nature take the form of ordinary enactments. The first category is easier to describe than to measure. Theoretically, at least, every statute, depending on both executive and judicial interpretations of it, contains a potential capacity to change the constitution, and it is even possible that years may pass before it is apparent that the constitution has been altered. The remarkable rise of the non-departmental administrative agency, a device known only in limited ways at Confederation and then under a different name, which blossomed during and after the Second World War into the basis for a second large public service, is a good example; yet each new crown corporation was created by a single incremental step, usually a statute. There is no evidence that any prime minister ever set out to produce a second public service, yet it happened. The same is true of those major institutions which are unlike either departments or crown corporations, whose heads report directly to Parliament, such as the auditor general, the chief electoral officer, and the commissioner of official languages.

Another flexible part of the constitution is found in legal amendments authorized by the terms of the written parts of the constitution, which permit changes by both Parliament and the provincial legislatures. Some of these arose from the need in 1867 to provide for Canada's immediate and also its future government, simply because it was not possible to clear up at one stroke all the alterations that went with putting three separate jurisdictions into five new ones. The Province of Canada, New Brunswick, and Nova Scotia had similar electoral systems, but they varied considerably in detail; the act of 1867 sensibly provided that for the new House of Commons the existing systems would prevail 'until the Parliament of Canada otherwise provides,' and in due course Parliament constructed a superbly efficient national electoral machine, a notable addition to the constitution. The provincial legislatures, under section 92 (1), could provide for 'the Amendment from Time to Time, notwithstanding anything in this Act, of the Constitution of the Province, except as regards the Office of Lieutenant Governor.' Under that power several provinces abolished their upper houses, and the provinces are now all unicameral.

Other amendments to the constitution, while not technically authorized by it, pertain to the federal-provincial arrangements assessed in the last chapter. One could argue, indeed, that the almost startling flexibility of the financial clauses is based on continual violations of the constitution; except that Parliament is broadly free to spend money any way it likes. (Presumably it cannot now spend money in ways that create discrimination forbidden under the Charter of Rights.) The first break with the original written terms – the grant of a better deal to Nova Scotia in 1869 – was challenged in Parliament, but the Colonial Office in London ruled that additional grants to the province were within Parliament's legal competence. Canadian governments have never looked back since.

A different amending power was added in 1949, when Parliament was granted the constitutional right to make changes in matters which concern only the federal government, subject to certain safeguards. The amendment of 1949, itself a formal enactment of the Parliament of the United Kingdom requested by Canada, states that the exclusive legislative authority of the Parliament of Canada should extend to all matters coming within the following classes of subjects:

The amendment from time to time of the Constitution of Canada, except as regards matters coming within the classes of subjects by this Act assigned exclusively to the Legislatures of the provinces, or as regards rights or privileges by this or any other Constitutional Act granted or secured to the Legislature or the Government of a province, or to any class of persons with respect to schools or as regards the use of the English or French language or as regards the requirements that there shall be a session of the Parliament of Canada at least once each year, and that no House of Commons shall continue for more than five years from the day of the return of the Writs for choosing the House; provided, however, that a House of Commons may in time of real or apprehended war, invasion or insurrection be continued by the Parliament of Canada if such continuation is not opposed by the votes of more than one-third of the members of such House.

Under that clause Parliament has so far (1986) passed five amendments, all of them concerning the Houses of Parliament or representation therein, and the patriation of the whole constitution with a comprehensive amending procedure in 1982 did not alter Parliament's power as set forth above. The Supreme Court, it should be recalled, took a narrow view of the clause when the government in 1978 referred to it a series of questions about abolishing or altering the Senate. The court held that the clause covered 'matters of interest only to the federal government'; each province had a stake in the Senate, and that put the Senate beyond federal competence alone.

There remains to be added a few observations on legal amendments authorized by the constitution. Ontario and Quebec were as new as Canada in 1867, so there are clauses, similar to those relating to Parliament, which begin 'until the legislature of Quebec [or Ontario] otherwise provides ...' The new capital cities are named in the act of 1867, the provincial seats of government subject to change by the provincial executives, Ottawa to be the capital of Canada 'until the Queen otherwise directs.' Those clauses sound innocuous, but since in each capital government has become a vast industry, the possibility of their being used to change things staggers the imagination.

THE LESS FLEXIBLE COMPONENTS

Formal amendments before 1980
As the previous section illustrates, a constitution can be changed both by altering the meaning of its words and by letting the words stand but adding to them. Attention must now be given to the more formal processes by which the actual written terms have been changed; and in the final sections the chapter will describe the most notable formal additions since Confederation.

It is a truism that the original British North America Act of 1867 contained no clause for its own amendment, a fact which has taxed the ingenuity of every generation of Canadian politicians. But it is equally true that there was no particular reason why an amending clause should have been included: the act was a statute of a sovereign imperial Parliament, and Canada was a colony; colonial politicians were accustomed to obtaining changes in statutes governing them by simple request. On the list of priorities in the minds of the Fathers of Confederation in the 1860s the amendment of a British statute did not seem to rank high. If the members of the legislature of the Province of Canada can be taken as representative, during the Confederation Debates they either assumed that the imperial Parliament alone could amend its own laws, or saw no problem anyway.

Until the 1980s there was no doubt about the purely legal position of formal amendments: only the Parliament of the United Kingdom could formally change the text of the British North America Act, and the convention quickly arose that it would not do so without a request for an amendment from Canada. As Canada moved toward nationhood the legal position as such became less important than the political paradox that Canada's constitution was an ordinary statute of another country's Parliament. Until 1931, furthermore, when the Statute of Westminster declared that no future British statute would apply to any dominion unless the dominion requested and consented to it, any British statute could technically apply to Canada as part of the empire, whether or not it appeared to affect the words of the British North America Act; from 1867 to 1931 several dozen British statutes had a direct or indirect application to Canada, and of these only a small fraction would qualify as genuine constitutional amendments. The doubt implied in the last sentence points up another paradox: it is not possible to state precisely how many amendments there were, or by what process or processes they were achieved.[1]

The important bona fide amendments can none the less be tabulated:

1 *1871.* An act to remove doubts as to the power of the Dominion to establish new provinces, to provide for the representation of those provinces, and to validate certain Dominion statutes regarding the government of Rupert's Land and of Manitoba. The act further stated that once the Dominion Parliament had set up a new province, it could not alter the act of creation except in regard to provincial boundary changes which could be made with the province's consent.

2 *1875.* An act to remove doubts as to the privileges, immunities, and powers of the Dominion Parliament and its members.

3 *1886.* An act to empower the Canadian Parliament to provide for the representation of territories in the House of Commons and the Senate, and to allow the Parliament to alter the representation of new provinces in the House of Commons and the Senate.

4 *1889.* An act to determine the boundaries of Ontario.

5 *1895.* An act to remove doubts as to the power of the Canadian Parliament to provide for a Deputy Speaker for the Senate and to validate a Canadian statute already enacted on the subject.

6 *1907.* An act to substitute a new section for section 118 of the British North America Act. It thereby raised the per capita monetary grants to the provinces and also the grants for the support of the provincial governments and legislatures.

7 *1915.* An act to alter the scheme of representation in the Senate and House of Commons. It provided as follows: (a) the number of senators was increased to ninety-six; (b) a new western senatorial division of twenty-four senators was created, each of the four western provinces being given six senators; (c) the members in the Senate might be increased under section 26 of the British North America Act by four or eight instead of three or six, representing equally the four senatorial divisions; (d) the senators to which Newfoundland would be entitled in the event of its admission to the federation was raised to six; (e) a province would always be entitled to as many members in the House of Commons as it had senators.

8 *1916.* An act to extend the life of the existing House of Commons by one year.

9 *1930.* An act to confirm the agreements which transferred to the Prairie provinces the natural resources which had been held by the Dominion since their admission to the federation.

10 *1940.* An act to give the Dominion jurisdiction over unemployment insurance. Section 91 was amended by adding as subsection 2 (a) 'unemployment insurance.'

11 *1943.* An act to postpone the constitutional redistribution of seats in the House of Commons until the first session of Parliament after the cessation of hostilities.

12 *1946.* An act to redistribute the seats in the House of Commons. This involved an entirely new draft of section 51 of the British North America Act.

13 *1949 (no. 1).* An act to admit Newfoundland to the federation.

14 *1949 (no. 2).* An act to give the Parliament of Canada power to amend the British North America Act except as regards provincial matters and subjects, constitutional

guarantees regarding education and the use of the English or French language, and the parliamentary annual session and five-year maximum term. In time of real or apprehended war, invasion or insurrection the five-year term may be extended by act of Parliament if the extension is not opposed by the votes of more than one-third of the members of the House of Commons.

15 *1951*. An act to give to the Parliament of Canada the power to make laws in relation to old age pensions, though not so as to affect the operation of any existing or future law of a provincial legislature on this subject.

16 *1960*. An act to retire judges of provincial superior courts at the age of seventy-five.

17 *1964*. An act to extend and clarify the pension amendment of 1951.

18 *1982*. The Constitution Act, passed by the Parliament of the United Kingdom and proclaimed in Canada in 1982, formally added a new section, 92A, to the act of 1867, enlarging provincial jurisdiction over non-renewable natural resources, forestry resources, and electrical energy.

Number 18 is part of the last amendment to the constitution of Canada that will ever be enacted in the United Kingdom.

To the above British list must be added five Canadian amendments authorized by no. 14 in the foregoing list:

19 *1952*. An act to provide a new safeguard for the representation in the House of Commons of a province whose population is becoming a relatively smaller fraction of the Dominion's; and to give a second member to the territories.

20 *1965*. An act to retire senators appointed after 1 June 1965, at the age of seventy-five.

21 *1974-6*. An act to adjust the basis of representation in the House of Commons.

22 *1974-6*. An act to confirm the representation in the House of Commons from the Yukon (one member) and to raise to two the representation from the Northwest Territories.

23 *1974-6*. An act to provide for the representation in the Senate of the Yukon and Northwest Territories; one each.[2]

It will be apparent from the above that the identifiable formal amendments have varied enormously in scope, some being intended only to clear up what the original enactment meant, some having only temporary application because of wartime, others making lasting substantive changes. Even these last cases vary in importance, from the addition of a senator or two on the one hand, to a significant enlargement of federal or provincial powers on the other. What the list does not make clear is where the amendments came from: in other words, if Parliament in London did not act on its own initiative but responded only to requests from Canada, who made the request? On three occasions (1875, 1895, and 1965) the Canadian cabinet did; and each instance occasioned a controversy, partly because on 27 March 1871 the Parliament of Canada had declared that 'no changes in the provisions of the British North American Act should be sought for by the executive Government without the previous assent of the Parliament of this Dominion.' On the other occasions requiring the amendment to British statutes, Parliament was consulted, the device used being a joint address from both houses. If one House wanted to amend the address, as happened in 1960, both had to agree on its final wording.

Agreement on a joint parliamentary address still left open the question of provincial participation, and until the Supreme Court spoke on this issue in 1980, there was no settled historical practice one could point to as clearly established. As early as 1887 an interprovincial conference asserted the provinces' right to initiate amendments independently of Parliament, but Parliament did not accept that. Ontario did agree to the changes in its boundaries in 1889, but that was specifically provided for in the first formal amendment, in 1871. Prior to the financial rearrangement of 1907, the provinces were not consulted about general amendments, and the negotiations that preceded the amendment of 1907 did not set a governing precedent. The federal authorities thereafter continued to proceed without provincial consent more often than not. However, where provincial interests were clearly involved, as in 1940, 1951, 1960, 1964, and 1982, the provinces were consulted.

Whether consulting the provinces involved the further step of obtaining their unanimous agreement to an amendment was never clearly settled. From time to time the compact theory was reasserted, for if indeed the provinces had participated in a treaty in 1867 (which legally and historically they had not) they could claim a right to participate in changes. The amendment of 1940 was held up awaiting the approval of Quebec, and then unanimity prevailed; but three years later, when the distribution of seats in the Commons among the provinces was being postponed, and the legislature of Quebec formally protested, the federal government went ahead, the prime minister, Mackenzie King, specifically rejecting the notion that the constitution could be amended only with provincial agreement. The 1943 episode portrayed in sharp relief yet another element: was the Parliament of the United Kingdom, knowing there was serious dissension in Canada over an amendment, none the less obliged to act on a request from the Parliament of Canada? The federal government said yes, but provincial refusals to accept that continued into the discussions that resulted in the Constitution Act of 1982. In one important sense the dispute is still going on: as this is written, Quebec has not yet accepted the revised constitution.

Proposals for formal amendment before 1982
Prior to the climacteric of 1980–2, an acceptable formula for amending the British

North America Act was sought for decades by Canadian politicians in a series of informal and formal consultations during which, it is fair to say, every conceivable approach was tried; and rejected. Exactly when the search began cannot be pinpointed, but in the 1920s the subject of amendment came up frequently in Parliament, though usually with no sense of urgency. In November 1927 amendment was on the agenda of a Dominion-provincial conference, the federal government proposing that amendments for some purposes could be made through Parliament after securing the consent of a majority of the provinces, with unanimous consent being required for changes of a fundamental nature. A lively discussion made clear that there were too many divergent views to make action then a possibility. In 1935 another conference proposed dividing the act into four sets of clauses, each of which would have its own process of amendment. In the light of subsequent developments they are worth repeating here:

1 Clauses concerning the constitution of the House of Commons and the Senate would be amended by the Dominion Parliament.
2 Clauses relating to the Dominion and one or more, but not all, provinces would be amended by the Dominion House of Commons and Senate and the legislatures of the provinces concerned.
3 Clauses relating to matters of mutual concern to the Dominion and provinces would be amended by the Dominion House of Commons and Senate and the legislatures of two-thirds of the provinces, provided that the population of these provinces was at least 55 per cent of the population of Canada. (This would ensure that either Ontario or Quebec was included in the two-thirds majority.)
4 Clauses relating to provincial and minority rights would be amended by the Dominion House of Commons and Senate and the legislatures of all the provinces.
   If the Senate should refuse to pass an amending bill sent from the House of Commons, and if the same bill should again be passed at the next session of the House, it would then go to a joint session of the two houses and final decision would rest with the latter body.

The general theme embodied in these proposals dominated constitutional discussions for at least four decades. The 1935 scheme got nowhere because of opposition from New Brunswick, but it did not disappear and variants of it surfaced at fairly regular intervals. As the discussions proceeded the proposals were enlarged and refined, but always some insuperable obstacles appeared. A 1950 conference came to grief over which clauses should be assigned to the several amending procedures; and in the 1960s Saskatchewan was the province which objected to the principle of unanimous consent for any proposal affecting the distribution of powers. The 1960s saw the emergence of a draft proposal justly celebrated as the Fulton-Favreau formula (named for two federal ministers of justice) but still resembling its ancestor of 1935; and in 1964 yet another conference, a nostalgic echo of the Charlottetown Conference of a century earlier, agreed in principle that it was time to bring the constitution home, with appropriate terms for amending it thereafter.

In 1971 another conference produced the Victoria Charter, which added among other ideas the creation of a constitutional bill of rights and a new amending formula which would guarantee regional consent to amendments, and reduce the Senate's power to delay any amendment. The Victoria Charter, strongly supported by Prime Minister Trudeau, came close to acceptance, but at the last Quebec was unable to agree to it. In retrospect, throughout the complex history so tersely summarized here, several basic propositions were gaining increasing respectability: (1) the constitution should be brought to Canada; (2) nothing would be gained by patriation alone, and a formula for future amendments was essential; and (3) a charter of rights was to be added. The main ideas of the Constitution Act, in short, were emerging from a half-century of gestation, with the help of cantankerous parents and quarrelsome midwives.

A bare outline of its actual birth is possible, but it can be misleading, for the whole chronicle was such that any mere recapitulation of outstanding events runs the risk of omission and misinterpretation; but the essentials are reasonably clear. The years preceding the Victoria conference of 1971 witnessed three formal meetings of a federal-provincial constitutional conference in 1968 and 1969, and several lengthy statements, under the signature of Prime Minister Trudeau, on such relevant topics as a charter of rights and federal-provincial finance, appeared in the same period. After the Victoria conference the flow of publications continued. A joint parliamentary committee heard vast amounts of evidence on the constitution and reported in 1972. The federal government's activities as a publisher continued, and it was joined by several of the provinces: British Columbia, Alberta, Saskatchewan, Ontario, Quebec, and Newfoundland all produced significant studies and discussion papers, the Quebec participation including not only *Quebec-Canada: A New Deal*, a government paper, but a response from the Liberal opposition, *A New Canadian Federation*. The Quebec referendum of May 1980, quoted below, led also to a federal determination to 'show the flag' by following up on the results with unmistakable action at the federal level. Considerable public activity on constitutional reform followed the referendum, and another round of meetings and conferences began, and went on until mid-September, when it was apparent that unanimous agreement on anything constitutional was impossible for the prime minister and the premiers.

Early in October 1980 the federal cabinet agreed to present to Parliament its own proposals for constitutional changes, and the House of Commons began debate almost at once. In due course the government invoked closure to move its resolution into committee stage, and a special joint committee began work the first week of November. In the meantime the provincial premiers, chafing over the federal government's unilateral proceedings and irked because the federal resolution had been extended without their consent to include provincial jurisdictions, met on their own to discuss strategy. The outcome was that only two provinces supported the federal course, and three went to court as described earlier. The final decision of the courts, rendered by the Supreme Court in September 1981 (by which time the federal government had redrafted its resolution, partly to meet opposition criticism and partly to recognize amendments proposed by the parliamentary committee), led the federal authorities to back off from their unilateral approach. More meetings began, and finally in November the prime minister and nine premiers reached agreement, Quebec alone now outside the fold. The resolution passed the House of Commons by 246 to 24 (the minority represented all parties), the Senate by 59 to 23; and the resulting constitutional amendment passed the Parliament of the United Kingdom in March 1982. All that remained then was the queen's trip to Ottawa to proclaim it in April.

That skeletal outline barely hints at the troubled atmosphere within which developments were taking place, the most troubled being in Quebec. It was in Quebec in 1970 that the federal government invoked the War Measures Act to cope with a perceived uprising, which included one murder but otherwise proved to be abortive. It was in Quebec again that in 1976 the Parti Québécois under René Lévesque won a provincial election on a platform that included separation from the rest of the federation. That goal was soon transmuted into sovereignty-association, on which the government planned a referendum for 1980. In preparation for the vote the government of Quebec produced over Premier Lévesque's signature the ringing polemic *Quebec-Canada: A New Deal*, urging the electorate to give 'one positive and resounding answer: Yes,' to a proposal seeking a mandate to negotiate new terms between the province and Canada.

It was hardly a reassuring situation for anyone interested in new constitutional proposals for Canada as a whole, including Quebec; but one such person was the prime minister from 1968 to 1979, and again after 1980, Pierre Trudeau. He too was from Quebec, and led a party with a strong base in Quebec. It is a wry footnote to the history of federal-provincial relations that *Quebec-Canada: A New Deal*, with the opposition between Lévesque and Trudeau having reached almost legendary proportions by late 1979, should actually have appeared during the short-lived Clark regime in 1979–80. The Quebec paper expected little from that change in government, since the constitutional situation 'is not one of its priorities.' But in any event, the Liberals under Trudeau won again on 18 February 1980, taking seventy-four of Quebec's seventy-five seats; traditional animosities could be resumed. The referendum, for which a negative vote was foreseen by

René Lévesque as a disaster which would send an entirely wrong message to the rest of Canada, encountered the electorate on 20 May; the vote was: yes, 1,485,851; no, 2,187,991.

It would be an error to assume that the federal government and Quebec alone played the major roles in the steamy prologue to the Constitution Act proclaimed in 1982, but the tendentiousness of the question voted on by the Quebec electorate in May 1980 is worth recording as a measure of one major province's attitude. The question itself, and the official paper preceding the vote, made clear that the Lévesque government did not see Quebec as a province like the others: it was none the less like the others in its sturdy single-mindedness where relations with Ottawa were concerned:

The Government of Quebec has made public its proposal to negotiate a new agreement with the rest of Canada, based on the equality of nations:

This agreement would enable Quebec to acquire the exclusive power to make its laws, levy its taxes and establish relations abroad – in other words, sovereignty – and at the same time, to maintain with Canada an economic association including a common currency;

No change in political status resulting from these negotiations will be affected without approval by the people through another referendum.

On these terms, do you agree to give the Government of Quebec the mandate to negotiate the proposed agreement between Quebec and Canada?

Varying interpretations were understandably given, to both the question and the emphatic 'No' vote, by the prime minister and all ten provincial premiers. But, like the Supreme Court's opinion in the following year on whether Parliament could amend the constitution unilaterally, the referendum provided another fundamental fact in the movement towards constitutional change – a conclusion whose significance can be assessed if one considers how different the negotiations would have become if 60 per cent of the Quebec voters had said 'Yes' instead of 'No.' But neither Quebec nor the referendum can be isolated from the rest of the chronicle. Apart from all the official documentation, the whole process caught the imagination of participants who felt compelled to record their experiences, of leading journalists, and of constitutional and other academic authorities, all of whom collectively produced an instructive literature covering a crucial short period in Canadian history, and one, indeed, far too comprehensive for even a short summary.[3]

The political stars were, of course, the prime minister of Canada and the premiers, and most of them were supported by a handful of leading ministers from their several cabinets. In both formal and informal conferences, these leaders variously coalesced and separated as issues arose and were settled or rejected. For a while a major grouping saw the federal leaders and those of Ontario and New Brunswick with the other provinces arrayed against them. The dissidents from the federal proposals were dubbed the Gang of Eight, a name which obscured the fact that in their arguing and recalcitrance, each was only working on behalf of his own province's interests as he saw them. When in the end an agreement was reached which only Quebec could not accept, the majority did not become popularly known as the Gang of Ten.

The long series of meetings that so often seems an indispensable prelude to political change included, according to close observers, clandestine meetings in hotel rooms and whispered conversations over meals, and these gossipy dealings were supplemented by more overt activities, some of them unusual for constitutional negotiations. The Gang of Eight at one point, having reached an accord, placed advertisements in newspapers lauding their stand, the premiers' signatures appearing with a red maple leaf: one of them was René Lévesque's. Confidential documents were of course leaked.

The provinces were not the only interested groups. Chief among the others were women's organizations, concerned that their struggle for equality should not be overlooked in a gaggle of politicians and advisers who seemed exclusively male; first the women's organizations seemed to be making headway, but in the event, they were dissatisfied with the final act. The natives' organizations (which in that usage mysteriously excludes associations of native Canadians of European or other ancestry) also had a difficult time, partly because they themselves exhibited internal disunity; nevertheless, their position, in Edward McWhinney's informed opinion, 'in strict legal terms, was much stronger than that of the provincial governments.' But it won them little; their lobbying in London was intense, and their representation received a sympathetic reading from the Foreign Affairs Committee of the British House of Commons, which none the less found 'that the UK has no treaty or other obligations to Indians in Canada';[4] their resort to British courts, based on the assumption that the treaties gave them a special relation with the crown, was also rejected. The groups which spoke for women and Indians both felt that they had been treated as pawns in a game.

The end was thus reached by a tortuous route. Almost the only consistently stable constitutional element throughout was the agreement of the two senior governments in London and Ottawa that the government and Parliament of the United Kingdom was bound to act on a request from the government and Parliament of Canada. That conclusion was based on long precedents, but in 1980–2 it was challenged not only by spokesmen for the provinces and the native groups, but also by the British parliamentary committee just cited, which observed in its *First Report* 'that the UK Parliament is not bound, even conventionally, either by the supposed requirement of automatic action on Federal requests, or by the supposed requirement of unanimous Provincial consent to amendments altering Provincial powers.' On the first requirement neither Pierre Trudeau nor the British prime minister, Mrs Thatcher, after an unclear start in Britain, seems to have wavered: British action would be automatic on a Canadian request. The main argument in Canada, which also reached the British Parliament, was over the substance and procedures of a proper request from Canada. There were, of course, other kinds of constants. Sensitive observers of the attempts of both women and native peoples to improve their respective constitutional positions have recorded the persistence it took for representatives of each group to maintain an effective advocacy, sometimes in defence of positions that had seemed to be already won.[5]

THE LEAST FLEXIBLE COMPONENTS, 1982 AND AFTER

And what indeed had anybody won? The whole performance concluded with three undeniable changes: the constitution of Canada in its entirety now rested in Canada; a Charter of Rights and Freedoms, wholly new, had been added; and so had a clear process for future amendments. But Quebec remained outside the final accord that led to the Constitution Act proclaimed in 1982, even though the recently elected Liberal government under Robert Bourassa has been sounding more conciliatory than its predecessor, arousing cautious hopes that Quebec would join the rest of the country in agreeing to the altered constitution. Bourassa's position, like that of his predecessor, requires the recognition of his province as a 'distinct society,' a claim not difficult to accept if it is mere rhetoric, but one that could create serious problems if it were taken to include extensions of Quebec's language policy (for years a contentious issue providing an off-stage obligato to the constitutional discussions) or frequently expressed provincial ambitions for broadcasting in the province. Quite apart from Quebec, the constitutional performance as a whole received some poor reviews, partly because of specific alleged weaknesses in the final document, partly because it avoided philosophical content in favour of pragmatic agreements that could be put into legal words.

Virtually all successful Canadian leaders have been pragmatists, and it is difficult to think of any who could not be so labelled, except possibly those who served such short periods as prime ministers and premiers that one cannot tell whether they were or not. A comparison of the federal government's early position of 1980, as expressed in its own words, with the final text of the act proclaimed in 1982 will show that pragmatism was at work. (One could, of course, start the comparison with much earlier documents, such as the Victoria Charter of 1971, or the proposed amendment bill of 1978.) Early drafts of the federal position do not involve a deity, but the act asserts that 'Canada is founded upon principles that recognize the supremacy of God and the rule of law.' Early drafts did not include particular recognition of native rights, perhaps because they were already assigned to Parliament under section 91 of the act of 1867, or perhaps because a charter of rights that protected everybody also protected native peoples. The act of 1982, in part II, recognizes and affirms 'the existing aboriginal and treaty rights of the aboriginal peoples,' and defines the latter to include Indian, Inuit, and Métis. A close examination of texts would reveal many such developments.

Most important for our purpose here (postponing for the moment the Charter of Rights and Freedoms) are those concerning formal amendments of the constitution. Early drafts echo the Victoria Charter of 1971. In essence, it was proposed that the general amending formula would require a resolution passed by each of the Houses of Parliament, and resolutions passed by a special majority of the legislatures of the provinces. What made the majority special was that it had to include every province whose population at any time had contained at least 25 per cent of Canada's population; two of the four Atlantic provinces containing a majority of that region's population; and similarly two of the four western provinces. Only Ontario and Quebec came under the 25 per cent rule (and as it was worded would have been the only qualifying provinces since Confederation) and that gave each of them a veto over any proposed amendment following the route just outlined. A later draft, the resolution which Parliament approved in April 1981, would also have permitted the constitution to be amended by a national referendum passed also by special majorities: a majority of all the electors voting, and provincial majorities in the several provinces as described above. Neither the veto for the central provinces alone nor the possibility of constitutional amendment by referendum survived to the final statute. The basic amending power is now defined as follows:

38. (1) An amendment to the Constitution of Canada may be made by proclamation issued by the Governor General under the Great Seal of Canada where so authorized by
    (a) resolutions of the Senate and House of Commons; and
    (b) resolutions of the legislative assemblies of at least two-thirds of the provinces that have, in the aggregate, according to the then latest general census, at least fifty per cent of the population of all the provinces.

That clause would allow one of Ontario and Quebec to veto a proposed amendment, but neither is guaranteed the power as a right. But another part of the existing amending power gives any province a veto:

41. An amendment to the Constitution of Canada in relation to the following matters may be made by proclamation issued by the Governor General under the Great Seal of Canada

only where authorized by resolutions of the Senate and House of Commons and of the legislative assembly of each province:

(a) the office of the Queen, the Governor General and the Lieutenant Governor of a province;

(b) the right of a province to a number of members in the House of Commons not less than the number of Senators by which the province is entitled to be represented at the time this Part comes into force;

(c) subject to section 43, the use of the English or the French language;

(d) the composition of the Supreme Court of Canada; and

(e) an amendment to this Part.

The two clauses quoted do not cover the whole of the amending process, but they are its core; and to them must be added two important notes, both integral parts of the new amending power. The Senate, although a resolution from it may appear essential from the above, can in fact only delay a constitutional resolution, not prevent its passage. If the Commons passes a resolution to authorize the proclamation of an amendment, the Senate has 180 days to consider it; but if after that the Commons re-passes the resolution, it does not matter whether the Senate passes it or not. More important, any province can opt out of any amendment 'that derogates from the legislative powers, the proprietary rights or any other rights or privileges of the legislature or government of a province.' The relevant sections do not state precisely who decides when derogation takes place, but presumably it is the provincial legislature, which is empowered to express its dissent before an amendment is proclaimed. A legislature can also change its mind and revoke a dissent to accept the amendment which offended it in the first place.

The extant amending process, it must be emphasized, makes the written part of Canada's constitution extremely inflexible. Action that requires the co-operation of Parliament and at least seven legislatures in provinces whose combined population is at least half the country's total is not often seen in Canada. Such action brings strong-minded federal and provincial partisans into close contact, each with personal and political goals, and the last time they reached the kind of agreement now demanded by the constitution was in the latest changes of 1982, the act here described. The latest Constitution Act was completed, and by peaceful means; but it was preceded by a mighty turbulence which not only isolated Quebec but left numerous scars on other participants. The literature which followed it revealingly included articles and books with titles like 'A Dangerous Deed: The Constitution Act, 1982' by Donald Smiley and 'The Constitutional Misfire of 1982' by Daniel Latouche; both are in the volume *And No One Cheered*. A book whose authors include Roy Romanow, the Saskatchewan minister who shared much of the constitutional spotlight in 1980–1 with his federal counterpart, Jean

Chrétien, is entitled *Canada ... Notwithstanding*. Further, specific institutions whose reform Canadians have long enjoyed discussing, such as the Senate and, in more limited circles, the Supreme Court, can now be reformed by a defined process, but the process can no longer depend on negotiation alone.

The rigidity of the amending process can be assessed against those two federal bodies. As recently as 1980, in deciding that Parliament did not alone have the legislative authority to alter or replace the Senate, the Supreme Court left open the question of what other legislative support (that is, provincial) would have to supplement Parliament's in any changes to the Senate. Again in 1981, in deciding that federal authority alone could not unilaterally amend the constitution where federal-provincial relationships or provincial powers were concerned, the Supreme Court concluded that any such action without the agreement of the provinces was unconstitutional in the conventional sense, 'no views being expressed as to its quantification'; in other words, the court left open again what 'the agreement of the provinces' meant. The new amending process is now clear: the Senate itself could only delay its own reform for 180 days, but reform would take at least seven provinces containing at least half the total population. And so with the Supreme Court: it was established, and thereafter altered, by statute, but its composition is now entrenched, so that the unanimous consent of all eleven Canadian governments is needed to change it.

The amending process is rigid in another way, one which perpetuates precedents that have often been criticized: once the proposal for amendment by referendum had gone from the federal proposals in 1981, constitutional amendment was left, in realistic terms, in executive hands. It is true that the amending formula now in force speaks of Parliament and the provincial legislatures, but what the elected bodies do is dominated by the cabinets they support. That confidence in executive power is often described as 'typically Canadian'; but citizens may take heart from the work of the typical Canadians who inserted in the Constitution Act of 1982 not only an amendment process but a Charter of Rights and Freedoms. The charter represents a notable departure in the philosophy of the constitution, inasmuch as before 1982 Canada's constitutional acts, apart from a few guarantees about language and education, assumed that the basic elements in the Canadian polity were the federal and provincial governments. The charter adds individuals.

THE CHARTER OF RIGHTS AND FREEDOMS

The charter, like the rest of the constitution, has its critics, of diverse views, ranging from those who challenge the need for a constitutional statement of rights in a parliamentary system, to those who hold that a charter is indispensable but the one adopted does not go nearly far enough. The second group includes conservatives who believe that the rights to own property should be guaranteed (it did appear in some early propasals) and those on another side who hold that every Canadian's right to gainful employment should be in the constitution. Those who challenge the need for a charter at all point to the partial charters already enacted, for example, in the electoral laws, or labour legislation which protects unionized workers. Parliament, they claim, is the safest and most adaptable source of citizens' rights, not a rigid legal statement whose ultimate meaning lies with courts.

General bills of rights, all of them ordinary laws until 1982, have been around in Canada for decades. Among the provinces, Saskatchewan led the way in 1947 when the recently elected CCF government under T.C. Douglas established a bill of rights as an integral part of its plans to restructure the governing of the province. Federally, John Diefenbaker used his influence as prime minister to give expression to a long-standing personal interest in the Bill of Rights enacted in 1960.[6] It was the personal will of another prime minister, Pierre Trudeau, that profoundly influenced Canada's progress toward the constitutional charter of 1982. That charter was itself a part of the troubled negotiations already referred to, and it too bears scars.

Some samples of changes effected during the negotiations are included in the following paragraphs, as illustrations of how alterations in wording can be significant steps toward agreement. Some of the changes may sound trivial, merely cosmetic in nature and not worth the long hours spent on them. But the precise wording of contentious clauses is one of the important matters that writers of constitutions must agree on and sometimes, paradoxically, an agreement on precise wording can be reached by escaping into imprecise words. If strong-minded negotiators cannot agree on the exact conditions to be attached to a particular action, they may be able to agree that, without listing any conditions, the thing must be done 'reasonably.' That leaves it to somebody else to decide later what reasonableness is in any given situation; and commonly that somebody is a judge sitting in court. Jurists have been known to characterize such semantic escape-hatches as 'weasel-words.'

The last chapter in the chronicle may be said to have begun with the federal government's first proposed constitutional resolution of October 1980. The preamble to that draft reads: 'The Canadian Charter of Rights and Freedoms guarantees the rights and freedoms set out in it subject only to such reasonable limits as are generally accepted in a free and democratic society with a parliamentary system of government.' That soon became, and remained, much clearer: the limits are now 'such reasonable limits prescribed by law as can be demonstrably justified in a free and democratic society.' The preamble remains vague, but limits prescribed by law can only be demonstrably justified to some person or persons, presumably those who sit in courts. Canadian history contains many examples of limits that were far from reasonable by modern standards, but each of which seemed demonstrably justifiable to a government at the time. The list includes the exclusion of Indians and Orientals from the franchise for prolonged periods; the exclusion from the franchise in 1917 of Canadians of several origins naturalized after 31 March 1902; the exclusion from the franchise until 1917 of virtually all women, and the discriminatory selection of women allowed to vote then; and the expulsion from British Columbia of Canadians of Japanese ancestry in the Second World War. All these varied discriminations were legal, and all seemed reasonable and justifiable to those promoting them. A lot depends, that is, on what the preamble to the charter is taken to mean, if anything.

When the charter moves into specifics, it starts off precisely. Under Fundamental Freedoms (section 2), 'everyone' has all the usual rights of conscience and religion, of thought and expression, of peaceful assembly and association. Freedom of the press includes 'other media of communication.' Such comprehensive statements of freedoms always seem appealing, and to every-body's advantage. For the first time in Canada queries like the following must now be seen as having a constitutional aspect: What will a guaranteed freedom of conscience mean to a convinced pacifist when he is an able-bodied young male eligible to be conscripted into the armed forces? How will the freedom of 'other media' apply to the copying of books, tapes, and videos freely available in libraries supported by public funds?

Democratic Rights are secured in sections 3 to 5, and they cover electoral and legislative rights already discussed: voting and being a candidate; ending each legislature's life (including Parliament's) at a maximum of five years except 'in time of real or apprehended war, invasion or insurrection,' when the life can be extended by a two-thirds majority; and each legislature must meet 'at least every twelve months.' This part of the charter further enshrines existing practices, but adds little new material.

Mobility Rights (section 6) ensures the right of Canadians to enter or leave the country, and within Canada to live and work in any province. The preamble aside, this is the first part of the charter to include a restriction on its own general terms. Other provincial 'laws or practices of general application' may govern mobility rights, for example, provided they are not discriminatory as far as present or previous residence is concerned. Minimal 'reasonable residency requirements' can be required for potential recipients of social services. And what are popularly called affirmative action programs – those that discriminate in favour of a disadvantaged group – are allowable if the province's employment rate is below the national rate.

Protection for mobility rights was not a particular favourite with all the provinces, and at one stage in the pre-1982 negotiations a proposal backed by most of them omitted mobility rights altogether. Any province's interest in mobility rights is bound to be less than the federal government's, whose interests have to go beyond provincial boundaries. Here again, history offers telling stories, and continues to do so. If offshore drilling for oil offers employment in Newfoundland's despondent economy, who is first entitled to any new jobs created, Newfoundlanders or other Canadians? On the occasions when Alberta's oil industry is flourishing, do unemployed workers from adjoining provinces have the same rights as Albertans to participate? Even within one province mobility rights can loom large. Is it proper for Nova Scotia workers from outports to flood the labour market in Halifax, or for electricians from Regina to take advantage of a building boom in Saskatoon? There is no simple answer to such questions or even, perhaps, a readily workable system of administration to put in place once a question is answered. The mobility rights in the charter may be hard to enforce, but they cannot be dismissed as rhetoric.

Legal Rights form sections 7 to 14 and, unlike Mobility Rights, they are fairly conventional statements of a kind difficult to challenge. The first clause sets the tone: 'Everyone has the right to life, liberty and security of the person and the right not to be deprived thereof ...,' and the following clauses spell that principle out in more detail, including all the essentials of a prompt fair trial for any accused. Section 12 forbids 'cruel and unusual treatment or punishment.'

Despite their general acceptability, the Legal Rights sections did not make their way through the negotiations without some buffeting. The administration of justice is under provincial jurisdiction, including courts of both civil and criminal jurisdiction, while the content of criminal law, including procedure in criminal matters, is assigned to Parliament. In early negotiations, some of the provinces were concerned that any Legal Rights clauses should be confined to criminal justice, leaving out provincial civil jurisdiction. There were also those reluctant to accept a statement of Legal Rights that did not guarantee a citizen's enjoyment of his property. Out of the complicated discussions in both federal-provincial meetings and the hearings of the joint parliamentary committee of 1980–1, the draft finally agreed on showed significant differences from the federal government's first proposals. The original, for example, said: 'Everyone has the right not to be subjected to search or seizure except on grounds, and in accordance with procedures, established by law.' The charter says positively, with a different qualification: 'Everyone has the right to be secure against unreasonable search or seizure.' A similar change was made to the original's statement on the right not to be detained or imprisoned: the 'except' clause was deleted, and the charter guarantees everyone's right not to be arbitrarily detained or imprisoned. The original proposal would have ensured that 'Everyone has the right on arrest or detention ... to retain and instruct counsel without delay'; the charter adds, 'and to be informed of that right.' (Women's organizations, incidentally, had a general objection to the charter's use of 'one' and 'everyone,' preferring 'person,' a word more familiar in law.)

Equality Rights, a single section with two clauses, guarantees to everyone a general assurance against discrimination, but in its passage through the discussions to the charter it aroused the particular interests of women's and native peoples' associations. In the first federal proposal it was entitled Non-Discriminatory Rights, and was a relatively simple declaration. The charter's clause reads in full:

15. (1) Every individual is equal before and under the law and has the right to the equal protection and equal benefit of the law without discrimination and, in particular, without discrimination based on race, national or ethnic origin, colour, religion, sex, age or mental or physical disability.
(2) Subsection (1) does not preclude any law, program or activity that has as its object the amelioration of conditions of disadvantaged individuals or groups including those that are disadvantaged because of race, national or ethnic origin, colour, religion, sex, age or mental or physical disability.

So comprehensive a provision might seem to cover every conceivable eventuality, but to the last it remained unsatisfactory to some. For example, 'every individual' with the stated protections is not in reality guaranteed access without discrimination to the electoral system. Elections take money and organization, and whatever the constitution and the law says, every House of Commons is dominated by males of European ancestry drawn heavily from particular professions and age groups. There are many similar examples, both in the public service and in private business entities. Furthermore, once categories of individuals are listed, it raises a question about omitted categories. The last four words of the clause, 'mental or physical disability,' were added to the original proposal; but what, women's organizations asked, of discrimination on the basis of marital status, sexual orientation, and political belief? Those three categories did not get into Equality Rights, although the last for some purposes could conceivably come under the first specific section of the charter, Fundamental Freedoms.

Official Languages of Canada, sections 16 to 22, starts off with an unequivocal assertion that 'English and French are the official languages of Canada,' and adds New Brunswick as a province where the same is true. The rest of the sections spell out in more detail, for Parliament and the legislature of New Brunswick, and the respective courts and public services under them, the circumstances in which the uses of English and French are constitutionally guaranteed. New Brunswick, for one major purpose, is actually made more officially bilingual than Canada: section 20 (1) begins, 'Any member of the public in Canada has the right to communicate with, and to receive available services from, any head or central office of an institution of the Parliament or government of Canada' in either language. The similar guarantee for New Brunswick reads 'any office,' i.e. not just a head office.

Quebec, oddly enough, is not mentioned in the language part of the charter, and that province is in any case made officially bilingual in section 133 of the Constitution Act of 1867; but so is Parliament, and the charter says a good deal about languages in Parliament. Behind that omission lies a long and contentious history. Of all the rights protected in the charter, those respecting language have probably in the past caused more provincial, regional, religious, and partisan outbreaks than any other, and commonly the turmoil was about the status of French outside Quebec. The election of the Parti Québécois in 1976 focused attention on the opposite – the status of English in Quebec. But that was not by any means the beginning, for the use of English in public institutions in Quebec had been under growing pressure for years, and in 1974 a Liberal government had secured the enactment of a statute which limited the rights of Quebec parents to choose the language in which their children would be educated. The Lévesque government went beyond that in 1977 to make French, in effect, Quebec's official language, with English the language of translation. The issue reached the Supreme Court, which ruled in 1980 (in *Attorney General of Quebec* v. *Blaikie*) that the language clause in the British North America Act of 1867 kept the two languages equal in Quebec for official purposes. The government of Quebec thus lost a crucial decision in a federal court in the same year as it was defeated on the referendum.

Lévesque's sensitivity in the pre-1982 period over attempts to entrench the English language more strongly in Quebec hardly needs further description, and it was matched during the constitutional negotiations by an equally firm reluctance on the part of the premier of Ontario to have his province join the bilingual world like New Brunswick. Manitoba also had a lively interest in language rights, for the Supreme Court decided, also in 1980, that a ninety-year-old provincial statute ending official bilingualism in the province, as set forth in the Manitoba Act of 1870, was ultra vires, so that Manitoba, though on a more limited scale than New Brunswick, is also officially bilingual. But there was almost no expectation in 1980–2 that Quebec could ever agree, as in New Brunswick, to provide services in English from 'any office of an institution of the legislature or government.' So Quebec, in what might strike any objective outsider of the Canadian scene as a peculiarity, is not mentioned in the charter under Official Languages of Canada. A Canadian reader of federal-provincial relations should feel no surprise.

Minority Language Educational Rights, section 23 in the charter, none the less brings Quebec in indirectly, though without naming any province. In legal terms it is complex, and in social terms it may become of great importance. Its leading statement is:

23. (1) Citizens of Canada
    (a) whose first language learned and still understood is that of the English or French linguistic minority population of the province in which they reside, or
    (b) who have received their primary school instruction in Canada in English or French and reside in a province where the language in which they received that instruction is the language of the English or French linguistic minority population of the province, have the right to have their children receive primary and secondary school instruction in that language in that province.

The clause is qualified, chiefly because it applies only where there are enough children 'to warrant the provision to them out of public funds of minority language instruction.' What it means in practice is that under some circumstances, if facilities are available, children born into an English or French minority can be moved about the country without losing the advantages of a public school education in their mother tongue.

Enforcement is the subject of section 24 of the charter, and it is an affirmation of a person's right to seek legal redress in cases where the rights in the charter may have been infringed. There follow seven sections of general application, variously protecting rights of native people recognized in the Royal Proclamation of 1763 (the root of their claim to be treated differently from Canadians or European ancestry); ensuring that the rights in the charter do not constitute a total list; encouraging the preservation of our multicultural heritage; and adding the Yukon and Northwest Territories to the charter on the same terms as provinces. The last general section, in a charter whose main purpose is to restrict law-making powers for what are considered good reasons, makes assurance doubly sure: 'Nothing in this Charter extends the legislative powers of any body or Authority.'

The remaining sections in the charter are partly routine, asserting what is already clear about its application to Parliament and the legislatures. But two are not. The sections dealing with Equality Rights did not take effect for three years, until 1985, the general purpose being to give law-makers time to prepare for the onset of equality. Clause 33 (1) deserves quotation:

Parliament or the legislature of a province may expressly declare in an Act of Parliament or of the legislature, as the case may be, that the Act or a provision thereof shall operate notwithstanding a provision included in section 2 or sections 7–15 of this Charter.

Parliament or a legislature, that is, may opt out of main parts of the charter by simply saying it is doing so. Its opting out will expire in five years, but it can renew it. Section 2 is Fundamental Freedoms; sections 7 to 15 cover Legal Rights and Equality Rights. It has already been recorded that the charter's first statement adds other limits (those 'prescribed by law as can be demonstrably justified in a free and democratic society'); and that a province can also opt out of certain kinds of amendments. The charter is thus by no means a script to be followed slavishly: *ad libs* are available.

It is important to note that opting out does not apply to several parts of the charter, including Democratic Rights and Language Rights. More important, two of the possible openings in it require opting out, not in, and the meaning of the third will be up to the courts. Opting in is a step that a law-making body can merely refrain from taking, and while it may be criticized for not taking it, it need not defend itself comprehensively. Opting out of major declarations on rights, in contrast, requires a positive action that will need explanation and defence, and under ordinary circumstances could be expected to make the leaders of a legislature move cautiously. One problem is, of course, that the circumstances under which opting out is considered seriously may never be ordinary.

The section quoted above has no provision requiring reasons: Parliament or a legislature can opt out of parts of the charter without a word of explanation. Experience in Canada so far suggests that the two provinces which have used the authority have treated the charter, despite its constitutional nature, as just another piece of legislation. As a legal precaution the government of Quebec, unable to accept the latest addition to the constitution, from the start used a blanket application of the 'notwithstanding' clause on bills presented to the legislature; and in 1986 Saskatchewan ordered striking public employees back to work 'notwithstanding.' When the Liberals returned to power in Quebec in 1985, they began quietly to drop the use of 'notwithstanding,' and it is not yet clear what that means: Quebec has still not signed in. The dispute in Saskatchewan has been taken by the union to the courts, and at this writing is not yet decided.

And therein lies a paradox. The 'notwithstanding' clause, like many parts of the charter, may easily become a two-edged sword. The Saskatchewan Government Employees Union, dismayed by a statute, turned from the legislature to the judicial system for redress. Many groups in Canadian society in the past, seeking to improve their lot, have often found legislatures more helpful than courts. Labour laws protecting rights to organize and strike were hard to win, but they are all the products of legislatures. Organizations of native peoples are in a different constitutional position than any other groups and they are still seeking, so far with no great success, a more satisfactory recognition of that; but they have also in recent decades shown increasing skills in political action. It is true that they have also won some notable legal disputes, and they may need more victories for their land claims. But if the recognition in the charter of 'their existing aboriginal and treaty rights' is to have content, a great deal of political negotiation remains. Women's associations have found new strengths in political action; in a revealing article on 'Women and Constitutional Process,' Chaviva Hošek has written of a parliamentary stage in the negotiations of 1980–2:

The deliberations of the Joint Committee afforded a crucial experience for women's groups, as it did for other groups of concerned citizens. The hearings raised the political consciousness of many people, and revealed the range and vitality of the opposition to the wording of the Charter and its approaches to human rights. Many people watched the televised presentations of the Joint Committee with fascination and a growing hope that the highly persuasive cases made by many civil libertarian groups would force the government to strengthen the Charter.

'The range and vitality of the opposition to the wording of the Charter' did not end in 1982. There can be no doubt that there is room within the charter for many groups to pursue their ends; but it is also conceivable – given the range and vitality of some of the court cases depending on the charter already under way – that we may find people demanding the use of the opting-out powers to bypass its existing wording.

We end the book where we began: Parliament, politics, the constitution; and television. And hope. The power to amend the constitution is now clear, and in Canadian hands. The apparent loophole in the charter, leaving legislatures free to set its core aside, also leaves citizens free to persuade their legislatures to use the power to bypass the charter. The opting-out clause may thus turn out to be a flexible element in the growth of the constitution. Conversely, if the courts take a narrow view of the charter, and legislatures cannot be persuaded to use their right to set it aside, it may not. For a book on democratic government in Canada, it would be difficult to find more appropriate last words. Except perhaps these: despite the profound significance of the charter, the first general agreement since 1982 to open up the constitution on terms designed to include Quebec, which led to an unprecedented unanimity among the prime minister and all the premiers, did not deal directly with the Charter of Rights and Freedoms at all.

Notes

I. POLITICAL PARTIES

1 Quoted in Hugh Townsend, 'Carving His Signature into History ...,' *Halifax Chronicle-Herald*, 29 Sept. 1981; reprinted in Donald C. Wallace and Frederick J. Fletcher, *Canadian Politics through Press Reports* (Toronto 1984), 97. For a thoughtful critique specifically of news coverage by television, see Robert Fulford, 'The Grand Illusion,' in *Saturday Night*, June 1984, 9–10.

2 Escott Reid, 'The Rise of National Parties in Canada,' *Proceedings, Canadian Political Science Association*, 1932, 193–4. See also J.M.S. Careless, *Brown of the Globe*, two vols (Toronto 1959 and 1963); Dale Thomson, *Alexander Mackenzie: Clear Grit* (Toronto 1960).

3 See Thomson, *Alexander Mackenzie*; Joseph Schull, *Edward Blake: The Man of the Other Way, 1833–81* (Toronto 1975); *Edward Blake: Leader and Exile, 1881–1912* (Toronto 1976).

4 On the Conservatives, see esp. J. English, *The Decline of Politics: The Conservatives and the Party System, 1901–20* (Toronto 1977); G.C. Perlin, *The Tory Syndrome: Leadership Politics in the Progressive Conservative Party* (Montreal 1980); on the Liberals, Christina McCall Newman, *Grits* (Toronto 1982); David E. Smith, *The Regional Decline of a National Party: Liberals on the Prairies* (Toronto 1981); Reginald Whitaker, *The Government Party: Organizing and Financing the Liberal Party in Canada, 1930–58* (Toronto 1977). Valuable earlier studies are: John R. Williams, *The Conservative Party of Canada, 1920–1949* (Durham, NC 1956); J.W. Pickersgill, *The Liberal Party* (Toronto 1962); J.L. Granatstein, *The Politics of Survival: The Conservative Party of Canada, 1939–1945* (Toronto 1967); Heath Macquarrie, *The Conservative Party* (Toronto 1965).

5 See W.L. Morton, *The Progressive Party in Canada* (Toronto 1950); Denis Smith, 'Prairie Revolt, Federalism and the Party System,' in Hugh Thorburn, ed., *Party Politics in Canada*, 2nd ed. (Toronto 1967).

6 A.R.M. Lower, *Colony to Nation* (Toronto 1946), 517. Admirable studies of the Social Credit party can be found in: John A. Irving, *The Social Credit Movement in Alberta* (Toronto 1959); C.B. Macpherson, *Democracy in Alberta* (Toronto 1953); J.R. Mallory, *Social Credit and the Federal Power in Canada* (Toronto 1954); see also W. Rose, *Social Credit Handbook* (Toronto 1968). The recent story of the Social Credit party is succinctly described in John Saywell, *Canadian Annual Review, 1960*, and subsequent years.

7 See Saywell, *Canadian Annual Review, 1967* and subsequent years; René Lévesque, *An Option for Quebec* (Toronto 1969); Pierre Laporte, *The True Face of Duplessis* (Montreal 1960). There is now a considerable literature on recent Quebec politics. See, e.g., L. Dion, *Quebec, The Unfinished Revolution* (Montreal 1976); D.H. Fullerton, *The Dangerous Delusion: Quebec's Independence Obsession* (Toronto 1978); R. Lévesque, *My Quebec* (Toronto 1979).

8 D. Lewis and F.R. Scott, *Make This Your Canada* (Toronto 1943), 117–19. See also Dean McHenry, *The Third Force in Canada* (Berkeley 1950); Kenneth McNaught, *A Prophet in Politics: A Biography of J.S. Woodsworth* (Toronto 1959); Stanley Knowles, *The New Party* (Toronto 1961); Leo Zakuta, *A Protest Movement Becalmed* (Toronto 1964); S.M. Lipset, *Agrarian Socialism* (Anchor ed., New York 1968); Walter D. Young, *The Anatomy of a Party: The National CCF* (Toronto 1969); Norman Ward and Duff Spafford, eds, *Politics in Saskatchewan* (Toronto 1968); I. Avakumovis, *Socialism in Canada: A Study of the CCF and NDP in Federal and Provincial Politics* (Toronto 1978).

9 See Smith, *The Regional Decline of a National Party* and *Prairie Liberalism: The Liberal Party in Saskatchewan* (Toronto 1975).

10 Hugh G. Thorburn, *Politics in New Brunswick* (Toronto 1961), 107

11 James Bawden, 'Is Parliament Good Television?' *Parliamentary Government*, Winter 1982, 16. That whole issue is devoted to 'Electronic Parliament.'

12 Whitaker, *The Government Party*, 249

2. PARTY ORGANIZATION

1 Canada Elections Act, 1984, s. 13(1); John Courtney, 'Recognition of Canadian Political Parties in Parliament and in Law,' *Canadian Journal of Political Science*, March 1978

2 See John C. Courtney, *The Selection of National Party Leaders in Canada* (Toronto 1973), esp. chaps. 1–4.

3 Liberal Party of Canada, *Constituency Organization Manual* and *Constituency Fundraising Manual* (Ottawa, n.d.)

4 Pierre Elliott Trudeau, Ontario Caucus Policy Conference of Liberal Party, Toronto, 2 Oct. 1976; excerpts from his speech are conveniently reprinted in *Globe and Mail*, 4 Oct. 1976.

5 Blair Williams, 'The Decline of Political Parties,' *Globe and Mail*, 4 July 1980; quoted in Donald C. Wallace and Frederick Fletcher, *Canadian Politics through Press Reports* (Toronto 1984), 168

6 *Constitution of the Progressive Conservative Association of Canada*, as amended 29 Jan. 1983; *Constitution of the Liberal Party of Canada*, as amended 7 Nov. 1982; *New Democratic Party Constitution*, Vancouver 1981

7 Canada Elections Act, s. 23; Courtney, 'Recognition of Political Parties'

8 Toronto *Globe*, 9 May 1893

9 Oliver Mowat, *Proceedings, Dominion Liberal Convention* (1893), 14. See also Courtney, *Selection of National Party Leaders*, chap. 4.

10 See, for example, Joseph Wearing, *The L-Shaped Party: The Liberal Party of Canada, 1958–1980* (Toronto 1981).

11 The growing number of studies of elections, political parties, and provincial governments is yielding a steady flow of information on party organization, but systematic studies of party organization as such remain relatively uncommon. See Leo Zakuta, *A Protest Movement Becalmed* (Toronto 1964), esp. chap. 3; Brian Land, *Eglinton* (Toronto 1965), esp. chap. 2; John Meisel, ed., *Papers on the 1962 Election* (Toronto 1964); Reginald Whitaker, *The Government Party* (Toronto 1977); Christina McCall-Newman, *Grits* (Toronto 1982); Courtney, *Selection of National Party Leaders*; Jeffrey Simpson, *Discipline of Power: The Conservative Interlude and the Liberal Restoration* (Toronto 1980); G.C. Perlin, *The Tory Syndrome: Leadership Politics in the Progressive Conservative Party* (Montreal 1980); Patrick Martin, Allan Gregg, George Perlin, *Contenders: The Tory Quest for Power* (Scarborough 1983); and Wearing, *The L-Shaped Party*.

12 Canada Elections Act, s. 2(1) and s. 10(2)(b)

13 See Wallace and Fletcher, *Canadian Politics through Press Reports*, 178; *Statutory Report of the Chief Electoral Officer of Canada*, 1983, esp. 29–30.

14 Courtney, *Selection of National Party Leaders*, esp. chap. 5

15 Martin, Gregg, and Perlin, *Contenders*, 80

16 *New Democratic Party Constitution*, 1981, articles XI and XIII; *Constitution of the Progressive Conservative Association of Canada*, as amended 29 Jan. 1983, articles 9 and 10; *The Liberal Party of Canada: Constitution*, s. 1.02

17 See Toronto & District Liberal Association, *Executive Handbook*, Jan. 1984; McCall-Newman, *Grits*, esp. Part 1.

18 Whitaker, *The Government Party*, 195

19 Martin, Gregg, and Perlin, *Contenders*, 22, 26; McCall-Newman, *Grits*; Wearing, *The L-Shaped Party*

20 See *Globe and Mail*, 22 and 29 Oct. 1984.

21 Toronto *Globe*, 1 Nov. 1911

22 John W. Dafoe, *Clifford Sifton in Relation to His Times* (Toronto 1931), 414–18

23 Courtney, *Selection of National Party Leaders*, 105; J. Lele, G.C. Perlin, and H.G. Thorburn, 'The National Party Convention,' in H.G. Thorburn, ed., *Party Politics in Canada*, 4th ed. (Toronto 1979), 77.

24 *Constitution of the Liberal Party in Ontario*, as adopted 29 Mar. 1969, article VII

25 See *Report of the Committee on Election Expenses* (Ottawa 1966), and Whitaker, *The Government Party*.

26 Martin, Gregg, and Perlin, *Contenders*, 6

27 Conventions had, of course, been held before these dates. The old Reform party in Upper Canada held conventions in 1859 and 1867, and the Conservatives in 1849. See Courtney, *Selection of National Party Leaders*, 25–8.

28 *Toronto News*, 9 Oct. 1909

29 W.S. Wallace, *Memoirs of the Rt. Hon. Sir George Foster* (Toronto 1933), 205. See Roger Graham, *Arthur Meighen*, 1 *The Door of Opportunity* (Toronto 1960), chap. II

30 A detailed account of these different methods of selecting Conservative leaders is given in R. MacGregor Dawson, *Constitutional Issues in Canada, 1908–31* (Toronto 1933), 380–97.

31 *Montreal Star*, 8 Aug. 1919

32 Saskatchewan New Democratic Party, *Constitution*, as revised Nov. 1978

3. PARTY ACTIVITIES AND PROBLEMS

1 As recently as 1976 a Saskatchewan Liberal leader on his retirement gave a frank departing interview in which he averred that when he was the province's treasurer the financial world treated him as a wizard; and when he went out of office he was ignored. Road contractors, he added, cluster around government and drop defeated politicians without remorse. Hon. Dave Stewart, *Saskatoon Star Phoenix*, 15 Dec. 1976. See also Duff Spafford, 'Highway Employment and Provincial Elections,' *Canadian Journal of Political Science*, March 1981, 135–42, and Norman Ward, 'The Politics of Patronage: James Gardiner and Federal Appointments in the West, 1935–57,' *Canadian Historical Review* 58, no. 3 (Sept. 1977), 294–310.

2 PAC, Macdonald Letterbooks, 10 Jan. 1871

3 Kenneth M. Gibbons and Donald C. Rowat, eds., *Political Corruption in Canada: Cases, Causes and Cures* (Toronto 1976), 9

4 Thomas Van Dusen, *The Chief* (Toronto 1968), 36

5 M. Grattan O'Leary, 'The Pork Barrel,' *Maclean's*, 15 Feb. 1924; see also John Saywell, *Canadian Annual Review, 1961*, 53–4; *Task Force on Government Information* (Ottawa 1969), vol. 1, 28–9; and Patrick Nicholson, *Vision and Indecision* (Toronto 1968), 333.

6 O'Leary, 'The Pork Barrel,' 198–201. See also Norman Ward, *The Public Purse: A*

Study in Canadian Democracy (Toronto 1962), esp. chaps XIII–XIV. For an account of the 'pork barrel' years ago, see *Canadian Annual Review, 1904*, 227ff; O.D. Skelton, *Life and Letters of Sir Wilfrid Laurier* (Toronto 1921; reissued in Carleton Library 1965), II, 265–70; Norman Ward, *A Party Politician: Memoirs of Chubby Powers* (Toronto 1968), 11–12, 358–9. For contemporary studies, see Gibbons and Rowat, *Political Corruption in Canada*.

7 Canada, House of Commons *Debates*, 1 May 1931, pp. 1191-2

8 James Scott, 'Political Slush Funds Corrupt All Parties,' *Maclean's*, 9 Sept. 1961. A bibliography on the subject is at the end of the first volume of *Report on the Committee on Election Expenses*.

9 See Richard Gwyn, *The Shape of Scandal* (Toronto 1965); Van Dusen, *The Chief*.

10 *Report of the Committee on Election Expenses*, vol. 1 (Ottawa 1966), 38

11 See F. Leslie Seidle, 'The Election Expenses Act: The House of Commons and the Parties,' in John C. Courtney, ed., *The Canadian House of Commons: Essays in Honour of Norman Ward* (Calgary 1985), 113–34.

12 Chief Electoral Officer, *Statutory Report*, 1984, chap. 2, appendix C. See also *Report of the Chief Electoral Officer Respecting Election Expenses*, 1984.

13 See Seidle, 'The Election Expenses Act'; and *Report of the Chief Electoral Officer*, 1984; *Thirty-third General Election: Report of the Chief Electoral Officer pursuant to Subsection 58(9) of The Canada Elections Act*, 1984.

14 *The National Citizens Coalition Inc.* v. *Attorney General for Canada*, Alberta Court of Queen's Bench, 25 June 1984; Chief Electoral Officer, *Statutory Report*, 1984, p. 73

15 When national and provincial members of the same party fall out, the dispute can become doubly bitter because of the family connection. Thus the Liberal government of Ontario under the leadership of Mitch Hepburn carried its dislike of the Liberal government at Ottawa under Mackenzie King to such lengths that it moved a resolution of censure on the latter's war policics. Many of Hepburn's followers disapproved of the quarrel, and the effects of these disagreements were soon reflected in the standing of the Liberal party in Ontario. The Saskatchewan Liberal party of the 1960s also had internal divisions over federal-provincial matters, and the Quebec wing of the party has commonly been an almost autonomous body.

16 *Manitoba Free Press*, 25 Apr. 1927

17 House of Commons *Debates*, 3 Apr. 1930, pp. 1227–8

18 *Grain Growers' Guide*, quoted in *Canadian Annual Review, 1923*, 715–16; R.V. Harris, 'The Advantages of the Union of the Maritime Provinces,' *Acadiensis* 8 (Oct. 1908), 247, quoted in Murray Beck, *The History of Maritime Union: A Study in Frustration* (Fredericton 1969), 36

19 These generalizations are, of course, subject to some qualifications. For an analysis of relevant material, see Howard A. Scarrow, 'Federal-Provincial Voting Patterns in

Canada,' *Canadian Journal of Economics and Political Science* 36, no. 2 (May 1960), 289–98.

20 *Canadian Annual Review, 1912*, 561–6

21 See Norman Ward and Duff Spafford, eds., *Politics in Saskatchewan* (Toronto 1968), 238–79.

22 Thus Wilfrid Laurier's first cabinet in 1896 included no less than three provincial premiers: Oliver Mowat, W.S. Fielding, and Andrew Blair. R.B. Bennett in 1930 made the premier of Nova Scotia a federal minister, and the premier of Ontario the high commissioner for Canada in London.

23 A most exceptional intervention was that of federal ministers in the Quebec election of 1939, but this could be attributed to the serious emergency caused by the Quebec premier's demand for popular support against participation in the war. On that occasion the four French Canadians in the federal cabinet announced that a victory for the Quebec Union Nationale party (under the premier) would be followed by their withdrawal from the federal government, and they threw their influence wholeheartedly into the provincial struggle, with conspicuous success.

24 *Montreal Daily Star*, 12 Oct. 1927

25 House of Commons *Debates*, 23 May 1923, p. 3048

26 Even this is not to be taken too literally. W.S. Fielding, a past and then a later minister of finance, said he had not voted for the tariff section in the Liberal platform, that he had never concealed his disapproval of it, and that it was not discussed at his election. Ibid., 6, 12 June 1922, pp. 2529–30, 2851

27 *Globe and Mail*, 21 Sept. 1966

28 *Constitution of the New Democratic Party*, 1981, article v

29 The minutes of a national convention in 1946, which was faced with 127 resolutions covering an extremely wide range, give this time with some exactness. Early resolutions apparently received a moderate allotment of time; but on the last day they were passed at the rate of at least thirty an hour, or an average of two minutes to each resolution.

30 See Evelyn Eager, 'The Paradox of Power in the Saskatchewan CCF, 1944–1961,' in J.H. Aitchison, ed., *The Political Process in Canada* (Toronto 1936), 118–35, for an excellent treatment of this problem.

31 *New Republic*, 16 July 1919

4. THE HOUSE OF COMMONS: REPRESENTATION

1 Canada, House of Commons *Debates*, 20 June 1940, p. 972. See also speech of Sir Winston Churchill, *British House of Commons Debates*, 22 Jan. 1941, p. 257.

2 See *Report of Task Force on Government Information* (Ottawa 1969), a document of interest partly because of the ways in which it has become outdated.

3 See John C. Courtney, 'The Size of Canada's Parliament: An Assessment of the Implications of a Larger House of Commons,' in Peter Aucoin, ed., *Institutional Reforms for Representative Government* (Toronto 1985), 1–39; House of Commons, *Minutes of Proceedings and Evidence of the Standing Committee on Privileges and Elections*, esp. 1982–6.

4 A full exposition of the system is given in Norman Ward, *The Canadian House of Commons: Representation* (Toronto 1950), 19–58; 'The Redistribution of 1952,' *Canadian Journal of Economics and Political Science* 19, no. 3 (Aug. 1953), 341–60; and 'A Century of Constituencies,' *Canadian Public Administration* 10, no. 1 (Spring 1967), 105–22.

5 House of Commons *Debates*, 9 Apr. 1952, pp. 1419–22

6 R. MacG. Dawson, 'The Gerrymander of 1882,' *Canadian Journal of Economics and Political Science* 1, no. 2 (May 1935), 197–221

7 Ward, 'The Redistribution of 1952, 354

8 See, for example, House of Commons *Debates*, 25 May 1933, pp. 5468–9; 21 Feb. 1947, pp. 698–9.

9 Ibid., 9, 17 Apr. 1962, pp. 2645–52 and 3040–9

10 See Ward, 'A Century of Constituencies'; T.H. Qualter, 'Representation by Population: A Comparative Study,' *Canadian Journal of Economics and Political Science* 33, no. 2 (May 1967), 246–68.

11 Halifax (city and county) and Queen's (PEI) were the longest surviving double seats. For the rest, see Norman Ward, 'Voting in Canadian Two-Member Constituencies,' in John C. Courtney, ed., *Voting in Canada* (Toronto 1967), 125–9.

12 For illuminating studies on the workings of the electoral system, see Alan C. Cairns, 'The Electoral System and the Party System in Canada 1921–1965,' *Canadian Journal of Political Science* 1, no. 1 (March 1968), 55–80; Duff Spafford, 'The Electoral System of Canada,' *The American Political Science Review*, 64, no. 1 (1970), 168–76.

13 See William P. Irvine, *Does Canada Need a New Electoral System?* (Queen's University, Kingston 1979); and 'A Review and Evaluation of Electoral System Reform Proposals,' in Aucoin, ed., *Institutional Reforms for Representative Government*, 71–109.

14 *Orientation Seminar for New Members of the House of Commons*, 9–10 Oct. 1984 (supplied by Don Ravis, MP)

15 *Report of the Commission to Review Salaries of Members of Parliament and Senators* (Ottawa 1979); *Canadian Legislatures: The 1984 Comparative Study* (Toronto 1984). Both these documents, the first federal and the second emanating from the office of the Ontario Legislative Assembly, are parts of invaluable series of publications covering details of elected bodies in Canada.

16 Ward, *The Canadian House of Commons*, 211–32. The pre-Confederation story is in

John Garner, *The Franchise and Politics in British North America, 1755–1867* (Toronto 1969).

17 Province of Canada, Legislature, *Confederation Debates*, 1865, p. 39
18 A full account of the origin and history of these acts is in Roger Graham, *Arthur Meighen*, I (Toronto 1960), chaps. 6–8. See also Ward, *The Canadian House of Commons*, 226–30.
19 The definitive modern work on election law in Canada is the series of volumes by J. Patrick Boyer, published by Butterworths (Toronto) beginning in 1981; not all are yet in print. The titles are: *Political Rights: The Legal Framework of Elections in Canada*; *Lawmaking by the People: Referendums and Plebiscites in Canada*; *Money and Message: The Law Governing Election Financing, Advertising, Broadcasting and Campaigning in Canada*; *Election Law in Canada: The Law and Procedure of Federal, Provincial and Territorial Elections* (two volumes); and *Local Elections in Canada: The Law Governing Elections of Municipal Councils, School Boards and Other Local Authorities*.
20 See Ward, *The Canadian House of Commons*, chap. XIV.

5. THE HOUSE OF COMMONS: PERSONNEL MATTERS

1 See Canada, House of Commons *Debates*, 8 May 1931, pp. 1407–14.
2 Mackenzie King's government, already defeated on a subamendment, had been in imminent danger of being defeated again by a vote pending in the House, and he had advised the governor general to dissolve. The latter refused, stating that as Arthur Meighen had the largest single party in the House and as an election had been held only eight months earlier, Meighen should be given an opportunity to form a government. King thereupon resigned and Lord Byng sent for Meighen. Meighen, although head of the largest party in the House, had no majority and was thus forced to depend on Progressive support.
3 *Report of the Commissioner to Review Salaries and Allowances* (Ottawa 1980), 19
4 This omits the abnormal six-year term, 1911–17. In 1935 the Parliament elected in 1930 was two days short of a full five years.
5 House of Commons *Debates*, 1 Apr. 1946, p. 473. See Eugene Forsey, 'Mr. King and Parliamentary Government,' *Canadian Journal of Economics and Political Science* 17, no. 4 (Nov. 1951), 451–67.
6 For financial and other details, see *Canadian Legislatures: The 1986 Comparative Study*; an annual publication of the administration office of the Legislative Assembly of Ontario.
7 Canada, *Permanent and Provisional Standing Orders of the House of Commons*, as amended to 1986, chap. XV
8 Sir T. Erskine May, *A Treatise on the Law, Privileges, Proceedings and Usage of*

Parliament, ed. Sir Gilbert Campion, 14th ed. (London 1943), 41. See Beauchesne's *Rules and Forms of the House of Commons of Canada with Annotations, Comments and Precedents*, 5th ed. by Alistair Fraser, G.A. Birch, and W.F. Dawson (Toronto 1978), 11.

9 See W.F. Dawson, 'Parliamentary Privilege in the Canadian House of Commons,' *Canadian Journal of Economics and Political Science* 25, no. 4 (Nov. 1959), 462–70; and *Procedure in the Canadian House of Commons* (Toronto 1962). There are many cases on this subject: for example, *Kielley* v. *Carson*, 4 Moo. P.C. 63; *Doyle* v. *Falconer*, 4 Moo. P.C. (N.S.) 203; *Barton* v. *Taylor*, 11 App. Cas. 197; *Fielding* v. *Thomas*, [1896] A.C. 600.

10 *Can. Statutes*, 31 Vict., c. 23, s. 1. The last clause (in quotation marks) creates a limitation that may not have been implied in the BNA Act

11 *Can. Statutes*, 39 Vict., c. 7

12 Beauchesne, *Rules and Forms of the House of Commons of Canada* (1978), 11ff

13 None the less, the MP Gilles Grégoire was arrested on 12 Feb. 1965, in connection with a relatively minor traffic infraction, and the Standing Committee on Privileges and Elections found that 'the privilege of freedom of arrest of a Member has not been infringed in the present case.' See its fourth report, 19 Mar. 1965 (House of Commons *Journals*, 1964–5, pp. 1141–2); and see also statement on the occasion of the arrest of Fred Rose, MP, House of Commons *Debates*, 15 Mar. 1946, pp. 4–8.

14 For an alleged threat against a member, see 1 Feb. 1939, p. 519.

15 See Dawson, 'Parliamentary Privilege in the Canadian House of Commons.'

16 See ibid.; and John B. Stewart, *The Canadian House of Commons: Procedure and Reform* (Montreal 1977), 57–8.

17 Norman Ward, 'Called to the Bar of the House of Commons,' *Canadian Bar Review*, May 1957

6. THE HOUSE OF COMMONS: ORGANIZATION AND PROCEDURE

1 John B. Stewart, *The Canadian House of Commons: Procedure and Reform* (Montreal 1977), 16

2 A. Paul Pross, ed., *Pressure Group Behaviour in Canadian Politics* (Toronto 1975), 2

3 See Pierre Duchesne and Russell Ducasse, 'Must Lobbying be Regulated?' *Canadian Parliamentary Review*, Winter 1984–5, 2–7.

4 Progressive Conservative Party, *PC Caucus Spokesman* (a brochure revised as needed). See also Paul G. Thomas, 'Parliamentary Reform through Political Parties,' in John C. Courtney, ed., *The Canadian House of Commons: Essays in Honour of Norman Ward* (Calgary 1985).

5 Rt. Hon. John Turner, Canada, House of Commons *Debates*, 30 Sept. 1986, p. 9. See also James H. Aitchison, 'The Speakership of the Canadian House of Commons,'

in R.M. Clark, ed., *Canadian Issues: Essays in Honour of Henry F. Angus* (Toronto 1961), 23–56; Gary Levy, *Speakers of the House of Commons* (Ottawa 1983).

6 See, for example, *Parliamentary Government*, Autumn 1982, 3–12; *Canadian Parliamentary Review*, Winter 1984–5, pp. 16–20.

7 *Permanent and Provisional Standing Orders of the House of Commons, 24 Feb. 1986*, chap. IV. For a history of the rules see W.F. Dawson, *Procedure in the Canadian House of Commons* (Toronto 1962); Donald Page, 'Streamlining the Procedures of the Canadian House of Commons, 1963–1966,' *Canadian Journal of Economics and Political Science* 33, no. 1 (Feb. 1967), 27–49; Stewart, *The Canadian House of Commons*

8 The problem of the bells was discussed at several sittings of the Special Committee on the Reform of the House of Commons, 1984–5. The 'bell rule' is now S.O. 13.

9 See Hugh G. Thorburn, 'Parliament and Policy Making: The Case of the Trans-Canada Gas Pipeline,' *Canadian Journal of Economics and Political Science* 23, no. 4 (Nov. 1957), 516–31; Eugene Forsey, 'Constitutional Aspects of the Canadian Pipe Line Debate,' *Public Law*, Spring 1957, 9–27.

10 The detailed procedure on public bills is in chap. XIV of the standing orders; that on private bills, chap. XIX.

11 These six points are based on an article by a deputy minister of finance: see W.C. Clark, 'Financial Administration of the Government of Canada,' *Canadian Journal of Economics and Political Science* 4, no. 3 (Aug. 1938), 391–419. See also Royal Commission on Financial Management and Accountability, *Final Report* (Ottawa 1979); Canadian Comprehensive Auditing Foundation, *Improving Accountability: Canadian Public Accounts Committees and Legislative Auditors* (Ottawa 1981); Douglas G. Hartle, *The Expenditure Budget Process in the Government of Canada* (Toronto 1978); Norman Ward, *The Public Purse* (Toronto 1962).

12 The Appropriation Bill is presented to the governor general in the name of the House of Commons only, and his assent is given in a special phrase (following English precedent), namely: 'In Her Majesty's name, His Excellency the Governor General thanks her loyal subjects, accepts their benevolence, and assents to this bill.' To ordinary bills the assent is given in these words: 'In Her Majesty's name, His Excellency the Governor General doth assent to these Bills.' For an enlightening analysis of parliamentary finance procedures, see Stewart, *The Canadian House of Commons*.

13 On the history of supplementary estimates and interim supply (a 'down-payment' granted to the government so that it can carry on until full supply is passed), and on governor general's warrants, see Ward, *The Public Purse*, especially chaps. XIII and XIV.

14 James J. Macdonell, Foreword to *Improving Accountability: Canadian Public Accounts Committees and Legislative Auditors* (Ottawa 1981), iii. See also S.L.

Sutherland, 'On the Trail of the Auditor General: Parliament's Servant, 1973–1980,' *Canadian Public Administration* 23, no. 4 (Winter 1980), 616–44.

7. THE HOUSE OF COMMONS AND THE EXECUTIVE

1 Canada, House of Commons *Debates*, 12 Nov. 1940, p. 33
2 Ibid., 11 Oct. 1968, p. 1095. See also 4 Oct. 1968, pp. 800–10; 15 Oct. 1968, p. 1133; 5 June 1969, p. 9813. Standing order no. 7 begins: 'Every member is bound to attend the service of the House ...'
3 House of Commons *Debates*, 12 June 1941, p. 3922. For the use of the old Committee of Supply made by members, see Norman Ward, *The Public Purse* (Toronto 1962), esp. chaps. XI and XIV.
4 Geoffrey Stevens, 'Controlling the Public Purse,' *Globe and Mail*, 21 June 1982
5 House of Commons *Debates*, 13–24 June, 8 July et seq., 1963, passim;. see also Saywell, *Canadian Annual Review, 1963*, 53–8 and 195–204.
6 See House of Commons *Debates*, 12 June 1941, pp. 3921–2; 19 Feb., 28 Mar. 1947, pp. 580–1, 1832–5.
7 R.B. Bennett in *ibid.*, 30 May 1938, p. 3339; see also Stanley Knowles, *The Role of the Opposition in Parliament* (Toronto 1957).
8 J.L. Ilsley in House of Commons *Debates*, 26 May 1942, p. 2774
9 Frank Oberle, MP, *Caucus Reform: Update '83*, p. 1
10 W.G. Moncrieff, *Party and Government by Party* (Toronto 1871), 58–9. For an insider's account of organization in the House, see Norman Ward, *A Party Politician* (Toronto 1968), esp. 261–310.
11 See 'Wives Complain to Trudeau,' *Winnipeg Free Press*, 21 June 1969.
12 Sir Gwilym Gibbon, 'The Party System in Government,' *Public Administration*, Jan. 1937, 19

8. THE SENATE

1 See Norman Ward, *The Canadian House of Commons* (Toronto 1950), chap. IV.
2 Larry Zolf, *Survival of the Fattest* (Toronto 1984), 151. See especially chap. 14, 'Paying the Party Piper,' and chap. 15, 'The Bagman Cometh.'
3 The agreement was actually in writing; see CCH Canadian Limited, *Ottawa Letter*, 1983–4, pp. 644–5.
4 Colin Campbell, *The Canadian Senate: A Lobby from Within* (Toronto 1978), 2; John McMenemy, 'Business Influence and Party Organizers in the Senate Imperil the Independence of Parliament,' in Paul Fox, ed., *Politics: Canada*, 5th ed. (Toronto 1982), 541–8. See also Zolf, *Survival of the Fattest*.

5 R.A. MacKay, *The Unreformed Senate of Canada* (rev. and reprinted in the Carleton Library, Toronto 1963), 149

6 Eugene Forsey, 'The Canadian Senate' (Ottawa, n.d.), 10 and 12; Campbell, *The Canadian Senate*, 32. The example given by Dr Forsey is by no means an isolated case: see Barbara Plant Reynolds, 'Amendments to Legislation Initiated by the Senate, 1968 to 1979' (Research Branch, Library of Parliament 1980).

7 Forsey, 'The Canadian Senate,' 8; Reynolds, 'Amendments to Legislation Initiated by the Senate.'

8 See MacKay, *The Unreformed Senate of Canada*; F.A. Kunz, *The Modern Senate of Canada* (Toronto 1965), and Eugene Forsey's review of it in the *Canadian Forum* 45 (March 1966), 285; John N. Turner, 'The Senate of Canada – Political Conundrum,' in Robert M. Clark, ed., *Canadian Issues: Essays in Honour of Henry F. Angus*.

9 Forsey, 'The Canadian Senate,' 13; Campbell, *The Canadian Senate*, 24 and passim. The Research Branch of the Library of Parliament has produced several relevant studies: e.g., Barbara Plant Reynolds, 'Standing Senate Committees' (1980) and 'Special Senate Committees' (1980); Diane Leduc, 'Special Editions of Senate Committee Reports, 1960–1985.'

10 MacKay, *The Unreformed Senate*, 112–28; Kunz, *The Modern Senate*, 304–14; Campbell, *The Canadian Senate*, passim; Zolf, *Survival of the Fattest*, 85

11 *Reference Re Legislative Authority of Parliament to alter or replace the Senate* [1980] 1 SCR 54; Constitution Act, 1982, ss. 38, 42, and 47.

12 There are a number of good accounts of the events up to and including the Constitution Act of 1982: *Canada Notwithstanding: The Making of the Constitution, 1976–1982* (Toronto 1984) has as one of its authors a leading participant, Roy Romanow (together with John Whyte, Howard Leeson); a constitutional lawyer, Edward McWhinney, has written several relevant works, including *Canada and the Constitution, 1979–1982* (Toronto 1982); a leading journalistic account is Robert Sheppard and Michael Valpy, *The National Deal: The Fight for a Canadian Constitution* (Toronto 1982).

13 See Donald Smiley, *An Elected Senate for Canada? Clues from the Australian Experience* (Kingston 1985).

9. THE MONARCHY AND THE GOVERNOR GENERAL

1 See Eugene Forsey, *Freedom and Order* (Toronto 1974), esp. Part I: 'Crown and Cabinet.'

2 See John Fraser's interview with the secretary general of the Commonwealth, Shridath Ramphal; 'Queen Takes Seriously Role in Commonwealth,' *Globe and Mail*, 11 March 1985.

3 See Sir John Kerr, *Matters for Judgment: An Autobiography* (Melbourne 1978); J.R. Mallory, 'The Office of the Governor-General Reconsidered,' *Politics*, Nov. 1978, 215–29.

4 See J.R. Mallory, 'The Appointment of the Governor General,' *Canadian Journal of Economics and Political Science* 26, no. 1 (Feb. 1960), 96–107. See also J.W. Pickersgill and D.F. Forster, eds., *The Mackenzie King Record, 1944–1945* (Toronto 1968), II, 435–6.

5 Imperial Conferences of 1926 and 1930; Conference on the Operation of Dominion Legislation and Merchant Shipping Legislation, 1929; Canada, House of Commons *Debates*, 5 Apr. 1943, p. 1829; *Statutes*, 2 Geo. VI, chap. 44.

6 *Letters of Queen Victoria* (London 1907) (second series), II, 631; III, 422

7 *Robert Laird Borden: His Memoirs* (Toronto 1938), II, 604

8 Letters to Lord John Russell, 1839, in J.A. Chisholm, ed., *Speeches and Public Letters of Joseph Howe* (Halifax 1909), I, 235.

9 See Thomas Walkom, 'Schreyer Leaves Record of Gaffes and Informality,' *Globe and Mail*, 24 Dec. 1983; 'Forsey Outraged at Schreyer's Career Musings,' ibid., 20 Apr. 1984

10 See Roger Graham, *Arthur Meighen*, I, *The Door of Opportunity* (Toronto 1960), 287–302.

11 See R. MacG. Dawson, *The Conscription Crisis of 1944* (Toronto 1962), and Pickersgill and Forster, *The Mackenzie King Record*, 1944–1945.

12 Walter Bagehot, *The English Constitution* (London 1872; 1908 printing), 143

13 See Dale Thomson, *Alexander Mackenzie: Clear Grit* (Toronto 1960), 268; E.M. Macdonald, *Recollections, Personal and Political* (Toronto n.d.), 487–90; *Borden Memoirs*, II, 603.

14 Sir Joseph Pope, ed., *Correspondence of Sir John A. Macdonald* (Toronto 1921), 203

15 O.D. Skelton, *Life and Letters of Sir Wilfrid Laurier* (Toronto 1921), II, 86n; 'The Imperial Conference,' *Journal of the Royal Institute of International Affairs*, July 1927, 204; House of Commons *Debates*, 4 Apr. 1967, p. 14479. In the same passage Diefenbaker paid tribute to the late Governor General Vanier.

16 See John T. Saywell, 'The Crown and the Politicians: The Canadian Succession Question, 1891–1896,' *Canadian Historical Review* 37, no. 4 (Dec. 1956), 309–37; Eugene Forsey, *The Royal Power of Dissolution of Parliament in the British Commonwealth* (Toronto 1943, reprinted 1968); H. Blair Neatby, *William Lyon Mackenzie King, 1924–1932* (Toronto 1963); Roger Graham, ed., *The King-Byng Affair, 1926; A Question of Responsible Government* (Toronto 1967).

17 See John T. Saywell, *The Office of Lieutenant-Governor* (Toronto 1957).

18 Frank MacKinnon, 'The Crown in a Democracy,' in *Dalhousie Review* 49, no. 2 (Summer 1969), 238–9

10 THE PRIME MINISTER AND THE CABINET

1 Joe Clark, 'A Prime Minister's View of the Office,' quoted in Paul Fox, ed., *Politics: Canada*, 5th ed. (Scarborough, Ont. 1982), 466. For more generalized studies, see H. Berkeley, *The Power of the Prime Minister* (Toronto 1971); T. Hockin, ed., *Apex of Power: The Prime Minister and Political Leadership in Canada* (Scarborough, Ont. 1977); R.M. Punnet, *The Prime Minister in Canadian Government and Politics* (Toronto 1977).

2 Henry F. Davis, 'Nature of the Privy Council,' *Canadian Legal Studies* 1, no. 5 (Dec. 1968), 305–6. See also Eugene Forsey, 'Meetings of the Queen's Privy Council for Canada, 1867–1882,' *Canadian Journal of Economics and Political Science* 32, no. 4 (Nov. 1966), 489–98.

3 See Roger Graham, *Arthur Meighen*, 1 (Toronto 1960), chap. 9; R. MacG. Dawson, *William Lyon Mackenzie King*, 1, *1887–1923* (Toronto 1958), chaps. 10–13.

4 Laurier clearly explained his action in the Commons on 18 March 1903 (*Debates*, 132–3). See also R. MacG. Dawson, *The Conscription Crisis of 1944* (Toronto 1962); J.W. Pickersgill and D.F. Forster, *The Mackenzie King Record, 1944–1945* (Toronto 1968); Norman Ward, ed., *A Party Politician: The Memoirs of Chubby Power* (Toronto 1966). Another ministerial crisis that resulted in the defeat of a government is chronicled in House of Commons *Debates*, 4–5 Feb. 1963.

5 Paul Bilkey, *Persons, Papers and Things* (Toronto 1940), 140–2

6 A first-hand account of a minister's varied duties is in Ward, *A Party Politician*.

7 Montreal *Gazette*, 30 Sept. 1947

8 Norman Ward, 'The Politics of Patronage: James Gardiner and Federal Appointments in the West, 1935–57,' *Canadian Historical Review* 58, no. 3 (Sept. 1977), 294–310; reprinted in Ronald G. Landes, ed., *Canadian Politics: A Comparative Reader* (Scarborough, Ont. 1985), 145–64

9 John Courtney, 'Reinventing the Brokerage Wheel: The Tory Success in 1984,' in Howard R. Penniman, ed., *Canada at the Polls, 1984* (Washington, forthcoming)

10 See Donald C. Rowat, 'The Right of Access to Public Documents,' in O.P. Dwivedi, *The Administrative State in Canada: Essays in Honour of J.E. Hodgetts* (Toronto 1982), 177–92.

11 Pickersgill, *The Mackenzie King Record*, 1, 25–6 and 385; II, 111–277

11. THE CABINET: FUNCTION

1 The serious literature on the general 'top management' in Ottawa is considerable and varied. A representative sample is: Audrey D. Doerr, *The Machinery of Government in Canada* (Toronto 1981); Richard D. French, *How Ottawa Decides: Planning and Industrial Policy-Making 1968–80* (Canadian Institute for Economic Policy

1980); *Report of the Royal Commission on Financial Management and Accountability* (Ottawa 1979); 'The Policy and Expenditure Management System in the Federal Government,' *Canadian Public Administration* 26, no. 2 (Summer 1983), 255–85; and Ian D. Clark, 'Recent Changes in the Cabinet Decision-Making System in Ottawa,' ibid., 28, no. 2 (Summer 1985), 185–201.

2 See G.V. LaForest, *Disallowance and Reservation of Provincial Legislation* (Ottawa 1955); E.A. Forsey, 'Disallowance of Provincial Acts, Reservation of Provincial Bills, and Refusal of Assent by Lieutenant-Governors since 1867,' *Canadian Journal of Economics and Political Science* 4, no. 1 (Feb. 1938), 47–59; J.R. Mallory, 'The Lieutenant-Governor's Discretionary Powers,' ibid. 27, no. 4 (Nov. 1961), 518–21.

12. THE PUBLIC SERVICE

1 J.E. Hodgetts, *The Canadian Public Service; A Physiology of Government, 1867–1970* (Toronto 1973), 143. The early history of the civil service, as well as an early view of it, can be seen in R. MacGregor Dawson, *The Civil Service of Canada* (Toronto 1929). For later views see Taylor Cole, *The Canadian Bureaucracy* (Durham 1949); J.E. Hodgetts and D.C. Corbett, eds., *Canadian Public Administration* (Toronto 1960); Keith B. Callard, *Advanced Administrative Training in the Public Service* (Toronto 1958); A.M. Willms and W.D.K. Kernaghan, *Public Administration in Canada: Selected Readings* (Toronto 1968); Hodgetts, *The Canadian Public Service*; Audrey D. Doerr, *The Machinery of Government in Canada* (Toronto 1981).

2 See D.P. Gracey, 'The Real Issues in the Crown Corporations Debate,' in Kenneth Kernaghan, ed., *Public Administration in Canada*, 5th ed. (Toronto 1985), 122-40.

3 J.R. Mallory in Dwivedi, ed., *The Administrative State in Canada* (Toronto 1982), 131–48. See also Mallory's later observations in his *The Structure of Canadian Government* (revised ed., Toronto 1984), 154ff. For earlier studies relevant to this theme see note 1 above; also John Willis, ed., *Canadian Boards at Work* (Toronto 1941); Lloyd D. Musolf, *Public Ownership and Accountability: The Canadian Experience* (Cambridge 1959); John E. Kersell, *Parliamentary Supervision of Delegated Legislation* (London 1960)

13. JUDGES AND COURTS

1 Canadian Bar Foundation, *Report of the Canadian Bar Association Committee on the Independence of the Judiciary in Canada*, 20 Aug. 1985, 7

2 Quoted in Ronald G. Landes, ed., *Canadian Politics: A Comparative Reader* (Scarborough 1985), 215

3 Perry S. Millar and Carl Baar, *Judicial Administration in Canada* (Montreal and Toronto 1981), 25

4 See James G. Snell and Frederick Vaughan, *The Supreme Court of Canada: History of the Institution* (Toronto 1985), esp. 135ff.

5 *Report of the Canadian Bar Association Committee on the Appointment of Judges in Canada*, 20 Aug. 1985, p. 9

6 Norman Ward, 'Called to the Bar of the House of Commons,' *Canadian Bar Review*, May 1952, 529–46; 'When the Losers Win,' *Canadian Parliamentary Review* 5, no. 1 (1982), 10–11

7 See Snell and Vaughan, *The Supreme Court*, esp. chap. 10.

8 W.R. Lederman, 'Democratic Parliaments, Independent Courts and the Canadian Charter of Rights and Freedoms,' in John C. Courtney, *The Canadian House of Commons* (Calgary 1985), 93; see also Peter H. Russell, 'The First Three Years in Charterland,' *Canadian Public Administration* 28, no. 3 (Fall 1985), 367–96.

9 Millar and Baar, *Judicial Administration in Canada*, 80; Canadian Bar Association, *Appointment of Judges*, 55. Both books are quoting from other studies.

10 Snell and Vaughan, *The Supreme Court*, 134

11 See Philip Rosen, *Major Proposals for Reform of the Senate and the Supreme Court of Canada since the 1971 Victoria Charter*, Research Branch, Library of Parliament, 1980; Roy Romanov, John Whyte, and Howard Leeson, *Canada ... Notwithstanding: The Making of the Constitution, 1976–1982* (Toronto 1984); Snell and Vaughan, *The Supreme Court*; and Robert Sheppard and Michael Valpy, *The National Deal: The Fight for a Canadian Constitution* (Toronto 1982).

14. THE ROOTS OF THE CONSTITUTION

1 The literature on representative and responsible government is too voluminous to be cited in full, but the following, for differing reasons, shed light on relevant topics: S.D. Clark, *Movements of Political Protest in Canada, 1640–1840* (Toronto 1959); John Garner, *The Franchise and Politics in British North America 1755–1867* (Toronto 1969); Norman Ward, *The Public Purse: A Study in Canadian Democracy* (Toronto 1962); G.M. Craig, ed., Lord Durham's *Report on the Affairs of British North America* (Toronto, Carleton Library 1963).

2 The voluminous literature on the Confederation period includes these books of particular interest. *Parliamentary Debates on Confederation of British North American Provinces*, 1865 (the Confederation Debates, reprinted in 1951 by the King's Printer); P.B. Waite, *The Life and Times of Confederation 1864–1867* (Toronto 1962); Donald Creighton, *The Road to Confederation* (Toronto 1964); W.L. Morton, *The Critical Years: The Union of British North America, 1857–1873* (Toronto 1964); standard biographies of such leaders as John A. Macdonald, George Brown, Alexan-

der Mackenzie, Joseph Howe, George-Etienne Cartier; relevant entries in *The Canadian Encyclopedia*.

15. THE NATURE OF THE CONSTITUTION

1 Interesting insights into the settlement of boundaries in a federation which grew after its creation can be found in Norman L. Nicholson, *The Boundaries of the Canadian Confederation* (Carleton Library, Toronto 1979).
2 The unprecedented role played by Canadians of Inuit and Indian ancestry in recent years has had to receive considerable attention in chronicles of the events leading to the Constitution Act of 1982. See, in addition, Canada, House of Commons, *Minutes of Proceedings of the Special Committee on Indian Self-Government*, 1983, and *Response of the Government*, 1984.
3 See text and bibliography in chap. 17 of Paul W. Fox, ed., *Politics Canada*, 5th ed. (Toronto 1982), 'Protecting Civil Rights'; Peter H. Russell, *Leading Constitutional Decisions*, 3rd ed. (Carleton Library, Toronto 1982), Part Two.
4 See, for example, Russell, *Leading Constitutional Decisions*; W.R. Lederman, ed., *The Courts and the Canadian Constitution* (Carleton Library, Toronto 1964); and works by Bora Laskin, W.R. Lederman, W.H. McConnell, and Edward McWhinney.
5 Russell, *Leading Constitutional Decisions*, 201
6 Some of the best chronicles on early federal-provincial arrangements are old: see, for example, J.A. Maxwell, *Federal Subsidies to the Provincial Governments in Canada* (Cambridge, Mass. 1937); *Report of the Royal Commission on Dominion-Provincial Relations* and supporting publications (Ottawa 1940); W.A. Mackintoch, *The Economic Background of Dominion-Provincial Relations* (Carleton Library, Toronto 1964).
7 Canada, House of Commons, *Report of the Parliamentary Task Force on Federal-Provincial Arrangements*, 1981; publications of the Institute of Intergovernmental Relations, Queen's University, Kingston
8 An invaluable and readily available source of up-to-date financial information is the annual *The National Finances*, published by the Canadian Tax Foundation. It summarizes pertinent statistics, and cites their sources. See also R.M. Burns, *The Acceptable Mean: The Tax Rental Agreements, 1941–1962* (Toronto 1980).
9 A relevant chronicle here is Christopher Armstrong, *The Politics of Federalism: Ontario's Relations with the Federal Government 1867–1942* (Toronto 1981).

16. THE GROWTH OF THE CONSTITUTION

1 See P. Gérin-Lajoie, *Constitutional Amendments in Canada* (Toronto 1950); and Guy Favreau, *The Amendment of the Constitution of Canada*. The area is re-

assessed, with few new discoveries, in the documentation leading to the Constitution Act, 1982.

2 The last three acts listed here are designated 1974–6 because those years saw one long session of Parliament; they were respectively titled: BNA Act (no. 2, 1974); BNA Act, 1975; BNA Act (no. 2, 1975). Because of the length of the session, what might have been BNA Act (no. 1, 1974) became no. 2 of 1975.

3 For example: journalists, Robert Sheppard and Michael Valpy, *The National Deal: The Fight for a Canadian Constitution* (Toronto 1982); participants, Roy Romanow, John Whyte, and Howard Leeson, *Canada ... Notwithstanding: The Making of the Constitution, 1976–1982* (Toronto 1984); constitutional authorities, W.R. Lederman, *Continuing Canadian Constitutional Dilemmas: Essays on the Constitutional History, Public Law, and Federal Systems of Canada* (Toronto 1981); Edward McWhinney, *Quebec and the Constitution, 1960–1978* (Toronto 1982); others, Keith Banting and Richard Simeon, eds., *And No One Cheered: Federalism, Democracy and the Constitution Act* (Toronto 1983)

4 The reports of the committee on the 'British North American Acts: the Role of Parliament' offer interesting views on the constitutional process as perceived in the United Kingdom (*First Report*, 21 Jan. 1981; *Second Report*, 15 Apr. 1985). The debates of the House for the 1980–1 session contain more.

5 See, for example, Chaviva Hošek, 'Women and the Constitutional Process,' in Banting and Simeon, eds., *And No One Cheered*, 280–300; and Douglas Sanders, 'The Indian Lobby,' in ibid., 301–32.

6 On pre-1982 rights, see, for example, *A Canadian Charter of Human Rights* (Ottawa 1968); F.R. Scott, *Civil Liberties and Canadian Federalism* (Toronto 1959); W.S. Tarnopolsky, *The Canadian Bill of Rights* (Toronto, Carleton Library 1975); and Thomas R. Berger, *Fragile Freedoms: Human Rights and Dissent in Canada* (Toronto 1981).

Index

An index in some ways resembles the platform of a political party. It contains a little something for everybody, and can serve as a guide or compass for whoever chooses to use it; at worst, it cannot do anybody any real harm.

Norman Ward, after preparing index